NATIONAL FILM ARCHIVE, PRAGUE
Knihovna Iluminace Series, vol. 26

in cooperation with Michigan Slavic Publications, Ann Arbor
Michigan Slavic Materials, vol. 58

National Film Archive, Prague, in cooperation with Michigan Slavic Publications, Ann Arbor, 2008

EDITED BY » JAROSLAV ANDĚL AND PETR SZCZEPANIK
TRANSLATED BY » KEVIN B. JOHNSON

CINEMA ALL THE TIME:
An Anthology of Czech Film Theory
and Criticism, 1908-1939

Manuscript Editor: Alice Lovejoy
Editorial Assistance: Kevin Johnson, Jindřich Toman
Proofreader: Fiona Gaze

Cover Design and Layout: Bedřich Vémola

First published 2008 by the National Film Archive, Malešická 12, 13000 Prague 3, Czech Republic
Publication no. 175; production no. 59-058-08.
www.nfa.cz

This publication has been supported through a grant from the Czech Science Foundation
(reg. no. 408/05/0868).

This is a reduced English translation of
Stále kinema. Antologie českého myšlení o filmu 1904–1950, ed. Petr Szczepanik and Jaroslav Anděl
(Praha: Národní filmový archiv, 2008).

ISBN: 978-80-7004-137-6 (National Film Archive, Prague)
ISBN: 978-0-930042-99-8 (Michigan Slavic Publications, Ann Arbor)

Library of Congress Cataloging-in-Publication Data

Stále kinema. English.
Cinema all the time: an anthology of Czech film theory and criticism, 1908–1939
edited by Jaroslav Anděl and Petr Szczepanik; translated by Kevin B. Johnson.
p. cm. – (Knihovna Iluminace; vol. 26) (Michigan Slavic Materials; vol. 54)
Includes bibliographical references and index.
ISBN 978-0-930042-99-8 (pbk.: alk. paper)
1. Motion pictures. I. Anděl, Jaroslav. II. Szczepanik, Petr. III. Title.
PN1994.S67713 2008
791.4301–dc22
2008024191

This publication is distributed
by Michigan Slavic Publications
University of Michigan
3040 MLB
Ann Arbor, MI 48109-1275
USA

www.msp.edu

CONTENTS

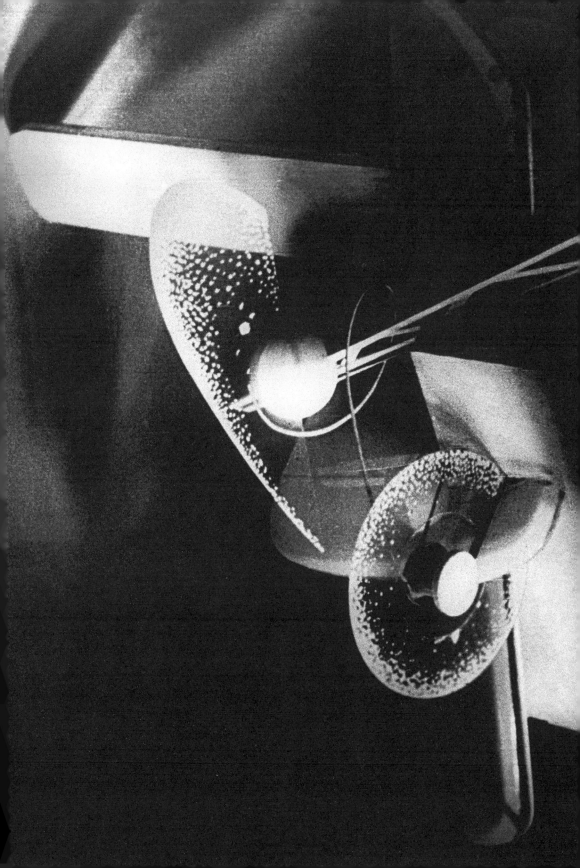

Preceding page: Still from the film *Světlo proniká tmou* [Light penetrates the darkness], dir. Otakar Vávra, Czechoslovakia, 1930.

Stanislav Kostka Neumann
FILM

I, too, am fond of film when it flies like the breeze,
urged by the whip of music in a frenzy.
Sing to me, torrent of people and things, machines, children, trees,
as you dash between the shores of an eternally dual destiny
of light and shadow.

Iridescent world, I love all mankind's abode
and hate all that tears us violently asunder.
Sing, cavalcades, rides, cruises, flights;
you are the storms of life and I'm a mistletoe cluster,
I gaze from a towering fir into wild worlds
while you press against my breast
with a firm and forceful fist.

Iridescent extract of the world, the world condensed,
by light and shadow shaped,
how you murmur, sing, sob, and cry,
though silent!
How you dash, reel, flow, and fly!
You rattle the tree of life;
from all the branches
fall fruits
down a grassy slope, into limpid waters;
they fill the streets, the paths and trails,
in seas and lakes they rock on waves,
tenements, workshops, cathedrals, and palaces
spinning as they're streaming down,
silence and roaring, gentlemen and beggars,
who here would not believe, who here could muster a yawn,

crime is so white and virtue so crimson,
instincts calculate and wisdom goes insane,
deeds walk on tiptoe, dreams disturb the curtains,
above the water a willow leaf is quivering,
love is turning red, hatred turning green,
the earth embraces the heavens.

Yes, I, too, am fond of film, and American first in line,
not a weepy novel, but a world that rushes.
What meaning the spasm of your heart, little human ant of mine,
within that amazing deluge that the mechanism channels
to the tiny rectangle, the piece of linen white!
What things you've created, constructed, made to trot and stride,
o man!
And what things you've erected, extended, expanded in all directions!

Yet among this all, like two crimson roses
your heart blossoms and the heart of your bride,
and oh, to what these roses are exposed!
You've connected continents, islands, and seas,
you've neglected to unite the nations and races,
you dry up swamps, not tears of sorrows,
and you know to be brilliant by philosophers,
though by law you're an old and simpleminded bloke
and lay your heart under the yoke.
The stories are ridiculous; kill yourself, if you like,
for superstition and prejudice, for mammon, delusion, and falsehood;
I suffered, now suffer like I have, in love, in hatred,
just leave life like a bullet fired
and whizzing forward unimpeded by hypochondria.

In that which you created you recognize yourself,
and to this, like a blessing, mighty nature lends its help,
build and suffer, deeds have outlasted you, deeds will outlast you,
the future will fashion from them its good fortune
like a wreath upon the head,
prudent and splendid.

Life, vast and frenetic, blazes upon my face,
the world from top to bottom like an eternal pilgrim oscillates,

reveals itself, disappears, shows a smile, bawls,
and down the avenues gallop cavalcades,
trains and cars, airplanes careen,
a woman is enraptured, a detective contemplates,
taciturn woods stretch into the distance and fields await their plows,
prairies, roads, bridges, tunnels,
a boat drifts upon a lake, factories gleam,
today we're on Italy's coastal rim,
perhaps on Sunday we'll go see the Buddha in Kamakura,
the sun sings to us, the wind flutters—o internationalism!
My homeland, beauty among beauties!
My world, globe! Compatriot! Man!
My sunken face stained with the flush of expectancies,
I sense the spreading honey of reconciliation,
the blood of socialism, which redeems the citizenry,
a harvest without the nobility.

And still I am but mistletoe upon a towering tree,
storms beat against my breast, they come to lift me
to pluck, lift, hurl me to the ground—
we also perish in a din of sound.

(1919)

ACKNOWLEDGEMENTS

This book has a thirty-year history. The original selection of texts and introduction were prepared by Jaroslav Anděl between 1978 and 1980 in Czechoslovakia. After Jaroslav emigrated to the United States in 1982, he continued to work on the project, and, in 1983, the Yugoslav journal *Filmske sveske* published a shortened version of the anthology as a special issue.[1] In the mid-1980s, Jonas Mekas generously proposed to publish the book through Anthology Film Archives, and, supported by Mekas, Jaroslav and American editor Deirdre Summerbell began to work on the texts, using several draft translations by Jitka Salaquarda previously commissioned by the Houston Museum of Fine Arts for the exhibition "Czech Modernism 1900–1945." However, there was not enough funding to continue, and the editorial work could not be completed.

In 2003, after discussing it with Jaroslav, Petr Szczepanik took over the project and found a new publisher for both the Czech and English versions of the book: the National Film Archive in Prague. With the support of a grant from the Czech Science Foundation, he selected thirty-one of Jaroslav's original seventy-six texts, added another three, restructured the book, reworked and expanded the introduction, and annotated the texts. Whereas Jaroslav's original introduction was written from an art-historical perspective and focused almost exclusively on the avant-garde and structuralism, this volume also emphasizes film's extra-artistic context (e.g., the history of cinema as an institution, socio-cultural conditions, and technology).[2] In 2006 and

---

[1]   Jaroslav Anděl, *Češka filmska teorija 1908–1937*, Beograd 1983 (a special issue of the magazine *Filmske Sveske*, vol. 15, no. 4). The other project that the current anthology builds upon is a two-volume Polish publication prepared with the cooperation of Andrzej Gwóźdź: *Czeska myśl filmowa. Tom 1: Obrazy, obrazki, obrazeczki* and *Czeska myśl filmowa. Tom 2: Reguły gry* (Gdańsk: Slowo obraz terytoria, 2005 and 2007, respectively).

[2]   The Czech version, entitled *Stále kinema* (published simultaneously with this English version), is based on a broader selection that spans the period from 1904 to 1950. Jaroslav's original group of seventy-six texts is noted in the Serbian publication mentioned above, which contains thirteen of these texts.

2007, two key collaborators joined in: first, Kevin Johnson as translator and Alice Lovejoy as manuscript editor. Both are scholars working on Czech cinema, speak excellent Czech, and, with Alice being an experienced editor, both were an ideal match for the project. It took close to two years to prepare the texts for publication, while, in the meantime, Jarmila Jandová, a well-known specialist in translating Czech structuralist texts into Spanish, generously offered to revise the existing translations of Jan Mukařovský's essays. Before the translation and editing was completed, an American co-publisher was found to ensure that the book received proper American and worldwide distribution: Michigan Slavic Publications, represented by Jindřich Toman of the University of Michigan, Ann Arbor. Jindřich did an excellent job of revising and adjusting the entire manuscript in its last stages. At the final stage of the process, Fiona Gaze, copy chief for the English-language weekly *The Prague Post*, proofread the manuscript.

The main principles by which the texts in this volume were selected and arranged are described in the introduction. To determine the originals upon which translations would be based, we compiled and compared all the published versions of each text and chose the textually most reliable version, preferring those published in the author's "selected writings." In cases where an author had changed his own text and published it multiple times (Karel Teige, Jindřich Honzl, Josef Čapek, Václav Tille), we decided to use the text's first version and comment on significant later revisions in the editorial notes. In several cases (František Langer's "Cinema All the Time," "The Cinema" and "A. W. F. Co." by Josef and Karel Čapek, Stanislav Kostka Neumann's "Pictures—Little Pictures—Tiny, Tiny Pictures," Emil František Burian's "Film and Music," Petr Bogatyrev's "Disney's *Snow White*"), the draft translations from the mid-1980s were used as a starting point and thoroughly reworked by Kevin Johnson. Minor changes to Alexander Hackenschmied's "Film and Music," originally published in English, were made by Alice Lovejoy and Jindřich Toman. In the case of Roman Jakobson's "Is the Film in Decline?," the translation by Elena Sokol, authorized by the author and published in his *Selected Writings*, was adopted virtually without changes. All three translations of Jan Mukařovský's texts, previously published in a volume edited by John Burbank and Peter Steiner, were reworked by Jarmila Jandová, as indicated above. The German originals by Lubomír Linhart ("Proletarischer Filmkampf in der Tschechoslowakei") and Jan Evangelista Purkinje (two chapters from *Beiträge zur Kenntniss des Sehens in subjectiver Hinsicht*) were translated by Kevin Johnson, and the latter revised by Jaroslav Anděl.

The typesetting of some of the texts from the 1920s presented a specific challenge. The original publication of Teige's "Photo Cinema Film" plays with different fonts in a sophisticated way that we decided to imitate to the best extent possible. The same applies for the manifestos by Jiří Voskovec ("*Photogénie* and Suprareality") and Artuš Černík ("The Tasks of the Modern Film Librettist"), whose original verse-like layout was preserved. In all other cases where the original uses a change in script to highlight a passage, we use italics. All footnotes were added by Petr (with several contributions by Jaroslav, Kevin and Alice) if they are not marked as "original." The aim of the notes is the following: 1) to identify film titles, quotes and allusions; 2) to provide a historical context for names and events whose meaning in the text may be difficult for the contemporary reader to decipher, with an emphasis on film history; 3) to reveal connections with Czech film culture of the time (premieres of the films discussed, journals, associations, production, and distribution companies), a task to which special care was devoted. Most difficult proved to be the identification of film titles from the early cinema period (for instance, in the text by Tille) and some of the numerous loose quotations from unspecified sources. In cases where our citation of a probable source is uncertain, it is clearly indicated as such. Where films mentioned in the texts had an English-language release, the title of this release is noted—along with its director, country of origin, and year of production—in italics next to the film's original title or, in certain cases, in the editorial notes. Where a film did not have an English release title, the original title alone is used, except in cases where a literal translation of the title (here noted in roman type) is particularly relevant to the discussion at hand.

There are a number of other colleagues and friends to whom we are indebted for reading and commenting on parts of the manuscript in Czech and for helping to solve practical problems that arose during the editorial process. Czech film historians Ivan Klimeš and Jan Svoboda provided invaluable suggestions on the introduction. Director of the National Film Archive in Prague Vladimír Opěla agreed to become an official guarantor of the project and graciously supported it at the most critical moments. The students in Petr's 2004 seminar at Masaryk University in Brno, "A History of Czech Film Thought," where a large part of this material was discussed, inspired him to rework the introduction. Others who offered assistance at one time or another include Soňa Weigertová of the National Film Archive, Tereza Frodlová and Pavlína Vogelová of Masaryk University, and film historian Karel Tabery. Finally, we owe a debt of gratitude to all the copyright holders, who generously granted us permission to use the texts included in this book.

Petr Szczepanik, Brno – Jaroslav Anděl, New York, 2008

TRANSLATOR'S NOTE

The majority of the texts in this anthology are being made available to English speak-ers for the first time, and for this fact I am greatly honored to have participated in this project. I am convinced that this book will fill an important gap in both film studies and Slavic studies, since to date there is little detailed knowledge in the English-speaking world of the innovative work on cinema produced in this part of Central Europe during the first half of the twentieth century. Some of the authors presented here (e.g., Karel Čapek, Alexander Hackenschmied, Roman Jakobson, Jan Purkinje, possibly even Karel Teige and Vítězslav Nezval), might be known to the ca-sual non-Czech reader, but many (such as Zdeněk Pešánek, Lubomír Linhart, Bedřich Václavek, etc.) are all but completely unknown outside the Czech context even though their writing is in active conversation with the work of other (better-known) European thinkers of the period.

With the exception of Hackenschmied's "Film and Music" (originally published in English) and the articles by Jakobson and Mukařovský, all of the translations, in-cluding that of the introduction, are my own. With several texts, however, my work was based on Jitka Salaquarda's unpublished translation drafts commissioned by the Houston Museum of Fine Arts in the 1980s. Two of the texts—Purkinje's dissertation and Linhart's "The Proletarian Film Struggle in Czechoslovakia"—were originally published in German and my renderings are based on these versions. I would like to extend my deepest gratitude to Petr Szczepanik and Anna Ryndová for their help in deciphering the more obscure Czech passages, and to Alice Lovejoy and Jindřich Toman for their numerous suggestions regarding English style.

The task of the translator is always a divided one: to communicate as much of the meaning behind the words of the original text while also maintaining as much of the aesthetic structure that lends each piece its unique character. Inevitably, certain sub-tleties of a text's linguistic style are sacrificed in submitting its ideas to a foreign vo-cabulary and grammatical system. I have strived for consistency in rendering specif-ic vocabulary across the texts, to maintain a sense of terminological continuity within the overall discourse, yet this was naturally hindered by differences in connotation between Czech and English. An illustrative example can be seen in the Czech words *tvar*, *výtvarný*, *tvárný*, and various other etymologically related forms. *Tvar* is generally translated as "shape," "figure," or "form," whereas the derived adjective *výtvarný* carries a wide variety of connotations whose emphasis can shift significantly depending on the context in which it is used. For example, the common construction *výtvarné umění* (and its equivalent, *výtvarnictví*) encompasses the English concepts of "visual arts," "graphic arts," "creative arts," and "fine arts." Since the texts in this volume generally emphasize the act of seeing, *výtvarný* has, here, mostly been translated as "visual." In some cases, however, authors such as Teige use the term to specifically describe institutional or high art, thereby emphasizing a hierarchical distinction between film and traditional art forms. Accordingly, my translation here reads "artistic" or "fine-art." At the same time, some authors emphasize the concepts of "form" and "shape" inherent in the root of the term *výtvarný*, for example when Obrtel speaks of "forming a new world." In such contexts, the translation clearly demanded alternatives such as "plastic" and "formal." This idea of "forming" or "creating" is more commonly described by the related adjective *tvárný*. This is particularly evident in Pešánek's writing, which presents light and film as "plastic elements" (*výtvarné prvky*), in the sense of being malleable and shapeable. Yet with other authors (e.g., in Josef Čapek and Teige), *tvárný* has been translated as "creative." Inevitably, such contextual variances in translation not only disrupt the continuity of discourse across the texts, but also eclipse the shared lexical and semantic relatedness of the Czech terms.

These writings originated in a period when the language used to talk about film was still being developed and this is reflected in the variety of nonstandardized terminology, particularly in the earlier texts. Whereas the occurrence of "film" in the English translations generally reflects the same word (*film*) in Czech, the word "cinema" serves as a gloss for a variety of terms borrowed from the international parlance of the period, e.g., *kiném*, *biograf*, *kinematograf*, etc. The usage of these terms varies from author to author, yet their meanings are more or less synonymous. The terminological variance in Czech is more a reflection of the discourse's lack of standardization than of differences in overall meaning. In other cases where authors have integrated foreign expressions into their writing, I have also attempted to keep the foreign words in italics. This is most notable with occurrences of *fotogenie* and *kinografie*, which these Czech authors clearly do not employ as general descriptive terms (e.g., photogeneity or cinematography) but as an invocation of a specific theoretical discourse, namely the writings of Louis Delluc and other French thinkers. Thus, the editors and I have opted to retain the original French terms—*photogénie* and *cinégraphie*—in the English translation. In certain instances, we have felt it necessary to supplement the English translation with the original Czech terminology indicated in brackets; such cases are generally accompanied by a brief explanation in the endnotes.

In addition to reflecting the origins of Czech film thought, these texts also display evidence of having been written at a time when Czech itself was still emerging as a language of intellectual discourse, exploring its own expressive idiom, and seeking lexical and grammatical standardization. (Here it should be noted that, when Purkinje was writing, German was the common language of scientific and philosophical communication in the Czech lands.) Thus, on the fundamental linguistic level, a sense of innovation and experimentation belongs to the zeitgeist of these texts. Although the translations "correct" many of the syntactic inconsistencies and linguistic archaisms, I have tried as much as possible to retain the overall feel of the pieces, to capture the essence of each author's literary voice. Each text posed a unique set of challenges in this regard. For example, the language in the pieces by Tille and the Čapek brothers reflects the search for terminology at a time when a common language for film analysis had not yet developed. Meanwhile, the writings of Teige, Nezval, and Neumann employ a vibrant poetic style, often testing the limits of expression with liberal and often abstract usage of metaphor. The vocabulary of Burian and Hošek breaks down the distinctions between discourses on film, music, and technology, whereas Kučera employs the language of architectural construction to describe the filmmaking process, and Pešánek applies sculptural terms to what is commonly thought of as a two-dimensional medium. I have strived for fidelity to the spirit and intention of the original language, even if the resulting English constructions might be slightly clumsy and the metaphors somewhat forced. In cases where the syntax of the original is unusual or the implied meaning not entirely transparent, I have tried to communicate this as literally as possible, without imposing my own interpretation onto the text. I did not attempt to illuminate the original with my own words, in the desire for the intended ideas to shine through with limited alteration. The task of generating meaning from these writings and the language behind them is left to the reader.

Since little Czech film theory has been translated into English, there were very few models available for my renderings of the present texts, which afforded me some amount of freedom in my work. More importantly, this volume represents a first step toward establishing an English-language discourse for talking about early Czech film thought. These texts are not intended only as a transferal of historically documented ideas from Czech into English, but can also reveal new possibilities for conceiving of and describing filmic phenomena in English, just as they did in Czech (or German) when they were first committed to paper. I am certain that there will be disputes with regard to my rendering of particular concepts or stylistic elements, but my deepest hope is that this anthology opens the door for further interest in Czech writing on film that will lead to greater knowledge and increased conversation in this field.

Kevin B. Johnson, Prague, 2008

Jaroslav Anděl – Petr Szczepanik
CZECH FILM THOUGHT: AN INTRODUCTION

This anthology is neither structured according to the established practices of chronology common to traditional writings on film history (e.g., according to the dates of historical events, changes in artistic movements, the introduction of new technology, etc.) nor is it organized in rigid categories corresponding to institutionalized branches of film studies (e.g., film history, theory, and criticism, etc.). Instead, the groupings of texts herein are intended to reflect basic transformations within the discursive construction of film as both a medium and a cultural institution, as expressed in writings on film from the period. These discourses do not describe film as a predetermined or externally evident object but rather actively shape it, seek appropriate names for it, break it down into its constituent parts, and demarcate it with respect to other objects of study.[1]

Each set of texts is grouped according to a specific discursive common denominator. The individual chapters see film as a means to educate the masses and extend human perception (Chapter One), a new artistic medium as well as a new formal model and source of themes for poetry (Chapter Two), an ideal tool for functionalist construction or ideological struggle (Chapter Three), and a new medium for recording and manipulating speech (Chapter Four). Furthermore, we turn to authors who envision alternative modes of film practice that radically deviate from the norms of classical narrative cinema and predate contemporary developments in multimedia

---

[1]   This way of conceptualizing an overview of writings on film and media is inspired by discourse history and the Foucauldian archaeology of knowledge. This is not the first time such an approach has been used: it is also applied in Albert Kümmel and Petra Löffler's volume of early German writings on media (*Medientheorie 1888–1933: Texte und Kommentare*, Frankfurt am Main: Suhrkamp, 2002) and in the exhaustive anthology of French film writing compiled by Richard Abel (*French Film Theory and Criticism: A History/Anthology 1907–1939*, Princeton: Princeton University Press, 1993). The present anthology only adopts historical discourse analysis as a point of departure, and does not rigorously apply the method. Instead, its goal is to acquaint the reader with the most compelling examples of early Czech film thought with an emphasis on film theory and artistic programs, to the necessary exclusion of many other genres and areas of reflection on the film medium.

and interactive art (Chapter Five), as well as to authors who seek film's aesthetic specificity in its signifying systems and spatial-temporal structures (Chapter Six). The organization of the anthology does not, however, lack a chronological dimension: Chapter One comprises texts from the beginning of the twentieth century, Chapter Two of texts from the first half of the 1920s, Chapter Three of texts from the period around 1930, and Chapters Four through Six of texts from the 1930s. The outbreak of World War II disrupted the continuity of both avant-garde and structuralist thought, thereby offering an appropriate temporal boundary for our selection of texts.

An ideal overview of the discursive construction of film would cover the entire spectrum of various genres of film writing. It is impossible to achieve such an ideal within a single volume, and thus this anthology includes only those texts that might prove most compelling to a wide readership, academic and nonacademic alike: programmatic texts of the avant-garde, artistic manifestos, the most important film-theoretical treatises, and reflections by specialists from other fields. Consequently, this volume excludes early texts that express general astonishment or indignation at the cinematograph as an invention and a new popular attraction, routine film reviews from magazines or newspapers, texts directly linked with industrial or state institutions, as well as creative works (such as poems and novels that invoke the film medium and the so-called "film librettos" of the avant-garde). From a historical perspective, all of these genres and ways of writing about film are no less interesting and deserving of in-depth study, but it was simply not possible to include them in a single book.

1. Kinéma: The Physiology of Vision, the Pedagogy of Perception, and the Cubistic Fragmentation of Reality

The anthology's earliest text is an excerpt from the doctoral dissertation of the multi-talented natural scientist and philosopher Jan Evangelista Purkinje (Purkyně in Czech). Published in 1819, Purkinje's dissertation was a foundational work on the physiology of perception. Purkinje intended to supplement existing knowledge of what was then termed "objective vision," with a particular focus on internal "subjective sense phenomena."[2] With this work, Purkinje promoted the method of empirical experimentation with one's own organs of vision. By systematically applying external stimuli (such as extreme light, pressure on the closed eye, limited blood flow to the head, or intensified breathing), he instigated various internal visual sensations that had no correlation to external reality. He then systematically described, sketched,

---

[2]   Jan Evangelista Purkinje, *Beiträge zur Kenntniss des Sehens in subjectiver Hinsicht* (Praha: Fr. Vetterl, 1819).

and classified these subjective sensory phenomena, recording measurements of their temporal duration, and comparing them quantitatively and qualitatively. He subsequently sought analogies with the other senses. For example, he likened the abstract shape of internal visual sensations to the so-called "sound images" that arise from the effect of sound waves on liquid or sand, as described by the German physicist and acoustics pioneer Ernst Chladni. From such analogies with sound, Purkinje came to the conclusion that sight, like hearing, is dependent on spatial oscillations, i.e., on some form of constant unseen motion, and that contact with external light is not the only way to induce these oscillations in the eye.

In the second part of the dissertation, particularly in the last two chapters, "Die Bewegungen des Auges" [Eye movements] and "Das Nachbild, Imagination, Gedächtnis des Gesichtsinnes" [Persisting images, imagination, the sense of sight's memory], the latter of which is included in this anthology, Purkinje offers a detailed examination of certain concepts that played a key role in the development of optical media in the nineteenth and twentieth centuries, namely the relationship between individual sense organs, binocular vision, and most of all the persisting image and visual memory. Visual persistence had been known at least since late antiquity, but Purkinje offers a new interpretation, one that, as he himself later specifically noted, was a prerequisite for the development of new technologies of the moving image (e.g., the thaumatrope and phenakistoscope):

> For several years now, I have been interested in the theory of these so-called optical magical wheels. Of course, this is merely a consequence of the observations I made long ago about the image that persists in the mind when the eye blinks, with the effect that the perceived vision of reality is not interrupted.[3]

In contrast to his predecessors, Purkinje did not simply define vision as an inertia-driven image of the external world, but rather as the result of a constructive operation equipped with its own "memory" and "imagination," and, furthermore, influenced by the neurophysiological and mental state of the human organism at the moment of vision.

Purkinje's dissertation is perhaps the earliest example of scientific discoveries that laid the groundwork for the rise of two major cultural developments of the twen-

---

[3]   František X. Halas, "Z neznámé korespondence J. E. Purkyně II," *Universitas: revue Univerzity J. E. Purkyně v Brně* 20, no. 2 (1987), 50; see also Jaroslav Anděl, "Pitture in Boemia–La nascita dell'artista e del critico moderno: arte, scienza e scoperta del tempo," in *La nascita dell'impressionismo*, ed. Marco Goldin (Conegliano: Linea d'ombra libri, 2000), 332–339; and Siegfried Zielinski, *Archäologie der Medien: Zur Tiefenzeit des technischen Hörens und Sehens* (Reinbek bei Hamburg: Rowohlt, 2002), 230–231.

tieth century: abstract art and new media technologies. The author himself attests to these connections in the chapter of his dissertation on "eye movements," where he predicts that, in the future, abstraction (which he calls "eye music" and identifies in nonrepresentational art forms and genres) will become an artistic program:

> When we look at regular geometric figures—spirals, circles, and wavy lines, symmetrical patterns, ornaments, and decorations—where order and necessity rule, the eye feels as if it is being pulled away from the outlines of the objects. The movements are easier, half automatic, so that they are transferred to the objects at which we are looking and that seem to manifest their own life and movement. This makes a strange impression and is also accompanied by sensations of tension in the eyeball. It would be worth the effort to define this kind of eye music as a separate art form, which beckons to us everywhere in nature and in the world of art. Surely this would open a new path for a creative genius, if the implementations were of sufficient magnitude. As of now, it does not seem that this art's time has arrived. It must serve as a slave to the adornment of clothes, buildings and gardens. Only in fireworks, dance and gymnastic performances, altars, flower gardens, transparent circles with movements in the center, and as of late in the kaleidoscope, did this art take on an independent life. However, because it marches through the world jointly with clowns, it is not recognized by aristocratic taste and is overlooked.[4]

The connection between Purkinje's work and later media is best exemplified in his encyclopedia entry on the "Kinesiskop," published forty-five years later, in which he forecasts not only the future shape of the film apparatus, but also its significance as a medium for science, entertainment, and art:

> This innovation [the introduction of intermittent movement] opens up a broad range of applications for this device, which one might call a magical device. It is of particular importance that this magic lantern can present a large public with diverse movements from natural, historical, and artistic performances, and it will even give rise to special branches of the science industry that will prove useful in schools and more generally for instruction and entertainment. [...] These performances can occur either on a small scale or can be enlarged as desired by optical means onto translucent surfaces. We can expect that, under the mastery of artists, this thing will eventually become

---

4   J. E. Purkinje, "Contributions to the Knowledge of Vision in its Subjective Aspect," in *Purkinje's Vision: The Dawning of Neuroscience*, ed. and trans. Nicholas J. Wade and Josef Brožek in collaboration with Jiří Hoskovec (Mahwah, NJ: Lawrence Erlbaum Associates, 2001), 106.

5   J. E. Purkyně, "Kinesiskop," in *Slovník naučný*, vol. 4, ed. František Ladislav Rieger and Jakub Malý (Praha: I. L. Kober, 1864), 657.

a special branch of visual art, where it will no longer suffice to create a single moment of an action in progress, but will also create entire actions and an entire people.[5]

Purkinje also made his mark in the history of optical media as an inventor and entrepreneur. In 1840, while teaching in Wrocław, he began to build upon the experiments of the Viennese professor of geometry Simon Stampfer, suggesting improvements and new applications for Stampfer's Stroboscope. Czech historian of precinematic inventions Jindřich Brichta sums up Purkinje's contribution to the field of stroboscopics and the development of moving pictures thus: "In separating the aperture wheel from the picture wheel, he created the first rotating shutter, which is still to this day used in all cameras and projectors (albeit with a different function)."[6] In contrast to other stroboscopic devices that also made use of the physiological phenomenon of the persistence of the image, such as Joseph Antoine Plateau's Phenakistoscope,[7] Purkinje divided the picture wheel into two parts that rotated on the same shaft: one with pictures of motion phases, the other with a series of apertures. In doing so, he eliminated the need to watch the rotating wheel in a mirror, which opened up the possibility of projecting the moving image. Purkinje made the first attempts to commercially exploit his invention as early as the 1840s, when he marketed it as an optical toy under the name "Phorolyt." After returning to Prague from Wrocław, he once again (unsuccessfully) put his invention up for sale, this time as the "Kinesiscope." Whereas the pictures in Purkinje's first stroboscopic wheels were hand-drawn (for example, a popular-scientific series of wheels showing the function of the heart and the circulatory system), he later began using photographs of motion phases.[8] At the beginning of the 1860s, he began experimenting with another precinematic principle: the intermittent movement of the picture wheel, which facilitated projection onto a large surface, thereby allowing a larger number of spectators than when a peephole is necessary to view the image. In this, Purkinje's work predated better-known inventions of the 1890s, when the introduction of intermittent motion became a key turning point in the development of the cinematic apparatus.[9]

As mentioned above, Purkinje's work belongs to the category of scientific hypotheses that anticipated the film medium as it would develop. Naturally, neither reflec-

---

[6]   Jindřich Brichta, "Jan Evangelista Purkyně a film," *Film a doba* 1, no. 5–6 (1955), 234.

[7]   Plateau's phenakistoscope, invented in 1832, had just one wheel with pictures of motion phases positioned between radial apertures. This wheel rotated in front of a mirror, and the spectator looked through the apertures to watch quickly changing scenes shown in cyclical movement on the mirror.

[8]   One preserved photographic series depicts Purkinje's own chest in ten positions as it gradually turns on its vertical axis. It belongs to the collection of the National Technical Museum in Prague.

[9]   See Brichta, "Jan Evangelista Purkyně a film," 235–236.

Figure 1. Picture wheel from Jan Evangelista Purkinje's "Kinesiscope," showing a series of photographs of Purkinje turning his head, ca. 1860. Karel Smrž, *Dějiny filmu* (Praha: Družstevní práce, 1933), 155.

tions on cinema as a technical invention, scientific plaything, or entertaining attraction nor the first thoughts about the nascent institution of cinema appear until later, at the turn of the twentieth century. If we disregard responses to the kinesiscope, phonograph, and other protocinematic devices, the first substantial array of written reactions to cinema in the Czech lands are the advertisements and reports that circulated in connection with the presentations of the Lumière brothers' Cinematograph in 1896 and the film projections of the first Czech filmmaker, Jan Křiženecký, two years later. The cinematograph, of course, does not mark the singular starting point of film history. At first, it was merely one in a series of machines showing "living pictures" and had the status of a "protomedium" that had not yet been constituted as an independent cultural institution. It is, therefore, no wonder that this emerging medium aroused the greatest interest in those fields to which it was closely related and which could, therefore, attempt to bring it under their own jurisdictions.[10] The greatest number of early reports and reflections on the cinematograph were published in photographic and scientific magazines such as *Fotografický věstník* [Photographic gazette], *Fotografický obzor* [Photographic horizon], and *Z říše vědy a práce* [From the realm of science and work]. These were followed by illustrated magazines and eventually by the daily press, whereas cultural journals took no notice of cinema whatsoever during this period. In those publications that did write about cinema, it was regarded primarily as a scientific-technological novelty and possibilities for its application were sought in the most diverse of fields, ranging from the natural sciences to education, criminology, medicine, and the military to journalism and, finally, entertainment.

Cultural critics only began to take notice of the cinema in the middle of the twentieth century's first decade, a time when fictional genres began to assume predominance over non-fictional genres in cinema programs, and the cinema was becoming, in the words of novelist and columnist Karel Scheinpflug, "a permanent attraction of *variétés*, wandering nomadically around the cities and even into the countryside," where it "triumphantly beats out the panoramas with stereoscopic viewfinders."[11] Of course, the first questions that these critics pose do not address the specificity of the new medium and its expressive means, but rather its effect on society, its "cultural mission" in relation to the established institutions of entertainment, learning, and education (e.g., the family, schools, adult educational facilities, the theater, travel, etc.). According to Scheinpflug, cinematic images' rather negative aesthetic and educational effect is determined wholly by the character of the phenomena they represent, whereby film techniques and staging practices can only corrupt their effect. Yet Scheinplug's text "Kinematograf vychovatelem" [The cinema as educator, 1904] is only a harbinger of a larger public discourse on the malignant effect of the cinema on children and youth that would become a predominant issue in writing on film in the 1910s. As in other European countries, the main figures involved in this dis-

---

[10]   For more on this evolutionary stage of cinema and the so-called "jurisdictional struggle" waged by established institutions for control over the nascent medium, see Rick Altman, "What it Means to Write the History of *Cinema*," in *Toward a Pragmatics of the Audiovisual: Theory and History*, vol. 1, ed. Jürgen E. Müller (Münster: Nodus Publikationen, 1994), 169–180.

[11]   Karel Scheinpflug, "Kinematograf vychovatelem," *Květy* 26, no. 6 (1904), 839. *Variété* (in the Czech original, *divadlo zvláštností*): the European equivalent of vaudeville; *variété* as well as vaudeville constituted the dominant context for film exhibition before 1905, and also provided a model for film form and for the structure of cinema programs; see Josef Garncarz, "Vom *Variété* zum Kino: Ein Plädoyer für ein erweitertes Konzept der Intermedialität," in *Intermedialität: Theorie und Praxis eines interdisziplinären Forschungsgebiets*, ed. Jörg Helbig (Berlin: Erich Schmidt, 1998), 244–256.

course were pedagogues, experts in adult education, women's organizations, and church leaders, and the aim of their lamentations was not the objective analysis of the new medium and the assessment of its possibilities, but rather to provoke the public and the authorities to more rigorous regulation of the hygienic conditions of the cinema auditoriums and morally unhealthy film content. Initially, only a very weak circle of film professionals stood in opposition to these critical voices. These were predominantly small-time entrepreneurs who lacked a platform from which to defend their interests, since film periodicals did not begin to emerge until the beginning of the 1910s, and even these were, at first, little more than narrowly focused, utilitarian trade journals. Gradually, though, arising from the protests of educators, an alternative vision of film as a tool for school lessons and adult education began to take shape. Although this vision never took predominance over the concept of cinema as a mass medium, until the late 1930s it continued to play an important role in the discourse of the cultural elite, citizens' groups, and state institutions, which attempted to integrate film into their concept of culture as education.[12]

The development of film writing that primarily addressed cinema's medium specificity, its aesthetics and criticism, began with Václav Tille's extensive study "Kinéma" (1908), and was followed with texts by other Prague theater critics, writers, and modern artists a few years later. As a professor of comparative literary history at the Charles-Ferdinand University in Prague, Tille focused on the study and translation of modern French literature and on the history of Czech fairy tales, whereas his journalistic activity was primarily dedicated to theater criticism. In addition, he also wrote about forty reviews, articles, and lectures that promoted ideas about film's educational potential and laid the foundation for Czech film criticism.[13] In "Kinéma," the most comprehensive of these, Tille sought to define the new medium's sociocultural meaning, as well as its particular aesthetic and ontological essence. In addition,

[12]   The first film journal in the Czech lands, *Der Anzeiger für die gesamte Kinematographen-Industrie* [Gazette for the entire cinema industry, 1907–1908], printed in German, was produced under the direction of Brno (Brünn) cinema owner Dominik Morgenstern. Czech-language film journals only began to appear several years later: *Český kinematograf* [Czech cinema] in 1911–1912, *Kinematografické listy* [Cinema magazine] in 1911, and *Kino* in 1913–1914. On the discussions of the malignant social effects of the cinema and its possible educational uses, see Ivan Klimeš, "Děti v brlohu: Boj proti kinematografům – bojem o dítě!," in *V bludném kruhu: Mateřství a vychovatelství jako paradoxy modernity*, ed. Petra Hanáková, Libuše Heczková, Eva Kalivodová (Praha: Slon, 2006), 193–236; and Jiří Pokorný, *Lidová výchova na přelomu 19. a 20. století* (Praha: Karolinum, 2003), 221–232.

[13]   See Lubomír Linhart, *První estetik filmu Václav Tille* [Václav Tille, the first film aesthetician] (Praha: ČSFÚ, 1968). Linhart's book contains all of Tille's texts about film, including unpublished handwritten notes. The article "Kinéma," however, was significantly shortened, omitting the first section, which presents a detailed history of the shadow play as a precursor to cinema. We have therefore chosen the original 1908 printing as the basis for the translation in this anthology.

he attempted to trace film's genealogical roots and to critically evaluate current film production. Above all, however, the most pressing question for Tille was whether film could truly be art. In terms of its theoretical ambitions and its coherence, "Kinéma" is probably the oldest text of its kind in the world, predating both Ricciotto Canudo's article "Naissance d'un sixième art" [The birth of the sixth art, 1911] and Vachel Lindsay's book *The Art of the Moving Picture* (1915).

"Kinéma" was written at and describes the important moment when cinema was liberating itself from its subjugation to other media and cultural forms (photography, *variété*, illustrated lectures), when the cultural elite began to comprehend it as an autonomous phenomenon, and when narrative was both emerging as its dominant aesthetic form and itself growing internally coherent. Using terminology borrowed from the "new film history," this was the period of early cinema's transition from a system that André Gaudreault and Tom Gunning have termed "monstrative attractions" (1895–1908) to a stage of "narrative integration" (1908–1914) in which film form was subordinated to narrative drive.[14] In this period (1908–1909), systematic thinking about film gradually started to emerge also in other countries, notably France and Germany, stimulated by increasing regularization of the production and distribution of fiction films.[15] There was no systematic film production to speak of in the Czech lands (which were still part of Austria) at that time; nevertheless, the stimulus for Tille's text can probably be attributed to changes within the systems of film distribution (centered in Vienna) and exhibition as much as to his own longtime interest in folk art, fairy tales, theater, and technical inventions. By 1908, the first permanent cinemas had begun operating in Prague and other Czech cities,[16] leading to a partial standardization of distribution and a transition from retail sales to wholesale rental circulation. At the same time, the supply of foreign fiction films (French and American melodramas, comic sketches, fantasy scenes, etc.) increased, and so-called "art films" of increasing length and complexity came to the Czech lands from abroad, attracting the middle classes to the cinemas. When one of these films, Albert Capellani's ambitious adaptation of Alphonse Daudet's drama *L'Arlésienne*, premiered at the Grand "Orient" Kinema (the most luxurious Prague movie house of the time, specializing in French "art films") in October 1908, it became the subject of Tille's first film review, which was probably the very first Czech film review

---

14 André Gaudreault and Tom Gunning, "Le Cinéma des premiers temps: un défi à l'histoire du cinéma?," in *L'Histoire du cinéma: nouvelles approches*, ed. Jacques Aumont, André Gaudreault, Michel Marie (Paris: Publications de la Sorbonne, 1989), 49–63.

15 See Abel, *French Film Theory and Criticism*, vol. 1., xv; Jörg Schweinitz, *Prolog vor dem Film. Nachdenken über ein neues Medium 1909–1914* (Leipzig: Reclam, 1992), 9–10.

16 The first permanent movie theater in the Czech lands opened in 1906 in Brno; by 1908, there were eight cinemas in Prague alone.

altogether.[17] Later that month, a number of films by the French Film d'Art company were also screened at the Grand "Orient" Kinema, and Tille discusses these enthusiastically in "Kinéma," which was published in November of the same year.

In "Kinéma," Tille describes some of the characteristics of the film medium that would play a key role in subsequent reflections on cinema, such as the tension between the realistic effect of the film image and its ability to give concrete form to fantasy, the conflict between continuity and discontinuity in filmic narrative, and the constructive possibilities of film editing. Additionally, we can see precursors to contemporary film terminology in such intuitive expressions as "how pictures are assembled" (i.e., editing), "the camera placed farther away" (the long shot), "forced pantomime" (silent acting), and "artificial breaks" (Méliès-style tricks). The primary context from which Tille describes filmic style is that of theater, which, he points out, is the source of film's expressive means, but from which, at the same time, film fundamentally differs. In contrast to the theatrical stage, whose fictional world resides in symbolic gestures and objects, Tille argues that the nature of the film image is rather like a slice of a larger world that, in the mind of the spectator, extends beyond the edges of the screen. Film also introduces a new style of acting founded on a "more faithfully detailed reality," on the interplay between facial expressions and realistic environments, and on the rejection of conventional theatrical gestures, make-up, and costumes. The structurally defining principle of filmic form is the dialectical relationship between fragmentation and synthesis; that is, rapid switches between different environments and temporalities are held in balance by an artificially constructed continuity. Tille succeeds in identifying several aspects of the film image that would later be singled out as indicative of its specific filmic, photogenic, and radically nontheatrical (or nonliterary) character: the composition of fantastic spaces from fragments of everyday reality; the special appeal of movement perpendicular to the screen (toward or away from the spectator), which amplifies a film's sense of plasticity; the visual effect of many figures milling around in one space compared with that of a wild chase; breaking down temporal continuity into a rapid series of moments, etc.

Tille's text also analyzes film's sociological dimensions by exploring the connection between film and the contemporary sensual and emotional experience associated with life in the (Western) metropolis, new forms of transportation, and social changes at the height of modernity. He places particular emphasis on film's ability to fragment and accelerate the perception of time and space, and on its inclination

---

[17]   Václav Tille, "Daudetova Arelatka v kinematografu" [originally published October 31, 1908], in Lubomír Linhart, *První estetik filmu Václav Tille* (Praha: ČSFÚ, 1968), 91–92. The film *L'Arlésienne* (Albert Capellani, France, 1908) was produced by the Société Cinématographique des Auteurs et Gens de Lettres (established by Pathé) and featured famous Parisian theater actors. See also Zdeněk Štábla, *Data a fakta z dějin čs. kinematografie 1896–1945*, vol. 1. (Praha: ČSFÚ, 1988), 108, 144, 147–148.

toward shocking spectacles, extreme situations, and (most of all) rapid motion. On multiple occasions, he turns his attention to "really exciting" situations, such as a cliffside chase, riding horseback along railroad tracks, a moving train, bomb attacks, and automobile explosions. Film strives to "forcibly captivate" the spectator with all means of sensory shocks and rapid emotional turns, as well as with "journalistic sensationalism," technological tricks, and grotesque acrobatic performances. For Tille, typical manifestations of this tendency are criminal and detective films, "whose ultimate goals are sensation and constant suspense, livened up with the use of diverse modern inventions rather than with old-fashioned sentimentality." The sensory and emotional effects of such films elucidate the very technological foundation of the film medium:

> The material of these stories adapts well to the accelerated vivacity of the cinematic projector and to its demand for brief, concise, and overt actions. This is produced by forced pantomime on the one hand, and on the other by the very mode by which movement is reproduced, since the faster and more precise a movement is, the more natural and less jerky the movement reproduced in a continuous series of images will be.

The anthropological dimension of Tille's thinking is expressed by his attempts to find analogies between, on the one hand, film's ability to materialize dreams and ideas, and, on the other, the age-old human endeavor to create visual, external projections of the "play of ideas from the inner parts of [the] mind" (whether in the form of a reflection on the surface of water, shadows moving in the night, or the laterna magica). Tille concludes his study with the assertion that film has introduced a means to mechanically copy the processes of human perception and imagination, thereby also providing artists with a medium for creating new, living fantasy worlds. While, in this sense, Tille's anthropological line of thought bears a strong resemblance to that found much later in Edgar Morin's book *Le Cinéma ou l'homme imaginaire*,[18] such comparisons between film and mental processes can be found as early as 1907, in Henri Bergson's work *Évolution créatrice*, which, according to Lubomír Linhart, it is likely that Tille read prior to writing "Kinéma." All the same, Tille generally maintained an unfavorable attitude toward the French philosopher, and their analyses differ.[19] Whereas Bergson's model serves to explain the rational capabilities of human consciousness, Tille's addresses the imaginative side of human consciousness and attempts to uncover the anthropological aspects of the new creativity introduced by cinema.

---

[18]   Edgar Morin, *Le Cinéma ou l'homme imaginaire* (Paris: Éditions de Minuit, 1956).

[19]   See Linhart, *První estetik filmu Václav Tille*, 15.

A more direct inspiration from Bergson can be seen in the work of poet Stanislav K. Neumann, whose article "Pictures—Little Pictures—Tiny, Tiny Pictures" (1913) characterizes illustrated magazines, photography, and the cinema as means of communication that serve the special needs of modern life. Neumann's positive assessment of film and, indirectly, of modern society in general is founded in his concept of "vitalism," which was inspired philosophically by Bergson as well as by Wilhelm Ostwald's notion of "energetism," and influenced artistically by Walt Whitman, Emile Verhaeren, and futurism. At the end of the 1910s, film came, in a sense, to symbolize life for Neumann and thereby also to serve as an inspiration for artistic creation, as evidenced by his poem "Film" (1919), with which we have chosen to introduce this anthology. This poem expresses a fascination with film as a typical expression of the dynamism, democracy, and internationalism of the modern era and as a creative inspiration for poetry, sentiments that anticipated the enthusiasm for film demonstrated by the young avant-garde headed by Karel Teige.

It is likely that Neumann was also affected by the literary works of the younger Czech generation that had preceded Neumann in "discovering" film. This is attested, for example, by Neumann's likening of film technique to the new literary approaches found in Josef Čapek's novel *Lélio* and the collection of short stories *Boží muka* [Wayside crosses] by his brother, Karel Čapek:

> In both books, we often come across examples of narrative and syntactic discontinuity between images, descriptions, and events that are not externally related, but seem to be illogically bound together with cinematic frugality into a single stream despite their occasional semantic, temporal, and spatial incoherence. Using this method, the authors achieve a purely poetic succinctness of content, a briskness that enraptures, an intensity of effect and magic that unwittingly restores to our minds the lost feeling of wholeness in the entirety of life, while at the same time dematerializing reality into pictures, as if it were being seen through a child's eyes. [20]

The features of the "new creative effort" Neumann describes were formulated by the younger generation of artists who constituted the Group of Fine Artists (Skupina výtvarných umělců), founded in Prague in 1911. Skupina's journal *Umělecký měsíčník* [Artist's monthly] was the most prominent Czech platform for new artistic programs, particularly cubism. The members of Skupina, including the Čapeks and František Langer, not only published the first programmatic writings on film by the Czech avant-garde, but also created the first serious artistic experiments in the realm of film

---

[20] S. K. Neumann, "Dvě knihy skutečně nové" [1918], in his *Stati a projevy, vol. 5, 1918–1921* (Praha: Odeon, 1971), 18.

production. Several months after the 1913 publication of his theoretical article "Cinema All the Time," discussed below, Langer wrote the scenario for the film *Noční děs* [Night terror, Jan A. Palouš, 1914], a production of the ASUM company, which had been founded by another Skupina colleague, Max Urban.[21]

The main impulse behind "Cinema All the Time" was not film praxis, however, but rather current discussions about the relationship between literary writing and film. A concrete example of this relationship can be seen in the collaborations between authors, of whom Langer was one, in writing film librettos (a.k.a. "Kinostücke") under the initiative of Kurt Pinthus, a German writer and dramaturge at Max Reinhardt's theater in Berlin. Pinthus's goal was to create a collection of original screenplays that would serve the development of film's expressive possibilities better than the adaptations of plays or novels that were common at the time. In addition to Langer, Prague authors Otto Pick and Max Brod, who wrote in German, also contributed to the project, which resulted in a collection of sixteen texts titled *Das Kinobuch*, published in 1914.[22] The contributing authors shared a thoroughly skeptical view of cinema, and their screenplay experiments were unbound plays of fancy written without the prospect of eventually being realized on film. Such a mixture of critical distance and fascination with the new medium is also expressed in Langer's article, which directly cites Pinthus's project.

At the same time, Langer's piece expands on Tille's observations about the differences between theater and film with its analysis of what would today be called the pragmatic relationships between a filmic text, its author, and its recipient. In contrast to the theater, Langer writes, film's most important players are its practitioners (the director and actors) as well as its spectators. These figures play an autonomous role, whereas the story's author and its spiritual implications are relegated to a tangential position. That is to say, film does not consider itself superior to its spectators and demands from them nothing more than rapt visual attention, because the full meaning of the events it depicts is revealed on its visible surface: "cinema is *a priori* something democratic, popular, created expressly for a broad public." Filmic events

---

21   Urban, an architect and film director, founded ASUM in 1912 together with actress Anna Sedláčková; the company's name was derived from their initials. ASUM's films emphasized their visual components over their literary components, and display many elements linked to cubism: rapid changes in the perspective and scale of the shot, dynamic movements through space, the integration of text and image, and a tension between events and their alternative interpretations that is similar to the distinction, in cubist painting, between an object and the various aspects of its appearance.

22   Kurt Pinthus, *Das Kinobuch* (Leipzig: Kurt Wolff Verlag, 1914). Langer's libretto is named "Der Musterkellner" [The ideal waiter]. In addition to anticipating the poetist "film poems" of the 1920s, the contributions by Langer and the other Prague authors to this collection mark the de facto beginnings of Czech screenplay writing; see Ivan Klimeš, "Z počátků scenáristiky v českých zemích," *Iluminace* 4, no. 2 (1992), 57–64.

offer spectators the pleasure of recognizing their own quotidian world as it is elevated to a nobler plane and objectified by the machine, thereby building up the common viewer's self-confidence. Langer demonstrates how film's ability to record simple objects and everyday work enables man to reassess his own life: "Now that he sees a piece of himself, he analyzes and objectifies himself, albeit only physically, but he does *recognize himself*." Langer associates film's ability to do this with the festive aspect of photographic representation and the ritualistic nature of the photographic act, which would later become one of the leading topics of photographic and film theory. His characterization of photographed objects as being "ceremoniously translated" is reminiscent of Marcel Duchamp's conception of the "readymade," which appeared the same year, and also anticipates the formalist concept of defamiliarization.

Langer also deals with the realism of cinematic direction and acting style. He argues that film acting is founded upon the simplification and separation of bodily movements into a series of static phases that correspond to the rhythm of the cinematic camera. By contrast, the goal of cinematic direction is to be perfectly transparent, to merge film and reality. With his emphasis on the spectator, for whom film is an "expansion of his life consciousness," on film's ability to "objectify" quotidian reality, and on the breakdown of movement into a series of unmoving positions, Langer's thoughts also bear certain similarities to cubism and neoclassicism, and, indeed, during the time he wrote this text, Langer was actively engaged in acquainting the Czech public with such contemporary art movements.[23]

The influence of cubist theory is even more evident in the texts of Karel and Josef Čapek. Their co-authored article "The Cinema" (1910) expresses an enchantment with the cinema as a form of popular culture, foreshadowing the avant-garde's interest, in the 1920s, in peripheral artistic genres and its relativizing of the hierarchy between high and low art. Karel Čapek's article "The Style of the Cinematograph" (1913) is undoubtedly the most profound theoretical study of film written in Czech during the 1910s. It not only offers a classification of genres and stylistic tendencies, but also a critical assessment of the attempted literary and theatrical reform of film at the time, against which he argues that the cinema must retain its fundamentally visual nature. Furthermore, Čapek provides an analysis of filmic language that he hopes will set the agenda for the future development of film as a unique art form. Beyond the influence of cubism, Čapek's thinking was also inspired by pragmatism, relativism, and modern scientific theories. Like Langer, he accentuates the idea of

---

[23] For example, in his essay "O novém umění" [On the new art], he discusses the work of Picasso and Braque; see František Langer, "O novém umění," in František Langer, *Prostor díla* (Praha: Akropolis, 2001), 14. The study originally appeared in a series of five installments in the newspaper *Lidové noviny* (June–July 1913).

"intensive and extraordinary realism," although Čapek connects this primarily with the principle of discontinuity, whereby variations in the viewing distance express "specific *objective and psychological relationships* between the spectator and the image." In the cinema, reality is accessible in various degrees of visibility. The spectator sees things from multiple angles and distances. Čapek's discussion of a "part that is greatly magnified and extremely actualized" may represent the very first description of a close-up to be found in Czech film theory.[24] According to Čapek, changes in the angle and distance of view, particularly magnification, result in an extraordinary expressivity and intensity of represented reality. Čapek considers this "analytic" process (which came to be labeled as "montage" after the 1920s) a stylistic quality specific to cinema as well as a conceptual blueprint for film art of the future. Cinema's task, he writes, is to show "a new, more complex, more expressive, highly detailed and dispersed vision of reality; to provide objects of intensive perception and inexhaustible interest."

Like his theories on film, Čapek's literary works also display characteristics typical of cubist painting, such as the desire to view objects from multiple sides, faceting, the juxtaposition of various perspectives, the analysis of spatial forms, and tension between the external and internal aspects of a thing.[25] Thus, we can understand his writings on cinema as part of his literary agenda, with cinema serving both as a source of inspiration and as a projection of literary ideals realized in another medium.[26] Parallels can also be drawn between Čapek's reflections on film and the constructivist theories of Dziga Vertov. The two are connected in their use of formulations such as the "organization of reality," their emphasis on film's documentary quality, the connections they draw between film realism and the discontinuity of time and space, as well as their attribution of equivalent value to actors and non-human elements in film. Likewise, the passages in which Čapek discusses the psychological characteristics and functions of film are reminiscent of Sergei Eisenstein's theories, which also highlight the psychological effects of montage on the spectator. Some of Čapek's ideas seem to anticipate Eisenstein's theory of a "montage of attractions" and his notion that the spectator's consciousness is a material to be forcefully molded by a series of shocks. In Čapek's words, film should seek "to gain the most powerful sensation from things" and to "impact the spectator directly, shape his interest, and force extraordinarily powerful, penetrating, and full perception upon him."

---

[24] The term "magnification" [*zvětšení*] was used to designate a close-up into the 1920s, whereas the current Czech term is *detail*.

[25] See, for instance, Čapek's short story "Utkvění času" [The suspension of time, 1913], or his later collections of short stories *Boží muka* [Wayside crosses, 1917] and *Trapné povídky* [Painful tales, 1921].

[26] See Jaroslav Anděl, "Cubism, Film, and Literature," in *Czech Cubism 1909–1925: Art, Architecture, Design* (Prague: Modernista, 2006), 378–383.

While the correlations between these two theories of the psychological aspects of montage can likely be traced to a common inspiration in the pragmatic philosophy of William James, it is important to note that Čapek's interpretation differs significantly from Soviet film theory and indeed from the majority of avant-garde movements of the 1920s in that it is not rooted in social and technological utopianism or in the artistic ideologies of collectivism and progress.

In the article "A. W. F. Co." (1917), which takes its title from the initials of the World Film Corporation (an American distributor of independent productions established in 1914), Karel Čapek professes his love for American film, which—like jazz and *variété*—was a key source of inspiration for his own literary writing. Josef Čapek then builds upon both of his brother Karel's texts with his article "Film" (1918), where he provides a concise overview of various national cinema styles, including his vision for the possible development of Czech film. Josef later included this article in his book *Nejskromnější umění* [The humblest art], which also contained reflections on photography, illustrated magazines, and urban folklore.[27] In the 1920s, this book would have a significant effect on the avant-garde artists of the group Devětsil [Nine strengths][28], whose programs and manifestos were inspired by film.

2. Construction and Poetry: Film as a Poetist Machine

Karel Teige's comprehensive programmatic study "Photo, Cinema, Film" first appeared in 1922 in the second annual volume of the anthology *Život: Sborník nové krásy* [Life: an anthology of the new beauty].[29] With its manifesto-like declaration of photography and film as the most modern artistic disciplines, Teige's text represents the consummation of the approach developed in the texts of the Čapek brothers and Neumann. Nevertheless, Teige advocated a significantly different artistic ideology that accented ideas of technological progress and collectivism, and his text is an indication of the important role these ideas played in the development of film theory in the 1920s, establishing a new position for film within the hierarchy of artistic disciplines and defining an ideological framework that molded many existing concepts and theories into a new whole. Furthermore, the ideas enabled the unification of two divergent conceptions of film: film as a synthetic art and film as a democratic and in-

---

[27] Josef Čapek, *Nejskromnější umění* (Praha: Aventinum, 1920).

[28] In Czech, this term also designates a plant known in English as a butterbur that was believed to have magical powers.

[29] The anthology was published annually beginning in 1921 by the traditional art association Umělecká beseda [Art union], which devoted this single volume to Devětsil.

ternational art, conceptions that stemmed from different genealogies stretching much further into history than film theory itself.

Teige's conception of film as a sort of super-art, a synthetic artistic discipline that unites the expressive possibilities of the traditional art forms, was first developed in the early 1910s by Italian theorist Ricciotto Canudo, whose thinking built upon older notions of artistic synthesis such as Wagner's idea of Gesamtkunstwerk.[30] The interpretation of film as a democratic art and an international language transcending boundaries of class and nationality, on the other hand, also has its roots in the nineteenth century, where it was linked to the appearance of new means of communication, including photography and film itself. This interpretation of cinema, however, did not take hold in modern artistic circles until the 1920s, due to the ambivalent stance that modern art initially adopted toward photography and film. With the uniting of these divergent conceptions of film (as a synthetic art and as a democratic, international art) under the ideological banners of collectivism and progress, film became the model for other artistic disciplines and the prototype for a new idea of art itself. Teige's manifesto does not contain completely original ideas, yet it is nevertheless an important representative text of the European artistic avant-garde due to its explicit formulations and the early date of its appearance. For instance, the slogans of functionality and standardization that Teige promotes were borrowed from the purist manifesto *Après le Cubisme* [After cubism] by Charles-Édouard Jeanneret (Le Corbusier) and Amédée Ozenfant.[31] With this text, furthermore, Teige was one of the first contemporaries outside France to reflect on Man Ray's experiments and the invention of the rayogram, and both this and other articles in *Život* attest to the impact on the Czech avant-garde of Russian constructivism, particularly as mediated by Ilya Ehrenburg's book *A vse-taki ona vertitsya* [And yet it moves], a portion of which was also published in the same volume of *Život*.

The study "On the Sociology of Film" (1924) by Bedřich Václavek, a theorist who led the Brno branch of Devětsil from 1923 through 1925, also explicates the artistic avant-garde's early ideas about film. Although its most direct inspiration comes from Marxist-oriented writing in Germany, this text has much in common with the theories found in the Soviet journal *LEF*, particularly Boris I. Arvatov's "formalist-sociological method," which equated art with technical proficiency and industrial

[30]   Ricciotto Canudo, "The Birth of the Sixth Art" [Naissance d'un sixième art, originally published in 1911], in Richard Abel, *French Film Theory and Criticism: A History/Anthology 1907–1939*, vol. 1 (Princeton: Princeton University Press, 1993), 58–66.

[31]   Teige's Czech translation of this manifesto also appeared in *Život*. The original manifesto was published in Charles-Édouard Jeanneret and Amedée Ozenfant, *Après le cubisme* (Paris: Ed. des Commentaires, 1918).

production.[32] Arvatov combined formalism with crude Marxism, similarly to Václavek reducing the sociological analysis of the literary process to the claim, as Victor Erlich puts it, that the "'material and form of a work of art are conditioned by the prevalent methods of its production and consumption' and that the latter, in turn, are determined by the type of economy prevailing at the given period."[33] Václavek's article clearly demonstrates an ideologically motivated interest in film and an adherence to the ideals of social and technological progress and their unity. For the artistic avant-garde in the 1920s (particularly in the first half of the decade), film represented the future of art and a new revolutionary society. In Václavek's text, we see Marxist-inspired postulates of the avant-garde aesthetic, while at the same time it also anticipates certain conclusions of later work on the sociology of film and mass culture.

In contrast with Teige's visionary attitude, Václavek considered himself more of a sociologist of literature and art (even though he had no real academic training in sociology).[34] With his positivist approach, he set himself apart from the then-dominant psychological critique spearheaded by literary critic František Xaver Šalda, while at the same time his emphasis on social context distinguished his work from that of the nascent Prague Linguistic Circle. In contrast with older sociological writing, Václavek was not concerned with thematic issues, seeking instead to identify determining factors and homologies in the relationship between the structure of society and the structure of a work of art. Borrowing a term from Inocenc Arnošt Bláha (the most influential Czech sociologist of the interwar period), Ivo Možný has labeled Václavek's approach "structural determinism."[35]

Václavek's interest in the cinema probably began in 1922–1923, a year during which he lived in Berlin, studying theater under Max Hermann, and deepened during his work with Devětsil, when he published several articles addressing the aesthetics of the film image, the image's relationship to reality, and even the contrapuntal relationship between music and image. However, he did not specifically focus on cinema as a mass product typical of contemporary capitalism until writing "On the Sociology of Film" in 1924. According to Václavek, film is dependent on industrial concentration, internationalization, advanced technology, and a precise division of labor. For this reason, film is especially suited to reflect the life of the average man of the masses and to satisfy, while at the same time to alter, his social needs. The

---

[32] *LEF*: a journal published in 1923–1925 by the Left Front of the Arts (Levyi Front Iskusstv), an ultra--leftist association of avant-garde writers, photographers, critics and designers in the Soviet Union, promoting ideas of constructivism and a utilitarian view of art. Boris Arvatov (1896–1940) was LEF's main theorist.

[33] Victor Erlich, *Russian Formalism: History, Doctrine*, 4th ed. (The Hague: Mouton, 1980), 113.

[34] See Ludvík Svoboda, *Bedřich Václavek jako sociolog literatury* (Praha: Orbis, 1947).

[35] Ivo Možný, "Bedřich Václavek jako sociolog masové kultury," *Sociologický časopis* 4, no. 3 (1968), 363.

structure of a film work (in Marxist terms, the "superstructure") reflects the laws of the "base," particularly those of mechanical production and the differentiated division of labor. By means of its direct and concrete visual nature, "which is not filtered beforehand by a network of concepts and words," together with the corporeality of its gestures and primitive schematic psychology, film expresses the intellectual views of the mass public better than any other cultural formation.[36] Václavek considered film's most valuable quality, however, to be its ability to unite isolated individuals into an active mass, "to revolutionize the masses via technology," thereby making it a potential tool for the proletariat's class struggle.

Václavek's theses on the structural correspondences between film and capitalism and on film's ability to refine the sensibility of modern man, thereby adapting him to a new social reality, might strike one as reminiscent of subsequent analyses by the theorists of the Frankfurt School, especially Walter Benjamin and Siegfried Kracauer. It is, however, highly unlikely that at the time he wrote "On the Sociology of Film," Václavek was familiar with Kracauer's series of articles for the *Frankfurter Zeitung*, which first began appearing at about the same time that Václavek was preparing his article. Rather, his direct sources of inspiration were the works of German leftist art historians (such as Wilhelm Hausenstein) and the film theories of Béla Balázs, whom Václavek repeatedly mentions in his book *Poesie v rozpacích* [Poetry in a quandary].[37] The most important model for Václavek's thinking on film is undoubtedly the German leftist politician and sociologist Carlo Mierendorff (1897–1943), whom Václavek cites by name in "On the Sociology of Film." Mierendorff's 1920 pamphlet "Hätte ich das Kino!" [If I only had cinema!] passionately criticizes the demands of the bourgeoisie to reform the cinema and praises the wild and primitive power of the new medium as constituting its political potential.[38] Václavek incorporates a number of elements from Mierendorff's manifesto into his own work, for example, theses on film's revolutionary effect upon the mass public and on the sensual immediacy of the film image. Václavek's article can be considered the first step in the Czech tradition of sociological thinking about film, with the caveat that it is a manifesto of its time, and, as such, its primary concern is not as much the objective analysis of film's social functions as the mobilization of film's role in stimulating the proletariat's revolutionary consciousness.[39]

---

[36]   Bedřich Václavek, *Poesie v rozpacích: Studie k sociologii umění a kultury* (Praha: Jan Fromek, 1930), 134.

[37]   See Možný, "Bedřich Václavek jako sociolog masové kultury," 366, and Václavek, *Poesie v rozpacích*, 134.

[38]   Carlo Mierendorff, "Hätte ich das Kino!," *Die Weißen Blätter* 7, no. 2 (1920), 86–92.

[39]   The foundations for a truly academic sociology of film in the Czech lands were established only in the 1940s, by Brno sociologist Inocenc Arnošt Bláha and his student Jiří Kolaja.

Social and technological utopianism were ideals shared by most of the European avant-garde movements of the 1920s, although this took on a different shape in each country, expressing itself in a variety of artistic programs and conceptions of film poetics. After its foundation in 1920, Devětsil's artistic program began to crystallize in the years 1922–1924, culminating in the 1924 publication of the manifesto "Poetismus" [Poetism], which would lend its name to an entire movement.[40] This manifesto presents film both as a key source of inspiration (together with technologies such as the radio, gramophone, and flying machines) and as a genre of poetist creation. The poetist enchantment with film had an effect on Devětsil's work in a number of artistic disciplines and inspired experimentation in the creation of new artistic genres, namely the so-called "picture poem" and "film poem." The picture poem was a visual creation similar to the dadaist or constructivist collage or photomontage, whereas the film poem was a literary work resembling a film libretto or screenplay in form. Both were intended to demonstrate poetism's ambition to merge modern painting and modern poetry. At the same time, both the film poem and the picture poem were also often understood as actual filmic projects, thereby representing a counterpart to Devětsil's theoretical and critical works about film. All of these elements combined to form a poetist aesthetic of film.[41]

Devětsil's pre-poetist phase (1922–1924) was characterized by a kind of intoxication with cinema dominated by the heroes of American adventure films and slapstick comedies, particularly Douglas Fairbanks and Charlie Chaplin.[42] The eventual formation of the poetist program brought with it a specific conception of film that Teige first hints at in his study "The Aesthetics of Film and *Cinégraphie*" (1924) and then

---

[40]   Karel Teige, "Poetismus," *Host* 3, no. 9–10 (July 1924), 197–204.

[41]   The film poem, with its hybrid form, was inspired by American slapstick films and by the librettos, or rather "cinematic dramas" (*drames de cinéma*), of Louis Delluc, Ivan Goll, and Ilya Ehrenburg, which appeared in Czech translations. In some cases, film poems were more akin to poetry, in other cases more like film scenarios, or even like screenplays. None of these were ever realized, but they were published in the mid-1920s, and their authors included Karel Teige, Vítězslav Nezval, Jaroslav Seifert, Jiří Mahen, Adolf Hoffmeister, Artuš Černík, František Halas, and Jiří Voskovec. More information on the film poem can be found in Viktoria Hradská, *Česká avantgarda a film* (Praha: ČSFÚ, 1976); Jiří Cieslar, *Česká kulturní levice a film ve dvacátých letech* (Praha: ČSFÚ, 1978), 62–75; and Karel Srp, "Optická slova (obrazové básně a poetismus)," in *Česká fotografická avantgarda 1918–1948*, ed. Vladimír Birgus (Praha: Kant, 1999), 56–62.

[42]   Fairbanks and Chaplin were declared honorary members of Devětsil and their names even turn up in poems from the period; for instance, in Vítězslav Nezval's "Podivuhodný kouzelník" [The marvelous magician, 1922] and Jaroslav Seifert's "Paříž" [Paris], the opening poem in the collection *Samá láska* [Only love, 1923]. For a detailed analysis of filmic sensibilities in the poetry of the period, see Luboš Bartošek, "Paprskem proboden obláček bílý... Filmové vlivy v české poezii dvacátých let," *Film a doba* 13, no 10 (1967), 540–548.

explicitly formulates in his subsequent article "Optický film" [Optical film, 1924]. The first of these texts takes its cue from Louis Delluc in criticizing the narrative-dramatic mode of film production and presents an outline for a new repertoire of subject matter that is clearly inspired by the aesthetic of the magazine *L'Esprit nouveau*. "Optical film" is a polemic against the aesthetics of abstract art and an attempt to stake out the poetist program, whose goal is "to provide the spectator with an artificial poetry that is an empowered equivalent to the poetry of flowing life." This is to be accomplished by inserting fragments, or what Teige calls "touches of reality," into an abstract compositional outline and by creating an international language "of optical standards, like those of semaphore and traffic signs."[43]

The fundamental dichotomy between constructivism and poetism, between "construction and poetry" (*stavba a báseň*), is a defining characteristic for both the program and terminology of the Czech avant-garde of the 1920s.[44] In his summarizing study "K filmové avantgardě" [On the film avant-garde], written at the end of the decade but not published until long after his death, Teige formulates this polarity in terms of "documentary" (*dokument*) and "poetry" (*poesie*).[45] In contrast, Václavek describes the opposition between "material film" (*věcný film*) and "pure film" (*čistý film*) in his 1930 book *Poesie v rozpacích*.[46] This polarization of film production into two fundamental tendencies corresponds with Teige's demand for a return to elementary purity as a solution to the crisis of film art.

Film also became an important model in other aspects of poetist thinking, for example in its materialism and its technological and biological determinism. In these contexts, film represented the promise for a revolutionary transformation of bourgeois culture by means of modern technology (speed, precision, unlimited reproducibility). At the same time, the poetists saw film as a symptom of art's paradigmatic shift away from intellectual reflection to direct contact with material reality and as a potential tool for cleansing the human sensory apparatus for the creation of a new "total man." Within their biologically based theory of cultural development, film appeared as evidence of a fundamental turn, within the pre-existing hierarchy of the senses, away from the auditory and toward the visual, toward a "new culture of sight."[47]

---

[43] All quotes from the above paragraph are taken from Karel Teige, "Film I. – Optický film," *Pásmo* 1, no. 5–6, (1924), 10–11.

[44] See Karel Teige, *Stavba a báseň: Umění dnes a zítra — Výbor statí z let 1919–1926* (Praha: Vaněk & Votava, 1927).

[45] Karel Teige, "K filmové avantgardě," in *Otázky divadla a filmu 3*, ed. Artur Závodský (Brno: Universita J. E. Purkyně, 1973), 308–327.

[46] Václavek, *Poesie v rozpacích*, 134.

[47] See Cieslar, *Česká kulturní levice a film ve dvacátých letech*, 49–51.

In terms of its arguments and concepts, Teige's notion of poetist film is reminiscent of Le Corbusier's and Ozenfant's program for purist painting, yet at the same time it also builds directly upon Delluc's theory of *photogénie*.[48] The concept of *photogénie* popularized by Delluc became a central theme in poetist film theory, featuring prominently in the texts of other Devětsil authors, especially poet Vítězslav Nezval.[49] Within film terminology, *photogénie* appears to have corresponded best with poetism's lyrical orientation and best expressed its sense of enchantment with new forms of visual art. The poetist texts describe photography and film as a type of miracle, an intensification of everyday life, a sort of luminous magic or a visual concentrate of individual components of represented reality. According to the central thesis of Jiří Voskovec's study "*Photogénie* and Suprareality" (1925), photography introduced a new sense of realism, because it is able to reveal "suprareality"—an optical distillation of normal reality.[50] Contrary to Teige's radical conception of pure cinema, Voskovec and Nezval chose a somewhat more compromising approach: in their perspective, the photogenic essence of cinema can be realized not only in "the lyric poetry of light," but also in dramatic action. Both authors stress that this is not achieved by the conventional adaptation of dramas and novels, but rather in plots that are constructed primarily as optical and rhythmic compositions. Nevertheless, it is clear (especially in Nezval's case) that this redefinition stems from their more pragmatic view of film as a form of popular culture that should communicate efficiently with the mass public. Indeed, both authors demonstrated their pragmatism several years later by collaborating on mainstream film productions: Nezval as a scriptwriter, Voskovec as an actor.

The poetist texts written in the second half of the 1920s demonstrate, in the filmic preferences of the avant-garde, a gradual turn away from the American and French films that fascinated them in the first half of the decade and toward the films of the Soviet Union, with Hollywood becoming a synonym of the capitalist film industry. Whereas the avant-garde was at first attracted by the synthetic nature of film, midway through the decade its interest instead began to focus on specific filmic means and its emphasis shifted to the medium's analytic aspects. Nevertheless, this transition still occurred within the framework of the same ideological model characterized above as the unity of social and technological utopianism.

---

[48]   See Louis Delluc, *Photogénie* (Paris: Brunoff, 1920).

[49]   For more on the importance of Delluc for Czech avant-garde reflections on film, see Vítězslav Nezval, "Louis Delluc," *Rozpravy Aventina* 1, no. 5 (1926), 62; for information on Nezval and film, see Vladimír Mlčoušek, *Vítězslav Nezval a film* (Praha: ČSFÚ, 1979).

[50]   This was the only work of film theory written by Jiří Voskovec, who was primarily known for his acting and writing for the stage and screen. For more on the context in which this article appeared, see Michal Bregant, "Několik poznámek na téma Jiří Voskovec a film," *Iluminace* 1, no. 1 (1989), 95–114.

In contrast with their German, French, and Russian counterparts, the members of the Czech avant-garde were not able to realize their own film projects during the 1920s.[51] For this reason, they were all the more concentrated on the search for parallels between cinema and other art forms and on attempts to introduce filmic techniques into their nonfilmic works. Film became more or less synonymous with the modern attitude within the individual artistic disciplines. It should not, therefore, be surprising that in 1924 writer Karel Schulz characterized the new Czech novelistic style as "filmic, cinematic, and therefore nearly photogenic."[52]

3. Film as Service: Functionalism and Ideological Struggle

As a consequence of the introduction of sound film, economic crisis, and the ascension of the younger generation, the beginning of the 1930s marked a crucial turning point in the development of the avant-garde's thinking. The harsh reality of the world economic crisis disrupted the vision of unity between social and technological progress and led to a radicalization of the avant-garde's leftist political attitudes. The movement's transformation is particularly evident in its altered conception of functionality. Whereas, in the 1920s, the demand for functionality implied a unity of concepts of technological and social progress, in the 1930s, the social aspect became a concern of its own, resulting in the development of a new program that placed primary emphasis on the social function of art. The new generation of film critics came to think of artistic production as a weapon for political struggle, and thus specific issues related to art were subordinated to the group's political goals: the critique of capitalism and the propagation of socialism and communism. The Second International Conference of Proletarian and Revolutionary Writers in Kharkov (November 6–16, 1930) is generally considered the watershed moment marking the divide between these two conceptions of functionality. At this conference, the Czech delegation (led by Bedřich Václavek and also including Lubomír Linhart) was familiarized with Soviet methods for instrumentalizing literature in the class struggle, for cultivating worker-writers, and for increasing the comprehensibility of literary language for the masses.[53]

---

[51] The complicated beginnings of avant-garde film experimentation in the late 1920s and early 1930s are discussed by Michal Bregant in "Avantgardní tendence v českém filmu," in *Filmový sborník historický 3*, ed. Ivan Klimeš (Praha: ČFÚ, 1992), 137–174.

[52] Karel Schulz, "Próza," *Pásmo* 1, no. 5–6 (1924–1925), 4.

[53] On the influence of the Kharkov conference on Czechoslovak literature, see Petr Šámal, "Beletrie, ženský komunistický tisk a problémy kontinuity (Na příkladu Rozsevačky)," in *Povídka, román a periodický tisk v 19. a 20. století*, ed. Michal Jareš, Pavel Janáček, Petr Šámal (Praha: Ústav pro českou literaturu AV ČR, 2005), 155–157.

This shift in thinking did not occur abruptly or unexpectedly. The groundwork for the ideological critique of film and for the utilization of film in the leftist intelligentsia's political struggle had been laid as early as the late 1910s and the beginning of the 1920s. In 1919, writer Emil Vachek had begun publishing his critical commentaries on Czechoslovak cinema in the social-democratic newspaper *Právo lidu* [People's right], and from 1921 onwards, the authors Ivan Suk (a pseudonym for Josef Suchánek), Jiří Weil, and Jaroslav Seifert, among others, regularly contributed similar articles to the Marxist daily *Rudé právo* [Red right].[54] Also in 1921, the freshly founded Communist Party of Czechoslovakia established its own organization for the propagation of proletariat culture, "Proletkult," according to the Soviet model. The secretary of this organization was Stanislav. K. Neumann, who had been a leading representative of pre-World War I leftist culture. For a period in 1921–1922, the Proletkult circle, which also published a magazine under the same name, and the avant-garde artists affiliated with Devětsil debated the preconditions for a true art of the people.[55] A central question in this polemic was whether the American comedies and adventure serials that dominated Czech cinemas at that time should be considered a template for proletariat culture, or whether it is first necessary to transform film into an agitational art. At that time, the enthusiasm for American films that infected Karel Teige, Artuš Černík, Jindřich Honzl, and many of the later poetists unequivocally prevailed over the skepticism of Neumann and proletarian poet Jiří Wolker, who saw commercial cinema as a product of petit-bourgeois culture that only served to diminish the mental capabilities of a passive audience. Proletkult quickly withdrew from this discussion and focused on the organization of educational film screenings for workers.

The situation changed around 1926–1927, though, as the influence of poetism began to wane and Soviet avant-garde films first reached Czech cinemas (particularly the widely discussed *Battleship Potemkin*, which had its Czechoslovak premiere in Brno on October 15, 1926, in a version re-edited by the Czechoslovak state censors). At the same time, a new generation of leftist film critics began to take shape, with the ambition of regularly evaluating current cinema programs, including Czech productions. (By contrast, Devětsil never developed any well-defined practice of film criticism and for the most part either rejected Czech films wholesale or simply ignored them.) This new group of critics centered around the communist journalists Julius Fučík and Lubomír Linhart, who in 1927 established a film column in the newspaper *Večerník Rudého práva* [Evening paper of the Red Right, later known as *Rudý*

---

54   See Cieslar, *Česká kulturní levice a film ve dvacátých letech*, 10–12, 39–44.

55   See Ladislav Cabada, *Intelektuálové a idea komunismu v českých zemích 1900–1939* (Praha: Institut pro středoevropskou kulturu a politiku, 2000), 72–80.

večerník, or Red evening paper]. In its efforts to reach the working class reader-viewer, this column focused on reviews of actual film premieres, rather than simply providing information about the offerings of film distributors, as was common practice. (At that time, routine film reviews often functioned as a covert form of marketing commissioned by the film's distributors.) Linhart's 1930 overview *Malá abeceda filmu* [A brief guide to film] became a sort of summation of the new group's film-aesthetic thinking with its combination of the poetist idea of pure film and the demand for the type of ideological effects promoted by Eisenstein.[56]

Also in 1927, the first film association of the leftist intelligentsia, Club for the New Film of Modern Film Workers (Klub za nový film moderních filmových pracovníků), was formed. The club's agenda mercilessly rebuked provincialism in Czech cinema and aimed to raise the standard of domestic production and propagate film art: "By confronting Czech cinema with foreign films, the former should learn to avoid petty provincialism and the cult of local stars, and instead finally pose meaningful and topical questions that address the script, photography, photogeny, as well as new artistic and technological techniques."[57] Even though the club existed for less than a year, it succeeded in bringing together the most important intellectuals involved with film in the last half of the 1920s: among others, its members included the theater directors Emil František Burian, Jindřich Honzl, and Jiří Frejka, the writers Karel Schultz and Adolf Hoffmeister, film critic Ctibor Haluza, and theorists Artuš Černík and Karel Teige. The strong disagreements that arose surrounding the club's utopian plans to organize an international film festival, a film congress, and film production itself attests to the paradoxical situation of leftist intellectuals, who on the one hand scorned the domestic film business yet on the other hand completely lacked the practical experience or the means to realize their own productions. The greatest accomplishment of the group was to expand the platforms and genres for critical writing about film, which established itself as a standard component of many leftist newspapers and journals such as *Tvorba* [Creation, 1925–1938], *Index* [Index, 1930–1931], *Signál* [The signal, 1929–1930], and *Čin* [Action, 1929–1939].[58]

From today's point of view, the leftist critical writing of the 1930s appears the most influential of the period due to the fact that it was the best organized and most closely linked with the theoretical thinking of the avant-garde. It even had an impact on some of the criticism that appeared in the film columns of many daily newspapers of various political leanings, many directly linked to specific political

---

[56] The book was based on Linhart's lecture "Moderní filmová estetika" [Modern film aesthetics], presented at the Philosophical Faculty of Charles University in Prague on January 21, 1928.

[57] "Filmové veřejnosti," *Český filmový svět* 4, 1927, no. 5 (January 15), p. 5.

[58] See Cieslar, *Česká kulturní levice a film ve dvacátých letech*, 110–112.

parties. From the first half of the 1920s through the beginning of the 1930s, these columns gradually became standardized and began to appear with greater regularity, usually in the form of a Friday overview of the previous night's film premieres. Newspapers that cultivated film criticism of a relatively high level included the legionnaire daily *Národní osvobození* [National liberation], with critics Jiří Lehovec, Alexander Hackenschmied, and others, the party organ of the National Socialist Party of Czechoslovakia[59] *České slovo* [Czech word], with Otto Rádl and Jan Kučera; the liberal *Lidové noviny* [People's news], with A. Jaroslav Urban and Artuš Černík; the Agrarian *Venkov* [Countryside], with Antonín M. Brousil; and the German-language newspaper *Prager Presse* [Prague press], with Willy Haas, which was closely tied to the state government. At the same time, several cultural-political magazines also began to print, with greater regularity, extensive studies about cinema, including the pro-presidential publication *Přítomnost* [The presence], with critic Franta Kocourek, and Otakar Štorch Marien's magazine *Rozpravy Aventina* [Aventinum discussions], with Karel Smrž.[60] In addition, specialized cinema journals also became a prime source for independent film criticism, particularly the newly established spectacular review *Studio* (1929–1930) and a revived incarnation of the magazine *Kino* (1931–1934).[61]

During this period of the 1930s, when film criticism placed more emphasis on the social and ideological effects of cinema, we also find authors who approached this subject from different perspectives than Marxism. A prime example is the brilliant journalist Otto Rádl (1902–1965), who contributed to the daily *České slovo* as well as a number of journals, including *Přítomnost*, and was editor of the film review *Studio*. Furthermore, the 100-page chapter he wrote for the monumental encyclopedic work *Dvacáté století* [The twentieth century] constitutes the most significant attempt at a cultural history of film written in Czech. In the introduction to this text, he formulates a number of theses that expand upon the primary idea that "the twentieth century found its most developed and most complete form of expression in

---

[59] Československá strana národně socialistická: a center-left party that combined nationalism with reformist socialism and opposed the communists; it bore no relation to the German Nazi movement (*Nazionalsozialismus*).

[60] Otakar Štorch-Marien was himself a prolific film critic as well as the publisher of the most lavish film journal of the interwar period, *Studio – Měsíční revue pro filmové umění* [Studio – monthly review of film art]; see Karel Tabery, *Filmová publicistika Otakara-Štorcha-Mariena* (Olomouc: Univerzita Palackého, 2004).

[61] For a factual overview of film journals and film-related newspaper columns, see Jiří Havelka, *50 let československého filmu* (Praha: ČSF, 1953), 15–22; for more on the history of Czech film criticism, see Jan Svoboda, "Filmová kritika," in *Teorie umělecké kritiky*, ed. Jiří Hájek (Praha: SPN, 1986), 197–210.

film."[62] In the first place, film is a "sociological source, [...] a registry of scientifically important sociological material" that offers "the analyst of human society and its problems the opportunity to peer into places that had been concealed to him in previous eras."[63] Second, film is always "an image of the thinking of the times," because it "contains a certain ideology, even when it pretends that its only goal is to provide entertainment." With critical mistrust, Rádl exposes the tendentiousness "of optimistic stories speaking about the fantasy career paths of poor young men" as well as that of Soviet films that "incited revolt against the old political and social order, assigned all the world's wickedness and degeneracy to the capitalists, showed intellectuals as mercenary traitors working for the capitalists, and allocated all traits of nobility and goodness to the oppressed, proletarian, and outcast peoples."[64] Third, film itself also alters perceptual reality and the disposition of the human sense organs: "It exceptionally accelerated the functioning of visual perception and expanded its memory for visual phenomena, transforming it into an entity with a far greater optical facility."[65] Fourth, as a globalized form of mass entertainment, "an art of everyone and for everyone," film has democratized culture in a fundamental way, with negative and positive consequences: on the negative side, film is not allowed to be "better than its spectators," to concentrate too much on film form or the psychological interiors of its figures, since it must also accommodate viewers of below-average intelligence; yet, on the positive side, it is becoming "a means for bringing people closer together and for discovering the human being underneath the mottled, superficial surface of national, racial, and social differences."[66] Rádl's humanistic and democratic approach thus constitutes a pronounced counterbalance to the radical leftist critiques of the 1930s, while also representing what was—within the Czech context—the most complex interpretation, for its time, of film as a socio-cultural phenomenon.

The next significant organization of intellectuals interested in film to appear after the disintegration of the Club for the New Film was the Film Club (Filmklub, 1930–1934), a nonpolitical association of film journalists formed under the initiative of Otakar Štorch-Marien, whose prime goal was to promote independent film criticism, opposing the attempts of distributors and producers to use film reviews as a type of promotion. (The club's leadership shifted between Štorch-Marien, O. Rádl,

[62]   Otto Rádl, "Film ve 20. století," in *Dvacáté století: co dalo lidstvu: výsledky práce lidstva 20 věku, vol. 8, Nové směry a proudy* (Praha: Vl. Orel, 1934), 28.

[63]   Ibid., 30.

[64]   Ibid., 30.

[65]   Ibid., 32.

[66]   Ibid., 34.

A. J. Urban, and A. Černík.) Nevertheless, the first organization of leftist intellectuals to have a fundamental influence on mainstream film culture did not arrive until the latter half of the decade, in the form of the Czechoslovak Film Association (Československá filmová společnost), which existed from 1936 to 1941. Similarly to the Club for the New Film, this organization brought together filmmakers, critics, and authors with the goal of propagating artistic values within Czech film production. In contrast with its predecessor, however, this new association had more realistic organizational ambitions (supporting the production of "cultural" and educational films, establishing film schools and archives), and, most importantly, it was able to successfully exert pressure on state cultural politics. This was achieved through Vladislav Vančura, the association's chairman, who sat as its representative on the Film Advisory Board (Filmový poradní sbor) established by the Ministry of Commerce, the most important state institution for cinema, where decisions addressing the import of foreign films and the support of domestic production were made.[67] Still later, in 1938, just prior to the outbreak of World War II, the Union of Film Journalists (Sdružení filmových novinářů) was formed as a branch of the Czechoslovak Journalist Syndicate (Syndikát čs. novinářů) under the leadership of A. M. Brousil.[68]

In terms of leftist film theory, the most pronounced expressions in the late 1920s and early 1930s came from the group known as the Left Front (Levá fronta), an organization of communist intellectuals founded in 1929 with the goal of promoting ideas of socialist justice and a new social order. When Devětsil was dissolved in 1930, a large number of its members joined the Left Front, with Karel Teige leading the way. The Left Front published a magazine of the same name from 1930 to 1933 and established specialized sections to develop its artistic program within individual fields: theater and literature, architecture, and finally photography and film, the latter as the Film-Photo Group of the Left Front (Film-foto skupina Levé fronty), founded in 1931. This mirrored analogous developments in other countries, leading to what were most often called "proletarian" or "workers'" art movements. In the field of photography and film, this first flourished in Germany, due to the specific economic and political conditions there. It is symptomatic of this that the first text to formulate a concrete program for the Czech film movement of this type, Lubomír Linhart's 1931 article "The proletarian film struggle in Czechoslovakia" (Der Proletarische Filmkampf in der Tschechoslowakei) was published in German in the journal

---

67   See H., "Kulturní pracovníci chtějí pečovat o čs. Film," *Filmový kurýr* 10, no. 43. (1936), 7; and Luboš Bartošek, *Desátá múza Vladislava Vančury* (Praha: ČSFÚ, 1973), 138–141.

68   During World War II, Brousil wrote several books about film (on film music, subject matter, and the national identity of Czech films). After the war, he was one of the co-founders of the Film Academy in Prague (FAMU) and the International Film Festival in Karlovy Vary.

Arbeiterbühne und Film [Workers' theater and film] prior to the founding of the Film-Photo Group.[69]

The manifesto of the "fi-fo" group, as it was affectionately abbreviated, was published in Prague in 1933 as part of the catalogue for the First Exhibition of Social Photography (První vystava sociální fotografie).[70] The term "social photography" gave a name to an entire movement and was also used by Linhart for the title of his book on the subject.[71] Linhart's book, like the manifesto for the catalogue, is dedicated to photography, yet its conclusions also found application in the realm of film production. In 1934, the trio of "fi-fo" artists Karel Kresl, Otto Vlk, and Václav Zelený directed a number of films building directly on the theories of the social photography movement in term of ideas, themes, and techniques. The group's filmic and photographic creations are marked by a rigorously ideological interpretation of represented social reality, for which they used techniques including "visual counterpoint" and "contrasting montage," with a focus on the confrontation between antithetical social phenomena.[72]

Even before "fi-fo" had become artistically active, though, the principles of the new film movement were formulated in critical writings that drew directly upon communist ideology, such as Linhart's 1932 article "Newsreels Show Us the World…" Another initial point of inspiration for the activities of the group was the screening of Soviet films, which were seen as ideal models for the creation of a socially functional work intended as a tool for social construction. Meanwhile, the state's acts of censorship against Soviet films provided an opportunity for leftists to criticize the existing social system.[73] Critical texts about Soviet films and their censorship, which followed the so-called "class" or "social" point of view, subordinated the discussion of specific artistic issues to the demand for social functionality. This led to a re-evaluation of the development of film production up to that point, and eventually resulted in the outright rejection of artistic experimentation and indeed the avant-garde

---

[69] The name of the Film-Photo Group of the Left Front was directly inspired by the famous exhibition "Film und Foto," which took place in Stuttgart, Germany, in 1929. For more on Czech avant-garde photography and its relationship to film, see *Česká fotografie 1918–1948*, ed. Anotnín Dufek (Brno: Moravská galerie, 1979) and Birgus, *Česká fotografická avantgarda 1918–1948*.

[70] This refers to the introduction, written by Lubomír Linhart, to the catalogues for the Prague and Brno exhibitions; see *Výstava sociální fotografie*, ed. Lubomír Linhart (Praha: Film-foto skupina Levé fronty, 1933); *Výstava sociální fotografie*, ed. František Kalivoda (Brno: Sekce pro mechanická umění, 1933).

[71] Lubomír Linhart, *Sociální fotografie* (Praha: Jarmila Prokopová, 1934).

[72] See Jaroslav Anděl, "Fotografie a filmová avantgarda," in *Česká fotografie 1918–1948* (see note 69), 104–107.

[73] For more on the public debate about film censorship and police actions against avant-garde film screenings, see, for example, "Anketa o filmové cenzuře," *Index* 4 (1932), 85–95 and 113–114; *Index* 5 (1933), 6.

movement altogether. According to this view, the only true avant-garde work is one that helps to achieve the goals of the proletarian revolution. Prime examples of this were found in Soviet works, whereas the creations of the Western avant-garde were seen as formalist playthings of bourgeois decadence. This is the specific conclusion that the Left Front organizer and hard-line communist Ladislav Štoll reaches in his review of the "Third Week of Avant-Garde Films" in Prague in 1931,[74] but similar judgments can also be found in the writings of Linhart and Teige from that period. Although the Left Front was *de facto* a relatively loose confederation of diverse groups, if we reconsider (in historical perspective) the collectivist rhetoric of its leadership, its indiscriminate attacks on political rivals, and its battles against various ideological "deviations" within its own ranks, we can deduce, as Ladislav Cabada does, that it was little more than an instrument of "bolshevization within the cultural program of the Communist Party of Czechoslovakia."[75]

This movement for socially critical art that conceived of film as a medium of political struggle can be seen both as a direct heir to the artistic avant-garde of the 1920s in its idea of collective utopianism and as an anticipation of the official aesthetic of socialist realism that would come after the communist takeover of 1948. It seems that the constructivist demand for the liquidation of art (which the Czech avant-garde also supported) in fact became the ideological precedent for the idea of liquidating the artistic avant-garde itself. This idea was already latent in the program of the proletarian art movement of the early 1930s, and soon thereafter became part of official Soviet cultural politics. The more prevalent the idea of social functionality grew within criticism and theory, the more militant and orthodox this criticism and theory became, and the more their programmatic aesthetics identified with their political ideology. Likewise, the more these artistic programs were transformed into a utilitarian instrument for use in political strategies and tactics, thereby losing their utopian charge, the less appealing they became to their original adherents.

In his numerous theoretical writings from the 1930s, Alexander Hackenschmied, photographer, critic, and leading initiator and creator of Czech avant-garde film, addresses some of the issues relating to the practical uses of film technology and the creation of utilitarian films (for instance, the production of advertising films, the relationship between film image and sound, montage, and editing),[76] issues that were directly related to his own films. Advertising films, which at that time seemed to of-

---

[74] Ladislav Štoll, "Avantgardní filmy," *Levá fronta* 1, no. 14 (1931), 3.

[75] See Cabada, *Intelektuálové a idea komunismu v českých zemích 1900–1939*, 140.

[76] See Alexander Hackenschmied, "O střihu," in *Abeceda filmového scenaristy a herce: Soubor přednášek scenaristického kursu Filmového studia* (Praha: Filmové studio, 1935), 73–91; "Propagace filmem," *Pestrý týden* 5, no. 5 (February 7, 1930), 5; and "Stíny, které mluví," *Pestrý týden* 4, no. 19 (May 11, 1929), 9.

fer a solution to the conflict between the avant-garde film movement and the film business, occupied an important position within Hackenschmied's creative output. Beginning in the mid-1930s, he worked for the Baťa company and helped build its modern film studios.[77] With Baťa, he worked as cameraman on a number of formally innovative advertising shorts, the most famous of which is Elmar Klos's 1937 *Silnice zpívá* [The highway sings], which promoted Baťa tires and won a prize at the World Exhibition in Paris that year.[78]

Like the works of other Czech filmmakers, Hackenschmied's filmic and theoretical output displays echoes of the three most prevalent ideological trends of the 1930s: functionalism, social critique, and surrealism. Most prominent in his programmatic writings are the ideas of functionalism, whose central thesis—"form follows function!"—and demand for functionality were dominant impulses in the development of documentary film. These ideas contributed to the popularity of advertising among the members of the avant-garde and helped to develop a specific means of filmic expression founded on a basic rejection of the concept of art (an idea that had similarly taken hold in the realm of photography). Jan Kučera's article "Regarding Better film, or Whither Art?" represents an interesting example of this conviction.[79] The young theorist Kučera was originally influenced by Devětsil's concept of pure film and joined the Club for the New Film, but later (like Linhart) began to place greater emphasis on the social function of film and the propagation of Soviet cinema. In this article, he reacts to the standardization of the avant-garde's techniques and applies the functionalist approach not only to the concept of art, but also to the very notion of an artistic avant-garde. The originality of Kučera's early writing lies in its detailed treatment of utilitarian non-fiction genres (such as newsreels and advertising), which he believed could regenerate film art by instilling it with the principles of functionality and objectivity, or with "the pureness of its supremely functional form," as he states in the article "Advertising and Cinematic Art" (1928).[80]

The concept of functionalism was most distinctly developed within the realm of

---

[77] The Baťa company was the largest Czech producer of shoes, and eventually expanded worldwide. In 1936, the company built its own film studio in the Moravian town of Zlín, which became Czechoslovakia's second-largest center of film production after Prague, and specialized in industrial films, advertisements, and documentaries. The team of young filmmakers employed by Baťa in 1935 included Alexander Hackenschmied and other avant-gardists, and their cooperation resulted in a unique symbiosis between Baťa's modern management techniques and avant-garde aesthetics. See Petr Szczepanik, "Modernism, Industry, Film: A Network of Media in the Baťa Corporation and the Town of Zlín in the 1930s," in *Films that Work: Industrial Film Production and the Productivity of Media*, ed. Vinzenz Hediger and Patrick Vonderau (Amsterdam: Amsterdam University Press, 2008).

[78] See Jiří Stejskal, "Zlínská filmová výrobna" (Doctoral dissertation, Univerzita J. E. Purkyně v Brně, 1972) and Jaroslav Brož, *Alexander Hackenschmied* (Praha: ČSFÚ, 1973), 41–46.

[79] Jan Kučera, "O lepším filmu, čili kam s uměním," *Studio* 3, no. 7 (1931–1932), 269–274.

architecture. It is therefore unsurprising that one of the most succinct formulations of functionalist theories appears in Kučera's article "Film and Building" (1933), which presents the author's explication of his film *Stavba* [Building], a documentation of the most extensive architectural realization of Czech functionalism, the General Pensions Institute building in Prague. The film production company Elektajournal negotiated with the General Pensions Institute to create a filmic chronicle of the building's construction, beginning with the demolition of the original buildings on the site. Reportedly, the building's architects Josef Havlíček and Karel Honzík also took part in the conception of the film.[81] In the end, though, the documentary chronicle was never completed and not even the rough material survives; nevertheless, Kučera's article remains as a record of the film's creative aims. Kučera's artistic manifesto stresses film's dynamic character, particularly its ability to interpret phenomena and objects in the form of a temporal process; likewise, in the spirit of functionalism's demand for functionality, it emphasizes film's documentary mission. The influence of the architectural model can also be seen in the terminology of Emil František Burian's article "Music in Sound Film" (1933): "Meters of sound [...] dynamically and rhythmically organize space on the film strip," "The sound engineer [...] will construct and make blueprints for kilometers of tones [...] and film shall have its tectonic space." Burian's article espouses functionalism with its emphasis on material and structure (e.g., the actual length of a sound recording) and with its functional point of view and anti-artistic sentiment, expressed, for example, in his endeavor to replace the term "composer" with the terms "sound technician" and "sound engineer."[82]

As a practicing architect, Vít Obrtel saw the relationship between film and architecture from an entirely different perspective than Kučera and Burian. Obrtel's only text on the topic, "Architecture and Film" (1926), reflects the ideological position of neoconstructivism, a theory he developed between 1926 and 1933 that, within Devětsil's architectural thinking, posed the most pronounced counterbalance to Teige's rationalist constructivism. According to Teige, modern architecture should be completely liberated from "bourgeois" art and dedicate itself to the purely functional and serial construction of "minimum dwellings" for the proletariat. Obrtel, on the other hand, maintained that functionality not only entails serving the practical needs of the body, but also the needs of the spirit, that is, the preferences, dreams, and temperament of the individual understood in a complex manner. According to Obrtel,

---

[80] During the second half of the 1930s, Kučera found a practical application for his enthusiasm for newsreels when he became director of the Czech weekly newsreel *Aktualita* (1937–1943); see Jan Svoboda, *Skladba a řád: Český teoretik filmu a televize Jan Kučera* (Praha: NFA, 2007), 39–42.

[81] See Svoboda, *Skladba a řád*, 45.

[82] Burian is discussed at length in the following section.

architecture should synthesize rational and emotional as well as scientific and artistic elements in order to express the "harmony between man, nature, and buildings as constituents of the world."[83] Writing during the pinnacle of the silent era, when film had become codified by the techniques of a classical construction of space and continuity editing, it is not surprising that Obrtel viewed it as the ideal medium for uniting functionality and fantasy, reality and "irreality," as a technologically based art form where space is "naturally arranged according to human criteria," while at the same time "form does not cease to be a function of the material." During the interwar period, Obrtel had great difficulty securing investment for his visionary projects and was therefore understandably interested in film as a possibility to visualize his theoretical concepts, to freely experiment with the "fantastical assemblage" of spatial forms; in other words, he saw film as a means of creating "momentary" architecture.[84]

Functionalist principles were also rigorously promoted in the publishing and organizational activities of František Kalivoda, architect, typographer, film and photography critic, and founder of the Film-Photo Group in the Brno branch of the Left Front. From 1934 to 1936, Kalivoda attempted to publish two international magazines, *Ekran* [Screen] and *Telehor*, dedicated to avant-garde visual culture, particularly photography and film. Although he only succeeded in publishing one issue of each, these magazines constitute a unique undertaking by European standards, in terms of their graphic design and their orientation toward multimedia art (to use today's terminology). Particularly international in character, *Telehor* was devoted to the visual experiments of Hungarian artist László Moholy-Nagy and featured texts printed in four languages. Kalivoda himself was neither a significant theorist nor artist, but rather a special kind of "mediator" whose career helps to illustrate the character of the European avant-garde as an international, decentralized network of media, disciplines, artists, and societies. He worked simultaneously within a number of fields, collaborating with leading personalities of the avant-garde movement like Moholy-Nagy and with international associations like CIAM [Congrès Internationaux d'Architecture Moderne]; moreover, he coordinated all of his contacts directly from Brno, independent of the larger Prague scene.[85]

---

[83]   Vít Obrtel, "Harmonie" [1927], in Vít Obrtel, *Vlaštovka, která má geometrické hnízdo: Projekty a texty* (Praha: Odeon, 1985), 60.

[84]   For more on Obrtel's theoretical work, see Rostislav Švácha and Rudolf Matys, "Vlaštovka, která má geometrické hnízdo?," in Obrtel, *Vlaštovka, která má geometrické hnízdo*, 307–354.

[85]   Moholy-Nagy's letter to Kalivoda, first published in *Telehor*, is a classic text in the history of the avant-garde. See László Moholy-Nagy, "Milý Kalivodo," *Telehor* 1, no. 1–2 (1936), 54–60. On the "network" nature of the interwar Central European avant-garde, for which Prague and Brno were key sites, see Timothy O. Benson, "Exchange and Transformation: The Internationalization of the Avant-garde(s) in Central Europe," in *Central European Avant-Gardes: Exchange and Transformation, 1910–1930*, ed. Timothy O. Benson (Cambridge: MIT Press, 2002), 34–67.

4. Optophonogeny: The Musicality of Film and the Plasticity of the Spoken Word

By the end of the 1920s, the Czechoslovak film industry had achieved a relatively high level of development in all the basic areas of cinematic production (production, distribution, and exhibition) such that the implementation of sound film was able to occur quite rapidly and effectively.[86] A detailed examination of the reactions to sound film by various critics, theorists, artists, technicians, and businessmen from the period reveals that ideas about future development of film art, entertainment, and media were widely divergent.

There are two basic trends that can be identified in the hundreds of articles in various periodicals that comment on the possibilities and consequences of the introduction of sound film. On the one hand, authors expressed concern that sound film would result in the decline of film art as it had evolved throughout the 1920s. The concrete consequences of the introduction of sound, they argued, would be that film would once again lean toward theater, thereby inducing a regression of its sophisticated visual "language," and furthermore that film production would be more subject to the laws of industrial production and the mass market. In this respect, Czech discourse did not differ greatly from arguments in the United States and Western Europe at the time. In addition to this, however, there were more locally specific concerns that sound film would result in the downfall of the national cinema, as there would be no interest in Czech-language films abroad and domestic demand would not be sufficient to cover the costs of production. At the same time, the local debate was also strongly influenced by avant-garde critics and academics in the humanities, who saw in sound film the beginnings of a new medium introducing new possibilities for progress. They expressed the hope that sound would enable the future development of film to fundamentally diverge from the classical form of narrative cinema that had thus far dominated the medium. Sound could then transform film into, variously, a medium for communication and news reporting that would be very similar to television today (as discussed by Karel Teige and Jiří Frejka), a recording medium enabling the archiving and linguistic study of everyday speech (Miloš Weingart), a medium of "optophonetic" poetry (Lubomír Linhart, Jan Kučera), a medium for

---

[86] The Czechoslovak industry had a relatively efficient infrastructure at its disposal, and as of 1932 it possessed studios with the most up-to-date technological equipment that were considered the most modern in the region after Germany. In addition, Czechoslovakia had the densest network of cinemas in Central Europe (calculated in terms of population per cinema seats) and was second only to Germany in terms of absolute number of cinemas, although these were typically small and of low quality. For a comparative overview of European cinemas for the year 1930, see Alexander Jason, *Handbuch der Filmwirtschaft. Band II, Film-Europa* (Berlin: Verlag für Presse, Wirtschaft und Politik, 1931), Übersicht 2 and 3.

synesthetic experimentation (Arne Hošek), or for artistic creation involving the "plasticity" of the spoken word, something akin to the genre of the radio play (Otto Rádl, Jindřich Honzl, Vladislav Vančura).

Undoubtedly, the development of this dialectic between catastrophe and utopia in the discourse of the period is linked to the fact that a significant amount of film criticism was written by members of the avant-garde, who, throughout the 1920s, never had the opportunity to apply their ideas in praxis and therefore projected these ideas into their theoretical reflections on sound. In addition, the linguists and aestheticians associated with the Prague Linguistic Circle (established in 1926) were equally important participants in the debate. Of prime importance to these authors was sound film's ability to record speech. This provided material for artistic work involving the signifying properties of the spoken word and brought new principles of metonymic contiguity to film narrative (Roman Jakobson); it also introduced new ways of conceiving the successive construction of space (Jan Mukařovský).

The best examples of the avant-garde and semiotic attitude toward sound film are found in the pair of texts by theater director Jindřich Honzl and writer Vladislav Vančura, published under the shared title "Contribution to the Discussion of Speech in Film" (1935) in *Slovo a slovesnost* [Word and literature], the journal of the Prague Linguistic Circle. Under the influence of Eisenstein and dialectical materialism, Honzl was inspired by the fact that the film sound track is materially separate from the image track, that speech is captured "photographically," and that the technology of reproduction enables its modification. Being thus distanced from reality, from the image, and from the unity of everyday sense experience, the "photographed word" invites free transformation and the establishment of dialectical confrontations with the image. According to Honzl, the materialistic film should not strive for naïve comprehensibility of speech and the synchronicity of sound and image, but should disturb the organic connections between the senses and create internal conflicts between them. Film should become an instrument for disrupting the organic unity of experience and for the scientific examination of the "spontaneity of *perception*" itself. Vančura, who, like Honzl, was also involved in film production, outlines a similar vision of film, whose dynamism is driven by "action focused on the spoken word." In his opinion, the talking film must seek the "veracity of its own order" not in the imitation of actual sound events and theatrical dialogues, but in the purposeful deformative intensification of sound expression, which in a practical sense means "sound superimpositions, sound grotesque, symphonies of detonations, etc." According to Vančura, the word itself must become action, the primary structural and rhythmic principle of the filmic form, and it should never inhibit filmic expression, for which many critics at the time had reproached it.

The advent of sound also introduced another subject to Czech film thought: music. The theorist who was most systematically dedicated to this issue was theater practitioner, composer, and film director Emil František Burian, who himself also worked on many film scores. The article "Music in Sound Film" (1933) has the character of an artistic manifesto and therefore provides an exceptionally concise summarization of Burian's creative principles. The titles of its sections ("The Meter of Film," "What to Do With Theory," "Structure," "Functional Sound," "Montage") mark the basic points of Burian's conception: to use the material defined by the actual length of a given sound recording as a starting point, to respect the structure of film, and to proceed from "the function of sound, rather than pure musical rules," a function that is defined by the "visual character of sound" and maintains montage as its basic principle. The article's point of departure is the premise that, for a composer, the music in a sound film represents, above all, the meters of actual length that constitute the sound recording, an idea that emphasizes the sign character of film sound and points to the essential connection between Burian's approach and structuralism. This connection is most clearly evident in the sections "Functional Sound" and "Montage," where Burian works from a point of view reminiscent of Mukařovský's analyses of semantic structures (see section 6, below), while at the same time echoing certain tenets of functionalism (see section 3, above.)

The discussions of film sound also shed light on the methods by which a given culture comes to terms with the arrival of a new type of media and the way in which a medium develops into a fully established social institution. This can be demonstrated using the case of sound film: first, a technological invention is tested on the market (short sound films, the temporary installation of sound systems in cinemas, and then their more permanent installation in the most luxurious premiere cinemas); it is subsequently modified into more effective forms (an optical sound track replacing sound on disc, songs and dialogues replacing simple musical accompaniment); finally, it leaves the stage of innovation and enters the stage of full diffusion and standardization. Contemporary culture must then find adequate reactions to the media innovation: it develops methods to adapt to the new medium or it suggests categories and metaphors that facilitate its naming and incorporation into an existing paradigm of reception. In Czechoslovakia, a small, young state that was confronting external threats from its more powerful neighbors as well as internal ethnic conflicts, the focal point of this process was naturally national language. It is, therefore, not surprising that sound film quickly became a hotly contested political issue, occupying the attention of the authorities and stirring passions on all sides of the spectrum (the most infamous example being the Prague demonstrations against German-language films in the fall of 1930).[87] At the same time, sound brought an increase in cin-

87   See Nancy M. Wingfield, "When Film Became National: 'Talkies' and the Anti-German Demonstrations of 1930 in Prague," *Austrian History Yearbook* 29, part 1 (1998, part 1), 113–138.

ema's public prestige, a fact that is evidenced, for example, by the fact that important state figures began to attend the premieres of "national" films such as *Fidlovačka* (Svatopluk Innemann, 1930). These included the revered Czechoslovak president Tomáš Garrigue Masaryk, who even had a personal cinema installed at his residence in Lány (a small town about thirty-five kilometers west of Prague).[88] It is also no surprise that important contributions to the discussion of the cultural and artistic aspects of film sound were provided by authors directly or indirectly associated with Prague structuralism and the activities of the Prague Linguistic Circle: Roman Jakobson, Vladislav Vančura, Jindřich Honzl, Miloš Weingart, and the young Jan Kučera.[89]

5. Creative Alternatives: Independent Film and Visions of New Artistic Synthesis

In some respects, the cusp of the 1920s and 1930s was a time of economic, artistic, and technological crisis for cinema (due, among other aspects, to the commercialization of film production caused by the advent of sound). It is therefore somewhat paradoxical that the Czech avant-garde embarked on film production precisely during this period. This occurred thanks to the rise of a younger generation who abandoned theoretical declarations and literary projects and began to create their own filmic works. One of the most interesting pieces documenting the formation of the avant-garde film movement is an unsigned report from 1930 in the film journal *Studio* called "Fotografie – česká avantgarda" [Photography – Czech avant-garde], which announces the attempt to form a group of avant-garde filmmakers and photographers around the journal.[90] Although a group like the one mentioned in the article never did take shape, the years 1930 and 1931 saw the organization of two collective exhibitions of modern Czech photography and three festivals of avant-garde film, which also featured works by young Czech artists. The main initiator of these events was Alexander Hackenschmied, who also made the first Czech avant-garde film, *Bezúčelná procházka* [The aimless walk, 1930], and wrote a number of articles addressing issues related to the film avant-garde and independent film.

---

[88] See, for example, "President republiky na premiéře *Fidlovačky*," *Filmový kurýr* 4, no. 52 (December 24, 1930), 22.

[89] For a more detailed analysis of Czech discourse on early sound film, see Petr Szczepanik, "Sonic Imagination, or Film Sound as a Discursive Construct in Czech Culture of the Transitional Period," in *Lowering the Boom: Critical Studies in Film Sound*, ed. Jay Beck and Tony Grajeda (Chicago: University of Illinois Press, 2008), 146–175.

[90] "Fotografie – česká avantgarda," *Studio* 2, no. 7 (1930), 220.

In contrast with the members of Devětsil, the primary focus of Hackenschmied's writing, as mentioned above, was his own filmmaking. His critical and theoretical activity in the 1930s grew out of concrete problems encountered in film praxis rather than from general artistic concerns. In his articles, Hackenschmied took issue with the negative effects of the film industry, film business, censorship, and sound film on the development of a cinematic avant-garde.[91] Thirty years prior to Jonas Mekas, Hackenschmied, in fact, coined the term "independent film," which was a broader concept than the idea of avant-garde film alone and enabled the unification of many various branches of film production into one movement (see his 1930 article "Independent Film—A World Movement" in this anthology). The idea of independent film helped the avant-garde overcome not only its hermetic sense of isolation, but also the commercialization of the movement itself. The point of the idea was to preserve the concept of the avant-garde, not to negate it, as was the case with the proletarian art movement. Hackenschmied states this explicitly in his article "Avantgarda žije" [The avant-garde lives, 1929–1930], which concludes with the sentence, "The avant-garde lives; only its historic epochs die."[92]

Creative alternatives to the dominant commercial use of film technology were not limited to the avant-garde and independent film, but also arose in the blurry border regions between film, fine art, and architecture. A unique example in this respect is the artistic and theoretical activity of Zdeněk Pešánek, a pioneer of kinetic art. Between the years 1924 and 1930, Pešánek created three different versions of a color piano (called a "spectrophone") and in later years he made a number of light and kinetic-light sculptures. In addition, he also published many works addressing the usage of light and motion in the plastic arts. By the mid-1920s he had already written an extensive theoretical treatise on kinetic art, which, due to lack of interest by publishers, was not printed until 1941 (with an introduction by František Kalivoda).[93] In his theoretical reflections and sculptural installations, which were often based on the concept of electricity as a carrier of energy and information, Pešánek promoted the principles of multimediality, programming, and global communication. Thus, from today's perspective, his work can be viewed as a forerunner to contemporary ideas about multimedia art and interactivity. Film occupied an important position in his concept of kinetic art, which was similar in many ways to László Moholy-Nagy's artistic program, and in 1927 Pešánek was chairman of the Club for the New Film. Further evidence of his interest in the medium can be seen in the chapter on film in his book *Kinetismus* [Kinetic art, 1941], in his 1928 sculpture bearing the title "Film,"

---

91   See Brož, *Alexander Hackenschmied*, for a selection of Hackenschmied's texts.

92   Alexander Hackenschmied, "Avantgarda žije," *Studio* 2, no. 9 (December 1930), 276.

93   Zdeněk Pešánek, *Kinetismus* (Praha: Česká grafická unie, 1941).

and in the 1926 script for his unrealized film project "Pomník letcům" [Monument to the aviators].[94] Conceived as an interpretation of and complement to one of his own sculptures, Pešánek's screenplay represents a unique undertaking for the period, and preceded a number of similar later projects, such as the film based on Robert Smithson's earthwork sculpture "Spiral Jetty" (1970). Pešánek further developed the ideas in this screenplay when he collaborated with filmmakers František Pilát and Otakar Vávra on the 1930 film *Světlo proniká tmou* [Light penetrates the darkness], whose subject is Pešánek's kinetic-light sculpture on the Edison electrical transformer station in Prague. Similarly to Moholy-Nagy's *Lichtspiel schwarz-weiss-grau* (*Lightplay: Black-White-Gray*, 1930) from the same period, this film not only served as a commentary to the artwork, but also as an innovative means for solving problems thematized in the work itself.

To various degrees, the texts of Kalivoda, Pešánek, Teige, and many of their contemporaries forwarded both the idea of synthesizing individual artistic spheres and the concept of synesthesia as principles of translation between the senses. The approach to synesthesia as a quasi-scientific program is most explicit in the work of Arne Hošek, architect, urbanist, acoustician, and creator of abstract "Musicalist" paintings.[95] He also conducted research on synesthesia, focusing on the possibilities for combining musical and visual-plastic systems of expression and conceiving of acoustics as a discipline wherein laws of "the melody of space" apply. Building upon the doctrine of theosophy, Hošek approached synesthesia as a metaphysical science, seeing it as a pathway to an absolute art that would establish harmony between the external and the spiritual world. As his article "Notes on the Aesthetics of Film" (1939) demonstrates, the source of his interest in sound film was the belief that the merging of sound and image with motion could lead to the creation of a synesthetic art that would become a new instrument for communication between both the artistic spheres and the individual senses. At the same time, he also explored film's potential as a new means of expressing abstract concepts and feelings, as is visible in his unrealized visionary scenario *Zdravý život* [Healthy life].[96]

---

[94] Pešánek wrote the screenplay for this unrealized project for the Elektajournal company. The manuscript is kept in a private collection in Brno, Czech Republic. See Jiří Zemánek, "Ve znamení hvězd: Pomník letcům," in *Zdeněk Pešánek*, ed. Jiří Zemánek (Praha: Národní galerie, 1996), 108–109.

[95] Musicalism: an artistic movement that attempts to recreate musical experience and the form of musical compositions in painting. See Hana Rousová, *Arne Hošek, souvislosti barev a tónů* (Praha: Galerie hl. m. Prahy, 1991).

[96] An undated manuscript from the second half of the 1930s; see Eva Strusková, "Arne Hošek a film," *Iluminace* 15, no. 4 (2003), 117–129.

6. Structure and Sign: The Prague Linguistic Circle's Approach to Film

Although it is commonly accepted that the origins of the semiotics of art can be traced to the interwar period in Central Europe and specifically to the Prague Linguistic Circle, the Prague structuralists' work on film theory is generally mentioned only in passing.[97] As with their linguistic pursuits, the film theories of the Prague Circle were informed by two traditions: Russian formalism and the Central European, in particular Czech, intellectual tradition. Just as Czech Vilém Mathesius anticipated several elements of structural linguistics in his writings from the early 1910s, so articles on film by Václav Tille, František Langer, and the Čapek brothers (included in this anthology), as well as the theater studies of Otakar Zich, were precedents for the film-theoretical works of the Prague Circle.

In 1923, Russian Petr Bogatyrev, who lived and worked in Czechoslovakia during the interwar period, published two studies of Chaplin that introduced the formalist method to film theory.[98] The differences between formalist and structuralist film theory can be clearly seen by comparing these early texts with Bogatyrev's later work and with Jan Mukařovský's first film-theoretical study from 1931, "An Attempt at a Structural Analysis of an Actor's Figure," which also focuses on Chaplin and specifically his film *City Lights*. In his analyses of the films *The Kid* and *The Count*, Bogatyrev shows that, in terms of both acting and plot construction, Chaplin employs a number of principles typical of literary and theatrical traditions (and specifically folk theater); for example, a fixed type of protagonist characterized by a mask, plots founded on parallels and contrasts, narrative retardation, etc. In his later article "Disney's *Snow White*" (1939), however, Bogatyrev works from the concept of the sign, which enables him to formulate and analyze issues that the formalist method fails to address, such as the transfer of signs from one artistic discipline to another and the signifying nature of drawn figures.

In this later article, Bogatyrev also points out some general principles at work in Disney's film, for example, the relationships between irony and banality, the comic and the tragic, avant-garde and folk expression, art for adults and art for children, etc. These issues, as well as the question of the interrelation between theater and film that introduces Bogatyrev's article, were also explored by E. F. Burian's experimen-

---

[97] See, for example, Robert Stam, Robert Burgyone and Sandy Flitterman-Lewis, *New Vocabularies in Film Semiotics* (London: Routledge, 1993), 14–15.

[98] Petr Bogatyrev, "Chaplin i „Kid"; Chaplin – mnimyi graf," in *Chaplin. Sbornik statei* (Berlin: Kino, 1923); Czech translation: Petr Bogatyrev, "Chaplin a 'Kid' — Chaplin falešným hrabětem," in Petr Bogatyrev, *Souvislosti tvorby: cesty ke struktuře lidové kultury a divadla* (Praha: Odeon, 1971), 5–19.

tal theater group "D," in whose journal Bogatyrev published his article. "D" was both inspired by film and directly incorporated film into its stage productions, not only as a new means for constructing scenery but also as an active counterpart to the live performance, thereby demonstrating "the creative treatment and adoption of signs from the sphere of one art to another" that Bogatyrev discusses in the introduction to his article. As was the case with Russian formalism, the theoretical work of the Prague structuralists developed in conjunction with contemporary artistic programs, often directly inspiring them, or being inspired by them.

Throughout the 1930s, the Prague structuralists developed their conception of the semiotics (or, more precisely, semiology) of art, i.e., the study of artistic works as semantic structures. The leading figure of this new discipline was Jan Mukařovský, who presented his programmatic article "Art as Semiotic Fact" (Umění jako sémiologický fakt) at the Eighth International Philosophical Congress in Prague in 1934. Several years earlier, his "An Attempt at a Structural Analysis of an Actor's Figure" (1931) represented one of the first works of semiotic analysis altogether and can be seen as the origin of the structural theory of film and theater.

At the very beginning of his article, Mukařovský defines "structure" as "a system of components aesthetically deautomatized and organized into a complex hierarchy that is unified by the prevalence of one component over the others," and in the remainder of the text he presents a model application of the structural method. First of all, he defines the individual components in the structure of the acting figure and divides them into groups: vocal components, expressive movements (gestures), and spatial movements. He then describes the interrelation of these groups and argues that, in Chaplin, the components of the second group (gestures, i.e., facial expressions, and poses) have the dominant position and subordinate all the other components. Within the line of gestures, Mukařovský consequently distinguishes between two planes: socially defined gesture-signs and individual gesture-expressions. In his opinion, a fundamental characteristic of Chaplin's figure is the interference of these two planes, that is, between two semantically different types of gestures. This interference is further reflected in the other components of Chaplin's acting and even in the distribution of supporting characters and the whole dramatic construction. Thus the internal structure of the actor's figure is projected onto the entire structure of the film, serving as its dominant unifying component. As we can see, Mukařovský first identifies and classifies the basic components, then, after defining their inner structure, i.e., hierarchy and function, he examines the relationship of these immanent structures to more general structures. The same systematic approach is used in his other two film-theoretical studies that focus on the analysis of film's two fundamental semantic components: time and space.

Mukařovský's analysis of filmic space appears in "A Note on the Aesthetics of Film" (1933), which builds upon Russian formalism (specifically upon the texts of

Yuri Tynyanov), and also indirectly upon older works by the Czechs Václav Tille and Karel Čapek. In this text, Mukařovský determines that the fundamental character of filmic space is successiveness, which can be expressed by a change in shot, a close-up, or the off-screen localization of sound. The succession of partial sections of filmic space that are presented with awareness of the unity of the total space, in other words, the succession of "partial signs," provides a semantic unity of space that becomes a meaning unto itself, which Mukařovský calls "space-meaning." Mukařovský attempts to formulate an inclusive conception of the film that can embrace all filmic forms and genres, as the conception's structural characteristics are present in every film—filmic time and filmic space. What links these two components is story, which is provided by a sequence of motifs and has the same successive nature as filmic space. Nevertheless, story is different than space, and the two create distinct semantic series that run simultaneously through the film in a hierarchical relationship. In general, space is subordinated to story, but in exceptional cases this hierarchy can be reversed, as in Dziga Vertov's film *Man with a Movie Camera* (1929).

In the article "Time in Film" (1933), Mukařovský first differentiates between two temporal sequences—the time of the action and the spectator's time—and points out their different proportions within drama and narrative. Whereas the time of the perceiving subject and the time of the action elapse concurrently in drama, in narrative these two temporal sequences are separated, thereby permitting the simultaneous presentation of different temporal levels, temporal condensation, flashbacks, etc. According to Mukařovský, filmic time is situated somewhere between dramatic time and narrative time: on the one hand, it bears certain characteristics of narrative time (e.g., flashbacks, condensed action), while, on the other hand, the time of the perceiving subject elapses concurrently to the time of the actual presentation, just as in drama. In film, a third temporal sequence also asserts itself: the time of the image projected on the screen; in other words, the duration of the filmic work that is "based on the actualization of the real time experienced by the spectator." Mukařovský labels this third temporal sequence "image time" or, more generally, "sign time." These three temporal levels are present in every art that is founded upon action, but only in film do all three levels have equal status, whereas narrative prose is dominated by the time of the action, drama by the time of the perceiving subject, and lyric poetry, which suppresses both of these temporal sequences, by sign time.

In Mukařovský's texts, we witness the growth of film aesthetics as a discipline concerned with defining the aesthetic norms of film art and as one that places particular emphasis on the epistemological investigation of the filmic material and its expressive means. Mukařovský's membership in the Czechoslovak Film Association bears testimony to the fact that, through the late 1930s, he was still interested in issues related to film production, even though he never returned to detailed examinations of film in his theoretical writings. In response to what he saw as the negative consequences of the introduction of sound, he proclaimed that film was an "extra-aesthetic phenomenon" that might strive toward art yet whose nature is not dominated by aesthetic function. Thus, in his view, film would always remain in essence an "industry; therefore, its supply and demand are determined by purely economic concerns to a far greater extent than by any sort of artistic concerns; therefore, film, like any industrial product, is forced to immediately and passively take on every newly discovered innovation of its technological and mechanical base."[99]

Another pioneer of structuralist film theory at this time was Roman Jakobson, who, like Mukařovský, was a leading figure in structural linguistics and a pioneer in the semiotics of art. In his only theoretical study of film, "Is the Film in Decline?" (1933), Jakobson argues against the widespread opinions that saw, in sound film, the decline of film art, due to the fact that sound represented a return to theatrical convention and the suppression of the specifically filmic principle of discontinuous narrative (see also the discussion in section four of this introduction).[100] Jakobson points out that the fragmented narrative style of silent film was primarily contingent on the use of intertitles, i.e., "elements of purely literary composition." The introduction of sound led to the elimination of intertitles and thereby (as Mukařovský also noted) a movement toward a nonfragmented style, one in which, however, specifically filmic qualities were not necessarily suppressed. On the contrary, Jakobson argues, the linkage of image and sound increases film's expressive possibilities (particularly in terms of plot construction) and clearly demarcates film's position between epic and drama.

Jakobson's main argument against the opponents of sound film, however, lies in his demonstration of the sign nature of film sound: for film, speech and noises are acoustic material in the same way that beings and objects are optical material. Filmic sounds, just like filmic images, are not primarily things, but signs, or rather, as Jakobson explains more precisely, things transformed into signs. Jakobson uses this principle of a thing being transformed into a sign to describe the process whereby part of a thing is captured visually or marked aurally. In film, these signs, these fragments of things (of time and space), are juxtaposed in two fundamental ways—in terms of contiguity, or in terms of similarity and contrast; in other words, according to the basic linguistic categories of metonymy and metaphor. The conclusion to Jakobson's study, which appeared as a chapter from a planned but never published

---

[99] Jan Mukařovský, "Estetická funkce, norma a hodnota jako sociální fakty" [1936], in Jan Mukařovský, *Studie* vol. 1 (Brno: Host, 2000), 91–92.

[100] A further text about film by Jakobson, although by no means a theoretical work, is his article about Vladimír Úlehla's ethnographic documentary *Mizející svět* [A disappearing world, 1933]. See Roman Jakobson, "Die entschwindende Welt: Ein Film der sterbenden Folklore – Prof. Dr. Úlehla als Filmregisseur," *Prager Presse*, no. 288, September 11, 1932, 5.

book titled "Předpoklady českého filmu" [The preconditions of Czech cinema], adopts a programmatic approach: he stresses that the absence of norms or an aesthetic canon is a highly positive condition of the current historical period and consequently predicts a blossoming of Czech cinema. This perspective reflects Jakobson's own practical involvement in film production: in 1933, the same year the article was published, he collaborated on the screenplay for the film *Na sluneční straně* [On the sunny side] with Vladislav Vančura, whose film *Před maturitou* [Before graduation, 1932] is directly cited in the article. In addition, he was also a founding member of the Club for the New Film (see section three, above).

A prime source of stimulation and inspiration for the development of the semiotics of art was avant-garde artistic practice, which problematized many of the traditional conceptions of art and raised theoretical questions that would be difficult to answer according to standard methods of interpretation. Not only were representatives of the semiotics of art such as Mukařovský, Jakobson, and Bogatyrev connected to avant-garde artists by their common interests and personal friendships, but they often worked with the artists on concrete projects (such as Jakobson with Vančura, Bogatyrev with the theater group "D," etc). Likewise, structuralist thought had a direct influence on artistic creation in the realms of literature, music, theater, and film. Furthermore, in their programmatic writings, some artists attempted to combine the principles of structuralism and those of the avant-garde into one conceptual whole, for example, E. F. Burian, Vladislav Vančura, Jindřich Honzl, and Jan Kučera.

* * *

Overall, we have discussed here—and presented in this anthology—primarily those examples of Czech film thought that are directly linked with film's evolutionary transformation as a medium, a cultural formation, and an artistic branch. Only a small portion of these fall into the category of film theory in the academic sense, and the significance of these texts for the time that they were written cannot be compared with the current status of "film studies" as a discipline. Instead, we have attempted to acquaint the reader with the exceptionally diverse range of genres and styles of writing that accompanied the formation and development of this new art form and emblematic component of modernity. In the first half of the twentieth century, film was seen as a medium that overturned the previously existing hierarchy of cultural values, and as a symptom of the radical transformations occurring in the spatio-temporal structure of everyday life and in individual subjective experience. The texts collected in this anthology seek to define the nature of this new medium, to determine its position among the other arts and media, to utilize it as an instrument within various artistic and political struggles, and to predict its future development.

For the most part, the authors of these texts did not work as professional film critics or film historians, but as academics, artists, and organizers within other disciplines such as literature, the visual arts, architecture, theater, music, linguistics, or even the natural sciences.

All these factors bear testimony to the uncertain position that film occupied in Czech culture of the 1900s–1930s. At the beginning of the twentieth century, film had to differentiate itself from the wide spectrum of optical media and artifacts of popular culture inherited from the nineteenth century and establish itself as an independent medium. In the early 1910s, it came to be defined as a primarily narrative form and by the end of the decade it had achieved, with some difficulty and many reservations, the status of a potential art. At the beginning of the 1920s, it came to be thought of as one of the most quintessential manifestations of modern technological civilization, and became an emblematic symbol for the international avant-garde. Yet, by the end of the decade, leftist critics and theorists saw film as sharply divided, with commercial production as exemplified by Hollywood on the one side and progressive, socially critical production based on the model of Soviet cinema on the other. In the early 1930s, due to the rise of sound film and the subsequent convergences between cinema and other sound media and artistic varieties (popular theater and music, radio, gramophone, etc.), film's identity underwent a new series of disputes and redefinitions. All of a sudden, what was once known simply as "film" now came to be understood as an old medium called "silent film" that was displaced by the new medium of the "talking film." This period also saw the first widespread development of a diverse spectrum of creative alternatives that competed with mainstream productions within certain areas of social and cultural life in Czechoslovakia: avant-garde films, independent films, amateur films, social documentaries, film as a technique in the fine arts and theater, etc. The texts collected here do not examine these struggles and transformations from an external, impartial point of view; on the contrary, they are an inseparable component of these transformations—their manifestations and agents.

Kinéma: The Physiology of Vision, the Pedagogy of Perception, the Cubistic Fragmentation of Reality

PART ONE

Jan Evangelista Purkinje
EXCERPTS FROM *CONTRIBUTIONS TO THE KNOWLEDGE OF VISION IN ITS SUBJECTIVE ASPECT*

Initially, an individual developing toward self-consciousness sees the whole world of objects only as something floating inside of him, like a dream, whereby fantasy and reality mingle together wonderfully; then he gradually places everything outside of himself and himself in opposition to everything, and begins to orient himself within the circle of his own existence. Yet something remains in the province of the senses that cannot be transferred outside the sphere of the individual organism.

In general, these are sensations that pertain to one or another of the senses, but that do not correspond to anything outside the body, and that—insofar as they imitate the qualities and forms of external things and therefore often cause deception—are in part rightly considered phantoms, mere illusions that do not correspond to any reality. Thus, with regard to the considerations at hand, these can be labeled as subjective sense phenomena. Yet it remains the undeniable task of the natural scientist to identify the objective foundation of these phenomena, while for common practical use it is enough to know that they are affiliated only with the sensory organs themselves and that there is therefore no need to search for corresponding objects outside the body.

Many of these phenomena were long ago appropriated by optics and have recently been appropriated by color theory[1]; many became the object of specific treatises without being attached to any existing branch of knowledge; physiology integrated many of them into its theory of the senses; but most were adopted by specialized pathology, owing to its particular task.

But, from the point of view of pure scientific research, pathologic conditions are just as rare as weeds for the biologist or rubbish for the chemist. These concepts are relative and have validity only insofar as they hinder the achievement of a specific goal.

---

[1] Purkinje alludes to Johann Wolfgang von Goethe's *Entwurf einer Farbenlehre* (1810). Purkinje's dissertation had a great impact on Goethe, whom he visited in Weimar in 1822 and to whom he dedicated his *Beobachtungen und Versuche zur Physiologie der Sinne. Neue Beiträge zur Kenntniss des Sehens in subjectiver Hinsicht* (Berlin: Reimer, 1825), another volume of his *Contributions*.

With the same passion with which he apprehends a law of nature that clearly penetrates the phenomena, the physiologist also apprehends the apparent entanglements and exceptions in the firm belief that they, too, will unravel into an all-pervading harmony.

If one wanted to bring the study of subjective sensory phenomena into union with the other guilds of knowledge, it would likely be difficult to immediately find its appropriate place, since any object can generally be viewed from various sides. Most likely, the first to accept it would be so-called empirical psychology, as long as nothing in the theory called for a closer identification of the material and dynamic relations within the individual organism itself. Physiology, understood in a somewhat stricter sense, only deals with objective realities and entirely excludes sensations as such. For physiology, sensations are merely letters and words through which it receives reports of things whose grammar could occupy a theory in and of itself.

From a less rigid point of view, however, all of these border distinctions are arbitrary and their value primarily consists in the fact that, the more divided they are, the more rigorously specific tendencies of the mind can be observed from all sides.

It would be better to categorize this subject, which stands at the outer edges of empiricism, within the descriptive natural sciences. There could also be a natural history of the senses and a sensory realm within whose borders sensations would be placed in harmonious groups, positioned against one another, in various mutual relationships.

Through observation and experimentation, each sense can be comprehended and presented both in its own unique existence and in its particular reactions to the external world; to a certain extent, each sense is an individual, hence the specificity of a simultaneous "self" and "other" in the sensations.

The only way to conduct such research is through strict sensory observation of and experimentation on one's own organism. Both are important branches of physical art in general and demand a specific orientation of the attention and a specific and methodical series of conditioning, training, and skills. There are certain objects of research in the natural sciences that can only be analyzed in this way, and about which we would otherwise have no idea.

In this way, physiography[2] would attain a subjective sphere in addition to the merely objective sphere it has now; whereby, of course, we should not be misled by the apparent disparity between them in terms of magnitude. The subjective sphere is just beginning to be examined, yet still provides a glimpse into a rich field of study that will arise once there is great enough competition between those who are able to focus their attention on the special limitations of the senses, especially in pathological states, and once the terminology necessary for mutual communication is developed.

---

[2]   Purkinje uses the term "physiography" to designate descriptive physiology, not physical geography.

I have discovered several things in this field that strike me as new, or that I have at least observed in greater detail than anyone else. In the present text, I proceed on the one hand descriptively, presenting the conditions of particular sensory perceptions together with their consequences, if they are known to me. On the other hand, I point out analogies I believe I have observed between individual phenomena themselves as well as between them and the external world. In doing so, I make no claims to successful explanations, for I am convinced that every object, so long as it is not grasped in the totality of its appearances, only permits a one-sided view, therefore keeping the mind in a condition of doubt, always awaiting a more perfect solution.

For now, I will concentrate only on the sense of sight.

[...]

Persisting Images, Imagination, the Sense of Sight's Memory[3]

I have often been amazed that the blinking of the eye does not disrupt vision, since I imagine that complete darkness must occur during a blink. But, under closer observation, I discovered that the open eye's field of vision, with all of its lights and images, persists in the sense for a short time after the eyelids have closed. The more attentively I regard a simple, not too expansive image, the longer I can maintain it in my sense after my eyes have closed. It is necessary to precisely differentiate this persisting image [*Nachbild*] from the afterimage [*Blendungsbild*][4]. The persisting image is held for a longer period of time only as the result of free agency, disappearing as soon as the will relents, but it can also be recalled again by the will. The afterimage floats involuntarily in the sense, disappearing and appearing again as a result of objective causes.

The sense's topicizing activity, the eye's sense of touch, proceeds to place the persisting image outside the organ, just as is the case with actual seeing. It can also de-

---

[3]   Purkinje uses the term *Nachbild*, translated here as "persisting image," to designate what is today described as two kinds of visual memory: iconic memory (sensory memory), and short-term memory ("primary," "working," or "active" memory). Curiously, Purkinje's concept of visual memory, especially when he distinguishes between primary and secondary sensory activity, is closer to today's understanding of the visual perception of movement (including moving pictures) than to the theory of visual persistence that for a long time prevailed in film and media studies.

[4]   The English translation of Purkinje's concept of *Nachbild* as "persisting image" and *Blendungsbild* as "afterimage" may sound counterintuitive, as the literal translation of *Nachbild* is "afterimage," while the literal translation of *Blendungsbild* is roughly "image caused by a blinding or glaring light." However, this terminological solution was necessitated by the specific meaning Purkinje ascribes to *Nachbild*; see note 3.

pict stereometrically limited images, and the memory image [*Nachbild*][5] maintains its original place and position even when the whole body is moved or turned. In contrast, the afterimage depicts only flat surfaces; it is located only in the eye and follows its movements. The liveliness of the memory image differs according to the differences in mood. It is particularly lively during heightened mental activity, after drinking spirits or ingesting narcotics, or when there is particular interest in a certain object; during a fevered agitation of the blood, particularly in the presence of cerebral affectations, it often approaches the level of hard objectivity. The afterimage, on the other hand, tends to persist longer during nervous moods or in asthenic states; the more energetically life flows through the organ, the more quickly it disappears. Furthermore, the closer the memory image is to the moment when the pattern was originally perceived, the clearer and more objective it is. With each passing moment it becomes harder and harder to maintain it in the sense with the same clarity. By contrast, the afterimage of weakly shining objects is confused in the first moments after seeing and only gradually forms to completion within the sense, which remains here only a passive observer.

I believe that, through an exercise in which, after the initial perception of an object, one would hold the image longer and more dearly, one could approach the reality of the original perception. This is an exercise that should not be unimportant in the training of memory and imagination.

One might ask in which organic structure the persisting image resides. With regard to the original image and the afterimage, it is most commonly believed that they are experienced in the retina, and the same could justifiably be claimed of the persisting image. In both cases, the empirical evidence is equally compelling.

Going a step further, it could be claimed that memory and imagination are active in the sense organs are themselves and that each sense possesses its own inherent memory and imagination—individual, limited powers subordinate to the general mental power.

In primary sensory activity, when sense is in direct interaction with the object, memory and imagination are already engaged and it is precisely here that they are the most vivid. Whereas they later appear only as shadows and auxiliary products of the actual sensory activity, memory and imagination reach their highest level of intensification only when their product approximates direct sensory perception. I assume that the distinction between this primary and secondary sensory activity stems from the fact that, with the primary activity, real movements and sensations take place in the organ, whereas, with the latter, only intended movements and sensations occur. Thus, in the former case, the eye follows the outline of the object with

---

[5]   In this context, the term *Nachbild* translates as "memory image" to indicate its broader meaning. Purkinje here describes working (short-term or active) memory.

actual movements, whereas in the latter case only the differentials of movements are stimulated within the relevant muscles, without the realization of actual movements.

It is easier to observe this type of movement in the speech organs, such as when we unexpectedly find ourselves engaged in self-conversation. This activity can be more crudely observed in larger muscle groups, for instance in the extremities, when the motion impulses of a muscle, resulting either from external or internal causes, strive to exert themselves but are inhibited by the will. In general, it can also be expected that each actual movement has a corresponding intended movement, just as each free natural power corresponds to a constrained one without being in principle distinct from it. Such concepts were formulated in physics long ago, prompted by phenomena such as weight, latent temperature, bound electricity,[6] and magnetism, or mutually limiting tensions and tendencies. The same is true for intended sensations. Each sensation is a unique modification of one's sense of self by external limitations. The tendency to bring about such a specific limitation by an inner stimulus would be intended sensation.

Just like their originals, both intended movements and intended sensations are mediated by the primary motor apparatus and the sensory organs.

It is unnecessary to assign memory and imagination (and their various forms) their own organs in the brain. The subjects of both as well as the direct sensations have been specified in the minutest detail. Why, then, would one want to allocate them to organs in the brain, whose detailed configuration is still so little known? To do so would only make matters more incomprehensible. The brain can be thought of as the seat and accumulator of the general free principle that flows into all other organs, a principle that only acquires its specific limitations in these organs.

For a long time, people have conceived of the senses as animals within an animal, thereby endowing them with their own identities. In addition to having their own lives, these individual animals are controlled by a higher, more powerful life form that brings them into a unity of action and consciousness.

Whenever this unifying principle loosens its grip, the individual subordinate life immediately begins to express itself according to its nature. Many a folly and madness can be seen as a detachment of one or more of the sensory and motor organs from the unity of mental activity, whereby its products appear alienated and its activities seem to rebel inexpediently against the harmony of the rest of the organism. Even during sleep, the senses seem to disperse, each going its own way. This can be easily detected by observing while falling asleep how often the eye and the ear dream completely different dreams at exactly the same time. One should also note here that

---

6   With the term "bound electricity," Purkinje likely refers to static electricity. This term might also allude to Volta's electric pile.

a dream is commonly occupied with fantasy images related to the sense that was most stimulated in the moments immediately preceding sleep.

What I have articulated here about the senses in general applies primarily to the eye. Whereas throughout the text I have been concerned only with what goes on within the organ connected to the sense of sight, particularly its physiological operation, I shall close here by drawing attention to the soul of this sense and its relationship to a higher principle.

(1819)

Václav Tille[1]
KINÉMA[2]

Across city outskirts, in carnivals, and on fairgrounds, there is a proliferation of wooden booths where the flickering, dappled pictures of various bioscopes[3] and cinematographs whir. The hotels, concert halls, and new buildings of the city are filled with permanent theaters of this type, of varying degrees of quality. In the production of living pictures, joint-stock companies dispatch their agents with cameras to all corners of the globe, arrange lively scenes on the streets even of small villages, and commission pantomimes to be performed on carefully prepared sets. They think up miracles and surprises, contract works from literary and artistic companies, and refine the technology of reproduction at break-neck speed. In terms of money, millions are caught up in fevered activity, and hundreds of thousands of people anxiously await new entertainment, new enjoyment evoked by an old visual medium—the shadow.

Neither shadows nor puppets are among the artistic visual media mentioned in Aristotle's *Poetics*. However, although we have no proof, it is highly likely that during

---

[1]   The information about puppets and shadow play was taken from Charles Magnin's *Histoire des marionettes en Europe* (Paris: Michel Lévy frères, 1852), and from Hermann Siegfried Rehm's *Das Buch der Marionetten* (Berlin: Fernsdorff, 1905). In addition, I studied the figures from Eastern shadow play and the puppets at the collection of the Ethnographic Museum in Berlin. Mr. Dawton from Ceylon provided me with some oral accounts of *wayang*. Data about Turkish shadow play are from Georg Jacob's books on the subject. [Original footnote]

[2]   *Kinéma*: there was no standardized film terminology in Czech at the time, yet Tille's term here can be equated with the more common form "kinema" as used by other Czech writers in the 1910s (e.g., František Langer and the Čapek brothers), which has essentially the same connotations as "cinema" in English.

[3]   The term *bioscope* (*bioskop* in Czech) was used to designate different technologies at various points in film history; for instance, in Berlin in 1895 by Max Skladanowsky, and in the United States in 1897 by Charles Urban. More importantly, *bioscope* was frequently a name for various traveling cinemas at the time Tille wrote his article. Tille (like the Čapek brothers) used the term interchangeably with cinematograph (i.e., *kinematograf*).

his time dramatic and visual artists in the East were already evoking artistic moods and enjoyment with shadows and puppets, the only visual media besides the human body itself with which it is possible to create life-like movement in art.

The shadow is a more workable and obedient visual medium than the puppet. It conjures a more consistent and deeper mood, is better suited to fantastic dreams, the most bizarre and grotesque creations of which it is better able to develop. Even in the ancient times of their most glorious cultural periods (from which many valuable mementos produced by artistic spirits remain), the cultured nations of the East found in shadows a medium for the creation of fantastic, wonderful, and colorful dreams; a medium to embody the most fragile creations of their fantasy; to construct unknown, mysterious worlds, populated with millions of fantastic, unearthly beings. We do not know where these radiant shadows of varied colors, flickering with dazzling brilliance on a taut screen, first emerged. Be it from India or China, these shadows spread throughout the Indian Archipelago, Siam, Japan, Samarkand, Arabia, Syria, Palestine, Persia, Egypt, Tunisia and Turkey. And still to this day, all of these lands are teeming with such fine little figures of transparent animal hide that, with their lightning-fast movements, excite the fiery fantasy of spectators. There is only a small handful of historical accounts from the depths of the past, yet the shape of the figures and the content of their plays themselves speak distinctly of bygone days, of the very sources of nations' spiritual lives.

Over centuries, the Indian Archipelago created a legion of shadow figures. The collection at Berlin's Ethnographic Museum has a delightful assortment of bold heroes, gracious princesses, wild bandits, giants, monsters, monkeys, and wizards, which gleam like the fiery feathers of a bird of paradise. They are clad in magnificent costumes, filled with weapons and jewels, and they possess expressive, soulful faces as well as slender limbs capable of life-like movement. These are not copies of human figures and faces, but fantastic apparitions that arose and grew over centuries from the vivid dreams of humanity. They are the servants of good and evil, a special race of heroes and demons that were born from and continue to live in the magical worlds of human fantasy. The noble and bold race of heroes have a slim, elongated neck. The central line of the forehead is extended into the line of the nose, forming a single meridian. The expressions of the heroic men and gracious young women are accentuated by oblong almond eyes and pursed, nearly smiling lips. They are slender figures with supple flanks, and delicate, tender limbs. Their hair flows loose below their shoulders or is tied up in a strong, untangled braid with the thin end returning up toward the head. The race of demons and evil ones have angular features with bulging, circular eyes, bared teeth and a craggy head set upon a stumpy neck that rises up from a burly body. Their hair and helmets are wildly unkempt. The bare skulls of the monsters, whose freakish bodies surpass even the most fantastical representations of Priapus, are covered with scraggly tufts of hair. All of the figures are painted with immeasurable care onto transparent buffalo hide mounted on a thin stem. Even thinner stems are used to manipulate their arms. What great artists cut and painted these delicate shadows of human fantasy! And with what love and zeal they breathed ravishing tenderness into the faces of the gracious young women, masculine courage into the expressions of the heroes, and fierce evil into the countenances of the demons! With what amazing diligence and taste they depicted the folds of their costumes, the tiny ornamentations on their jewels and weapons, the expression in their eyes, and the tender contours of their bare bodies!

Along with the kings, heroes, princesses, and demons, there appear whole throngs of soldiers, monkeys, giants and other demons. They are cut with miraculous artistry from whole swaths of bull hide, upon which the heads of bizarre figures are painted hundred-fold.

On Java, during weddings and births, at anniversary celebrations, and at the parties of affluent Malaysian households, a luxurious carpet is laid out on the floor. The women and girls huddle close together in front of a wall measuring five meters in length and more than half a meter in height, pulled taut over a thin bamboo frame. The men sit behind the wall, around the carpet. With a cup of coffee and an opium pipe, the director of the play, the *dalang*, sits in the center of the carpet, surrounded by musicians, boxes, little bells and figures. In front of him, high oil lamps with thick wicks cast evenly diffused light down onto the white screen. Heroes, demons and legions of soldiers are already grouped together and planted along both sides of the screen, arranged in tight rows that become gradually smaller as they approach the center where there looms a hill, *gunung'an*, on which there stands a symbolic tree. Finally, the *dalang* is finished with the preparations, music begins to play, the hill disappears from the center of the screen, the figures of the heroes and the king with his courtiers appear, and the plot starts to unfold with the tempo of a slow and serious epic poem. *Wayang*, the shadow play, has begun.

These are not mere children's entertainment or light plays of impulsive fancy. The shadow play is a serious proceeding, initiated with a sacrifice. The *dalang* is a person who enjoys considerable respect. The stories illustrated by the figures on the screen are parts of a hundred-, perhaps thousand-year-long national tradition. The oldest of these are remnants of ancient, wonderful Malaysian myths about the creation of the earth. The same myths that gave rise to those amazing and manifold Malaysian carvings and to most wonderful pictures and stories. With their primitive ideas of cosmogony, told with fascinating and moving symbolism, these stories have no equals. Mingled with the old myths are long stories from the *Mahabharat* and the *Ramayana* (filled with exciting scenes such as battles with giants and demons) and also stories from the extensive tales of Panji (about a bold hero and his endless adventures). The hero undertakes bold quests and wrestles with giants. The scenes rapidly alternate between heroic, romantic, and comical. The jesters that accompany the hero mock the lumbering giants. Great armies fight countless battles, each one bloodier than the next. And when day breaks, the powerful oil lamps are extinguished. The heroes are victorious and indulge in a celebratory feast, after which the gracious *gumbjong*, a splendidly decorated wooden dancer, performs a charming dance with natural movements. This dance, with its clamorous music, concludes the *wayang*. Throughout the night, the multi-colored, glaring whirl of fiery shadows blazes on the white screen. The shadows beam with such passionate love, wrath and hate, and their masters speak and sing so perfectly with such a range of sharply and soulfully nuanced voices that they could even succeed in inspiring the cold imagination of a European. The flickering shadows achieve such life and such inner expression, and they are so perfectly and artfully stylized that they awaken the same deep moods as any perfected work of art. It is the pure and beautiful art of the naïve soul. It is the art of the gentle painters who created the figures, of the actors who breathe life into them with such passion, and of the creators of the cosmic myths, heroic stories, and adventurous tales of the immortal figures of Indian poetry.

In Siam, the mood of the shadow play is even more serious. The play of luminescence and shadow takes priority over the creation of colorful effects. The play, called *nang* [shadow], is performed only during sad and solemn celebrations, during mourning for the dead and during the burning of the body. The plots of the *nang* come from one solitary source: the endless stories of the *Ramayana*. The hero Rama lives exiled in the jungle with his gracious spouse, Sita, and his step-brother, Lakshmana. The multi-headed Ravana, king of the Ceylonese demons, kidnaps Sita. Sugriva, the king of the monkeys, and his wise counselor, Hanuman, help Rama search for his spouse. The monkeys build a bridge to Ceylon. In the end, Ravana is killed, and Sita proves her purity by a test in which she walks through fire. What seeds for wild and tender episodes are sowed within this simple framework! How many bloody battles, murders, magic spells, intrigues and cunning tricks the actors are able to render with their grotesque little figures dressed in typical Siamese festive costumes with spiraled and pointed headdresses! The transparent leather on which the moveable figures are painted and the long piece of hide speckled with hundreds of soldiers, demons and monkeys are both punctured with thousands of tiny holes that carefully mark out gems, weapons, and the folds in the clothes. When the light from behind the curtain illuminates these dead shadows, thousands of glowing spots light up the dark outlines, forming complex lines that describe bodies, clothes, weapons and whole legions, which the assistants to the actor manipulate with miraculous skill. The ceremonious show is accompanied by the performance of several solemn live characters, by the jokes of a comic figure, and by the declamations of two orators reciting the national epic. All the spectators know these passionate and heroic scenes by heart. Rama and Sita, Lakshmana and Ravana are their own personal friends and enemies. They all know in great detail the fate of the characters in advance, yet time and again the audience is captivated by the solemn rhythm of the poetry. They listen breathlessly to the simple yet passionate songs and melodious prose. With great pleasure, they watch the whirl of radiant sparkles and shadows on the white screen, the living shadow of ancient history, the tradition from which the spirit of the nation grew.

Chinese shadow play disengaged itself from the literary tradition. It is not merely shadows of old myths and national epics. It does not merely create vivid figures of the imagination, but is also focused on real life. In addition to dragons, demons, wizards and miracles, the shadow play presents cities and streets, the bustle of people on public squares, the interiors of tearooms, opium dens, bazaars and harbors with boats. Figures taken from real life act out humorous, frightening, solemn and grotesque scenes. The innumerable sounds of street commotion, the whistling of birds, and comical dialogues resound from the screen. The performing artists feel and see life around them and transfer onto the screen their own impressions and feelings, as well as the perceptions of contemporary people. These are artists with a deep and accomplished visual sense who use scenery, acting and declamations with extraordinary technical skill to evoke ardent moods. This art form was perfected by a tradition spanning hundreds and hundreds of years. The oldest evidence of shadow play, dating from the eleventh century, comes from China. The Chinese artists who performed shadow plays for the son of Tamerlane in Samarkand were already capable of faithfully depicting a wild horse dragging an old man by the hair.

Citing modern plays, Siegfried Rehm describes the following scene: in a magical gloom, a pagoda is reflected in the quiet waters of a lake. A man whose mother has died enters the scene. He offers a sacrifice to the deity. The smoke from the sacrifice wafts toward the sky as the son implores the lord of the underworld to release his mother's shadow. Then the strings of a Chinese zither ring out and the pagoda disappears into a swirl of colorful rings, in which the shadow of his beloved mother appears. She tells the secrets of the other world; her breathing is labored, her breast heaves, and her face shows excitement. When her voice finally fades, the shadow disappears. Once again the pagoda is seen reflected in the quiet water. The moon shines and swans float on the lake.

This is not merely a creation of fantasy, but the mood and illusion of life that is able to overcome the laws of the real world and realize human dreams thanks to the technology of visual representation.

The little figures, scenic decorations and lighting effects utilized by Chinese shadow plays in their comical, moody and grotesque rendering of life are more complex than those used in Siam or in the Malaysian Archipelago. The ancient native tradition is even displayed in the costumes of the figures, as well as in their segmented, moveable limbs and in their grotesquely drawn yet expressive faces and high, lavishly fashioned hairstyles. The figures emulate the movements of the human body more faithfully than do the Siamese or Javanese figures, whose immobile bodies and mobile arms are mounted on sticks from below. The three-segmented arms and two-segmented legs of the Chinese figures are suspended on wires from above, which allows them to smoothly and faithfully perform even the most passionate and complex movements, thereby appearing far more realistic than the figures from the Indian myths and epics with their stiff and stereotypical movements. In Japan, besides a tradition of shadow play that was even richer and more fully developed than in China, there also arose a fondness for magnificent puppets.

We know that the Arabs have executed wonders with the tiny figures of their shadow plays since ancient times. Their sovereigns, among them the famous Saladin, are known to have followed the nimble shadow play with passionate fondness, despite the fact that it often boldly commented on serious matters through caricature and satire. For quite some time, shadow play took the place of drama in Arab culture. (Even in the Archipelago, Siam and China, animated shadows have existed longer than puppets and live actors have.) The Arabs even brought their shadow play with them to Egypt and to Europe. In the El Escorial monastery there is a manuscript of three shadow plays by an Arab physician († 1311), which present a multitude of varied characters and complex, eventful scenes. The plays are of a literary nature and one of them bears a striking resemblance to the wonderful, spirited allegories of the European Middle Ages. The play begins with a ram-fight, a cockfight, and a bullfight. Then al-Mutajjam has a feast prepared with the meat of the defeated bull. He arranges for a large amount of wine and invites everyone from the streets to drink. Many bizarre and horrendous guests arrive. These allegories of human vice in the form of realistic characters take part in the feast and drink themselves into a stupor, until the final guest appears—the angel of death. Full of trepidation, al-Mutajjam, an Arab precursor to Don Juan, asks if there is not still time for repentance. The angel of death bides his time as the sinner breaks into a repentant confession and praises God almighty. Then, forgiven of his sins and with a prayer on his lips, he ascends to the gates of heaven.

These animated shadows romped about on white screens throughout the Arab lands for hundreds of years. They did not, however, merely enliven literary fantasy and portray simple scenes of everyday life. They also critically attacked and satirized political matters. In the sixteenth century, in Cairo, the government was even moved to suppress a dangerous shadow play that was inflaming a revolutionary movement.

In Siam and the Indian Archipelago, satirical, derisive, grotesque, and sexual elements were of only secondary importance to the sacred ceremony, and, in China and Japan, they formed the foundation only for special plays that were outside the realm of serious and spirited taste. Yet these elements dominated the thoroughly modern shadow play in Turkey, which developed a tradition with its own unique and novel variations and situations. The accounts of Turkish shadow play in the thirteenth century are highly dubious and of the seventeenth century we know only that shadow play flourished under the reign of sultan Murada IV. There are references to Turkish shadow play by European travelers in the eighteenth century, but it is not until the nineteenth century that it was systematically studied in its new, established form, primarily in the works of Jacob. Apart from exceptional performances, it was restricted to the month of Ramadan. Traveling among coffee houses, bazaars and small inns, it made do with a stage of approximately one square meter in size. Within scenes of streets, canals, bazaars and public squares, the black shadows of tiny leather figures, pressed against a white screen with thin, crossed rods, engage in unending dialogues. The primary subject matter is the exploits of the wily rogue Karagöz and his sophisticated friend Hacivat. The hero of the awkward and lascivious stories, Karagöz, is dim-witted, wily, sensual, gluttonous, vulgar, and funny. He is a perennial figure of that grotesque type that resurfaces over and over in world literature in the most varied of guises: Dandin, Trubert, Eulenspiegel, Sancho Panza, Falstaff, Leporello, Harlequin, Kašpárek et al.[4] Karagöz is typified primarily by his sensual inclinations and also for his awkward jokes, with which he makes both young and old laugh with wonderful ease. They are simple stories, sometimes consisting merely of dialogue, that feature characters such as a wild arnaut[5], a comical "Franconian," a foreigner, a European doctor, a wily and noble Jew, an Arab, a Persian, Karagöz's wife, Hacivat's daughter, a stubborn donkey, a barking dog and a dragon. The stories are highly realistic imitations of everyday situations, primarily Karagöz's predicaments, amorous expeditions, and business endeavors. Of course, the actors also take advantage of the opportunities offered to them by shadow-reproduction. For example, when Karagöz wants to hide, without hesitation he stands still to resemble an immovable post to which someone then tethers a horse, or he transforms his body into a bridge across a canal, which is then traversed by carriages and people. Apparently, *hayal*, the Turkish shadow play performed by artful and intelligent *Hayalis*, is very comical and played with extraordinary skill and vitality, often digressing into risqué erotic episodes. Indeed, the more popular form of *hayal*, in which Karagöz and his friend Hacivat continually outdo one another with their crudeness and extravagances, is extremely vulgar. This type of shadow play is performed in the Turkish and Arab lands, as well as in Syria, Palestine, Egypt, and Tripoli and reaches the most extreme perversion and crudeness in Tunisia.

---

[4]   These are references to comedic characters from theater plays, novels, and larger literary or dramatic traditions: Molière's comedy *Georges Dandin ou le Mari confondu*, Douin de Lavesne's novel *Trubert*, the German stories of Till Eulenspiegel, Cervantes's *Don Quixote*, the Shakespearean character John Falstaff, Don Giovanni's servant Leporello, Arlecchino from Italian commedia dell'arte, and Kašpárek (or Kasperle) from the Czech and German puppet-theater tradition.

[5]   An Albanian, specifically one serving as a soldier in the Turkish army.

The bad as well as the good plays use similar techniques to elicit laughter from the audience, whether through the use of comic or racy situations, constant word play, or their characters' false eloquence and mistakes in reasoning. They also have a special penchant for making a mockery of European doctors and travelers. The ceremonious solemnity, deep tragedy and entrancing moods of the Eastern shadow play have disappeared for good in the naïve, grotesque and crude fluttering dance of shadows on a small white screen. This type of shadow play humbly and impudently panders to the non-demanding audience with mere sensual jokes, mockery of foreigners, and naïve silliness. Such a decline of ideals, which we trace from East to West and from the past to the present, is gradually spreading to other countries. It is even evident, for example, in Persia, although neither the technical skill of the acting nor the inventive fantasy used in creating grotesque scenes has decreased in quality.

These Eastern shadows reached European culture at the end of the eighteenth century. They became an amusement at King Louis' court approximately a quarter century before the revolution. At Versailles in 1780, the young actor Séraphin François entertained the ladies of the court and the king himself with his *ombres chinoises*. For several years, he even treated the common Parisian citizens to this royal entertainment at the Palais Royal. French authors gladly wrote fantastical and sentimental pieces in the Parisian style for him and his successors, who maintained the theater until the time of the Franco-Prussian War (1870–1871). The Parisian literary and artistic communities embraced this new visual medium with a passionate fondness, creating fantastic and extraordinarily charming marvels of dark shadows and color at the famous Chat Noir. This theater far surpassed its imitators throughout Europe with its comedies, oratorios, mysteries, sensational plays, pantomimes and grotesque fantasies.

Yet despite their charm, the "Chinese shadows" of the Versailles court were nothing more than the bizarre plaything of a decadent society weary of delights, and despite its amazing level of excellence, the shadow play of the Chat Noir was nothing more than a diversion for the highly sophisticated art world. These shadows did not become an integral part of the national art and culture as they had in the Orient. For centuries the Europeans had been interested in animated shadows, but not as a visual medium for representing human fantasy. From Da Vinci's sketches for the *camera obscura*, in which one could behold colorful, moving images of reality, to the experiments of the loquacious adventurer Della Porta, in which transparent images were projected with the help of lenses, Europeans strove to evoke mysterious phenomena with animated shadows. These shadows, which depicted life-like forms of devils and dead bodies on screens and in shifting clouds of smoke, were a cause of great concern for the Inquisition, until the Jesuit Athanasius Kircher won official recognition for these "unholy apparitions" with the introduction of his "magic lantern" in the seventeenth century. In the eighteenth century, all efforts were directed toward the invention of various devices with which the Europeans strove to realize shadow visions and to achieve strange effects by combining them in various ways. These effects were often employed in mysterious charlatan séances. Yet one problem remained unsolved. The *camera lucida* was able to mimic the movement and color of reality on a flat surface and on a reduced scale, but it did not succeed in capturing and maintaining this constantly changing picture, thereby liberating it from the real object. The *camera obscura* (first with daguerreotypes, then with wet plates and finally with dry plates) was indeed able to capture a permanent picture of reality, but without color and without movement. At the same time, the peculiar mutoscopes were, in a primitive way, attempting to represent characters and objects in motion by means of a rapidly spinning series of pictures.[6] Finally, all three of these elements were combined to create a band of snapshots of reality and a medium was invented that generated animated shadows on a screen, mechanically faithful reproductions of objects.

In ancient Eastern shadow play it was necessary to create moveable objects that were then used to combine animated shadows on a transparent screen, whereas the European *laterna magica* reproduced immobile pictures on a screen. With the help of photography, the cinematograph made moving pictures, liberated from physical objects, and thus captured the continuous movement of reality.

Science seized upon this invention and used it to precisely illustrate the flight of birds, the movement of humans and machines, and the growth of plants. However, private entrepreneurs also seized upon it and began to create a new type of shadow play, a shadow play that was at once a copy of reality, a wonder of technology (generated with those new visual media), and a creation of human fantasy. Yet for the time being, as is often the case, this art form remained in the hands of business entrepreneurs and technical craftsmen, people who cater primarily to the taste of the consuming masses and who are guided primarily by the desires of their audience when it comes to the choice of subject matter and the refinement of technology. And so new formats arise at a dizzying speed: cinematographs, bioscopes, and moving picture theaters, with diverse programs that alternate images of foreign landscapes with comical, magical, sensational, and sentimental scenes. The composition of the scenes is determined primarily by the visual medium itself, by its particularities as well as by its shortcomings.

The reproduction of real foreign landscapes falls into the field of popular science. The employees of cinematographic companies undertake expeditions to far-off

---

[6]   Mutoscope: a coin-operated peep-show device that was a mechanized version of the "flip book," patented in 1894 by Herman Casler.

places, from the Arctic Circle to the equator. From all corners of the world, they select the most diverse landscape tours, war scenes, and images of industry and transportation. All of these things become subjects for their camera lenses, which by the day achieve higher and higher degrees of reproductive perfection. For the most part, the pictures are true to reality and only rarely require a little retouching. Inserts from a zoo complement endless scenes of stalking from a lion hunt that was actually played in an unseen garden somewhere near the shore but is deftly relocated to a tropical rainforest. A picture depicting the hunt for a polar bear includes pretty images of the wide sea along the northern coast of Germany in sequences that show the shooting of auks or seals, but the polar bears inserted into this landscape are from other recordings; and when the hunters finally encounter the polar bear, the white giant is replaced with a rather tame little bear from the Hagenbeck Zoo.[7] Student life on the Boul' Mich' is indeed truly portrayed by amateur volunteers, but the nighttime can-can at the Bal Bullier is quite obviously the work of hired ladies on a stagy set under artificial lighting.[8] In such cases, though, composition and imitation are only used to help overcome the technical difficulties involved in reproducing reality. At the very most, the visual arts can help this process only in terms of the choice and arrangement of the subject. This, of course, if it is at all possible to speak of art, when the choice of subjects conforms for the most part merely to the tastes of the traveling studio employee.

There is even less genuine artistry in scenes based on literary themes, in comedies, or in sentimental and sensational dramas that are intended to arouse a certain mood within the audience. Thus far, the invention has been entirely in the service of making money, and its operation has been entrusted to people who lack any sense of taste or literary consciousness.

The composition of a scene is dependent to a large extent on the mode of production. Photography captures reality most vividly and effectively by either filming a fast, exciting scene in one place, or by filming a fast movement in a direction perpendicular to the spectator. Consequently, dramatic and sentimental pieces adopt one of two compositional modes: they either try to amass in one space an abundance of intense and marked pantomime movement that requires no verbal explanation

---

[7] A famous zoo in Hamburg, established by Carl Hagenbeck in 1907. Throughout the late nineteenth century, Hagenbeck was renowned for displaying wild animals collected from around the world as well as for his "ethnographic exhibitions."

[8] The Boulevard Saint-Michel, a central street in the Latin Quarter of Paris, was famous as a hotbed of student life. Likewise, the Parisian dance hall Bal Bullier was originally frequented mostly by students. As Jay Leyda wrote in a letter to Lubomír Linhart included in Linhart's monograph on Tille (*První estetik filmu Václav Tille*, Praha: Filmový ústav, 1968, 191), Tille is probably writing about the film *Les étudiants de Paris* (*The Paris Students*, Harry Ray, France, 1906).

(thus far, the lack of spoken language has been overcome only by the gramophone, and with only minor success), or they assemble a plot founded on an violent escape and chase that is directed either toward the spectator, or away from him in an open setting (which must be as plastic as possible or else crossed with perpendicular lines, roads, a path of a river situated in the direction toward the spectator). As a result, these sequences become rather monotonous. They permit only a limited range of really exciting scenes (e.g., a chase along cliffs, jumping into water, running down the street, riding horseback along railroad tracks, a moving train, boats in the current, etc.). Furthermore, the choice of subjects is narrowed due to the fact that as objects recede into the distance, they rapidly decrease in size and relatively quickly begin to lose their plasticity. Herein lies the as yet unresolved problem of the gap between theater and reality. Theater relies only on a flat image, a backdrop that creates a sense of perspective projection—and the spectator has grown accustomed to this unreality. In reality, for a spectator to follow dramatic action as it moves away from him, he must maintain a uniform distance between himself and the action or it will rapidly disappear from his range of vision. The cinematograph is, of course, able to make use of scenes arranged in a theatrical fashion, yet in such cases it is too easy to see through the illusion. Alternately, the cinematograph can break up the action and follow it in rapid intervals from various perspectives; however, this technique has yet to overcome the difficulty of maintaining the interconnected coherence between the individual moments of a highly active scene.

Compared with theater, the cinematograph has the advantage that it is able to compose a scene regardless of the sequence in which its individual elements are created. Scenes between which there were breaks for preparation that lasted many hours can be linked together on the screen with only brief instants between them, without regard to changes in the set, terrain, clothing, etc. A romantic story that takes place on an actual London street, continues in a restaurant, then on a boat traveling to South Africa for several weeks, and finishes on a Boer battlefield, is composed of pictures taken at all of the locations where those people actually performed. In contrast with theater, the cinematograph's spectator is constantly aware that the composed action is unfolding in a copy of reality and not in constructed scenery. Therefore, the cinematograph achieves a more intimate connection between art and the real world, thereby increasing the intensity of the scene for the spectator.

A typical example of how pictures are assembled is the nicely conceived scene in which a young girl is rescued from a rock during high tide by a dog and a horse. The young girl is playing with her dog and pony in the yard of a villa. She gets permission to run to the sea with her dog. She runs through tall dunes to the edge of the water. It is low tide. She takes off her stockings and wades out into the water to a low-standing rock. She plays with the dog on the rock. The tide starts to come in, floods the area around the rock and continues to rise. The girl sends the dog out into the waves to run home and get help. The dog swims and the camera follows him to the shore. We see him run through the flooded dunes and up to the villa. He runs into the stable and calls out to the pony. Both of them race back to the sea and swim out to the rock, which is now only barely protruding from the waves. In the meantime, however, there is a different, older girl on the rock and her image is reduced accordingly in that the camera is placed farther away. This girl makes a rather daring leap onto the horse, a leap that would have been dangerous for a young child. The girl then continues to play her role very believably. Completely soaked and worn-out, she is barely able to hold onto the horse, which eventually delivers her to the shallows. The horse then arrives back at the villa, where the parents are frantically searching for their child, once again with that young girl riding on his back. It is merely an oversight that the director has allowed her to arrive in a dry dress and with stockings on her legs.[9]

The actors in such a scene must, of course, adjust their make-up and bodily expression completely differently than when performing on the theater stage. In the theater, verisimilitude can be disrupted by a faithful copy of life that is not created expressly for the stage and according to its demands. In the cinematograph, the demarcation of a picture does not function as a frame does for a work of art. On the contrary, the picture is merely a slice of reality, unlimited by a frame, and it must permit the spectator to forget that he is observing life through a rectangular opening. Whenever a director's arrangement leans toward the theatrical, it comes across as comical or, at the very least, awkward, even in the most dramatic of scenes. Wigs, glued-on whiskers, theatrical gestures, and grimaces are downright repulsive. The animated shadows on the screen do not permit theatrical conventions, and the eye of the spectator demands a much more faithfully detailed reality than that seen on the stage, which calls for a conventional arrangement in terms of framing, perspective and lighting. The cinematograph is still at its most successful with comical, grotesque scenes and with dramatic situations from everyday life. Comic actors tend to be outstanding acrobats who can successfully perform awkward rides on horses or on bicycles, execute somersaults into water, participate in brawls, and enact wild chases along cliffs with masterful virtuosity and miraculous agility. The exaggerated grotesqueness of these situations attracts such a high level of attention that the rather shabby imitations of movements (intended to express emotional states) and the often-artificial set escape the eye. Likewise, dramatic scenes of intense action, assaults, murders, bomb attacks, and fires divert attention from the often-forced composition; nevertheless, the necessary transitional and preparatory scenes completely disrupt the illusion. Still, it is more than apparent that the cinematic author is a technically

---

[9]   According to Leyda, the film described here is *Dumb Sagacity* (Cecil Hepworth, 1907).

skilled director who cares primarily about creating a moving scene that forcibly captivates the viewer, and not about the artistic and balanced treatment of the material. This pursuit of abrupt and violent effects, this attempt to continually maintain tension with a series of moving scenes and to distract attention from the deficiencies of the reproduction is the fundamental flaw in the direction of such pantomimes. In intellectual terms, whether comedy or tragedy, such scenes are completely pitiful, entirely dominated by farcical humor, sappy sentimentality, and schmaltzy or pulp sensationalism.

Some pantomimes operate purely by virtue of artificial, unnoticed breaks, which they can use to construct a suspenseful scene without endangering the live actors. A baby girl plays at the feet of her father, who is loading bullets into a revolver. He is called away by the postman and leaves the revolver on the table. The girl takes the revolver and proceeds to suck on it, primarily on the mouth of the barrel. With all her force she tries to press the taut trigger. Her mother enters the room and faints. The girl continues to play with the revolver. Her father returns and with deathly trepidation entices the girl with goodies and toys until he finally succeeds in carefully taking the gun from her hands. He then shoots all the live rounds into a target. Not being aware that the loaded revolver left on the table was switched out during an un-photographed break, so that the girl was playing with an unloaded gun, the spectator experiences deathly anxiety, not even taking note of the superficially slapdash performance of the actress in the role of the mother.[10] Yet, having no other intention than to achieve a sensational effect, such scenes at least attain their goal, without regard for literary and artistic criticism. Pantomimes that strive for artistic composition, that try to achieve a new form of theater, however, turn out worse. As a rule, their intellectual foundation is nothing more than sappy sentiment, journalistic sensationalism, or the virtuosity of a thrilling novel. Quite oddly, it is impossible to find even a trace of real feeling or thought in these seriously and dramatically composed cinematic plays, which, after all, by their very mode of production should necessarily be more realistic than theater itself. This visual medium is evidently still too new, too dependent upon those who are able to master its technology, to be fully accessible to modern dramatic authors. And consequently, in the composition of these dramatic pantomimes, we find merely those scraps of intellectual creation from past ages that circulate in cheap publications among the lower social classes, whether they be the superficial opinions about local events in the popular press, which inject daily gossip into the minds of the public, or pulp fictions about Indians, conspirators, criminals, and detectives, skillfully calculated to titillate the imagination.

---

[10] According to Leyda, the film described here is probably *Terrible angoisse* (Lucien Nonguet, France, 1906).

Take, for example, *Vendetta*:[11] a dance scene in a Spanish bar amongst sets from *Carmen*, with extras of a completely international nature and with theatrical costumes; a duel over a mistress, a murdered adversary and a chase. A small house somewhere in the countryside, an old father with wads of cotton on his eyebrows and around his mouth, a mistress with tights simulating brown skin on her legs, and a murderer fleeing from Italian *carabinieri*, whose uniforms have been simplified in anticipation of further deployments. The chase proceeds along cliffs, across a creek, along the sea and through vineyards. The *carabinieri*, with their enormous riding boots and sabers at their sides, are hot on the heels of the nimble fugitive, always staying just close enough that they do not disappear from the view of the photographic lens. Then the return to the cottage, a shootout, and finally the suicide of the murderer followed by the final scene in which the theatrical old man rolls his eyes, and with wooden, theatrical pantomime indicates to a young boy that he must avenge his father. Regardless of its awkward composition, who today is still interested in this theme, which prior to Solferino was so popular?[12]

Another example of socially ethical sentimentality: a doctor's little daughter is a bit ill; the doctor leaves his impatient wife and child; he goes to the company of a splendid *demimonde* and gets drunk on champagne. At home, the little girl is now suffocating to death with diptheria; the desperate mother sends for the father; a servant brings the drunken man home. In front of his choking little girl, the unfaithful man becomes sober; he refreshes himself with water and proceeds to perform a tracheotomy, thereby saving the child and becoming reinstated with his family.[13] The individuals do not come across as preposterously as those in the previous play; in particular, the little girl acts with extreme virtuosity. In such plays, children, dogs, criminals, and murderers act the most naturally. Yet even their gestures and facial expressions reek repugnantly of those belletristic supplements to family magazines, just like the whole piece stinks of the morality in the closing chapters of a bad novel.

Avid newspaper readers are easily satisfied, for instance, with a nihilist assassination that is filled with more dangerous ideas than sensational journalistic gossip. A meeting of nihilists and the drawing of lots; a young woman draws the lot and must carry out the assassination. A letter of warning is received in the office of a high-ranking Russian bureaucrat. He says farewell to his children and, disregarding the warning, drives off in an automobile. These scenes alternate rapidly in a most diverse and realistic set. The car drives (using the beloved effect that presents vertically oriented roadways with sudden turns); there is a bomb attack and the automobile

---

[11]   Tille refers to the French film *La Vendetta* (*The Vendetta*, Ferdinand Zecca, 1905).

[12]   A reference to the bloody Battle of Solferino between the Franco-Sardinian Alliance and the Austrian army in 1859.

[13]   According to Linhart, the film described here is *Vater! Dein Kind ruft* (Germany, 1909).

explodes. There is an artificial, unnoticed break between the attack on a real auto-mobile with a harmless bomb and the fake explosion of a wooden automobile in the same location, which can only be discerned from the obviously flimsy and wooden appearance of the pieces of the smashed automobile. Then there is a hunt for the young nihilist woman by Cossacks on horseback (with the effect of a prolonged chase with an artificially protracted perspective). Once again the nerves are affected as the nihilist woman is tethered to a horse and brutally dragged off through deep snow. And finally the shamefully sentimental ending. The murdered man's widow and her children visit the nihilist woman in a canvas set made to look like a prison. The widow forgives the young nihilist and provides her with her overcoat and hat so that the nihilist can escape. Then the widow herself informs the guards of what she has done.[14]

Working above all to strike at the compassion of the viewer, such tragic scenes are generally poorly conceived, yet occasionally they contain moments that play out rather naturally and truthfully. For example, I have seen *Death of a Blind Man*,[15] whose theatricality is rescued by the natural performance of a dog conducted with virtuosity by an invisible director. The dog plays affectionately with the sickly blind man on a bed; he runs to the doctor with a note; he traverses a straight path through the maze of streets full of people and vehicles; the doctor comes and writes a prescription, then he gives the blind man some money; the dog now runs off to the pharmacy; with gestures, he makes it understood that he is asking for medicine. He waits for the medicine to be prepared, then he returns to the blind man, who is already in the throes of death. The saddened dog toddles along persistently behind the funeral car; he lies down at the graveside and refuses to be driven away by a guard who shoos him away several times; he even refuses to be lured away by the treats offered to him by compassionate people. The impression left by the play is completely natural, successfully evoking compassion through the obedient animal's deep sorrow.

Relatively speaking, the best composed tend to be criminal and detective plays. The actors perform with extraordinary accuracy and naturalness; no doubt many are not too far removed from such scenes in their real lives. The only bothersome aspects are two tricks that recur too frequently: a throng of people in one place to create exaggerated vivacity in thrilling scenes, and a long chase sequence directed perpendicularly toward the spectator, as is necessary to intensify the visual effect. More intellectually satisfying nowadays are the fashionable detective stories whose ultimate goals are sensation and constant suspense, livened up with the use of diverse modern inventions rather than with old-fashioned sentimentality. Furthermore, the material

---

[14]   The film discussed here is probably *Le Nihiliste* (France, 1906).

[15]   Tille likely refers to the film *The Faithful Dog* (a.k.a. *True to the End*, France, 1907).

of these stories adapts well to the accelerated vivacity of the cinematic projector and to its demand for brief, concise and overt actions. This is produced by forced panto-mime on the one hand, and, on the other, by the very mode by which movement is reproduced, since the faster and more precise a movement is, the more natural and less jerky the movement reproduced in a continuous series of images will be.

I am reminded of two examples that are not lacking in deftness of composition in a literary sense. In one example, a detective pursues a group of counterfeiters. Forged money is brought into a police station and the commissar calls in a Sherlock Holmes type, who sets out on the hunt with the obligatory pipe in mouth and hands in pock-ets. He sits in the American bar from where the fake money came. He comes across an elegant gentleman in a tuxedo, who pays with fake gold. He follows the man's car to a ramshackle building in the woods. Then, with a group of policemen, he enters a secret tunnel. The counterfeiters' workshop is in full operating mode; a guard an-nounces the invasion of the police; the criminals lay a trap with ammunition car-tridges and flee. The detective anticipates an explosion and prematurely detonates it himself, then sets off after the criminals. The policemen and criminals who have been shot tumble down a considerably high rock face. The pursuit of the leader is drawn out simply to allow for interesting visual effects, until finally the crime leader and the detective find themselves facing each other with drawn revolvers atop a tall, sheer bluff. At a decisive moment, the detective tucks away his gun with a smile and, with gentlemanly gestures, points out to his elegant opponent that there is a chasm in front of him and a row of detectives on the steep pathway below him. Precisely as in Jókai's *The Black Mask*, the man in the tuxedo realizes his situation and shoots himself in the head.[16] Back with the policemen, the detective, then, exactly like Mr. Holmes, removes the pipe from his lips and tips his obligatory cap in front of the dead body. Readers of Jókai and Doyle are filled with blissful satisfaction.[17]

In a more American style, an automobile is robbed at gunpoint. A man on a mo-torcycle stops in the middle of a road and lays his machine down to block the path. He draws two Browning pistols and waits until a car filled with gentlemen and ladies arrives. With gunshots, he forces them to stop, throw their money and jewels from the car, and then drain all the gasoline from the tank. The facial expressions and arm gestures are performed with virtuosity. The man mounts his motorcycle and rides off. A second automobile arrives and the people set off for the police station and after the criminal. The police attach a portable telegraph machine to the wires

---

[16]   A reference to the main character of Mór Jókai's 1860 novel *Szegény gazdagok* (*The Poor Plutocrats*, 1899).

[17]   Leyda thought Tille might be referring to the third episode from the series *Nick Carter, le roi des dé-tectives*, titled *Les Faux monnayeurs* (Victorin-Hippolyte Jasset, France, 1908).

on a telegraph pole and alert a police station further up the road, in front of the fugitive. The robber is cornered in a tavern, but manages to slip away. He then forces the chauffeur of an automobile at gunpoint to drive him off at an insane speed. The cars tear along one right behind the other; they cross railroad tracks barely in front of a train; they dart through the town until they enter a forest, eventually ending in a marsh. The criminal takes off again on foot and the contest ultimately ends in a river where the robber is finally defeated.[18]

In such pieces, action is combined with landscape images. Other scenes that manage to link a simple story with the presentation of a striking landscape may perhaps express a reduced desire to create effects, yet, on the other hand, such scenes have a higher degree of taste and restraint, and therefore leave a more profound impression. One of the most successful realizations of such a scene is in *Accident in the Mountains*,[19] which was photographed amongst the actual scenery of the Austrian Alps. In the early morning, the leaders, porters and other members of a mountaineering club assemble at an inn in a valley. They ascend through the forest and through the firn until reaching a glacier. They crawl along icy ravines and climb up a snowy ridge until they reach a deep glacial crevice beneath the icy, snow-covered saddle with black peaks. One of the expedition leaders lowers himself into the crevice and finds two dead bodies at the bottom. He has their packs and picks pulled up; he wraps the heads with cloth, puts the frozen bodies into bags and ties them up; then he has himself and the bodies lifted up from the crevice. Then, with stretchers in tow, the whole expedition undertakes the difficult journey across flatlands and ravines to a tiny lake, where small boats carry the dead bodies to the opposite shore.

Throughout the long story, I was unable to discern from faces of the participants or from the transported bodies any indication of whether the scenes were theatrically arranged or not. The arrangement, however, was so simple and so potent that it worked very earnestly and artistically. In cases where the arrangement of figures and movements is not too awkward or theatrical, the effect on the imagination and emotions tends to be very powerful. This is all the more reason to lament the fact that reproductive technology and forced pantomime have not yet permitted a more perfect artistic rendering of serious topics.

Extensive studies and much experimentation will be required before human creativity can adapt to this new visual medium, and until artists finally gain effective command of it.

---

[18]   The film described here is *Brigandage Moderne* (*Modern Brigandage*, France, 1905).

[19]   Unidentified title (in Czech, Tille indicates the title *Neštěstí v horách*). This is possibly a reference to the film *Catastrophe in the Alps* (France, 1907).

With its shadowy facial expressions, movements among easily changed settings, easily prepared scenes, and the technical assets with which it is possible to create the impossible in a real picture, this visual medium proves much more rewarding in the creation of grotesque and comical scenes than in the creation of serious dramatic works. This comic genre, which has up to this point been more compatible with the mental capabilities of the directors and actors, besides producing an abundance of trash, has in fact also produced some innovative and effective compositions. To be sure, these works do not have the same value as great literature, but they are nevertheless technically very well made. With the exaggeration and amplification of apparently real situations, they create effects that overstep the bounds of possibility. They often utilize the technical assets of shadow play (as already partially known in the Orient) to comically and skillfully transpose reality into the realm of impossibility, dreams, and wild fantasies. Some extravagant effects are achieved merely by the performances of actors and the direction of the action. Directors select accomplished acrobats who perform dressed as common people on the street or in nature, and carry out common, everyday operations in an incredibly deft and exaggerated style. Everyday mishaps and stunts are executed with miraculous showmanship: they set up collisions of cars and horses with pedestrians, the destruction of entire houses by one strong man, a whole squad of policemen clambering through the façade of a five-story building, a bicycle jump from a high bridge into a river, brawls during which people are thrown in huge arcs out of second-story windows, a whole group of people falling through the fourth floor down to the ground floor, etc.

The photographic apparatus itself allows for further deviations from reality to comical and grotesque effect: a person suddenly disappearing from his clothes, the substitution of one person by another in a bed or in a hideout, the changing of the scenery around the actors, the quivering of streets and houses around a teetering drunkard, the realization of a gold-digger's dreams, impossible images in a telescope, etc. These are all the result of games with photographs of real life that are carried out with such technical skill that they evoke living fantasies and illusions of reality in the mind of the spectator. Yet this technical craft is still in diapers and will certainly yield much more sophisticated and effectively composed creations in the future.

Today, this medium operates primarily on the basis of its novelty and shows a tendency leading toward peculiar, autonomous compositions that aspire to be nothing more than a magic production. The magic it performs comprises optical illusions, which are, so far, very few in number. It is possible to photograph moving pictures together with other moving pictures that are smaller in proportion relative to the first ones. Thereby it is possible to have tiny girls dancing on a table or in a mirror in the presence of other life-sized living persons; to insert a living girl's head into jewelry, a belt buckle or the gemstone on a ring; to have living beings arbitrarily disappear and re-appear in the air or in the mist above a pond; to release brightly teeming throngs of figures from tiny walnuts; to chop off a living head; to summon forth ghosts in graveyards; to animate the frightening shadows of Richard III, etc.—and all in an amazingly life-like way. Just as in other genres, the imagination of the directors conjuring up these ghastly and miraculous apparitions is still very tame, naïve and sometimes quite tasteless. The Eastern shadow play commands its own primitive means with far more proficiency, virtuosity and refinement. In contrast with this, the cinematograph is still in the embryonic stage, but in the hands of real artists it can germinate from this embryo into a new and extraordinarily effective artistic genre. In the near future, the means of reproduction will be mechanized to such a high degree, and the people operating the apparatus will be technically trained to such a degree of proficiency, that writers and visual artists will be able to create real works of art with this new visual medium without a care for the technical obstacles that now plague them. These artists are now in the process of acquainting themselves with the peculiarities, difficulties, and advantages of this new medium. When the technical obstacles are overcome, shadow, the ancient visual medium of the Oriental dramatics arts, now in a new, more perfect form, unchained from the actual objects that create it and independent of artificially created models and figures, will become the material with which the European artist will be able to create works of art that awaken moods and evoke impressions within the spectator, works of art whose foundation is the depiction of real-life movements and facial expressions in real-life environments. The shadow is, of course, a very brittle and ephemeral material to use for artistic creation, yet its very versatility, volatility, swiftness, and malleability allow for the extraordinarily powerful flowering of human fantasy, and the intricate and complex preparation required by the material creates a space for the boldest of compositions.

Thus far, the production of such scenes has not progressed beyond the experimental stages and is limited to Western Europe and America, where the first attempts are being made to leave the cinematograph in the service of creative artistic spirits.

The French literary community is the most active. On the Rue Chauveau in Paris, Formigé has established a small theater where a team of actors, writers, and artists create artistic scenes for the cinematograph.[20] Anatole France, who visits the new shadow play with great fondness, is the enthusiastic advisor of a new institution whose literary curator is Henri Lavedan and whose director is Charles Le Bargy of

[20]   The French architect Jean-Camille Formigé (1845–1926) was a co-founder of the Film d'Art Co. (Société Film d'Art), which was established with the ambition of adapting prestigious stage plays to films starring famous actors, directed by eminent theatrical directors, and complemented by original musical scores. In doing so, it attempted to attract intellectuals and a bourgeois public into movie theaters. The company built a studio designed by Formigé on the rue Chauveau in Paris in 1908.

the Comédie Française. At first, this institution attempted to adapt Rouffe's old pantomime *La main rouge* under the title *L'Empreinte ou La main rouge*.[21] Then Lavedan wrote the script for *The Assassination of the Duke de Guise*,[22] for which Saint-Saëns himself composed a score, and Jules Lemaître prepared the screen adaptation of *The Return of Ulysses*, for which Georges Hüe created musical accompaniment.[23] Sarah Bernhardt, Madame Bartet, Paul Mounet, Jean Mounet-Sully, Delaunay, and other superb Parisian actors filled the lead roles. These initial experimental pictures are now traveling throughout Europe under the name "Film d'art." The arrangement of the scenes and the acting are still too theatrical, and the verbal accompaniment with a gramophone does not evoke an ideal illusion. Using a different approach, the acting company Odeon also made attempts at artistic creation for the cinematograph. They performed Alphonse Daudet's *L'Arlésienne*[24] not on a theatrical stage but in its own actual, natural environment: on a country farmstead near Arles; in the old local arena, on whose seats the love affair between Frédéric and the Arlésienne unfolds as the bull fights take place below them; in the quiet city street; in the fruit orchards; in the deep heart of the forest; and on the fields near the well, below the tree where the shadow of his fickle lover appears in the thoughts of the unhappy, love-struck young man. Compared with scenes performed in theatrical costumes amongst artificial sets, these actual, natural environs are far better suited to the virtuously performed mimetic scenes and grant the actors much freer and more natural possibilities of motion and facial expression.

Without a doubt, there is something seductive in this new visual medium. In those silent, nimbly and playfully flickering swarms of shadows there is something astonishing and alluring, something that so vividly evokes in the soul the impression of our own dreams, mysterious and unimaginable images that flash on and off inside our consciousness. These images light up involuntarily in our brains, and, conjured forth by imperceptible impulses, acquire grotesque forms, grow pale or become colored. The intellect and consciousness constantly strive to capture and hold onto this whole play of ideas from the inner parts of our mind, yet it sinks once again below the threshold of consciousness, either in a turbulent whirlwind or in the sluggishly plodding haze of thought. For primitive man, a colorful reflection in water, the moving shadows of bodies or clouds, the eerie shadows of objects in moonlight, a fata morgana or mountain specters were enough to awaken astonishment, to stimulate his imagination and compel him to contemplate supernatural and divine matters.

---

[21] *L'Empreinte ou La main rouge* (Henri Burguet, France, 1908).

[22] *L'Assassinat du duc de Guise* (André Calmettes, Charles Le Bargy, France, 1908).

[23] *Le Retour d'Ulysse* (André Calmettes, Charles Le Bargy, France, 1909).

[24] *L'Arlésienne* (Albert Capellani, France, 1908).

Still today, the unsophisticated minds of civilized culture continue to project their dreams in the murky, moving contours of nighttime shadows, from which they spin their heavenly and hellish visions. The modern photographic apparatus has mechanized the creation of these visions on a screen. It has mechanized this process by which a real object is transformed on the retina of the human eye into a picture that penetrates the consciousness. The apparatus has thereby provided creative artists with a medium with which living pictures of moving reality can be used to create the moving, living world of human fantasy on a screen. So far, this world is populated only with scraps of antiquated thoughts and by unskilled attempts to realize banal impressions of reality, created without imagination from news headlines, the common wares of novels, and the comedy of circus clowns. Yet one can sense that the germ of a new artistic genre lies within the fierce yet clumsy, blundering yet frenzied activity with which the modern shadow play continues to develop.

(1908)

František Langer
CINEMA ALL THE TIME

Writers' interest in the cinema [*kinema*] can be attributed, to a major degree, to the fact that this invention appears to be close to the theater, and thus happens—perhaps only seemingly—to touch upon the métier of the writer, who says to himself: "Maybe something can be done here," because the structure of cinema is based on plot and thus resembles a drama. The factors that shape a drama are arranged in the following sequence: (1) First of all is ethics, a view of the world, culture, or anything of that sort; this is the precondition for the creation of a drama. (2) Then there is a poet, or, to put it less uncompromisingly, the writer as creator. (3) Then come the director and the actors as the practical executors of the drama. (4) And, finally, the spectator, the listener, a passive yet extremely valuable factor on whose behalf, and, as a result of the factors indicated under number one, the poet and, subsequently, the director and actors were initially motivated. In cinema, the order is completely different. In the first place are the two groups of theater practitioners. In the second place—if there is any such place at all, it is only by chance—the literary writer. The third and, as a general rule, the second independent factor, is the spectator. And, if there is something higher, more spiritual in the cinema, it is rather a matter of chance, a consequence of the spectator's state of mind at a given moment, than the result of anything else.

The Director and Actors

First of all, we should be aware that the poetry of the cinema has a purely practical character. Now and then it is possible to see what might be termed a photographic–artistic kind of film in which shadows and lights create an effect of vivid contrasts. With the exception of simple landscape photographs, those are the only images that produce any optical impression in the spectator, just as with art photography in general, which today is beginning to replace the old art of painting. When we see actors in a film arranged as *tableaux vivants*, it immediately strikes us as tasteless and disgusting, just as any photographic image of that kind would. So, with the exception of the photography of light and shadow, there is nothing of visual interest for us. In addition, there are two more complex things that arouse our interest: the interplay of actors, which is the director's concern, and the play of gestures, which is the actor's realm. These are the two aspects of dramatic performance that arise solely from the practical activity of theater professionals.

Generally speaking, the director is the representative of theatrical practice in the same way the writer is the representative of theatrical idealism—hence the eternal disputes between them. In cinema, direction is the most practical activity imaginable. Its duty is to reach a point at which it becomes totally invisible, at which the hand of the director blends with the resultant reality, making any intentionality entirely unnoticeable. A film's direction must blend with reality—this is the *style of cinematic direction*.

The actor's activity is rather nuanced. The actor must contrast his natural behavior with the ever-present awareness that he is performing in front of an apparatus that takes a certain number of pictures every second, and that this apparatus will reproduce his mimetic activity. This means that the actor's natural state is *rhythmically modified*, that his performance is bound by a different rhythm than that dictated by his natural self. You can see right away which actor performs for the pictures professionally and which is a dilettante. It is not only in the number of gestures that they differ. (The professional uses just a few, very marked movements, a kind of sign language in which certain gestures always have the same meaning. The amateur uses a great number of gestures, arbitrarily.) At first glance, they differ rhythmically. The acting professional seems to feel the projection speed of the chain of pictures, as if he had learned how to put his gestures into a series of static states to be captured in a fraction of a second by the apparatus. The amateur—for example, any of the local actors who play in the films of Prague companies—thrashes around waving hands and legs; he is in too much of a rush and gets ahead of the tempo of the pictures, so that in the end the entire film is nothing but a smudged photograph.

Today, we can already make qualitative distinctions among the most frequent performers in film stories. Film needs new types of actors: extremely expressive faces and figures. There are two popular types among the top film artists. Those of the first type are popular because of their factual substance as actors, for the genuine art of their acting: Asta Nielsen, skinny and ugly but perfectly exhaustive in facial expressions and gestures, albeit executed with extreme simplicity; M. Prinz,[1] a minor actor of young roles, is of the same quality; Bumry,[2] a fat man but an incomparable

---

[1]   Langer probably refers to then-world-famous French comedian Charles Prince (1872–1933), who was known in Germany as "Moritz." He was considered Max Linder's strongest rival.

[2]   Bumry: Probably a period nickname for "Fatty" Arbuckle (1887–1933).

comic with mimics as plastic as conceivably possible. From American films I still remember a little blonde who was good on horseback and whose face suited every part, from Shakespeare's girlish and lovelorn Juliet to the energetic and resourceful young American woman.[3] Other favorites rise above the mainstream either through their willingness to put up with beatings, falls, and foolishness, or by the elegance with which they represent the world of the upper crust to the cinema-going public, in other words, by purely external characteristics unrelated to acting. I am otherwise unable to explain interest in such bad actors as Max Linder, Valdemar Psilander, and Henny Porten.[4]

The Writer's Role

The writer's role consists of really only one thing: to create the foundation for direction. This means the writer lends the cinema his spiritual property, which is still *untreated* in a literary sense, because it will never reach the point of verbal expression. The writer supplies the director with his configuration or fantasy—in short, with his idea. Even in those cases where the director is dealing with already completed works (such as, for example, *Les Misérables*, *Quo Vadis*, *The Tragedy of Man*, etc.)[5] he does not extract literary content from them but draws only on their imagined, invented substrata, i.e., their plots. The cinema does not even like content that arises from fantasy, i.e., the most literary content, if I may put it that way. And, since it is possible to find a configuration or a casual idea in any average citizen, it is not even necessary to turn to a writer. Thus there is no relationship at all between the cinema and the

---

[3]   This is probably a reference to Florence Turner (1885–1946), the main female star of Vitagraph Studios, sometimes called the "Vitagraph Girl." She played Juliet in *Romeo and Juliet* (J. Stuart Blackton, USA, 1908) and *Indian Romeo and Juliet* (Laurence Trimble, USA, 1912).

[4]   Paradoxically, film historians today consider these three actors to be much more important than some of those mentioned previously by Langer (e.g., Turner and Prince): Max Linder (1883–1925) was a French comedian, the most popular comic film actor in Europe before World War I, and an inspiration to Mack Sennett and Charlie Chaplin; Valdemar Psilander (1869–1917) was the biggest male star of the Danish Nordisk company, who played sporty lovers and elegant *bon vivants*; and, finally, Henny Porten (1890–1960) was the first female star of the German cinema, representing the prototype of the common German woman. Clearly, Langer was not a specialist in film actors: in the original, he misspells Porten as Porden, and Valdemar Psilander as Waldemar Psylander.

[5]   Although Langer mentions these famous literary works as mere examples, he could also be indirectly referring to the already-existing film adaptations of the novels by Victor Hugo, Henryk Sienkiewicz, and Imre Madách, i.e., to the film series *Les Misérables* (Albert Capellani, France, 1912), the short Film d'Art adaptation of *Quo Vadis?* entitled *Au temps des premiers chrétiens* (*In the Time of the First Christians*, André Calmettes, France, 1910), or to another adaptation of the same novel called *Quo Vadis?* (Enrico Guazzoni, Italy, 1912).

writer. The writer can bring a casual idea to fruition, but it is not his duty to appropriate or take command of this luminous stage. A somewhat greater amount of script content is supplied only by the director's selection from the material that he obtained from people who do not need to be designated by their profession. This fall, Kurt Pinthus will publish in Leipzig a book of such subjects for film.[6] It is quite irrelevant that only writers contributed to it. I doubt film can give a writer any inner satisfaction; at most, it can offer a sense of activity or occupation, the feeling of pleasure one might have with a toy, something like the common pleasure one experiences when a joke goes over well at the café table.

Some might object that the possibility exists for the cinema to have a style and to therefore potentially become an area of artistic activity in the future. Maybe. Probably. Then again, maybe not; maybe cinema will remain interesting only as long as its novelty is irritating, and then it will lose its attraction for the next generation. And style? Yes, but this would be a matter for some new studio hacks whose interests will be neither literary nor visual. For the time being, there is really no work here for a writer; it is entirely the director's affair. Cinema is the photography of direction. The writer can only contribute by writing the script. But this book will never make its own appearance on the stage.

The Spectator

In art, the spectator, the reader, the listener is a problematic subject. Any creative spirit is completely indifferent to him. However, in an invention like the cinema, the spectator has an important role, because cinema is *a priori* something democratic, popular, created expressly for a broad public, and is so not only from a financial standpoint but also in its core essence. What is the fundamental difference between theater—i.e., good theater—and cinema? (With a few changes, we could also be discussing variety shows, the circus, sports spectacles, and the like.) In regard to its relationship with the spectator, theater assumes a superordinate position. In order for somebody to be a good member of a theatrical audience, a certain and at times even considerable talent is necessary. Similarly, the listener at the opera or a concert must have either a natural or a cultivated musical talent. A good spectator (listener) is a passive artist, and sometimes even a considerably advanced one. But cinema, a movie [*snímek*], is on the same level as the filmgoer. Cinema is a photograph of reality; that is, it is a testimony of something seen with one's own eyes—figuratively by

---

[6] Kurt Pinthus, *Das Kinobuch* (Leipzig: Kurt Wolff Verlag, 1914). For more on Langer's cooperation with Pinthus, see the introduction to this anthology, p. 30.

the camera lens, but it could have also been witnessed by human eyes. Film is therefore an *event*, and the spectators are pedestrians in the street who have stopped to look, just as they would stop on the street to look at some interesting incident, be it a fallen horse, or ice-cutting and loading down by the Vltava river. Thus the relationship between the picture and the spectator is the simplest one imaginable. Of course, more can be seen in film, events that are much less common, like an automobile accident, a domestic quarrel, games of chance, a safe robbery, a murder, and all in the same context with everyday events—family lunches, lovers' engagements, traveling, comings and goings, work, etc. And thus the spectators simply watch, nothing more.

Do they also think? It is probable that a spectator will, in his mind, infer some events previous to the action shown on screen, or some small, transitional incidents that were not shown, although these are actually derived from the whole context. But, on the whole, a movie does not offer much food for thought; its images change quite fast, albeit reaching, at best, a speed equal to the mental agility of the average movie-goer. The images thus proceed simultaneously with and at the same tempo as comprehension, and require only visual perception and attention.

Does the spectator feel something? This answer belongs in the final chapter.

Spiritual Results

The greatness of any act can be measured only by the greatness of the feelings it provokes, because a fact, an act, is something objective and may become measurable and valuable only relative to a subject. I have said that cinema is a representation of facts, of events, and not spiritual, but material, or at very least real facts. We can find out what kind of feelings the cinema evokes in two ways: first, through self-inspection, by observing ourselves, and second, by logically considering the trains of thought in the minds of other spectators. Sometimes they are so kind as to communicate their sentiments quite loudly behind you. Actually, only once in my life did I have a powerful feeling in the cinema: somewhere in Rome, where I was wandering for several weeks among the stones of architecture and sculptures, I saw in one film a part of the Rhine, small quiet turns and leafy forests with grass and bushes. And I was seized by such a tremendous longing to laze on the banks of the Sázava river, a terrible homesickness for forests and quiet nature. At other times a quietly powerful and pleasant feeling comes over me when I see some place that I know and where I have enjoyed being, like catching a glimpse of a dear, well-known face.

In the simple spectator, the strongest and most predominant feeling is probably one of compassion when disaster strikes and when sadness overtakes the figures on the screen. This feeling can be quite naturally powerful, because what the spectator sees is a photograph, which does not lie, and thus the spectator is directly affected by the photographed reality.

Quite common after this are suspense, horror, etc.: feelings provoked by certain situations, feelings that are perhaps most attractive for the spectator since they excite him most agreeably. More scarce is malicious pleasure induced by the injuries suffered by funny people (cuckolded husbands and such). There is also a feeling of moral superiority, most frequently among women. And pride in the physical and moral abilities of one's brother and fellow man, which unfurls before the spectator on the white projection surface.

Then there is yet another thing—actually quite sufficient on its own—that makes the cinema very valuable. An example: in the middle of a normal film plot, a young girl sees the execution of simple household chores—sometimes the watering of flowers on the windowsill or the care of a canary, at other times the setting of the table, etc. For a simple girl, this means an elevation of her plain life into the higher world she sees in the film. It means that some value is accorded to the work she has been doing until now without any special awareness. Let us also keep in mind what the act of photography means to simple people: they are accustomed to being photographed only on very special occasions—when a man joins the army or gets married, when a girl is confirmed, or at the weddings of one's children. Such occasions have a sense of elevation, which is why people have such rigid Sunday faces and figures in the photographs. But now the simple man sees the photography (and with it the ceremonious translation) of simple things, of his daily work and other matters that are not nearly as important to him as those great life events. He therefore pays attention to them, now that he sees a piece of himself, he analyzes and objectifies himself, albeit only physically, but he does *recognize himself*, and this is a tremendous expansion of his life consciousness. This result is barely noticeable, and I myself would have also missed it had not a young girl who sits only in the cheap seats of the cinema [*biograf*[7]] said to me: "Now I like to wash, clean, and do the laundry much more since I have seen how pretty it looks in the cinema."

[1913]

---

[7]   The term *biograph* (from the Greek *bíos*, or life, and *gráphein*, to write) derives from the film projector of the same name developed in 1895 by the American Mutoscope and Biograph Company. The biograph was known for its still (non-flickering) images, and by the end of the nineteenth century was among the most commercially successful film projectors in the United States; see Charles Musser, *The Emergence of Cinema: The American Screen to 1907* (Berkeley: The University of California Press, 1990), 145–160. In Czech, the word *biograf* was used for movie theaters and at times also for cinema in general.

Stanislav Kostka Neumann
PICTURES—LITTLE PICTURES—
TINY, TINY PICTURES

In a recent article, someone vented their indignation over the excessive surge in pictorial weeklies[1] and other periodicals filled with reproductions of more or less timely photographic images. To a certain extent, this critic was correct, but not entirely.[2] This phenomenon is just like that of motion-picture theaters and similar contemporary attractions aimed at the broadest public. They must be considered an inevitable consequence of serious causes. Our point of view here must be grounded in a positive attitude toward modern life, and so we are not going to bemoan the fact that they exist, but we shall, first of all, ask why they exist, and then—and here we shall reach our main topic—examine whether they really meet given needs, and, if they do, whether they do it well or badly. This is the only correct way to reach an appropriate judgment, which should not be *a priori* futile, but purposefully critical and fruitful.

We cannot destroy something that has healthy roots with cheap anathema unless we are also able, or want, to remove the roots from their soil. If the people of today thirst for contemporary images of near and distant worlds, they are going to get them despite the moralists' ire. And they really do thirst for them, because, for all of us, regardless of party allegiance or intelligence, these images have become, to a certain extent, a basic need.

I am not one of those who feverishly gobbles up life. I do not fly into a frenzy out of desire for riches, impatience for success, or eagerness for pleasure. I am not in

---

[1] Although the Czech *obrazový*, which Neumann uses here, might be more appropriately translated as "illustrated," we have used "pictorial" here and throughout the article to maintain Neumann's emphasis on the word "picture," as introduced by the article's title.

[2] In this essay, Neumann argues against an article with the same name that was published anonymously in the journal *Přehled* 12 (1913–1914), 78. This article criticized illustrated magazines that suppress their textual aspect and provide information solely through photographs, thus supposedly overshadowing more serious literary journals in much the same way as film and theater; see Milada Chlíbcová's editorial note in S. K. Neumann, *Rozumět umění* (Praha: Československý spisovatel, 1976), 487.

a hurry for anything, and I can make do without much. Mainly, I like to sample things slowly and thoroughly. One proper experience lasts a long time with me. Sometimes I think that life is like a good wine, which should be piously sipped.

In reality, life is much more like a great feast with far too many dishes. For this, it is necessary to have a well-trained stomach, not to mention a well-stuffed wallet. If we do not have these, though, what is to prevent us from being sated by eating two or three dishes, and then observing, fed and satisfied, perhaps even a little ironically, how one nice dish follows another? At least the eyes can have their pleasure, although the stomach is already indifferent.

Sometimes I am sated like that, filled to the hilt with an idea, an experience, effort, or worry; nothing more can enter my innards, yet my sight, hearing, smell are nevertheless, due to an incurable habit, on the prowl. Even though I am extremely busy with my affairs, something would be missing if, for example, I did not receive my newspaper in the morning. Perhaps I will just skim over the headlines and some local news items, maybe I will not hold the magazine in my hands for more than five minutes, but it is only once I do that my little soul finds peace.

And, just as I need, from time to time, sometimes more and sometimes less, newspapers and even some topical pictures of the world, so I also need someone to talk about those things which are not mentioned in public. And I know that everybody today who is not backward, capricious, or otherwise mentally unhealthy needs such reporters.

We want to be informed, we want to be at least cursorily informed; even if we ourselves love life at a calmer tempo, we want to follow, at least from a distance, the rhythm of contemporary life, which we cannot or do not want to experience at its very epicenter. That is one of the consequences of the primeval human desire for knowledge, which has been awakened, generalized, and democratized by the ease and means of modern communication. Our entire life is already built upon this desire; today, everything happens with the presumption that everyone can learn about it in the shortest time possible. This tendency in our life can only be widened and deepened; it cannot be reduced, it cannot be stopped or deflected.

That is why uninformed people are corruptible; they are unfit for anything healthy, not for use as a foundation or even as material. Only swindlers rely on uninformed people, and clericalism—the quintessence of all swindling—consistently builds on uninformed people. We can boldly say that the foundation of modern life is information [*informovanost*][3] and that the organism of modern life functions best where

---

[3]   Here, and in the following paragraphs, Neumann uses the peculiar Czech term *informovanost*, which roughly translates into English as "informedness" or "the state of being informed." For better readability, we have translated most occurrences of this term simply as "information."

information is at its highest, and it functions poorly where there is less of it. And the natural development of our world requires ever more perfect information.

If the informational function of the responsible authorities is not yet as perfect and reliable as we would expect given the current level of communication means and inventions, it is not the general tendency of our social development that is at fault. The fault generally lies in the ill will of a minority, disharmony in the womb of society, the internal predicament of the economic system, which on the one hand commands that much should be kept secret and falsified, and, on the other hand, is in no hurry to elevate the information level for the broadest strata of society.

To be informed is an inevitable complement to modern man's education and enlightenment and, in fact, modern life is more likely to pardon some gaps in an ordinary citizen's education than his insufficient level of information.

However, there is another reason we wish to keenly follow the rhythm of contemporary life. There is something vertiginous, uplifting, invigorating, and captivating in this rhythm, even if it tends to be more feverish and precipitous than perhaps is healthy. It is not even necessary to adjust to all its fevers and madnesses in order to feel its beauty and dignity and to become internally one with it.

The immensity, the mightiness, the complexity of modern efforts, unequalled by anything that has yet existed in the West and even less so in the East, prove that the new deists and all those who today seek God are led astray by futile and fruitless speculation. They seek God and a new religion out of habit, out of momentum; they search for the forest among the trees, unable to find points of view that would allow them to embrace with one glance the sea of its beautiful treetops, majestically singing and rumbling, and to feel the power of the enthusiasm from which everything is born and which springs from eternal human longing. And this longing for a more intensive earthly life needs no treatises on the greediness of nature and matter nor professorial demarcations of the road to the superman, and least of all dogmas or theology; it only needs an open path in order to rise to that enthusiastic "yes" to life from which moral strength and heroism are born...

I shall return to this matter of "new deism" elsewhere, since it does require a special chapter. And therefore I will now only conclude briefly: captivated by the rhythm of modern life, by its intoxicating quality and its depth rather than by its speed, we feel at one with it, and it offers us the gifts of faith and power before which all the old-time pondering about the futility of everything and about the divine creator falls silent, before which everything that repelled us from the earth and life toward the supernatural or nirvana falls silent. And this is what we and each of our fellow citizens need: this unification with the earth, with life, with the cosmos, whereby all hypochondrias are countered; this sense of certainty that is superior to the ancient pantheism and modern monism, a hundred times more beautiful than all deisms; this feeling that is already overflowing from the lips of the new poets as well as from the throats of nightingales.

We would begrudge our fellow men the supreme joy of life if we were to oppose the dissemination of this feeling, this intuitive understanding of the dignity of life. And this is what would happen if we were to, in any way, oppose the increase of information.

I often remember the insight into this matter presented some time ago by František Langer in his article on the cinematograph. He had heard a girl express the view that she will take much more pleasure in doing her housework now that she has seen how pretty it looks in the cinema.[4] I believe this could be generalized as follows: the more varied the life that people see pass by them daily as if on a theater stage, the more manifold charm they will find in life and the more life and its rhythm will captivate them and turn them into participants, thus leaving them less time for thoughts that cripple them and lead them astray from the earth and the world. The results of this could be immense. Let us therefore be happy that people today are expressing such great hunger in this direction, and let us wish them thorough satiety.

The flourishing of cinematographs and magazines with reproductions of contemporary photographs proves that the process of informing through words and letters awaited its picture complement. That is something the nation of Komenský[5] should have no trouble understanding. However, if we compare the speed and versatility of informing through letters, especially in newspapers, with the present level of informing through pictures, we find that the latter must still be considered highly insufficient, primitive and slow. There is, therefore, even less justification for the voices protesting the "picture mania."

Contemporary inventiveness in the corresponding areas anticipates something quite different. The time is likely near when cinemas—where it seems to me that the informative and instructional side is already gaining the upper hand over the depraved qualities—shall turn into "live journals," and pictorial weeklies will become dailies...

Let us, however, stay with that which we presently have; namely, those pictures and those little pictures. Several entirely just reproaches can be expressed here. We have *Český svět* [Czech world], *Světozor* [Worldview], *Týden světem* [A week in the world]—that, I believe, is how the name of that third weekly goes[6]—not to mention

---

4   Neumann refers to Langer's 1913 article "Cinema All The Time," in this anthology.

5   Jan Amos Komenský (1592–1670), known also as Comenius, a seventeenth-century philosopher, theologian and pedagogue, is famous for his work *Orbis Pictus*, in which pictures were, for the first time, used for teaching purposes.

6   Neumann refers *to Týden světem. Obrazová revue pro život kulturní* [A week in the world: an illustrated review of cultural life], published by Alois Wiesner in 1913 and 1914.

two "illustrated magazines" of very low quality.[7] Three such weeklies does not seem a high number, and yet it is. Even if it does not actually happen, it could very likely occur that we would find the same or practically the same little picture in five weeklies simultaneously, and likewise also in *Zlatá Praha* [Golden Prague], another weekly, and in *Rudé květy* [Red flowers], published every fortnight. There are even more possibilities.

In these petty circumstances of ours, therefore, it would be healthy if at least the three competitive weeklies that are dedicated to pictorial information of a nobler kind would somehow become more specialized in their main sections, leaving only a lesser part to those topical little pictures that they seem unable to do without. In this way, they would at least double their informational importance. They could even more than triple it, if they would only exclude all those unimportant, stereotypically repetitious scenes of high society pastimes or of the activities of indifferent associations and similar little pictures, which are as similar to each other as one egg to the next, do not instruct, and please only the most backward taste. Whenever the trivial or bad predilections of the public are at issue, a serious periodical should always consider whether anybody would actually miss such a bad thing, rather than whether their periodical will be more pleasing if it turns up on their pages. If our periodicals really had the will, many bad things could disappear from them without anybody missing them. Public taste is dictated to us much more than we generally believe.

The second defect of the pictorial periodicals is their textual content, particularly when it is fiction. A stupid rhyme or story, or some blabbering that aspires to be a literary feuilleton, often spoils the pleasure of quite pretty and interesting little pictures; they do this simply by their mere presence, which people can sense even if no further attention is paid to them. On the other hand, the textual accompaniment to illustrations is often totally insufficient.

The social-democratic *Rudé květy* is undergoing a characteristic development from an illustrated educational and literary monthly to a pictorial-informational biweekly. As is the case with all social-democratic activities, less imitation of bourgeois manners and more originality would do them some good. I was reminded of this recently as I was perusing the latest issue of *Styl* [Style], which is devoted to social art, or better, to social architecture, particularly that of factories. What a hymn to labor those factory colossi sang to me, particularly Behrens's exquisitely beautiful monster of the Frankfurt gas works! And with what daring irony did the brutal women's jail in Würzburg and the military stockade in Berlin glare at me! And so the thought struck me of how nice it would be if *Rudé květy* would and could completely, resolutely, firmly, and without any compromises, dedicate itself to composing from pic-

---

[7]   Neumann probably refers to the periodicals *České ilustrované listy* [Czech illustrated magazine] and *Nové ilustrované listy* [The new illustrated magazine].

tures a well-thought-out hymn to labor. Of course, they frequently do have little pictures of the workers' life, from factories, etc., but it is all somehow haphazard and uninteresting, not edited for social expressiveness designed to move and captivate...

It happens to be my weak point that I like to dream about what people could do if they wanted and if, perhaps, there were fewer obstacles.[8]

Thus, with these reservations, I consider the informative pictorial magazines to be quite useful and good, regardless of the fact that nothing in the world, especially not moralist anger, will, for the time being, stem that flood of pictures, little pictures, tiny, tiny pictures, which will keep on growing and growing. Despite its all-too-human shortcomings, it will be a blessing, bringing the glory of life from all parts to all corners of the world, helping man to gain a sense of unity with everything that is and that flows.

This flood of images, which, as I am convinced and have already said, is only at its beginning and promises at the very least, large dailies with information based on images, is being criticized for turning people away from "serious" art and "serious" literature, just as cinematographs are criticized for turning them away from "serious" theater. If we stop to think about it, this is hardly a justified criticism. It is quite unthinkable that a serious lover of good art, good reading, good theater would allow himself be turned away from these things by pictorial weeklies or cinematic productions. And, on the other hand, it will be no disaster if some *Český svět* or cinema does at times turn an average citizen away from what is generally called serious art, theater, or literature. On the contrary, the average painting, writing, and acting that are within reach of such a person are much less useful and pleasurable to him than the varied information in the pictorial magazines and motion-picture theaters. It is, of course, quite possible that in certain circles the contemporary pictorial weeklies do displace other periodical literature; for example, "serious" literary weeklies such as *Máj* [May] and *Zvon* [Bell], but this only means that people are thereby getting their hands on periodicals that are useful and read with interest, unlike those periodicals that used to lie about the house unread, or, if they ever were read, produced mortal boredom. There must be some progress even in such circles.

(1913)

---

[8]   At the time this article was published, Neumann had already planned to launch a well-designed illustrated periodical. Since the summer of 1914, the brothers Josef and Karel Čapek and the publisher František Borový had also been involved in the project. In 1915, the journal acquired a more concrete form (the contents of the first issues, graphic design, etc.) and was given a name: *Nové Čechy* [New Bohemia]. Neumann was unable to realize the project because he was called up for military service; however, after World War I he implemented some of his ideas in the journals *Červen* [June, 1918–1920] and *Reflektor* [Spotlight, 1925–1926]; see S. K. Neumann, *Rozumět umění*, 487.

Karel Čapek – Josef Čapek
THE CINEMA[1]

The modern audience has been given a new stage—a luminous quadrangle projected onto a vertical wall. Movement is contained in this quadrangle: people walk and act, trees bend under the wind, animals crawl or gallop, and all of nature, living or not, is in motion, with all of its physical acts. Movements create dramas and farces. People jerk about tragically, escaping from someone or pursuing somebody else; they throw themselves into water, from rocks, into danger, they fight for their lives, overcome the most terrifying obstacles, scramble frantically, win, or die. Reality is the milieu. Bamboo groves, cities, castles, sea, and land—everything here is a physical reality with the most palpable predicates and suggestive details, except for color. How could anyone not believe in such a perfect, rich and mobile reality? And who will not be astonished and convinced by the optical and aural reality of the perfected sound cinema [*kinematofon*][2] of the future, where each movement will be accompanied by sound, each blow by a clap, and each action by acoustic evidence? Then the power of suggestion will be insurmountable and the illusion entirely complete: the play of shadows will seem truer than the acting of real, material actors.

This is because the other quadrangle, the old hieratic stage, is exhausting its final options with planks, canvas, and mock-ups. For almost four centuries, that which is called theatrical technique has been developed, applied, and perfected. The struggle for reality on the stage and illusion in the audience has been going on for four centuries. And now, in the course of some four years, the cinema [*biograf*] has overtaken those four centuries and seized the all of reality, seized illusion, seized comedy and tragedy, seized forms and movements and the dramatic character of forms and movements, and in the future it will also seize that of words and music.

---

[1]   The Czech title of this article is "Biograf." For information on the etymology and Czech usage of this term, see note 7 in František Langer's "Cinema All the Time," page 97 of this anthology.

[2]   An invention of this name never existed. The Čapeks probably derived the name from Edison's Kinetophone, or perhaps they composed it as a fusion of "cinematograph" and "gramophone."

There is no doubt that the theater has a new and quite ruthless competitor in the cinema [*kinema*]: will the stage engage in a competitive match with the film projector? Such an excessively unequal struggle will hardly take place: the theater and the cinema are much more likely to divide their rights to existence with an unspoken agreement. Shadows will never have an eternal human heart; shadows will always write on the screen only the external outline of man and the outer embossing of tragedy and fate; they will not feel, suffer, love, and have passions; the shadows of people will not be dynamic, they will be merely kinetic. On the other hand, the theater will *perhaps* limit its optical realism, its attempts to be a spectacle. The stage will become simplified, enlarged, and more severe, and everything excessively visible will give way to that which can only be felt. It is on such grounds that humanity shall appear with its great internal feelings and suffering.

In the meantime, the cinema [*biograf*] shall take the path of unlimited possibilities. Perfect combinations of films placed one over the other,[3] retouching, deft arrangements, quick exchanges of objects and scenes shall eliminate the border between the physically possible and the impossible. There is nothing impossible for the cinema. Here, objects that are not alive become free, move, and act; a little figure drawn by a child's hand becomes alive and starts running around the world; it is pursued by fate, and it may live and die tragically; lions surge out of their cage and run around the city; a bottle can become alive, it can turn into a man or a dog and then vanish again on the luminous square; people appear here and fall prey to the most tragic or grotesque destiny. For in the cinema [*kinema*] there are no natural laws of gravity, motion, impenetrability, or possibility.

The most remarkable thing, however, is that everything and anything that happens here, all that is absurd, impossible, and nonsensical, is seen as physical and undeniable reality, monitored by the eyes, and in future also by the ears. The most eccentric action takes place so thoroughly and gradually, with so many matter-of-fact and determining details, that no skeptic could possibly be so clairvoyant as not to be surprised and shocked, to not feel the most nonsensical of powers over this refined and nonsensical reality.

Furnished with all these technical possibilities, full of hope for complete and limitless freedom, the cinema awaits its genius. Then we shall see supremely cruel and tragic stories, dreamt up by the most perverse fantasy and realized with satanic precision and delight; we shall be tormented by entirely new horrors and new powerful impressions: all the cruelty of the most refined literature shall be surpassed by a leap of reality. Or we shall find ourselves looking at new miracles, at a new magic that surpasses all physical laws. No age, not even the most infantile or superstitious, ever

---

[3]   The Čapeks refers to double exposure, or superimposition.

dreamt such eccentric and extreme wonders as we shall see, and something approaching a modern fairy tale for adults and decadents shall come into being. We shall also see a new and unusual comedy able to avail itself of all that is impossible and utterly inventive. In the movie theaters [*kinematografs*] of the future, we shall live to see practically physical fables play out before us, fables that were once merely fantastic and nonsensical inventions. The inanimate world may speak to us in words that have never been heard before. Thus a totally new grotesqueness will be able to come into being: the most eccentric acoustic grotesqueness. Perhaps we shall see the day when plucked roses cry, stones sing, horses begin to preach, and people speak in the most beautiful cornet voices. What more is still possible here? The luminous projected square of the cinema [*bioskop*] has the capacity to become not only a new stage but also a new world, unrestricted by the material limitations and laws of this world.

In the first place, it has the capacity to become the basis for a certain new fantasy, that is, for a certain new art, if we shall live to see the cinema [*bioskop*] earn the right to call itself art.

(1910)

Karel Čapek
THE STYLE OF THE CINEMATOGRAPH

There are those who already consider the movies [*biograf*] one of contemporary man's essential needs; it is telling, they say, that he requires short, fast, and intense entertainment amidst his long-term occupations or his even more perpetual disinterest, which consumes him. Yet, even if this entertainment is so urgently necessary, it is still inevitably restricted in character—it is utterly fleeting. The same film repeated twice crushes us with boredom, and viewing multiple film sketches of the same kind is torturous. Hence the expansive character of the contemporary cinematograph. It must constantly release something new and unseen to the world. Cameramen fan out across the whole world; screenwriters think up new sensations and seek out new settings; film companies compete with each other with spectacular sets and numbers of extras, with their triumph over difficulties and their record achievements; production costs rise to absurdity and inventiveness becomes ever more intricate and sophisticated from one day to the next. Today's film enterprises aspire to continually surpass the limits of what has already been accomplished, to realize images that were impossible yesterday and to tirelessly expand the territory of their business. Twenty years ago, theater was similarly struck with the fever of spectacle and exhausted all possible means of theatrical machinery to the point of absolute weariness, and still, to this day, operetta revues in Paris and Berlin display an analogous pursuit of ever-newer and more splendid scenic astonishment. Of course, cinema, experimenting with reality rather than with theatrical illusion, has a disproportionately wider field and a richer supply of possibilities. Nevertheless, its rapid development is possible only within certain limits, beyond which it meets with unavoidable exhaustion. Even the range of optical tricks presently seen in the movies [*biograf*] has its limits, to which cinematic slapstick humor is already coming alarmingly close.

It is obvious that this headlong development contributes very little to the consolidation of the cinematograph, which notwithstanding continues to rise in popularity and familiarity among the general public. Naturally, then, reformers speak out, calling for style or art in the cinematograph; others emphasize the pedagogical role of luminous pictures, which is not an entirely foolish thought. Furthermore, the cinema itself has discovered its own proper and enduring domain—to chronicle the world with images from far-off lands, army parades, the visits of kings and presidents, celebrations and large public operations, the life of people in Africa or America; all that is of interest to contemporary man, who wants to see and experience everything. At the same time, the endeavor to make the movies literary is an unfortunate reform. Again and again there are attempts to bring an entire novel, such as *Les Misérables* or *Quo Vadis*, to the screen. An experiment was made to cinematically execute the complex psychological drama *Der Andere* (*The Other*) under the direction of Lindau and with the famous actor Bassermann.[1] Soon we will see completely cinematic literature, great novels and historical pieces, Shakespeare and Ibsen on film. It will be a very stupid spectacle: we will witness excellent actors as they vainly take great pains in the struggle to overcome the burden of silence that weighs on their acting, using all means of sophisticated and realistic pantomime; we will see how they exhaust themselves to express in artificially fragmented movements and gestures that which the spoken word can express accurately and simply. The director's patient ingenuity will be occupied with the superfluous labor of figuring out how to fiddle with and paraphrase literary content, how to meticulously elaborate the optical surface of the dramas, and how to overcome, as smoothly as possible, the difficulties presented by the useless surrogate actions of the performers. This sort of literary or theatrical reform of the cinematograph is a grave and unnecessary mistake. Cinema will never become literature, let alone dramatic art, for in the cinematograph, a running horse or the photographed image of a prominent personality is often just as good an actor as the best mime. The cinematograph bears the stamp of reality too distinctly for film acting to ever assert itself purely as art.

Yet there is no doubt that it would be possible to gain from the movies [*biograf*] a certain level of artistic or stylistic interest. In order for cinema to achieve this goal, however, it must discover its own formal means and a reliable autonomy of expression; it must cease to be a surrogate for literature or a half-baked form of theater in order to become the cinematograph, purely and genuinely. Its progress towards style is only possible on its own foundations. There is a new, wide field and real creative invention here that should not be applied to width, but rather to depth. Since cinema produces *images*, this invention should be fundamentally visual, not literary. And here we see that the cinematograph has its very own prominent assets, which we find

---

[1]   In fact, the film *The Other* (Germany, 1913) was directed by Max Mack. Paul Lindau merely wrote the script, which was, in turn, based on his own theater play. Among other period film adaptations, the Italian epic adaptation of Henryk Sienkiewicz's 1896 novel *Quo Vadis?* (Enrico Guazzoni, 1912) gained considerable attention in Prague, where it premiered in March 1913, just two months before Čapek published his essay. The adaptation of Victor Hugo's novel *Les Misérables* (Albert Capellani, 1912) aroused public interest as well—its first screening in Prague took place in October 1912.

scattered among contemporary films and which could be clearly developed. Most importantly, its material is not the theater play, but rather reality; and cinematic operations have access to this reality not only in its limitless diversity of phenomena, but also in its *variable degrees*. A given action can be depicted from up close or from afar, in more or less detail, small or magnified, perhaps even microscopically projected, thus in various degrees of visibility, urgency, and intensity. The cinematograph is not restricted to the so-called *ideal distance* that is the rule for contemporary theater. On the contrary, it utilizes *very real distances* that express specific *objective and psychological relationships* between the spectator and the image, since those aforementioned "degrees" of reality also represent higher or lower degrees of interest, cooperation, and attentiveness from the spectators. An object or action opens up in front of the movie spectator like a fan: the spectator sees things from multiple distances, he approaches them, observes them from the closest proximity; he surveys the whole or becomes attached to some part that is greatly magnified and extremely actualized. (Examples from recent films: in a robbery scene, the large image of a hand suddenly appears, slowly opens a drawer, and removes a watch. Elsewhere, the apparatus projects an enormously magnified head with an expression of pain and resolve in a moment of utmost psychological importance. In another case, there is a scene of departure: a carriage arrives, the boarding is rendered in the greatest detail, then the camera follows the departure down a very long street. There are many such examples and what is at stake here is simply the systematization of these techniques. Everywhere we are surprised by the *minute details* of human behavior that are normally overlooked, and at the same time by the extraordinary *expressivity* of things and human movements, which we do not otherwise notice as we do here.) If it is possible to call this process analytical, it is a special form of analysis that does not disturb its objects. It is *sui generis* realism: not ordinary, but rather intensive realism, which greatly surpasses the common observation of reality. In life, we look at objects summarily and hastily; as a rule, our perceptions occur carelessly and superficially, without interest in penetrating reality more deeply or more comprehensively. We do not circle an object, but merely walk past it, content with random and fleeting glances of the things happening or existing around us. And perhaps precisely here is where the task of the cinematograph emerges: to show us a new, more complex, more expressive, highly detailed and dispersed vision of reality; to provide objects of intensive perception and inexhaustible interest. The more the cinematograph thus surpasses the superficial realism of normal summary vision, the more spirited and stylized it will become. For rooted in every object there is something extraordinary that we become aware of as soon as we cast off the ordinary mode of seeing. This extraordinary something is at once the urgent richness of perceived reality as well as the intensity and freshness of our interest.

It is important that the material of the cinematograph is reality in its breadth and richness as well as in its various degrees of intensity. In both areas, the material is so immense that the special task of the cinematograph should be to organize it and demarcate it in a visual sense. It is precisely this immensely variable intensity of reality that can offer the creative mind an open space for experimentation and entirely new findings. This should not be merely an effective arrangement of scenes constructed by a practitioner, but rather the genuine activity of thought and methodical perceptivity, an activity that itself seeks to gain the most powerful sensation from things. The genuine film "composer," starting with actions that are elementary instead of theatrically complex, should compose with great pleasure using precisely those various degrees of reality that emerge through successive approximation, magnification, minute details, rotating, and countless other methods. He should do this in order to achieve that which is the movies' exceptional quality: an intensive and extraordinary realism that has artistic merit. The "composer's" work method would aim to give objects a character that is not cursory, but rather as expressive and intense as possible. Thus the dead realism of photography could be re-evaluated as something more elevated and spiritual, and not as a mere reproduction of visible reality. There is no doubt that the character of images attained in this way would be purely modern, internally aligned with modern acuity and taste, and with the interests of contemporary people. Therefore, the task of such a composer would not be to merely enact a story and give it continuity, cadence, and clarity, but rather to impact the spectator directly, shape his interest, and force extraordinarily powerful, penetrating, and full perception upon him. This would no longer be the typical role of a film practitioner, but rather that of a psychologist who also possesses the facility to intuitively penetrate below the surface.

(1913)

Karel Čapek
A. W. F. CO.

That big, strong man is Holbrook Blinn, the American film actor, or rather a long-shoreman, a man smoking a cigar, a bum who spends his time in bars or outside in the sunshine, a lazy athlete and a champion boxer, so lazy and stubborn that even a friend, a man of the cloth, cannot persuade him to take up a better life. Both then wander lazily along the docks and look at the beautiful ocean liners. At home, the champion boxer does the dishes for his mother, and we, the spectators, smile that he has such a good heart.

Bets on the coming boxing match are made in the bar and we see with pleasure many American faces; everyone throngs to the spectacle. We are not, however, in the first row of spectators; it is only through the legs of the front-rowers that we see the legs of the boxers dance on the mat; or we run up to the gallery and from above see only the shoulders of the contenders while the musicians in the cinema play a languid waltz as an accompaniment.

From the bet he wins he sets up a saloon. We see his longshoremen buddies. His plan, however, is to establish a great freight forwarding company to compete with and destroy the company for which he formerly worked. In the meantime, he simply looks at the enormous ships and New York dock warehouses with the eye of a conqueror.

American World Film.[1]

---

[1]   The American company World Film Corporation (hereafter A. W. F. Co.) was established in 1914 primarily as a distributor of independent productions, but it also made its own films. It was headed by general manager Lewis J. Selznick and production managers William Aloysius Brady and Lee Shubert, and focused on film adaptations of theater plays. The company was dissolved shortly after World War I. The company was quite important for the Czech market, because by 1916 it alone had managed to renew the import of American films to the Czech lands, which had been blocked by Austrian economic restrictions and by other obstacles related to the ongoing war. A. W. F. Co.'s products, which made their way to Prague via Switzerland and Vienna, gained acclaim in the press for their sensational stories and truly filmic style of acting. At the same time, their popularity might have also been the result of nationalistically motivated dissatisfaction with German and Austrian films,

That lovely girl is Alice Brady, film actress, daughter of the old freight forwarder and a beautiful blossom of wealth. She is not really beautiful; every third girl is prettier than she, but how should I say it? None is more enchanting, never before have we seen such marvelous manners.

The champion boxer, plebeian of all plebeians, is in love with her. Strength courts beauty. The American king fights for his happiness.

And the film unrolls further and further.[2]

But you who sit here as if you were in the theater or at a concert, why does it excite you, why do you hold your breath when the victorious champion horribly and calmly suffers with his vain love? It is, after all, only a film, a pantomime of shadows and surrogate drama;[3] little more than shadows on the wall made by a child's hands, a deceptive art, dumbness, falsehood and sensation; not a painting, or theater, or a concert, just film.

* * *

The A. W. F. Co. recognizes justice and order the same way the spectator does; its film cannot do without character just as a Greek drama cannot be without Fate; for this company, public court proceedings are a manifestation of the world order.

Due to its innate optimism, the A. W. F. Co. loves a happy end. Only occasionally will it film some European novel with a sad ending, perhaps to reveal the twisted character of the Old World. Its own, domestic branch is, however, full of confidence: everything shall end well, as the American philosophy urges.

The A. W. F. Co. casts no shadows on life. Its vision of life is firm and chivalrous. It relishes able and honest men who know very well how to wear their professions as well as their clothes, be they coattails or workers' dungarees; it enjoys their physical capability as well as their moral character. A woman, however, is a weak and lovely creature.

The A. W. F. Co. views a woman with a mixture of respect and a secret awareness of male superiority. Above all, it views her as something lovely, infinitely lovely in

---

which comprised the majority of the films seen in the Czech lands at that time. Other A. W. F. Co. films exhibited in Prague in 1916 and 1917 but not mentioned by Čapek include *Hearts in Exile* (James Young, USA, 1915), *The Almighty Dollar* (Robert Thornby, USA, 1916), *Trilby* (Maurice Tourneur, USA, 1915) or *The Face in the Moonlight* (Albert Capellani, USA, 1915).

[2]   The film Čapek describes here is the social drama *The Boss* (Emile Chautard, USA, 1915), featuring Holbrook Blinn in his first major role (as Michael R. Regan) and Alice Brady (as his wife, Emily Griswold). The film was produced by William A. Brady Picture Plays, Inc. and distributed by World Film Corporation.

[3]   The film was based on the play *The Boss* (1911) by Edward Sheldon. Holbrook Blinn starred in the stage production, which he co-directed with William A. Brady, the producer of the film.

thousands of little movements of life. In all situations, it finds the time to stealthily and tremblingly glance at her eyes, the slipper in the fold of her dress, and her covert look at the mirror, how she powders her nose and dresses up, how she prattles in society and plays cards. The A. W. F. Co. loves elegance and endows its women with feathers as if they were Indian chiefs, and not with feathers alone: also with the magic of delight and spontaneity.

I hereby declare that Alice Brady has no equal.

The A. W. F. Co. loves New York, automobiles, nature, and children, society, wealth, and family; love and marriage are the greatest possessions; the most beautiful legend is about love and strength; life has meaning only in love and happiness.

* * *

The A. W. F. Co. refuses to imitate stage drama and its whole bag of tricks.

It rejects false moustaches, wigs, theatrical scenery, machinery, and illusions.

It also rejects the division of the world into leading and supporting roles, into actors and extras, into good actors playing lovers and bad actors playing servants. It recognizes only good lovers and good servants; a chance pedestrian who barely flashes through the background of the film must be a great pedestrian, nonchalant and marvelous, overflowing with realistic invention.

The A. W. F. Co. believes completely in the reality of the external world: all that can be seen is real, and the better it is seen, the more realistic it will appear to us. And here the A. W. F. Co. has made a new discovery: the more realistic a thing appears to us, the more wondrous and magical it becomes.

This discovery shows the road for the A. W. F. Co. to follow: to invent phenomena, the fantasy of reality, and to magically unveil the visible world.

A natural movement is the most unexpected movement, spontaneity is the most mysterious of all movements. But all things have their semblance of spontaneity: there are moments when they appear to brim with mystery and cause a nearly fantastic impression with their bare and strange matter-of-fact quality. There are times when the things in our room, our own table or bed, or even our own hand surprise us with their appearance, when they stand up urgently before us, sliding out of the worn surface of habit. This surprising, childlike vision is the magical aspect of reality.

The A. W. F. Co. loves reality and never loses the hunger to convince us of this; it will just as soon cut out a scene as show it in its entirety, it will show it from different sides, it will take one or two faces and enlarge them to monstrous proportions, looking at them from an exciting and pressing closeness, taking frightening account of their fear or pain; and all of a sudden it will show what is happening outside at the same moment, behind the walls of the house; it will reveal the whole of New York.

It photographs a street: there is an automobile going down it, rushing, making a turn; there is a lovely woman in the car, hurriedly powdering her nose; a man is suppressing a yawn; another man is deep in thought; once more we see the entire long street, from which the automobile is disappearing (*A Butterfly on the Wheel*).[4]

A young man remembers his love; the memory becomes an image, both illusion and reality; his present torment and delightful memory are projected into one and the same mirage (*Camille*).[5]

Blanche Gordon defends herself in court: first the entire courtroom is shown, then the jury alone, and now, very close up, the tall defendant: the judge, enlarged more than lifesize, rings a bell; the district attorney hits the table with his fist; the counsel rises; the key witness is sworn in; Blanche's husband is here, her girlfriends over there. Blanche is speaking and the action she speaks of is projected onto the screen. Blanche wrings her hands in hurried movements of desperation; the district attorney waves his hand at her: this carries no weight with us (*The Rack*).[6]

The A. W. F. Co. works on an epic scale; it dwells with delight on details and monumentalizes them like Homer did with Achilles's shield. If it wants to express a man's love and anxiety, it can show him bending down with an unexpectedly loving smile to children he doesn't know. In truth, rarely have I read a more touching confession of love: to thus comprehend each action in all of its spontaneous appearances requires a tremendous knowledge of the world.

Reality is a mighty stream and every moment is inexhaustible. Theater simplifies it. Film dissects it. It scrutinizes it from different angles, it turns it upside down; but wherever it penetrates, it always finds complexity and inexhaustibility: the human face and its expressions will never cease to captivate the viewer.

The virtue of the theater is its economy. Film is the opposite of theater. Film's strength lies in its lack of economy, in its wastefulness and excesses. Only when film is the least like theater does it become a new and strange delight, a new and fantastic spectacle.

In reality there is neither unity nor economy. Every real action is a cluster of countless events, chances, and jumps; causal connection and theatrical connection are equally artificial constructs.

---

[4] The society drama *A Butterfly on the Wheel* (Maurice Tourneur, USA, 1915) features Holbrook Blinn in the main role (as Mr. Admaston); it was produced by Shubert Film Corporation and distributed by A. W. F. Co.

[5] *Camille* (Albert Capellani, USA, 1915), an adaptation of Alexandre Dumas's *La Dame aux camélias*, does not feature Blinn or Brady; it was produced by Shubert Film Corporation and distributed by A. W. F. Co.

[6] Alice Brady appears as Blanche Gordon in the drama *The Rack* (Emile Chautard, USA, 1916); the film was produced by William A. Brady Picture Plays, Inc. and distributed by A. W. F. Co.

The A. W. F. Co. renounces unified causality, unity of action, one-dimensional time, and a stationary point of view. Each action is understood as a cluster, taking place here and there, in many places, jumping, simultaneously or at various times. We can circle each individual thing, see it close up or from afar, and only through these changes is its surprising reality felt. The wealth of phenomena that the world offers film is inexhaustible and cannot be compressed into a rational unity. Its place is taken by speed and fullness, for reality itself happens rapidly and without gaps.

The A. W. F. Co. does not show the world as we see it, but more realistically than we are capable of seeing it; hence the uncanny appearance of the world in film. In film, just as in literature, the image of reality arises from invention, not from imitation. Yet all invention is actually an act of creation, and the invention of beauty is art.

Beautiful is the shimmering light that envelops things, beautiful the transparent grayness in which phenomena appear with a bare, monumental, matter-of-fact quality. No other films achieve a more beautiful light. Utilizing light, the framing of the image, the sizes of objects, a combination of black and white, the choice of costumes and environment, and with hundreds of unexpected inventions, the A. W. F. Co. achieves new and unusual motifs of pictorial beauty. How often have I wished that the fleeting, changing shadow would linger for a little while, but the most beautiful images in film, just as in life, have escaped me before I could capture them forever.

I would like that lovely, accidental movement to wait; I would fill my sight with all those details that escape me with every passing second, and with each second that disappears before it has shown its wealth to my eyes. I would like to prolong the magnified proximity of this luminous face, since I can never get enough of proximity or of the human face.

(1917)

Josef Čapek
FILM

American films are the best of all. I will not provide here a lengthy enumeration of all their merits. These have been written about elsewhere. Nor will I discuss the ways in which many of their characteristic traits converge with some traits of modern painting and literature, which may well have even gained something from cinematic technique.

American films—the most valuable among them being undoubtedly the very few that we have seen from the American World Film Company—distinguish themselves with their perfect execution and also with a new and highly refined conception; their frequently tendentious and moralistic stories are presented with a powerful and, at the same time, spirited realism that is completely removed from any of the common schlock concocted for the European public. French productions, which love to turn older novels into films and provide for excellent acting, are also generally good. From novels with a rich, full, and touching story, by authors like Dumas and Sardou, the French can create good film plays. By contrast, the stories of German films are generally very thin, weak, and nonplastic, devoid of any literary or dramatic value. It is the Anglo-Saxon concept that builds most upon the contemporary world, its type of hero is generally a working man, daring and successful, but the dramatic conflict rests in the emotional, in love gained, lost, and regained, where the heart crushed by injustice achieves happiness by redressing and overcoming evil. However, the story is never overburdened or constricted by the moralistic tendency; its moralism seems, here, to be a natural part of the outlook on life, and even its aesthetic effect cannot be disregarded: the story should end with the victory of truth and goodness. Of course, such satisfying finales are not completely novel, but the American concept does not favor the artificialities of fate and chance; an especially virile and vital trait is visible everywhere; the ideal is strength, which takes aim at obstacles and errors on a path to correctness and goodness. Also, we must not forget fragile emotionality and nonsensual ardor, which are as important for the Anglo-Saxon race as hardness. In contrast to this, the Latin outlook is more passionate, more sensual; man is much more a toy of fate and chance, which rule over him without recourse and often quite harshly; evil is more powerful and ineradicable, and tragic guilt is a more absolute element of the drama.

Closest to French films are the Italian ones, which work with beautiful and spectacular scenery and are usually played well and full of suspense; Italians are born mimes. Danish and Norwegian films are rather boring and commonplace; they are made with little taste, played and constructed without tempo and acuity; on the whole, they are shoddy and too akin to factory products. Apart from a few exceptions that were the result of well-thought-out direction rather than a proper film concept, German films are fabricated without any emotion and taste; the story is usually nonsensical, bordering on stupidity; and frequently downright coarse or unbearably sentimental; the great majority are products that can satisfy only the basest demand. The worst of all are their farces, vulgar and spiritless, most often built upon an incredibly low and undignified concept of man and life, upon the downright shameful devaluation of all human emotions and qualities.

I make no secret of the fact that until now the majority of film production has been entirely poor, even stupefying, and has served no good purpose. This is, however, no reason not to believe that it can indeed be elevated artistically as well as morally.

Since I have written about photography,[1] I am right now most interested in how a good American film appears to the eyes. It has a much better effect than other films due primarily to its clarity and graphic presentation, and in most cases also by a good, well-sensed ratio of figures and details in proportion to story. The story is set in the picture format with utmost expressivity, consistently filling the screen with greatness, fullness, and as convincingly as possible. And the story is usually well balanced, composed into very picturesque and plastic images for the delight of the eye and the memory. The composition proceeds from the natural and tries to be as natural as possible; the scenery is grandiose, chosen with good taste and understanding.

Film can adeptly focus (limit) the spectator's interest by jumping to or gradually narrowing in on the story itself, on the main figure, on his or her face, or on a single, *truly* fundamental characteristic or trait. Figures can be large and can grow larger as needed for emphasis, they can even reach supernatural size, so that we can observe them even better and more powerfully than if we saw them close up; on the other hand, the story can be aided elsewhere by the use of greater distance, a removed perspective. The suggestive shifting and movement of the field of vision allows the spectator to participate in the story, and American film technique often uses

---

[1] This article was originally published in 1918 in the journal *Cesta* [The journey]. In the previous issue of the journal (no. 17, September 27, 1918), Josef Čapek published an essay on photography titled "Fotografie našich otců" [Photography of our fathers]. Two years later, he included both articles in a collection of essays titled *Nejskromnější umění* [The humblest art, Praha: Aventinum, 1920].

these possibilities truly *dramatically*. The spectator's suspense and participation escalate through this visual dramatization of the story, and the film becomes richer and more dynamic. Here we can say without reservation that the Americans know how to work very expressively and picturesquely in film.

So the first possibility film offers is to most effectively sharpen and focus the moment of dramatic suspense. Simultaneously, it is possible to support and extend suspense to maximum fullness through a multidirectional spatial widening, through the cooperation of several views; the story or a figure can thus be endowed with maximum plasticity according to need and time. It is possible to disassemble an instant and fix it in several dramatic moments and views; remote instants and places can be presented in simultaneous, directly connected pictures; it is possible to freely and plastically shape space and time in a thoroughly creative manner.

These, then, are thoroughly new creative elements that can be artistically and expressively exploited for quite special and specific effects unachievable by real theater. Besides, the cinema [*biograf*] simply cannot compete with the theater by imitating it, nor can it supplant it in any capacity. Therefore, it must strive to achieve its own particular form that honestly and sharply differs from the art of the theater. We also correctly sense that intertitles with excessive amounts of explanatory text are detrimental to film, since they are a far too primitive and unsuitable substitute for the spoken word of the theater. Also, when a film merely optically translates a complete theatrical play, recording just its exterior, it becomes mute and empty. The technique of the theater and the technique of film should not have anything in common and should not be identified with one another. Of course, in both instances the dramatic action rests on actors, and even for cinema [*biograf*] the actor should play as perfectly as possible. In film, however, the creative execution of the story has its very own and special laws, because in its very essence film is action in space.

All of film's open possibilities lend themselves directly to artistic creativity and also to a responsible presentation of the world; to a completely new and penetrating intervention in dramatic material, which has thus far not been treated in this manner. It is a penetrating and multifaceted look at the human drama performed by the actor and at the world, i.e., at material reality, since film can very easily do without a theatrical backdrop. Film's picturesque quality can emerge only from a sense for truthfulness and from a new poetic imagination, *because this world and reality of ours should be presented as an immediate dramatic reality*. This, of course, does not lie in the carefully selected picturesque and interesting details, but in the rare sense of realism that does not see the world merely as a heap of objects but as a space and environment for dramatic action.

American films are truly the best made, with the greatest scientific knowledge, with the most lively and enterprising sensibility; they achieve truly new, surprising, and seemingly fresh effects. A new and vigorous power has begun to take action here, and it has undertaken its new task very conscientiously. These films are thereby outstanding due to their generally more highly refined execution. Their photography has an incomparably more beautiful tone than that in German films, for example, an extraordinary gentleness and a rich smoothness of transition, and thereby also a more subtle expressivity as well as quieter luminescence and depth. It also excels because of the clearer and more monumental way it positions things in space, and its grandiose modulation from dark to light. For these reasons alone, reality does not to appear as superficial, petty, and tortuously prosaic as it does in the poorer European films.

An expert has explained to me that this balance of tones and the sophistication of work in general can be explained by the perfection of the material; for example, the sensitive layer on the plates, films and even papers of Western production is allegedly thinner than on the German ones, such that they work in an incomparably gentler, softer, and simultaneously more expressive manner; they also apparently work with more light. However, I believe that the attempt to improve material must be especially motivated by taste, otherwise there would be no need to improve the tools when comfort, speed, or ease of work are not at stake, since the goal is to produce the most beautiful picture.

In the Czech lands, practically nothing has been done in this field. If the very few experiments that have already been carried out signify the beginning of future work, then the question of how our domestic production can compete with foreign production arises. It cannot be with marvelous or adventurous scenery, as, for example, Italian films indulge in; it cannot be with pictures of the struggle for life amidst large human and industrial agglomerations, as in American films; neither could it or should it be with high-society stories set in fine and rich surroundings, which abound in the majority of the remaining film production. Actually, in many ways the question is already answered by the type and character of the natural live scenery here. I do not believe that we should limit ourselves only to history and to the endless exploitation of Old Prague. It is, of course, entirely conceivable that several of our historical films could gain more general interest if they were perfectly executed. Besides them, though, there is another open path to original and valuable work, and that is to turn the concept of scenery and story away from splendid exteriority to a higher level of inner intimacy, to a serious deepening of concern, to a warm and compassionate feeling for less dazzling things, for the value of life, for the life of being born here and the hard struggle toward freedom; these are conceivable pictures for us and they are truthful pictures in the purest human and social sense.

[1918]

Construction and Poetry:
Film as a Poetist Machine

PART TWO

Karel Teige
PHOTO CINEMA FILM

MODERN ART. New art. These adjectives have been overused and abused; *epitheton ornans* has become *epitheton constans*, and, in the end, people do not have faith in either of them anymore: there is simply no faith in novelty (the public instinct is always conservative, of course), and *modern* has been unjustly equated with *modish*. It has even fallen out of fashion to be modern: many contemporary neoclassicists strive with all their might to be thoroughly old-fashioned. It has been acknowledged that nothing ages quite as rapidly as true modernity. Yet the result of this acknowledgement has not been to continually revive novelty and modernity, to recharge them again and again with relevance and active animation. Instead, refuge is taken in eternal values. Egyptian pyramids, East Asian sculptures, Greek temples, Gothic cathedrals, and Baroque palaces have survived centuries and millennia. The Ferris wheel and the Eiffel Tower are modern, and behold, today the Ferris wheel has already ceased to exist and the Eiffel Tower's days are also numbered. For his poem of the world "Zone," Apollinaire would now have to choose a different shepherdess to watch over the lowing herd of the Paris bridges. And Jean Cocteau, that fine, modern, and ironic spirit, who is also an avowed "opponent of modernity," would be forced to find a different setting for his charming play *Les Mariés de la Tour Eiffel* [The Eiffel Tower wedding party], someplace other than the magical and poetic environs of the Tower's first platform. It is not our task to demonstrate that the difference between the eternal quality of the Egyptian pyramids or the Doric temples and the ephemeral quality of the Eiffel Tower and the Ferris wheel is rooted merely in the difference in materials, the difference between stone and iron, or in greater or lesser artistic value. On the other hand, we do not wish to defend here the opinion that there are only ephemeral truths, which would be another extreme. We do not aim to demonstrate that all of those so-called eternal works were extremely modern in their day, that contemporaneity is one of the prerequisites for that much-desired eternity; that the contemporary, topical, fashionable, and modern Seurat, even if the colors on his canvases were to turn black, is more assured of this eternity than the outdated and lofty Bouguereau. There is no point, and this is not the place, to develop and discuss these matters. We merely wish to make the simple assertion:

MODERNITY IS NOT AN EMPTY WORD, BUT A PRIVILEGE AND AN ACHIEVEMENT.

It is not necessary to extensively demonstrate this assertion. It is verified by any and every fact in the world. Everything is an argument *in its favor*. The Red Star Line is much more perfectly developed than the Argonauts' ship. The Goliath airplane is more perfectly developed than the mythological wings of Icarus or the first Montgolfière hot air balloons. Surely you would much rather ride in Pullman cars on express trains than in an idyllic stagecoach. Radiotelegraphy is better than signaling with torches or using homing pigeons. Modern medicine is something of which the quacks of yore could not even dream. Yes, this modernity—an achievement and a privilege—quite simply represents advancement and progress.

Yet, you might argue, art does not know progress. Art has been put on display and emphatically reproduced multiple times such that its evolution cannot be compared to progress in the real world. Evolution is a process of continuous change; progress is advancement and accumulation of achievements. If we do not differentiate between the concepts of "evolution" and "progress," but rather consider the two identical, we could even assert that art does not evolve, and would thus apparently be unable to presume that Picasso or Derain are at a higher stage than Giotto, Negro sculpture, or Minoan painting.

Evolution in the sense of progress exists solely in matters of practical human needs and in the sciences, not in philosophy or in art, unless we, perhaps, consider that there can be long periods of decline in these areas. Art today is not a matter of practical human needs. For example, the form of the violin evolved for quite a long time until a form was found that was absolutely perfect, functional, and satisfactory, and henceforth unchanging and *standard*. Here its evolution came to halt; it had arrived at perfection, at a standard, at a permanent position for typified production. This is the case and will continue to be the case in all other products of human labor. This is precisely the case in technology, mechanical and civil engineering, and it could even be the same in architecture, if it were truly a form of structural engineering, instead of that which it so ambitiously desires to be—applied art and decorativism. The case is different in art, however, where there can apparently be no talk of progress, advancement, or the accumulation of achievements occurring parallel to the passing of the years. Indeed, in abstract or absolute terms, neither Paul Cézanne nor Henri Rousseau is a "more advanced" or "more perfect" artist than Ghirlandaio or Fra Angelico. Yet it is possible to speak of progress and perfection in a relative sense, in terms of a specific prevailing tendency within a specific span of time. The impressionism of Monet and Renoir is more advanced than the impressionism of Manet, and possibly even Turner. Derain's post-impressionist synthetism is more perfect than Cézanne's initial attempts. And, what's more, it is possible to speak of progress in all periods in which art itself was also a matter of practical human needs, when it was an integral part of the world and of life, one of life's important facts, subject to all other achievements of the period and to the vast, almost unlimited possibilities of progress. Unfortunately, contemporary art is too far removed from the contemporary world and contemporary life, which are modern, intense, improving and ever improvable, advanced, and progressive. The academic art of today strives to be nonmodern, timeless, classical, unchanging, mystical, and untouchable in its absoluteness.

We have introduced these remarks *firstly* in an attempt to show that modernism is a privilege, an achievement, progress, and perfection. It is not ephemeral, it is defined by evolution toward more or less absolute perfection, *standardization*, permanent existence, and eternity; and, *secondly*, because we wish to discuss an art form that is utterly new and modern, an art form that presumes evolution as a process of permanent progress and refinement, as the constant advancement towards superior perfection, and not progress as merely the occasional transformation in character over time. We wish to discuss an art form that was born not long ago from scientific progress and the desires of the human heart, an art form that is not a matter of academic aesthetics but an event that is important to the world and to life, with a profound public significance. We wish to discuss

CINEMA.

The invention of the CINEMATOGRAPH opened up a rich new territory for art; it was almost literally the discovery of a new world, the discovery of America. And just as America was known before Vespucci and Columbus, just as it is impossible to attribute the invention of gunpowder solely to Roger Bacon or the printing press to Gutenberg, just as both Franklin and Prokop Diviš discovered the lightning-rod conductor, and both Nicola Tesla and Marconi the radiotelegraph, likewise the cinematograph is not the exclusive invention of Edison or the Lumière brothers. Precisely speaking, it is never possible to attribute great inventions to one individual person. A great discovery is nothing more than the culmination of protracted collective effort, a product that always has numerous predecessors and distant origins. The collaborative work on great events and on great feats is always done by a collective, and the inventor is nothing more than one worker in this community. Einstein's theory would have been unthinkable without its predecessors.

Although a recently born invention of the new age, cinema is, nevertheless, evidence of a specific tradition with ancestors that date back centuries. On the one hand, it can be traced back to *Chinese shadow plays*, which are founded on the idea of projecting a moving image onto a flat surface. This practice was brought to Europe in the eighteenth century, when shadow theaters were established in Versailles and in Paris at the Palais Royal. Henri Rivière and Caran d'Ache, the well known humorous caricaturists of the 1880s, projected *French shadows*, delicately drawn and finely articulated silhouettes cut from zinc plates, at the Théâtre d'application and later at the cabaret Chat Noir in Montmartre. On the other hand, cinema's direct predecessor is the *laterna magica*, the invention of Athanasius Kircher. Combined with the *fantascope*, which contains little rotating colored lenses, the *laterna magica* enabled Cagliostro to simulate his miracles and enabled Robertson to present mysterious phantasmagoria to astonished Parisians in a Capuchin monastery.[1] When Reynaud then combined the *laterna magica* with the *praxinoscope*, the first step was made toward the projecting film apparatus.[2] Comprehensive discoveries continue in a parallel fashion, opening up new possibilities in the realm of photography: Janssen's astronomic revolver, Faye's chronophotography, the invention of transparent plastic film, Edison's *Biographe* and *Bioscope*—until 1895, when the Lumière brothers' company projected their cinematographic works, and the *first cinema in the world* was opened in the Salle des Conférences on the Boulevard des Capucines.[3] Animated painting, which had previously been a laughable utopia or a mystery of sorcerers' magic, became a reality whose mere existence exceeded all expectations. Life itself appeared on the projection screen. At that time, no one suspected that they were

---

[1] Guiseppe Balsamo (1743–1795), alias Alessandro di Cagliostro, was an Italian occultist and swindler; Étienne-Gaspard Robert (1763–1837), alias Robertson, was a Belgian scientist, magician, and inventor. After 1798, he became famous as a presenter of "Phantasmagoria," ghost shows based on the principle of the magic lantern, which he often staged in abandoned Capuchin crypts in Paris. He patented the Fantascope in 1799.

[2] In his Praxinoscope, the French inventor Charles-Émile Reynaud (1844–1918) used perforated film and hand-painted images to project what was later recognized as a forerunner to the animated cartoon.

[3] Teige refers to the French astronomers Hervé Faye (1814–1902) and Pierre-Jules-César Janssen (1824–1907). Faye was the first to propose the idea of tracing the movements of Venus with a series of photographs. However, it was his colleague Janssen who was in fact the first to successfully photograph the various phases of Venus's path between the Sun and the Earth in 1874. He did this by means of his own invention called the Photographic Revolver, which enabled him to take a series of 48 pictures in 72 seconds at regular intervals. In his mention of the Biographe and Bioscope, Teige likely confuses Edison with Georges Demenÿ, who registered both of these inventions in 1895. The Bioskope projector was also patented in 1895 by Max Skladanowsky. In 1896, the American Mutoscope and Biograph Company, co-founded by Edison's former employee William Kennedy Laurie Dickinson, presented a projector called the Biograph, which surpassed Edison's older Vitascope projector. The first public screening of films by the Lumière brothers took place on December 28, 1895, in the Salon Indien of the Grand Café at Boulevard des Capucines 14, Paris.

standing on the threshold of a grand future. The opinions at that time held that those performances would be merely a temporary trend that would soon lose hold of public curiosity and that the perfected *laterna magica* would only be of service to scientific work. In the meantime, cinema has conquered the whole world. It is active everywhere, and the public everywhere indulges in this uniquely new and bold spectacle. Today, there are more than 70,000 cinema theaters on the surface of the globe.

So, this is a century of new discoveries and new lighting, a century in which optics (the science of light) has become the science of miracles (just as Descartes predicted centuries ago), giving birth to cinema, an art form that has become the art form of miracles, a miracle itself. It is developing at an amazing and giddy pace. Its progress is noticeable from one day to the next. The achievements of centuries, from the Chinese shadows and the *laterna magica* to the Lumière brothers' apparatus, have been overshadowed by the evolution of cinema, which has lasted only a few years. If you compare the first French films, the short scenes and stories that are, for instance, still projected today at the variété-cinéma, with contemporary American serials or the dramas of D. W. Griffith or Thomas Ince, you can notice an undreamt-of advancement in quality and rapid technical improvement. So we, the citizens of the first decades of the glorious, grand, and revolutionary twentieth century, are the assistants in the birth of this new, glorious art form. It is the most lively and intensive of all art forms. Its novelty is not a fashionable *haute nouveauté* or a seasonal curiosity, but an important cultural factor. Its powerful, lively, and captivating beauty speaks to the public, which does not want to be lectured or educated but demands sensation above all, just like the man who is not permitted into the banquets of our contemporary high-class pseudo-culture (Oh! *Panem et circenses*...!). An immeasurable power lies in the popularity, common character, and utter internationality of film, which speaks to the masses of all nations and races on the planet. It is a proud hymn of earthly beauty that can be an effective weapon in service of humanity's revolutionary ideals.

The young French writer Marcel Raval once said jokingly that modern poetry was born from Arthur Rimbaud and the fairy of mechanics. Cinema, just like almost everything else in the world, is the offspring of mechanics—of the machine—and human ideals. Yet, being the successor to the once-glorious and powerful art form of the theater, which has perished and continues to perish, and being, like the theater, a consortium of other individual art forms, film's origins are markedly more complex. We have seen the maternal line of cinema's family tree develop from shadow images to the *laterna magica*, from there to the inventions of the daguerreotype and chronophotography, and finally to the Lumière brothers' discovery. But, in addition to this scientific, technical, and optical tradition, cinema also has another tradition that, for lack of a better term, we will call "artistic." Yes, cinema is something of a *super-art*: it unites lyrical poetry, epic poetry, the novel, satire, comedy, visual beauty, music, acting, dance, in short, all art forms, in a splendid synthesis. Cinema is visual art, cinema is spectacular art (something like theater), cinema is poetry, cinema is ballet; it alternates between each of these and it is all of them simultaneously. At present, there are already several valuable tendencies in the direction of cinema aesthetics. These are primarily the writings of the astute and bright Louis Delluc (*Photogénie, Cinéma et Cie, Charlot*). If it wants to define the unique, new, and universal beauty that characterizes film, the future aesthetics of cinema must above all specify the relationships of

CINEMA TO THE VISUAL ARTS
CINEMA TO LITERATURE
CINEMA TO THEATER

PHOTOGRAPHY mediates cinema's relationship and connection to the visual arts, to painting. Film is a *cinéplastique* art, just as dance is a *méloplastique* art.[4] It is a living, luminescent painting, an animated image. Its rapid and remarkable technical progress from its beginnings to products of the present day is particularly determined by the continual refinement of photography, for the beauty of film is not literary or dramatic but PHOTOGENIC.

The representatives of modern painting are first and foremost the French; or better and more precisely: Paris; Montparnasse is the homeland of modern painting. The contemporary homelands of photography are England and above all *America*. The Cabots and Yankees[5] comprehended photography from the time when it still consisted only of primitive, embryonic daguerreotypes,[6] and today they create with it magnificent PHOTO JOURNALISM and *documentary* photography that is powerfully enchanting and possessed of its own unique poetry. *The modern cabinet of curiosities [panoptikum]*[7] is the illustrated weeklies and visual magazines of England and America. That which was once the French and European Empire style of picture-

---

[4] This is likely a reference to the famous essay "De la cinéplastique" (1922) by Élie Faure.

[5] Teige seems to invoke the symbols of the established North American elite to suggest that even its members understood the value of photography. Any specific connection he sees between the Cabot family and photography is not clear.

[6] From the beginning and particularly in the last third of the nineteenth century, daguerreotypes were distinguished by a certain visual expressivity, breadth, and simplicity, by well-balanced sharp detail, well-modeled and graceful compositions; in short, by beautiful pictorial qualities, as keenly described by Josef Čapek in his interesting book *Nejskromnější umění* [The humblest art, Praha: Aventinum, 1920]. [Original footnote]

[7] At the time this article was written, common Czech and German usage of the term "panoptikum" did not refer to Jeremy Bentham's prison, but rather to a form of popular entertainment that could be translated in English as cabinet of curiosities or wax museum.

making is now the American illustrated magazine. And this modern photography, even a simple snapshot, has just as much beauty in it as an elaborate documentary–like engraving in the Empire style, which amazes not only modern spirits but also antique collectors. The beauty of photography, just like the beauty of modern artillery technology, is provided by its simple and utter perfection and is contingent on its functionality. The beauty of photography is of the same ilk as the beauty of an airplane or a transatlantic ship or an electric light bulb. It is the product of a machine as well as the work of human hands, the human brain, and, if you will, the human heart. The physiochemical productive process, the photographic developer, the chemical baths, the exposure, etc., are all controlled by people, by their capability and their aptitude. Photography is therefore no less of a human art, because the photographer's abilities are further multiplied and regulated by the impeccably operating mechanical brain of the camera, which does not submit graciously to being violated by the erratic tastes of the salon, which, for its part, wants to *standardize* beauty, aesthetics, and the rules of photography. The refinement of photography multiplies its beauty and enhances its clarity, its realism, and its documentary aspect. These qualities, which constitute the intrinsic sense of photography, are betrayed by the typical "artistic" photography of Europe, the nonsense of which we will address later. When perfect photography comes alive on the cinema screen, on that gray screen of our earthly heaven (to use the words of Ivan Goll),[8] thereby revealing to our eyes without falsehood and trickery the giddy epopee of life, visual drama (photogeny[9]), and all things of the world; when this happens it is evident that photog-

---

[8]   Ivan (Yvan) Goll (1891–1950) was a German-French poet, who began as an expressionist in Berlin, then joined the dadaists in Zurich, and later the surrealists in Paris. From 1918 to 1924 he was engaged in a debate among literary writers about the aesthetic potential of the new medium of film (*die Kino-Debatte*), and in 1920 he published the manifesto "Das Kinodram."

[9]   *Photogénie* (in English, photogeny; in Czech, *fotogenie*): etymologically, *photogénie* derives from the Greek *photogéneia* (the production of light). The term was first used in France in 1851 to designate an object that reflected enough light to produce an imprint on a photographic plate. With the gradual development of more efficient light-sensitive emulsion, the word's original technical meaning was replaced with a reference to a certain aesthetic quality of the photographed object, which appears unique, poetic, or delightful in the photograph. After World War I, the term was adopted for cinema, most notably in the writings of theorists Louis Delluc and Jean Epstein, who focused on the ways in which a filmic image represents reality in its uniqueness, but at the same time—especially if using close-ups, slow motion, or special lighting techniques—sensually and emotionally augments it. In modernist film thought of the 1920s, the term refers to a painterly or poetic concept of cinema that is nonliterary and nontheatrical and that stresses spatial compositions or revelatory depictions of faces or landscapes over dramatic action unfolding in time. Czech avant-garde writers (including Teige, who exchanged letters with Delluc, as well as Vítězslav Nezval and Jiří Voskovec) used Delluc's conception of the term to designate a specifically modern optical poetry found especially in the American films of Chaplin and Fairbanks, which they considered expressions of the mechanical and circuslike qualities of the modern world. Thus, *photogénie* became not just a key term for cinematic specificity, but also

raphy is the most qualified of all the arts to interpret the rhythm, poetry, and incessant drama of events around the globe in the most pregnant and authentic manner. The film band is able to capture more of the world's beauty than a hymnal poem—as in Apollinaire's "Zone": film's lyricism is not literary, soaked with alizarin dye or printer's ink, but immediate and real.[10] It is reality, and reality does not need to be sung hymns of praise in order to be beautiful, captivating, and poetic. It is so. And therefore it is captivating, splendid, and poetic. Léger's pictures of machines and Marinetti's poem "À mon Pégasse" do not bring additional beauty to machines or to limousines. The beauty of the machine and of the automobile is the beauty of reality and pure form, which does not need to be adorned with ornaments or festooned with poems. Yes, *in reality and verisimilitude lies the morality of photography*. After all, veracity is always held as a virtue and it is in accordance with the function for which photography was invented. For painting, photography represents liberation from naturalism, that malodorous mold that was eating away at painting's solid and constructive artistic laws. With the intervention of photography, painting was able to develop its aesthetics, which will be henceforth anti-naturalistic, and it is now aware of its new mission, its new, concrete role and new function in modern life. The credit due to photography for curing painting of impressionism is immense, but painting has repaid photography badly: it has infected photography with the disease of impressionism, making it into artistic photography, something like an art industry, a false art.... Also, with regard to *cinégraphie*, it is fitting to show favor for American photographic culture and attitude over films of French and Italian direction. Although these are perhaps capable of playing with light, shadow, and chiaroscuro with noble taste, and are able to elicit marvelous lyrical effects (for example, in *Mater Dolorosa, La Dixième symphonie, J'Accuse!* and other productions of the Pathé company),[11] they are at times alarmingly inclined toward the allure of art photography. "Artistry" in this sense is an unquestionably dangerous element for film; and a cowboy serial often contains more photogenic and dramatic beauty than *film d'art*.[12]

---

an important inspiration for modern Czech poets and for the art movement called poetism [*poetismus*]. See Jacques Aumont & Michel Marie, *Dictionnaire théorique et critique du cinéma* (Paris: Nathan, 2002), 156–157.

[10] In the original Czech, Teige uses the term *pásmo* (strip, zone) as a dual reference to both the celluloid strip and to Guillaume Apollinaire's "Zone," the first poem in the poet's collection *Alcools* (1913). See note 5 in Teige's "The Aesthetics of Film and *Cinégraphie*," this anthology, p. 148.

[11] *Mater Dolorosa* (*Sorrowful Mother*, Abel Gance, France, 1917); *La dixième symphonie* (*The Tenth Symphony*, Abel Gance, France, 1918); *J'accuse!* (*I Accuse*, Abel Gance, France, 1919). In fact, only the last of these was produced by Pathé Frères Company.

[12] A reference to the highbrow film movement *film d'art* as well as to the French company Film d'Art, which produced two of the three films mentioned here—*Sorrowful Mother* and *The Tenth Symphony*.

But, on the other hand, what wondrous photogenic reality American film offers us, filled equally with power and with tenderness! Here we have seen perfect scenes of dark and rainy nights, the clarity of raindrops in the lucid darkness of space (in *Daddy-Long-Legs, Bread,* etc.),[13] the lights from a lighthouse's reflectors striking into the nighttime mists, the light of arc lamps in a damp harbor evening at the New York docks, the opalescence of illuminated advertisements from skyscraper heights above the city streets. The magic of this filmic and photographic chiaroscuro is not borrowed from Rembrandt or Leonardo. In fact, it is even more enchanting. But the poetry of night, the darkness and effects of artificial light, and the electric nights of the big city are not the only subjects of photography and film. There is also the broad light of day, clear and glorious, the azure sky above the California plains, on the pampas, or in the Mexican mountains! For, let us not forget, photo and film are not hunters of artificial lighting effects. They are first and foremost documentary. They are evidence and proof that the world is beautiful and the mere reality of film and photography thereby wholly refutes the gibberish of pessimistic philosophy. Until the invention of cinema and the refinement of the photographic camera, philosophy was able to proclaim that reality does not exist, that everything is illusion. But just one issue of an illustrated weekly, just one film episode—for example, a plane taking off or a Gaumont newsreel[14]—is irrefutable evidence of the existence of reality, a direct expression of the ambiguous drama of modern life. Philosophy lied. Photography cannot and may not lie.

Photography lies when it becomes "artistic." This is falsity, hypocrisy, and in the end a qualitative decline in terms of photography's own innate beauty. After all, photography does not require gallery-style chiaroscuro or impressionistic haziness to make it beautiful. Likewise, ornament and décor do not contribute to the beauty of modern architecture. When painting abandoned impressionism, photography inherited the wardrobe that fine society had cast off. Expressionism has already run its course, yet photography and film have donned expressionist garb (for example in the pointless German experiment *Das Cabinet des Dr. Caligari* [*The Cabinet of Dr. Caligari*]!).[15] Artistic photography, just like the art industry, is undignified, trashy, dim, and unhealthy. Its photo-plastic power has been drowned in the half-hearted aestheticism of Whistler.[16] Bleakness and boredom, inappropriate and false *art pour*

---

[13]   *Daddy-Long-Legs* (Marshall Neilan, USA, 1919), *Bread* (Ida May Park, USA, 1918).

[14]   The French production company Gaumont began releasing its weekly newsreel in Czechoslovakia in 1920 under the name *Gaumontův týdenní přehled.*

[15]   Robert Wiene, Germany, 1919.

[16]   James McNeill Whistler (1834–1903), American-British painter and proponent of the "l'art pour l'art" credo.

l'art. How much more beautiful are the clear, sharp photos we see in the Anglo-American illustrated magazines or on the screen during a Wild West film! They possess the genuine lyricism and hymnal beauty of Whitman's poetry.

As we have said, the home of modern photography and the refuge of *photogénie* is America. But we must also remember that America is not only the homeland of Walt Whitman, but also the fatherland of Edgar Allan Poe, as we now examine the peculiar, astonishing, and extraordinary artistic work of the American photographer living in Montparnasse, Paris—MAN RAY.

THE CASE OF MAN RAY: MAN RAY, this American Jew, friend, and colleague of modern French painters and poets, was a second-rate cubist painter. As with many second-rate cubist painters, he followed the trend of the times and became a dadaist. As a dadaist, he stopped painting and began to construct the meta-mechanical images "dada mecano New York." These were something rather similar to the suprematist constructions of the Russians Rodchenko and Lissitzky, a kind of utopian machinery, antennas, planes, etc. He then photographed these meta-mechanical constructions; he photographed them beautifully and meticulously, with a precise knowledge of the craft of photography (with which he earned his daily bread, by the way). He soon realized that the photographs of these constructions were even more beautiful than the constructions themselves, that the photographs faithfully interpret the sober beauty and photo-plastic, material expressivity of the constructions. This expressivity is not of an artistic type and is not even entirely attributable to the work's creator. And here he was witnessing the birth of a new branch of visual art: photography that is truly visual, that is truly art, that almost ceases to be photography and becomes something akin to painting and graphic art, something different than the common quasi-artistic studio photography that we have designated as part of the art industry. Here, photography gains its own independent and competent language. Nowhere, not even here, can photography abandon reality; it can become *super-real*, though. *Surréalisme* is the defining quality of Man Ray's photographs. It is the defining quality of modern creative art. Man Ray is thereby a brother to Juan Gris.

Photography is beautiful, even if it is not art, and the same is true of film. However, they are able to become art without losing their beauty, and, at best, they can alter and re-evaluate beauty. The director D. W. Griffith has succeeded in this, as have T. Ince, J. B. Mille, and to some extent Antoine and Abel Gance.[17] Man Ray has also succeeded, most consistently of all.

A photograph of an egg in a glass is a magnificent light play and a poem of light founded on supreme technical perfection. A paper spiral hanging from a stick, which

---

[17]   Teige likely refers to American director Cecil B. DeMille and French theater and film director André Antoine.

for the nihilist taste of dadaism is an example of modern sculpture and therefore art, is for Man Ray but a transitional bit of reality that provides the beauty for his photographs. Only photography that first develops in the darkroom, sometimes even after its real subject no longer exists, only that photography can become art. Yet true photographic poetry, a magic that is almost sorcery, can be found in Ray's most recent experiment "Champs délicieux," twelve 18 × 24 cm photographs published together in one album with an introduction by Tristan Tzara. Here, for the first time, photography stands side by side with painting and graphic art, consistently and without any evidence of half-hearted "artistic photography." The beauty of these works is analogous to the beauty of other fine-art works in recent history. In creating these "direct" photographs, Man Ray completely abstained from using photographic plates or lenses. They are subjects unto themselves; they are picture poems. The application of this photographic process, commonly used in the sciences, creates aquatint tones and delicate tonal transitions, nearly unachievable by graphic arts. At times it is almost phantasmagorical.

Picasso not only pasted newspaper clippings to some of his paintings, he even pasted photographs of pears onto some of his "still lifes" as well. George Grosz and Max Ernst not only pasted entire photographs onto their paintings, they also created entire works from pasted-together photographs. "This has nothing to do with painting," says the public, whether justly or unjustly, shaking their heads critically at these experiments. Man Ray would say *that it has nothing to do with photography*, one must be aware that:

photograph : painting = cinema : theater = orchestrion : piano = the forthcoming photo-plastic art : sculpture.

Just as cinema, with its resolute intervention, liberated theater by eliminating its multiple varieties and branches and making its aesthetic more precise, photography has liberated painting by freeing it from the yoke of naturalism. In turn, Man Ray's discoveries, inventions, and works are liberating photography from the decadence of "artistic photography" that has set in. They liberate it from the prevailing form of "artistic" photography (i.e., impressionism) by simply eliminating it. Through photography, they create a truly surrealistic art, an art that, according to Apollinaire, begins precisely where imitation ends. Whereas painting, freed from the dangerous elements of naturalism, is now returning to reality, from abstraction to the concrete, the photography of Man Ray, freed from the allure of Whistlerian idiom, is approaching the formal play of Picasso, Braque, and Gris. As soon as cinema seizes upon Man Ray's invention in the same way that it has appropriated all other new photographic achievements thus far, it will find itself at the threshold of a new, undreamt-of realm.

On the other hand, the perfection of color photography will, of course, also be a great enrichment to film.

As we have indicated, THE RELATIONSHIP OF FILM TO THE FINE ARTS is mediated by *photography*, which likewise acts inversely as the mediator in the relationship of the fine arts to cinema. New painting stands to learn quite a bit from cinema and by studying photography. Actually, it is precisely in film that art can most readily and most easily realize its own sense and purpose. Cinema has a sizeable influence on art, which is certainly not limited merely to superficial modifications, themes, etc. Many young painters are just as enthused by visions of cowboys as they are by the spectacle of the circus and the variété. This influence will surely not remain on the surface, but will grow deeper over the course of time. Yet to expand on the relationships between cinema and painting, or rather between photography and painting and vice versa, is beyond the scope of this article.

CINEMA AND POETRY. Cinema lives by a different poetry than does theater. It is unacquainted with the sentimentality and hysteria of Maeterlinck or Claudel and does not know the senile language of Ibsen. The lyricism of cinema is neither symbolic nor futuristic. It is not in the least bit academic. In our opinion, Dumas and Hugo are not well suited for the cinema, in which case it would be necessary to fundamentally rework and violate the text of the novel. Sentimental and historical literature is inappropriate for cinema, as are academic literature, official theater repertoire (e.g., *Lady of the Camellias*), and literature with a cultured niveau (i.e., poetic art). Being the spectacle of the people, cinema lives by the lyricism of the literature that is read by the people: Jules Verne, Karl May, Nick Carter, Buffalo Bill stories, *Uncle Tom's Cabin*, *The Heroic Captain Korkoran*, *Around the World in 80 Days*, *The Children of Captain Grant*, *Old Shatterhand*, the sharp-eyed Sherlock Holmes and Arsène Lupin, Bret Harte's stories from the far West and London's novels from the snowy plains, Upton Sinclair, Jensen, Mark Twain—in short, literature that is popular, adventurous, exploratory, and sensational, the so-called sleazy literature of colportage.

This literature offers modern, sensational entertainment. Adventure and fantasy are its domain. There is no space here to point out its often very healthy, unsentimental, active morality or its new, modern, active philosophy, yet they are both indisputable. It is the child of a new world, of modern social and cultural circumstances. It breathes the steamy airs of America, seduces with the magic of far-off places, intoxicates the masses; it is bored with sentimentalities and academism. It was born in an age when the vision of the world became sharper and more precise, imagination more surprising, and its emotional, expressive power has not lost its intensity. It is this literature, not the academic, Parnassian lyricism, but rather the truly popular literature that is, however, also very modern; simultaneously lyric, epopee, and drama; a literature that exists not so much in the studies and *libraries*, but rather on the backdrop of the wide heavens, free as a bird, or in the swift whirlwind of life—this literature is the foundation of cinema. Their poetry is of the same stock.

The poetry of cinema appropriates all elements of reality: automobiles, airplanes, steamships, cities, farms and farm boys, American Indians, astronomy, suburban hovels, feasts, landscapes from across the globe, wigwams, skyscrapers, prairies, etc. It contains all feelings and emotions. In this, the sister of cinema is the poetry of WHITMAN and the other American poets who are his students (Sandburg, Lindsay, Masters, Treat, Ridge, Ezra Pound, Oppenheim, Kreymborg, et al). Using only the slightest of means, it is able to produce an exact and complete image of the environment. Not only trains, boats, flying machines, or a band of Indians, but also tramway tickets, railroad signals, a letter with a seal, a business card, a notebook, a clock, a ring, a tropical helmet, even these little objects can become effective "actors" and meaningful events in film. In one sense, such allusiveness comes close to the technique of the detective novel, but it is also reminiscent of the taste and magic found in the poetry of Jean Cocteau and other modern poets.

The lyricism of cinema moves people with its exoticism, yet it is not the decadent exoticism of Baudelaire or Gaugin, but rather modern cosmopolitan exoticism. It is not the exoticism that escapes from the hypercivilized lands to the dreamy paradise of Tahiti or the Orient, but the exoticism of the Trans-Atlantic, of Pullman cars, or the Canadian Express Pacific, the exoticism of travel diaries, illustrated magazines, and a globetrotter sensibility that possesses a constantly fresh perception of the world. The images on the cinema screen change rapidly, because life itself is excessively fast. From time to time, an express train passes before our eyes. Paris, London, New York, and St. Petersburg hang on the screen by illuminated beams of light. San Francisco borders with Melbourne. Cinema looks at the world through the prism of a cosmopolitan, international spirit.

Modern literature and new poetry are open to the powerful, beneficial influence of cinema just as it is to the influence of that so-called sleazy literature that is the source of story material for American film. Novellas have adopted the cinematic narrative technique of simultaneity. Jules Romains, Blaise Cendrars, Jean Cocteau, Max Jacob, Ivan Goll, Apollinaire, Ehrenburg, Birot, Edschmid, Tzara, Epstein, Mac Orlan, Hamp, L. Delluc, and others, including the Czechs Černík, Nezval, Schulz, and Seifert, have integrated the essence of cinema into their poetic style. Some of them have even actually written film librettos, the most famous and most interesting being Goll's *Chapliniade*.[18] (A more detailed exploration of the influence of cinema on modern literature would be an interesting subject for a literary-critical study, but it is beyond the scope of this article.)

CINEMA AND THEATER. To put it simply: cinema is theater in the same way that an aeroplane is a flying person, to quote Honzl. Theater is centripetal, a concen-

---

[18]   Ivan Goll, *Die Chapliniade: Eine Kinodichtung* (Dresden: Rudolf Kaemmerer Verlag, 1920).

trated impression; film is centrifugal. Theater synthesizes to the extent of creating symbolic suggestions and abbreviations; film, as a rule, has epic expansiveness and is infatuated with expressive details. Theater has and will always have its limits, its limited scripts; film's stage is the world itself, the contemporary world spreading out into the unending distance, and the enormity of life, for film is the glorious "life-writing"[19] of modern art. Whereas theater is essentially monistic and synthetic, film is pluralistic and divisionary. These are more or less the basic aesthetic differences and mutually antithetical relationships between film and theater. Yet, under the influence of contemporary cultural and social circumstances, the formal attributes are growing ever more sharply and strictly divorced. Whereas cinema is expanding at a dizzying pace, theater is falling into ever farther, ever deeper decline. Whereas the movie houses are filled every evening with the international masses of all parts of the world, the theater auditoriums yawn in emptiness. The declaration "Do not build theaters" is complemented by the request "Build popular cinemas [*biografs*]!" Max Jacob ("Cinéma et Théâtre," *Nord-Sud*)[20] describes the relationship between cinema and theater thus: theater is a statue on a pedestal; it is not life. On the other hand, cinema cures us of all epidemic and endemic diseases of the theater. In cinema, it is bandits who are applauded, not elegant snobs. The foundation of theater is convention; the foundation of cinema is unpretentious reality. We defend cinema as a realistic art and refute theater as pathetic and academic art. While theater thrives on gesture and posturing, cinema thrives on certainty. Theater is entertainment for romantics and the petite bourgeoisie; cinema is entertainment for modern spirits and a source of refreshment for those who look to the future. It is an exaltation of humanity that can be displeasing only to misanthropes and to enemies of the world and of mankind.

Theater long ago ceased to be a celebration for broad strata of society, as it once was in ancient Greece. Nobody today will cry at the closing of theater houses except for the snobby, elite audience that had gone there as a pretentious manifestation of their cultural standing. In modern cultural life, it has been succeeded by cinema, the popular spectacle. Just as photography made the existence of naturalist-academic painting impossible, so does film make the existence of naturalist-academic theater impossible. These are both merely unnecessary atavisms that will soon die out anyway. The theater will fall with the bourgeoisie. Cinema lives on with the proletariat, the broadest stratum of society.

Being an innovation of our age, cinema, like photography, lacks a tradition of old masters. Just as photography went astray when it borrowed effects from Rembrandt

---

[19]   Most likely an allusion to the Greek roots of the early term for cinema, "biograph."

[20]   A reference to one of Jacob's contributions to the avant-garde journal *Nord-Sud*, founded in 1917 by Pierre Reverdy: Max Jacob, "Théâtre et cinéma," *Nord-Sud* 12 (February 1918), 10.

and Whistler, cinema also certainly went astray when it strove to be conventionally theatrical. The literature that cinema appropriated is not in the least bit official or academically sanctioned, and, likewise, the theatrical tradition upon which cinema instinctively and rightly rests is not the official, academic theater. Being the spectacle of the people, cinema has its tradition in the heretical mutations of theater that are likewise spectacles of the people and "pleasures of the electric century," that is:

IN CIRCUS AND VARIÉTÉ,
IN BALLET, PANTOMIME, MELODRAMA, MUSIC HALL,
THE CAFÉ-CONCERT, AND CABARET,
IN FOLK CELEBRATIONS, SUBURBAN DANCE HALLS, ETC.,
IN SPORTS.

The freedom of modern art was born in the circus, the variété, and the music hall. Here is where true modern poetry lives—brisk, electric, and extremely non-naturalistic. This is the home to new forms of humor, clowning irony, sentimental *gaminerie*,[21] brisk sketches, miraculous tricks of equilibrists, jugglers, equestrian girls, exotic dance, "eccentric-girls," and Japanese acrobats; this home is poetic and romantic. If romanticism is truly an eternal power that pervades history, and if it is true that every age, even an absolutely realistic age like our own, requires at least some romantic spice, then this romanticism can be found today in the circus, the variété, and the music hall, it is represented by acrobats, comedians, clowns, singers, and dancers, as well as by the famed boxers that are applauded and beloved by the masses. It is a nomadic romanticism, the romanticism of modern wandering minstrels, of globetrotter troubadours, who are citizens of the world. Nomads have been and will always be romantic, and what they produce is not empty art.

Given that the relationship of cinema to official theater, "artistic" direction, and acting as well as to classical, naturalist, and psychological drama is defined purely as strained antithesis, it is possible to consider circus, variété, and music hall as closely akin to cinema, and as predecessors to cinema, in more than one respect.

Of all of those unsanctioned mutations of theater and spectacle, the *circus* and *théâtre variété*, by virtue of their character, their meaning, and their vital mission are most closely related to cinema. They are exotic, like cinema. They are international, their expressive language being some sort of artistic Ido or Esperanto, just as with cinema. They are spectacle without literature and beyond literature. Variété stars, "eccentric-girls," jugglers, sketches, the brutal dialogues of extremely short clown scenes, something like the legacy of *commedia dell'arte*, exquisite equilibrists

---

21 From the French term for "childishness, impishness."

and their risky, break-neck performances, beautiful and energetic wild-beast tamers, unusual, artful, and exotic dances, graceful equestrian girls in vermillion dresses with green sashes and thousands of bangles, each attraction more sensational than the last—all of these fantastic, outlandish, intoxicating, nearly miraculous things are enticing to modern artists, who have grown bored with the pathetic vacuousness of the theater. Seurat, Toulouse-Lautrec, Picasso, Kubišta, Archipenko, and Léger mined their paintings from these environs. The poetry of the jungle and of far-off lands, the breath of the circus, were the inspiration for one of Neumann's most successful and most characteristic poems.[22] Yet at the same time, circus and variété are spectacles of the people, for their strength lies in healthy, playful, and ravenous reality, in grotesque, potent caricature and satire; and in this way they are akin to film.

The same can be said of *music hall, pantomime, the café concert,* and *cabaret.* They are nonacademic, ingenuous, and primitive, in the specific modern sense of the word. They are popular, or least they should be. As F. T. Marinetti said, they contain the complete range of laughter and are a tireless ventilator of the overheated brain. Whereas the circus nowadays has its home above all in France, the most important circuses being the Paris MEDRANO (*Boum! Tous les soirs Boum!*) and the NOUVEAU CIRQUE DE PARIS, the birthplace and current home of the striking, synthetic art of music hall and *caf'conc'* [*café-concert*] is principally the Anglo-American world. Charlie Chaplin and even Fatty grew out of the British Fred Karno pantomime company based in London. Exotic revue, travesty, parody, farce, dance, dance and more dance, nonacademic ballet (and Anna Pavlova from the Russian ballet even ventured to perform on the music hall stage in the United States), Loïe Fuller, Max Dearly, and Mistinguette of the Casino de Paris, the Eldorado, and of film (*Les Misérables*)[23], who, with her impish taste, revived the fantastic, wild, uninhibited, and mischievous dance, the *danse gavroche* in the soil of the variété, in the art of melodrama, and raised it to the same level as the hieratic dances of Isadora Duncan, Harry Pilcer, and Gaby Deslys, Mme. Roberty of the Parisian music hall Concert Mayol, Mme. Paulette Pax, Pearl White, Musidora (from the film *Les Vampires*),[24] Vernon Castle, Max Linder, Stacia Napierkowska—this is cabaret, music hall, variété, the modern lively, electrifying, and poetic theater, art that is not officially recognized or appreciated, but that at least lacks old-fashioned modesty. It is untrue that this art is some kind of inferior spectacle, some sort of lower-quality theater, simply because it does

---

[22] A reference to Neumann's poem "Cirkus," first published in 1914.

[23] Mistinguette was the stage name of famous French entertainer Jeanne Bourgeois; Casino de Paris was a music hall on the Rue de Clichy and Eldorado was a *café-concert* on the Boulevard de Strasbourg (both in Paris); Mistinguette played the role of Éponine Thénardier in the 1913 film series adaptation of Hugo's *Les Misérables* (Alberto Capellani, France, 1913).

[24] *Les Vampires* (Louis Feuillade, France, 1915).

not recognize the morbid aesthetics of the day. On the contrary, modern theater, truly modern theater, the aspiration of young poets and several experimental theaters in France and revolutionary Russia, is becoming the brother of cabaret (e.g., the Russian Theater of Revolutionary Satire),[25] magical plays, *comédie-bouffe*, ballet, and vaudeville, while cinema has taken the place of grand theater and great drama in the modern era.

Incidentally, it is necessary to remark that the flowering of variété and cabaret has been described as a product of bourgeois pseudo-culture. To some extent, especially for us Czechs, this is in fact the case. The first-class stages are explicitly bourgeois, not only in their external design but also in their programming. In the Czech case, Hašler represents an example of this. Yet at the same time, it is clear that these stages have a political element. Next to the old bohemian cabarets Chauve Souris and Lapin Agile in Montmartre, we find the luxurious revues Ba-Ta-Clan, Folies Bergère, Olympia, and Alhambra. Yet there are also popular suburban spectacles and, in Montparnasse, the Rue de la Gaîté is home to both the nationalist cabaret Bobino and the socialist Gaîté-Montparnasse. It is known that the Russian revolution itself resurrected cabaret, and just as Napoleon declared that Beaumarchais's *The Marriage of Figaro* was a complete representation of the French Revolution, so does the lyricism, power, rage, suffering, and defiance of the current revolutionary movement lie concealed in the erotic and proletarian revolutionary chansons of some contemporary cabarets. This is also found in the lyricism arising from the atmosphere of the periphery and *fortifs*[26] as well as in the social pathos of some films. The characters whom proletarian audiences admire, such as Sherlock Holmes, Arsène Lupin, Apaches, and pirates, are not the products of bourgeois aesthetics, philosophy, morality, or lyricism. These characters are to the common people what John Gabriel Borkman or Des Esseintes[27] are to bourgeois aesthetes. There is no philistinism or snobbism in such cabaret. Bourgeois theater loves polished and contemplative dialogue, fateful psychology, traditional dramatic structures, individualist yet nevertheless conventional heroes. The little theaters of the people love brave Apaches; fine sailors; little ditties; lighting effects; twinkling spotlights; the colorfulness of posters; simple, ever-fresh, and bright events. In a spectacle without beginning and without

[25] *Terevsat*: the Theater of Revolutionary Satire was an officially sanctioned theater movement that combined folk dance, gymnastics and song as a propaganda tool to spread communist ideology in post-revolutionary Russia.

[26] The areas around the former Parisian military fortifications (also known as "La Zone"), which had been occupied by the poor and homeless.

[27] John Gabriel Borkman is the title character of a Henrik Ibsen play of the same name from 1896. Esseintes is the protagonist of the 1884 novel *À rebours* by Joris-Karl Huysmans and the most famous prototype of a decadent aesthete.

end, these theaters translate life's ceaseless drama into a rapid sequence of numbers. Just like popular dancing events, they are a refreshing entertainment of the modern world and modern style, "the pleasure of the electric century." Nevertheless, we must emphasize here that it would be a mistake and a sin to consider real life to be like Eden, Luna Park, or Magic City, as is often done nowadays. In real life, we do not move from attraction to attraction.

THEATER AND FILM. Cinema went astray when it tried to imitate theater. Film had nothing to learn from the worn-out, degenerating, yet vainly resuscitated, theater save for a few vices, false pretensions to *film d'art*, which it quickly shook off. On the other hand, theater can take valuable instruction from film, which is full of vitality, as well as from the circus, variété, and cabaret. In every aspect, film dramas and serials surpass and discredit traditional feature dramas, which do not really pose any competition whatsoever, and narrative plays of lower literary value (à la *Excelsior!*),[28] because its faculties are far superior to the rather imperfect tricks of the theater, even those of the Châtelet stage. Bearing testimony to the decomposition of traditional theater, modern dramatic production shirks the antiquated dramatic structures that, in building upon conversation, psychology and God knows what else, have lost their *raison d'être*. Instead, modern dramatic production consciously and programmatically opens itself to the influence of cinema, the repertoires of small popular stages, cabaret, and the circus, and, just as with circus and film, is closely linked to exoticism. The experimental works of young authors rely on new techniques of staging and direction that differ from the traditional theatrical norms. In the foreword to *The Breasts of Tirésias* (*Les Mamelles de Tirésias*), Apollinaire speaks of the necessity for a double stage, one in the center of the audience (as in Japan), and a second that encircles the audience in a wide band. Birot's plays, which are full of circus attractions and variété exoticisms, are conceived for clowns, jugglers, and acrobats. Ivan Goll's satirical piece *Methusalem* is permeated with cinematic scenes. Just as futurist painters place the observer in the middle of the picture, modern theater wants to have the observer in the middle of the play, in the middle of the spectacles and dramatic events. Vaudeville, pantomime, ballet, and the attempts at purely optical theater (Pitoëff): these are spectacles equally lyrical and dramatic in spirit and purpose, just as the characters Fantômas, Buffalo Bill, and Chaplin are equally dramatic and lyrical. Of course, we are not talking here about symbolist lyrical drama, but rather about something whose harbingers were Synge's *Playboy of the Western World* and Jarry's *Ubu Roi*. Perhaps these experimental works are sometimes

---

[28] *Excelsior*, by the choreographer Luigi Manzotti and composer Romualdo Marenco, was an 1881 ballet that celebrated the scientific and industrial progress of the nineteenth century. The renowned Czech poet Jaroslav Vrchlický wrote a libretto for the ballet, which had performances in the Czech National Theater in Prague.

strongly burlesque, but burlesque must be filled with the spirit of lyricism if it is to be art. This lyricism is reflected in song, dance, laughter, gesture, set design, and costume. It is the common lyricism of everyday life, modern lyricism that is not narrowly literary, that successfully weds itself with the most urgent dramatism. To make the point clearly: sporting events are, for example, irreproachably dramatic and do not lack a strong modern lyrical accent. The unification of lyricism with dramatic events is possible only when the traditional rules regarding the three unities of action, space, and time are abolished, and replaced with the modern element of simultaneity.

CINEMA AND SPORT. Whereas film is in no way bound to theater, it is exceedingly indebted to sport, athletics, and acrobatics. Is it necessary to expand on this obvious fact? Just as much a collective work as soccer, film only rarely chooses its actors from the milieu of theatrical tragedy, and American film in particular never does so. (French cinema is relatively closely tied to theater both in the practices of directors such as Abel Gance: *Mater Dolorosa, La Dixième symphonie, J'accuse!*; Louis Feuillade: *Judex, Tih-Minh*; Charles Burguet; Pouctal: *Au Travail*; Antoine: *Les Travailleurs de la mer, La Terre*; and with its actors from the theater: Gabrielle Robinne, Éve Francis, Marcel Lévesque, Sarah Bernhardt, and Séverin Mars.) In the vast majority of cases, however, film finds its unique performers among the ranks of sportsmen, athletes, acrobats, and circus clowns. Chaplin's friend Carpentier, the famous boxer, now plays in film. Only sport of a very high level of perfection can provide film with such "smart" automobile drivers, equestrians, and cowboys as Rawlinson, Fairbanks, Marie Walcamp, Helen Holmes, Pearl White, Maciste,[29] Harry Carey, W. Hart, Ruth Roland, and others. Cinema as art is the crowning example of modern intellectual culture, which is nevertheless also a celebration of modern physical culture. It establishes a balance between the two, and therein lies its significant moral importance.

CINEMA AND MUSIC exist in a reciprocal relationship that is not as simple and straightforward as it appears, but is in fact highly complex. Quite simply, film requires musical accompaniment. Theatrical performances nowadays are unthinkable without an orchestra and, likewise, the images on the cinema screen turn into gruesome and bizarre apparitions when not teamed up with the melody of music. Psychologically speaking, this is entirely natural. Yet the question remains whether music will still be required in the future, when perfect color films are projected in the broad light of day. For the time being, however, musical accompaniment is an ab-

---

[29]   This is apparently a reference to the actor Bartolomeo Pagano, who played the character Maciste in a series of Italian films from 1915 to 1926.

solute necessity. Each accompaniment should be appropriate for the given film and modern musicians should take great interest in the programmatic selection of music. Mozart's *Abduction from the Seraglio* and sometimes *The Magic Flute* are played for oriental films. Offenbach, Beethoven, Dvořák, Smetana, Bizet, and Schubert are played; and in France even Debussy is played from time to time. Chopin is used for Chaplin's *The Vagabond*. Yet behold how precisely modern music coincides with the character of film: Stravinsky with his rag-piano and pianola, and modern dance and marching music of the world: the Salome Foxtrot, Indianola.... The rhythm of modern dances is an authentically modern rhythm, it contains something of the rhythm of pounding trains and city life. How perfectly fitting a jazz band accompaniment is for film! Of course, being that film is mechanical theater, the most fitting would certainly be mechanical music (gramophone, orchestrion, pianola), because music, which should function as the accompaniment, illustration, and backdrop to the film drama, should not ignore the instruments of modern technological achievements. Let the music roar with the din of dynamos, Morse telegraphs, and automobile horns, with the squeal of express trains and aeroplanes, let the throbbing of the typewriter replace the traditional throbbing of the nightingale in the poetic summer night! Such "touches of reality," which were sought after by the futurists with their "noise machines" and by Erik Satie in his *Parade*, can have the same meaning for music as newspaper clippings, playing cards, pieces of material, etc., have for cubist still lifes. Picasso, Braque, and Juan Gris use these things to freshen up the abstract geometric structure of their work, bringing to it some aesthetically unfiltered vitality, the reality of raw material. The most favorable musical technique in this sense is *jazz*, which outdoes Russolo's noise machines through its expressivity. For that matter, the job of these noise machines can be done better by phonograph recordings that accurately capture the clamor and tumult of the city, train stations, promenades, harbors, great mass assemblies, and the thunder of proletarian demonstrations.

Modern music cannot work for the dead theater. There are no truly new operas and there never will be, just as there will not be new dramas. We shall rather expect musical novelty in operetta, which is closer to popular taste and mentality. Let music start working for film. Here it can discover an extensive realm of beautiful tasks, albeit difficult ones that demand responsibility. Some authors of Romance modernism are already making such attempts, notably the members of the Parisian 6 ("*Le Six*"). Darius Milhaud, for example, has composed a "Cinéma-symphonie" and scores for some of Chaplin's works.[30]

---

[30]   Milhaud's surrealistic ballet *Le Boeuf sur le toit* (1919) was subtitled "a cinema-symphony" and was originally created by the composer as an accompaniment to Chaplin's films.

As we have attempted to indicate, the *artistic value of film* is immeasurable. If we today hesitate to award film the label "art" (in 1921, the Parisian Salon d'Automne named film the "tenth Muse"), it is only because its beauty, vitality, and quality tower above the quality of contemporary art. There is a series of names connected with film that future historians and critics will place alongside the celebrated figures of the art world.

Charles Spencer Chaplin, Charlot, or Charlie is the most omnipresent film artist. He belongs to the proletariat of all nations and races. His works circulate the entire world. He is the greatest individual film artist, the greatest figure in contemporary art. He is the Molière and Aristophanes of today. Young poets of all nations pay homage to him. His pitiful sadness provokes indefinable happiness for the masses. He is more than an actor. He is a clown. A poet. The inventor of new, utterly modern expressions of humor and irony that are tinged with delicate and paradoxical sentimentality. He is one of those great humorists who "goes into the corner and cries" (Neruda).[31] He lives "a dog's life," he is a vagabond, immigrant, waiter, floorwalker, piano mover, fake count, glazier, adventurer, fireman, soldier, pawnshop assistant, policeman, and drunkard; a jack of all trades, master of none.

Douglas Fairbanks, as with Whitman, can be said to conduct his heroics from a particularly American standpoint, embodying with his work the true modern poetry of athletics and sport. He is the hero of Arizona, the avenger of injustice Zorro, a crestfallen man and a man of the world, bandit and nut, sanitarium owner, Robin Hood and d'Artagnan from the *Three Musketeers*, whom he unwittingly modernizes with his simple naturalism.

Sessue Hayakawa, the greatest contemporary tragedian, William Hart (Rio Jim),[32] Mary Pickford, Jack Pickford, Pearl White, Mrs. Vernon Castle[33], Fatty (Roscoe Arbuckle), Dustin Farnum, Marie Walcamp, Mae Murray, Mae Marsh (*Intolerance*), Ruth Roland, Norma Talmadge, Lincoln, Fanny Ward,[34] Alice Brady, MacLaren, Coogan, Edna Purviance, and Eric Campbell (partners of Chaplin), Dorothy Phillips, C. Kimball Young, Harry Carey, O. Thomas, Marie Doro, P. Dean, S. Milovanoff (orphan Jeanette),[35] Mathot (*Au Travail*),[36] Biscot, Musidora, Peggy[37], Ève Francis, Nazimova, Gémier (*Mater Dolorosa*), Sjöstrom, O'Brien, etc., etc.

---

[31] A quote from the 1878 collection *Písně kosmické* [Cosmic songs] by the Czech poet Jan Neruda.

[32] W. S. Hart was known in France as Rio Jim.

[33] The first name of Vernon Castle's wife was Irene. Although they were a ballroom dancing team, she was the only one of the pair to make significant appearances in film.

[34] Also known as Mrs. Thomas Ward.

[35] In *L'Orpheline* (*The Orphan*, Louis Feuillade, France, 1921).

[36] *Au Travail* (*Work*, Henri Pouctal, France, 1920).

[37] This is likely a reference to ballerina and actress Marguerite de la Motte, who had the nickname Peggy.

Directors: the foremost is D. W. Griffith (*Intolerance, Dream Street, Broken Blossoms, Way Down East*), Th. H. Ince, Mack Sennett, Loos,[38] Emerson, DeMille, Antoine, Abel Gance, Capellani, etc., etc.

THE NEW PROLETARIAN ART—the art that the perceptive Ehrenburg has predicted will someday cease to be art—is INTERNATIONAL, POPULAR, AND COLLECTIVE; it is the mission and style of the future. Of all the contemporary arts, film is closest to proletarian art, most notably in the works of Chaplin (*The Kid, The Vagabond, Shoulder Arms, The Immigrant, Easy Street*) and Fairbanks. The epic quality of modern life and the enormity of the world are palpable in these works; it is not merely the world in pictures, but a poem of the modern world itself. Film is stormy and fierce, yet also succinct. It is bountiful and its possibilities know no limits. It is the only art for the contemporary proletariat, but it is not yet a purely proletarian art. Its social significance is immeasurable. If we close all the theaters, exhibitions, galleries, reading rooms, and churches, only a small handful of people will mourn helplessly. The world will keep turning. Yet perhaps it would indeed stop if the film projectors of all lands stopped turning. Several kilometers of revolutionary film will conquer the world, just as a number of contemporary films have already conquered the heart of the proletarian public.

(1922)

---

[38]   Probably a reference to writer and producer Anita Loos.

Karel Teige
THE AESTHETICS OF FILM AND *CINÉGRAPHIE*[1]

The achievements of contemporary art are nothing more than the end results of a new, contemporary sensibility and mentality, directly linked with the permanently regenerating newness of the world. They are a reflection of the external conditions and the satisfaction of the poetic needs of the modern man: these achievements are not concerned with the domain reserved for science, philosophy, or ethics, and make almost no appeal to Kantian "pure reason," of whose meaning and even existence we are rightly skeptical. The landscape we bisect at a speed of 100 km/h with an express train or a car no longer has descriptive and static value for us; our senses are saturated with a sense of completeness and synthesis. We stand by the windows of an express train, unmoving, with our legs firmly astride, hands in our pockets and pipe in our teeth, with an immense ravenous desire in our hearts; meanwhile, the space of the landscape hurtles past us with the velocity of a steam engine and the apparently turning plate of the earth races back, winding itself into a ball of a swiftly experienced past. We are experiencing *an entirely new vision of the world*. It can arguably be said that today's man experiences a hundred times more impressions than a person of the Middle Ages did. We are a people of an express-train mentality, with a stirred-up and enthralled sensibility whose elasticity enables all possibilities for development. Our world is a patented invention, with the dynamic beauty of speed, me-

---

[1] *Cinégraphie* (in Czech, *kinografie*): *cinégraphie* defines film as a specific modernist art form that differs from other arts and from conventional cinema and uses its own form of "language" or "writing." First used during World War I by filmmakers and critics Emile Vuillermoz and Marcel L'Herbier, the term was redefined in the early 1920s by Louis Delluc and Léon Moussinac to designate, as Richard Abel puts it, the "rhythmical or structural ordering of *photogénie* throughout a film." In contrast to *photogénie*, *cinégraphie* refers not only to the optical qualities of a filmed object or its filmic depiction, but also to the "grammatical" or "rhetorical" principles by which filmic images are linked together. In Czech, Teige and Voskovec used the term in accordance with the French meaning, but sometimes also simply to designate filmic art as such. See Richard Abel, *French Film Theory and Criticism: A History/Anthology 1907–1939*, vol. 1 (Princeton: Princeton University Press, 1993), 206–213.

tallic and fiery, with the vibrant color of great hope. It is an environment of electrical exchanges, Americanism, news reports, and radiotelegraphy. Just like Einstein's theory, the speed of transportation has granted us a novel and proper understanding of space and time. The world is neither a paradise nor a garden of youth nor a hell of work. It is simply a time-space continuum and its art is the *chrono-spatial poem.* The modern muses are daughters of the big city who visit the intellectual centers. Our world is truly organized *"selon l'Esprit nouveau"* [according to The new spirit][2] by engineers and *constructeurs*, embellished and fueled by merry visionaries, poets, clowns, and acrobats. The Americanized Europe is becoming a single, chaotic, and cinematic metropolis, and the social transformations taking place there will render it, sooner or later, a harmonious international city. In this Europe, on the membranes of our dreams, like bright films, *electrogenic poems of luminous signs* are sprouting up, garishly colored *affiches*; the illumination of busy avenues converses with us, as do traffic lights, signaling colors and signs, semaphore, the nervous tapping of Morse code, and the extremely brief jargon of telegrams and advertisements. These poems of the world do not scan into Alexandrines. This is the source of modern poetry's condensed and diverse nature and the impetus for its destruction of pre-established forms. It springs from the rapid tempo and massive pressure of the modern era. This tempo has exponentially accelerated the evolution of the soul; under such pressure outdated atavisms disintegrate, safely and immediately. This speed arouses the need for yet greater speed, and likewise awakens the desire for rest and calm to allow for meditation. Indeed, the comfortable lounge chair and "air-express" are illustrations of this situation. Given that kinetic speed and the rapid sequence of facts, ideas and observations indeed bring about a simultaneity of perception, it is possible to illustrate our times with the following picture: *a comfortable lounge chair in the cabin of an "air-express."* Today we *simultaneously* experience the most severe *psychological contrasts, sharpened to the point of paradox*; we feel and comprehend concurrently; sensibility and intelligence are in permanent operation, mutually complementing each other. Consequently, we are *neither* intellectualist philosophers *nor* sensitively creative poets, we do not even alternate between these two options; we are both, simultaneously and reciprocally. To utilize a term from Epstein, we are *lyrosophes.*[3]

---

[2]   *L'Esprit nouveau* [The new spirit]: a magazine published monthly between 1920 and 1925 by architect Le Corbusier (Charles Édouard Jeanneret) and painter Amédée Ozenfant. The magazine represented purism, a movement that combined classical and constructivist ideas in a modern aesthetic whose hallmarks were simplicity, logic, and order.

[3]   *Lyrosophy* is a term coined in the early 1920s by French filmmaker and theorist Jean Epstein (1897–1953), who believed that cinema was destined to reveal the nonrational logic of the unconscious. Epstein dubbed this logic *lyrosophy* and understood it as an epistemological basis for film art.

Being opponents of weepy sentimentalism, it has not been uncommon for us to feel a sort of lack and lifelessness from the traditional artistic disciplines, from painting, sculpture, literary poetry and all of their variations. In *cinema* [*kino*] an *entirely new art form* has been revealed to us, more perfectly suited than any other art to respond to the character, needs, and exigencies of today. We have come to understand that cinema is the cradle of all truly new art: a live radio-concert in which all the diverse voices from all cities of the world will be collected; profound, magical and melancholy songs where unseen images and unknown lights burn like radiant ephemeral stars in a veil of locomotive smoke. Cinema's possibilities are limitless; its sources are rich and infinite. Its poetry, a 100% modern poetry, is all-encompassing, precise, succinct, and synthetic. It is the poetry of the travel journal, the Eiffel Tower, Baedeker, the poster, and the postcard, of maps, anecdotes, and slapstick comedies, the poetry of nostalgic souvenirs, for memories of cities are like memories of love; it is the poetry of cafés filled with lamps and smoke, the song of the modern sirens of the Red Star Line,[4] the tourist poetry of long corridors of hotels and argosies, with their mysterious, numbered doors to rooms and cabins. Globe-trotting and frivolity, clownery and adventure, equipped with the utmost comfort.

Even the calmest among us, the contemporary inhabitants of the electric century, are bombarded daily with a myriad of fierce sensual emotions and frenzied bits of information. What we require in order to relax, in order to catch our breath, is not the piercing and titillating nothingness of nirvana. On the contrary, we require deft and concise art, sudden and ephemeral sensations, a lyrical and poetic charge of direct expression and of cutting innuendos, something like jazz, radio, and especially *film*. For a long time, objections have been raised by those sickly and marasmic arts whose claims have, from the beginning, been threatened by film's expansion, to the effect that cinema is a poor and lowly pseudo-art that requires the intervention and collaboration of theatrical and literary luminaries. It was deemed that westerns and adventure serials fall below the level of academic drama, and as a result our screens are today filled with wretched and ransacked dramas. *The separation of film from theater*, which is absolutely necessary for its healthy development, has not yet been carried out systematically enough. After all, there is no relationship between theater and film aside from unfriendly antagonistic tension. Whereas theater is centripetal and comprises concentrated impressions, film is centrifugal and infatuated with the expressive minutiae that play such an important role in life. The theater has its limits and its limited script, and will always have them as long as it remains theater. Film has the entire world as its stage, the whole contemporary world fanned out in its nev-

---

[4]   Teige refers to the famous American-Belgian passenger ocean liner of that name, which transported numerous emigrants from Europe to the United States.

er-ending expanses. We could say that theater is *monadic and synthetic*, whereas film is *pluralistic and divisionist* in its methods. It is the art of earthly beauty, burning topicality, and captivating fantasy; it is *a cross-section of the contemporary world*. Being, after all, a poetic chain of images,[5] film was able to avoid becoming a Babylonian confusion of languages; it is international like Ido or Esperanto; it writes its verse in all humanly imaginable languages and jargons.[6]

Baudelaire said that beauty is founded on astonishment. The beauty of film is founded on nothing other than this. Accordingly, its aesthetics is the aesthetics of astonishment, the aesthetics of surprise and the unexpected. Several years ago, the late Canudo initiated film sessions at the Salon d'Automne,[7] whereby film (perhaps in answer to Apollinaire's long-standing wish) was officially recognized as art, a privilege that is, incidentally, very dangerous. Canudo favorably characterized cinema like this: it is a phantasmagoric world of human miracles whose manifestations are infinite, renewing themselves week after week; it is a total image of the life of all beings and objects scattered across the whole globe, each of which is the flower and resultant of its specific environment. Cinema is above all an outstanding instrument that, regrettably, is often under the control of inept dolts, as if an absolute beginner were to play on a Stradivarius.

It should have been clear from the very beginning of cinema, from the first slapsticks and burlesques, that we are dealing with good art that has the potential to become better and to be perfected.[8] But, because the idea of perfection is rather sad,

---

[5] In the original Czech text, Teige uses the term *pásmo* (zone, strip) in reference to the Czech avant-garde's poetic technique of free-associating verses, emotions, ideas, and dialogues to build a manifold, dynamic flow or image. The term was first used to this effect by Karel Čapek, who gave the title "Pásmo" to his 1919 translation of Guillaume Apollinaire's poem "Zone" (first printed in 1913 in Apollinaire's *Alcools*). The translation strongly inspired the Czech avant-garde poets, above all Vítězslav Nezval and Jaroslav Seifert. *Pásmo* was also the title of a journal started by the avant-garde group Devětsil in 1924, in which Teige, Artuš Černík, Jindřich Honzl, Bedřich Václavek, and others published articles on film. At the same time, Czech poets (among them, Vítězslav Nezval and Jaroslav Seifert) writing a special kind of film libretto—which were, in fact, more associative poetry than film scripts, and never realized as films—spoke about the "filmové pásmo" (film strip) in reference to the poetic potential of filmic montage as well as to the technical basis of the medium (i.e., the series of images on a celluloid strip).

[6] Teige made some changes in this paragraph when he re-edited this essay one year later for his book *Film* (Praha: Václav Petr, 1925). Instead of contrasting the centripetal and monadic qualities of theater with the centrifugal and pluralistic qualities of film, in the later version he focuses on the literariness of theater as opposed to the immediacy of film.

[7] Beginning in 1921, Ricciotto Canudo (1879–1923), an Italian art theorist who established the foundations of film aesthetics and theory, organized special screenings of film excerpts at the prestigious Parisian annual exhibition of painting called the Salon d'Automne, in order to promote the notion of cinema as high art.

the fact that it is still not yet perfect is gladly welcomed. Of course, it is true that throughout the entire dizzying process in which the technology was being perfected, film was never in such a worrisome state as it is today. Its development is at a crossroads and its misgivings are those of abundance; it could evidently benefit from a dose of disinfecting medicine in the form of *aesthetic minimalism. Non multa sed multum.*[9] Nowadays there are excessively artistic films that (just like the art industry) unscrupulously borrow effects from other artistic disciplines, particularly from the theater, rather than working with the intrinsic and innate elements of filmic art itself. Here, as in other parts of the world, we most desperately require a revision of values, *a radical cleansing of the creative means* and a forward-looking clarity of spirit that is precisely aware of its purpose and its mission. Clearly, film has endured this crisis for quite a long time now. Incidentally, this is becoming a chronic crisis, fed by the financial speculation of film entrepreneurs striving after "grand spectacles" and *chef-d'oeuvres,* while we, the devotees of cinema, are beginning to talk about film's downfall, which is becoming more and more evident as time goes on. Yet, when we consider some of the most poetic, photogenic, and modern contemporary films, it is possible to believe that marasmic cinema is indeed on the wane and thus we continue to set our immense, spirited hopes on this *supra-real art.* But, when criticizing film, we must be knowledgeable of the standards and criteria of judgment. We absolutely require an *aesthetics of film.* This contemporary state of confusion needs to be dispersed. Some principles of cinematic aesthetics need to be formulated more clearly and precisely. Most of all, the relationship of film to theater, literature, and painting needs to be clarified, and this borrowing of heterogeneous values that is turning film into an undignified art industry, i.e., *"film d'art,"* needs to cease.[10]

Film is a *living image.* An enormous visual orchestra, a drama of lines and substances in motion. It is a *cineplastic* poem [*kinoplastická báseň*][11] thrust into time, so that it has persistence and action. It is a *time-space poem.* A poem that requires "not words, not music or rhyme, [...] not custom or lecture, not even the best"—as was the dream of Whitman.[12] It is a painterly creation that does not become rigid with time.

As Černík[13] correctly observed, due to its terseness, film is more of a poem than a novel to be read in countless installments.

Film is living photography. Photography is truthful imagery. Above all, film aesthetics should operate in conjunction with the aesthetics of photography; the development and perfection of film aesthetics depends on this. Here again, the optical aspect is of primary importance. Once again we should point out, just in passing, the interesting experiments of the American photographer *Man Ray*, who was the first to bring photography to the level of great visual art.[14] He liberated his photography from the fallacies of art photography by simply doing away with art photography altogether.

The present age throws bookish literature, studio tableaux, and all manner of statues onto the scrap heap, while the new masses welcome the spectacle of silent film art with applause.

Old novels and epics, musty and archaic, are sometimes adapted into quite satisfactory films. The loss of live, spoken, and melodic words has ushered in a *new expressivity*. Being a poem without words, film is an example of modern poetry, which day by day becomes more visual and optical in order to compensate for the diminishing value and efficiency of words. Film actors have no need to recite literature, they are acrobats, jugglers, and clowns; the prosody of film is not the prosody of elevated speech, but the *prosody of bodies in motion.*

Guillaume Apollinaire, that brilliant spirit who foresaw so many future developments, speaks in one of his stories of a painter who is "positioned at the edge of life, facing the wide realm of art" and feels his position undergoing a 180° turn, such that he will be "on the edge of art, facing the wide realm of life." If this turn in artistic orientation is actually under way, it is so thanks in no small part to the powerful intervention of film. The new art, which ceases to be art, positions itself in the center of life by overstepping the boundaries of art.

Illuminated advertising projections, photographs in illustrated magazines—is this still painting?

Hangars, elevators, lighthouses, train stations, factories—is this still architecture? Office furniture, uniform tourist clothing, English Dunhill pipes, fountain pens, typewriters—can this be called the art industry?

---

13 Theater and film critic Artuš Černík was dedicated to promoting modernist trends in art. He also wrote several lyrical film scripts (or "librettos") in the spirit of the poetist movement of the era. These scripts were, however, never realized.

14 As the later version of the present text indicates (see note 6), Teige was interested, above all, in Man Ray's experiments with photograms (also referred to as *rayographs*), photographic images made without the use of a camera by placing objects directly on the surface of photo-sensitive material.

Journals, feuilletons, travel guides, the tragedy of the Titanic or the Lusitania—is this still literature?

Mast-filled harbors, a beautiful night with electric moons, a sailboat on the sea, disappearing into the distance—is this still the lyricism of books?

The shimmy, blues, tango, and even aviatic foxtrot parades above the roofs of the city—is this still dance and choreography?

The boxing-match, demonstrations, soccer—is this still theater? *All of these things can be actors in a film.*

All of this is the realm of modern, purely *vital poetry*. *Poetism* contends that, nowadays, after the burial of artistic tradition, there is only *one singular art with many forms*, and this is living *poetry*. Aesthetics is the aesthetics of poetry. It is possible to evaluate film in the same way as all other art forms. *Legibility—visibility—rapidity* are just as much poetic qualities as they are optical, kinetic, pictorial qualities: *transposition instead of description; an indication of photogenic details, an optical system, rapid and unexpected technology, a life of ideas, mechanical precision, an atmosphere of reality made simultaneous with dreams, ideographic schematization*—this is how the laws and the standards of poetry, images, and film are formulated.

The modern spirit is the spirit of construction. It is the spirit of wisdom. But, in every piece of wisdom, there is a healthy grain of madness. In order for cheerful madness to have value and meaning, it is crucial that it perform its comedy upon a firm foundation of life-wisdom. In order for the Japanese acrobat to not kill himself on the trapeze, it is necessary for the trapeze to be solidly mounted and well constructed.

Two tendencies are the expression of the times. *Constructivism* and *poetism: neither is an artistic -ism in the traditional,* narrow sense of the word.

Constructivism is a method of work; poetism is the atmosphere of life. Constructivism has rigorous rules. Poetism, being both free and without borders, knows no regulation or prohibition. It is the art of life and therefore expresses itself in a delicate, harmonious *bon ton* of life. The poetry of life was germinated in a constructive foundation and grew in harmony with it: clowns and *fantaisistes*[15] are brothers to laborers and engineers. This foundation is *the machine* that satisfies all of our primary and daily needs. Modern art must come to terms with the machine. It does so much more appropriately with photography and film than was the case with futurism. Modern images and modern poetry conjoin and interfuse in film. The visual and poetic emotionality of cinema is unconditionally dependent on cinema's technical perfection. New inventions in photography and projection (e.g., color film, sound film) can lead us directly, without morbid aesthetic speculations, toward new poetic

---

[15]   In Czech, Teige uses the neologism "fantaisista," derived from the French "fantaisiste," which means fantast or dreamer, but can also refer to a music-hall artist.

expressions. Slow motion (as in *When the Clouds Roll By*[16]) provides the illusion of dreaming. Rear projection, matte shots, and the like achieve finesses and effects that were denied even to the most sophisticated poetry.[17] Film does not have developmental labyrinths, peripeties, and variations like the art of the past. Only in the present crisis has it deviated from its own true course. Its path of development corresponds to the process of technological progress and perfection.

We have stated that in the present crisis film production vitally needs to formulate its aesthetic rules more precisely. Its main objective should be to fully utilize and combine its own optical elements with sophistication.[18] It should shut out elements that are foreign to it, carried over from the academic arts. It should mark out its own sovereign space, free of psychology and literature, and without "Caligarism." Yes, *The Cabinet of Dr. Caligari*[19] is the best illustration of how the so-called "art" film has gone astray. This unhealthy, hysterical film is not even a film at all; the hypersensibility of a madman is not modern art.

The theatrical and deformed sets did not translate into a cinematic form, but remained poor paintings. Real persons appeared as ghosts in the unreal scenery. The director forgot that, in film, dramatic character as well as pertinent deformations (even those going to the extreme of caricature) must have an optical and photographic quality. It was a fatal misunderstanding.

In contrast to this deterrent example of an "art" film, it is fitting to bring up some examples of perfectly realized *film art*, particularly of American origin. The films of Harold Lloyd are fascinating not only because of their intense comical nature, but also because of their flawless and exquisite photography. They are a joy for the eyes and the soul. The dramatic nature and suspense of the film *Hurricane's Gal*[20] with Dorothy Phillips can be explained by its pure photogenic quality. Chaplin's exemplary films do not even need to be mentioned here.

It was Louis Delluc who best formulated the photogenic foundations and principles of film. He pointed out that film is *not primarily a narrative art* and that adventure and detective novels featuring Sherlock Holmes, Fantômas, and Buffalo Bill do not yet qualify as film. A shot of a hydroplane taking off is more characteristic of film. For film is *primarily an optical art*. Living painting is an art of spectacle and, be-

---

[16] The adventure-comedy film with Douglas Fairbanks *When the Clouds Roll By* (Victor Fleming and Theodore Reed, USA, 1919).

[17] In the later version of the essay (see note 6), Teige provides an example of such techniques: the German film *Die Straße* (*The Street*, Karl Grune, 1923), which was praised by Siegfried Kracauer and others at the time for its modern visual style.

[18] In the later version (see note 6), Teige gives an example of such an optical element: new film lenses.

[19] *Das Cabinet des Dr. Caligari* (Robert Wiene, Germany, 1920).

[20] Allen Holubar, USA, 1922.

ing just this, it is *a dramatic poem of movement*, the sister of the circus, the cabaret, and the music hall. The filmic muse can learn a valuable lesson in the Medrano.[21] Clowns and acrobats are its instruments. The contemporary film regime believes, perhaps too much, in the dictatorship of movie stars. It is right to boast about Hayakawa, Nazimova, Fairbanks, and Pickford,[22] but its biggest reason to boast are precisely those performers who represent the closest bond to the circus—the clowns, whose ranks include so many poets, Chaplin being the greatest among them.

If film is to refine its aesthetic, it must first master the optical aspect. In the age of the radio concert, we can expect the invention of the *radio film.*

In the meantime, the *"Pathé-Baby"* device enables the introduction of the *home cinema.*[23] Filmic chamber music. You will have cinema in your home just as you have books of lyric poetry and gramophone discs. You will presumably not be projecting adventure serials at home, though, as they should have the participation of a mass audience. It is entirely proper to make the careful distinction between public art (posters, frescoes, street music, etc.) and private art, lyrical poetry, and intimate, lyrical film. Such a film becomes an intimate, lyrical poem of photography and image, without plot, only motion. The principles of photogenic aesthetics can be most distinctly and securely demonstrated in this type of film. Literature and dramaturgy have no business here. It is pure *cinégraphie*, a drama of black and white, a moving optical poem, and the most modern visual surface. The film scores of Hans Richter, W. Gräff, and V. Eggeling[24] are neo-plastic pictures presented in rhythmic motion.

Inextricably and completely bound together with the optical and photogenic emotionality of cinema is its poetic emotionality. Here is where we encounter mod-

---

21 The Medrano was a renowned Parisian circus.

22 Sessue Hayakawa (1889–1973), Alla Nazimova (1879–1945), Douglas Fairbanks (1883–1939), and Mary Pickford (1893–1979) were among the most famous American film stars in Czechoslovakia in the 1920s.

23 Pathé-Baby was a 9.5 mm film format with central perforation developed in 1922 by the Pathé company for the general public and film amateurs, with cameras and projectors that were easy to handle. In Czechoslovakia as well as in other countries, Pathé established a special cinémathèque of 35mm films that were shortened and transferred onto 9.5 mm, which it then sold or rented for home projection.

24 Hans Richter (1888–1976) and Viking Eggeling (1879–1945) were pioneers of abstract cinema. Richter, for example, experimented with the movement of geometric shapes and lines. Werner Gräff (1901–1978) worked as cameraman and scriptwriter with Richter. In the later version of this essay (see note 6), Teige adds a third name: Russian designer and photographer El Lissitzky (1890–1941). In addition, Teige supplements the main text with a photo from one of Eggeling's abstract films and a short profile of the director that focuses on the interrelations between film and painting in his work, particularly in his dynamic visual compositions. Teige also mentions some other avant-garde techniques, such as photograms, fireworks, and reflectorial plays, and lists the names of various painters experimenting with film or photography at the time (e.g. Vladimir Baranoff Rossiné, Victor Brauner, Charles Sheeler, Mieczysław Szczuka, Teresa Żarnowerówna, et al).

ern poetry. Through cinema, the poet speaks to a public made up of simple people, tired laborers who want nothing more than to refresh their nerves, which are consumed by the exhausting struggle for life. He speaks to a public that does not want to be lectured, that has no concern for academic art, but wants only to *watch* and *be entertained*, which naively demands sensations, just like the man who is not permitted into the banquets of our contemporary upper-class culture.

The poet can most effectively find a connection with his audience by means of the cinema. Poets sense that, when writing for the cinema, it does not suffice to simply throw down on paper a rough sketch for the director to develop. Instead, they must record the entire story from the optical point of view, a story conceived directly for cinema. They must construct an entirely cinematic dramaturgy. Such are the librettos of Birot, Epstein, Delluc, Goll, Herbier, and Mahen.[25]

So much for the aesthetics of film.

Is it necessary to say something about the ethics of film?

The ethical mission of cinema only extends as far as the ethical mission of poetry does. Rather than seeing film as a magnificent *agitational* and *tendentious* artistic instrument, an instrument more suitable for this purpose than tendentious rhyming verse, I consider film a *poetic* art, a universal art that represents the complete repertory of life on the globe.

Its daring spirit and intoxicating exoticism, together with its beautiful optimism, could have a most marvelous ethical influence.

This optimism that keeps on smiling through the harsh stages of today, the dangers and eternal uncertainty of tomorrow, and the Yankee optimism of bluff is the most healthy exorbitance. It brings us to laughter at the crossroads of existence. It turns the world topsy-turvy, head over heels, and like a clown in a circus it awakens loud laughter and unmediated joy and merriment.

It preaches merriment as a worldview.

Nothing more.

Isn't that enough?

(1924)

---

[25] Pierre Albert-Birot (1885–1967) is a modernist poet, dramatist and filmmaker who was an adherent of Apollinaire. Louis Delluc (1890–1924) was concerned with film both theoretically and practically. He was an important source of inspiration for the Czech poetists. Marcel L'Herbier (1890–1979) was involved with the French avant-garde of the 1920s, during which time he produced a series of films. Jiří Mahen (1882–1939) is considered among the most important figures in Czech literature from the first half of the twentieth century, and also participated in film events as a journalist. In the later version of the essay (see note 6), Teige adds the names of three Czech poets who published poetist film librettos in 1924–1925: Vítězslav Nezval, Jaroslav Seifert, and Artuš Černík.

Bedřich Václavek
ON THE SOCIOLOGY OF FILM

The sociologist's primary interest in film must be its *production*. Rather than analyzing production in a comprehensive manner, we will merely state here a few facts that contribute to a sociological explanation of the film-product, of the filmic work of art.

The film industry is the youngest of the major industries. In a quarter-century it has passed through all stages of development, from an individual small-scale enterprise to a large capitalist concentration, phases that the other industries passed through much more slowly. This concentration, however, is only organizational and financial—in the interest of film's diversity, production itself has been decentralized and even systematically divided on a geographical basis. Film production today spans the entire globe. In this way, the film business has become international. As an industrial product and a commercial item, film is an industry and a business like any other. Thus the same factors that apply to the socialization of industrial production and the organization of distribution in general also apply to the future of film, for film is a necessary part of life today and therefore cannot remain the plaything of capitalist interests as it has primarily been until now. Of course, the film industry, like every technologically advanced form of production, is closer to this process of socialization than technologically antiquated branches of production (because of the collaboration of a large number of people, the public interest, the system by which companies are granted licenses, etc.).

Film is a typical *product of the times*. It was brought into being by the frantic tempo of contemporary life and a worldly imagination marked by intense topicality. It was formed by technology and the audience. The audience: people who during the day are utterly stressed by their occupation and rush around anxiously, even when they are enjoying themselves. For others, whose occupation is generally defined by boredom: here they wish not to be bored. For this reason, film became the most entertaining and most serious art form of the times, the most modern entertainment for the masses. It took the place of theater, which lost its position because its appeal became limited to the small social class of the educated. The billions spent on the production of films during times of economic distress are the charge humanity must pay for its fantastical illusionism. Statistics show that film exists primarily for modern people who let themselves be carried by the current of the times and live unwittingly by the laws prescribed by the present. Therefore, frequent visits to the movie theater belong today to the industrial worker's standard of living. Film is not, however, of such importance to people whose profession is anchored in the economic systems of older periods (for example, craftsmen) or those who separate themselves from the wider public out of their own personal interests (e.g., scientists).

Film is a *new art form* emerging *from altered technological-economic and social-intellectual conditions. The machine* plays an eminent role for film. Even the intellectual content of film rises and falls with technology. Film is art generated by a machine. It is a true piece of *collective work*. The scriptwriter, the director, and the actor: although individually indispensable, each is merely one component in the great industrial apparatus, and their function is always subordinate to the whole.

Film responds to intellectual needs created *by the division of labor*. The organization of labor in large-scale productions disrupts the close relation between an individual and his occupation in life. When his activity becomes mechanized, a person seeks compensation by striving to fill his leisure time as pleasantly as possible. With the division of labor, an individual's life becomes very one-sided. The division of labor affects not only the factory worker, but has also spread to other occupations. For this reason, the modern person strives to transcend the narrow confines of his life, to enrich his world with the most diverse experiences, to receive spiritual nourishment for his mind. Nowadays, he finds this primarily in the movie theater. As a result of the elevated demands placed on humanity by a century of mechanized labor and the intensified tension and expenditure of strength brought on by the struggle for life, the other side of daily life—i.e. rest and recuperation through entertainment without purpose—had to assert itself, thus providing a counterweight to the tension. Theater and literature, following the path of intellectual ideals, withdrew from daily life by demanding great intellectual strain to comprehend them. But a person is not capable of doing this after work and thus seeks out cinema, which is simply pure play without didactic interests. There, one enjoys the simple *pleasure of looking* and the *desire for poetry*. As if on cue, film appeared at a time when human life was becoming more and more restricted and mechanized—and also less hazardous—as a sort of corrective measure to satisfy *mankind's instinct for adventure*, which through long decades had grown increasingly dormant. Film's rich technological and fantastic-illusionary capacity made this possible.

Many of film's qualities have met *the sensibility and mental constitution of the modern age*. The most characteristic element of film, movement, meets the *dynamism* of modern times, to which it is much closer because of its *primitivism*. — Contemporary speech is a logical filigree. The contemporary poet aims for basic communication. Having no speech, film is limited to psychological elements that can be expressed physically; that is to say, it is based on primitive mental relationships that existed prior to speech. With mere suggestions of gesture, film conjures up a whole free complex of ideas. It is ultimate mechanization, but at the same time ultimate primitivism. Film is thus becoming comprehensible to people of all races and cultures who have no common denominators except for elementary emotions. — Film *meets modern visuality*. Mankind is increasingly losing the gift to create the world from the word. It lives silently. On the floors of tenement blocks, in restaurants, on the streets and in streetcars, people pass each other silently. The newspaper editorial more and more frequently replaces public speeches. Modern man understands a picture without effort and film, for him, is the poetry of vision. Photography has revealed to him the tremendous objectivity and beauty of life.

Modern man is completely oriented toward everyday life. Historical orientation is foreign to him; he has no sense for the problems and questions of classical drama; he is entirely anchored in the present. He is interested in current *social realities* of the contemporary world rather than in history and imaginary problems. For this reason, "social" quickly became the most frequently used word in film advertisements. The social themes depicted by film are characterized by a strong *typification*, by concrete examples. Film drama reaches people by entering their everyday lives. Film meets the tendencies of the modern times with social themes presented typically and concretely, with mundanity and *worldliness*. When it steps beyond the worldly realm, it touches on another typically modern quality: the fantastic. Yet the fantastic in film is simply reality that has been elevated beyond the limits of practicality. Film meets the collectivist-materialist tendency of the times and the *undifferentiated and unproblematic* nature of modern man, particularly the proletariat. Not having a voice, the proletariat is protected in advance from a differentiated psychology.

The cinema has greatly increased mankind's feelings of happiness. It counterbalances the gloomy side of today's mechanized life. Mechanized and standardized work leaves a great empty void in the human soul. Film fills this void with experiences. The excitement and expanded consciousness offered by film provide people with a state of balance that their own narrow, restricted existences could never afford them. Film releases restless energy that has built up in the souls of its spectators. For urban youth, it is a substitute for the activity of play, and it has a hygienic effect on the souls of adults.

Having arisen out of the conditions of the modern spirit, film acts upon it in return and forms it. The cinema educates its public much more rapidly than does a book or the theater. It pulls a person at a remote end of the world out of isolation and connects him to the whole world. It is "everyone's general instruction." It informs. *It teaches a new sociability*. In the cinema, country villagers see the hustle and bustle of the metropolis, its flood of lights, cars, hotel façades, and train stations. City dwellers see wooded mountain ranges, the melancholic lines of telegraph cables along isolated paths, and the serenity of the countryside. Central Europeans see deserts, seas, China, India, and life there. The Japanese participate in American and European life. A *new consciousness of world unity* emerges, a consciousness of world omnipresence that finds its way into modern poetry. The cinema was one of the leading originators of this new cosmic consciousness. The expansion, clarification and refinement of individual consciousness through increased knowledge of the world contribute to the expansion and refinement of the world conscience.

Cinema contributes to man's liberation from the domination of the machine, resulting in his own metaphysical domination over the complex nature of world events. In experiencing the daring adventures of film heroes, a person discharges energy (formerly invested in war ventures) from a theoretically inexhaustible source and neutralizes it.

Film is more social that an individualist book; filmic writing is the most social form of poetry. Poetry was a temporary measure that arose from necessity, a monotonous and unpopular substitute for direct communication. Film leads from the individual to society. It is the art of an age that realizes that the earth belongs to *the people*, that the deepest and loftiest matters are common to people everywhere.

The cinema is a cabinet of curiosities [panoptikum][1] *for the mass public,* of those who live without books, whose vocabulary is the poorest, who never touch a book, who at most come into contact with a pamphlet or an orator shortly before elections, but then fall back once more into their anonymous existence. A public that has no name but exists nevertheless; a public that with its great numbers is the bearer of grand events of spirit and the driving force of the world. A mass that must be won over if an attempt to create a new society is to bear fruit. The cinema is the path to this public, and in particular to the proletariat. *The cinema* these days is *first and foremost a proletarian matter.* The majority of film enthusiasts belong to the lowest social strata. There are not that many filmgoers among the typically petit-bourgeois classes who do not possess the same vivacity of spirit and longing to expand their spiritual horizons as the proletariat. There are very few workers like the one who proclaimed in a survey that he is repelled by film because "good" (meaning the dominant classes) always wins. Since the time that it was discovered as an art form and became "gesellschaftsfähig,"[2] film has certainly fallen and become bourgeois. The first films were full of adventure; they were diabolic and swept spectators away in their

---

[1]   See note 7 in Karel Teige's "Photo Cinema Film," page 128 of this anthology.

[2]   German for "socially acceptable."

maelstrom. But risqué, daring and outrageous matters later disappeared from film and bourgeois high-mindedness became rooted in their place. The bourgeoisie triumphed. Being itself too cowardly for eccentricity, it permitted only one thing in film: shallowness. The captivating tempo was taken from film and obese middle-class ideals became nestled in it. Adventure disappeared as family tragedy and drama emerged. To hell with it! Bomb assassinations are preferable to scenes from family life, provocative impudence preferable to sentimental and weepy tragedy!

But this attempt to rob film of its revolutionary edge did not succeed. The auditorium remains empty during sentimental stories from the petit-bourgeois life, which are particularly abundant in German productions, while, on the other hand, American adventure stories and slapstick fill the seats. Nevertheless, the bourgeoisie displayed good insight when it tried to rob film of its own domain and meaning, for even though film does not specifically advocate proletarian ideology, it does *revolutionize the masses via technology*. It informs and unites the socially oppressed of all nations. It sharpens their sensibility and turns them away from the antiquated poems, novels, and dramas that have been penetrated to the core by the drowsy and inactivating bourgeois attitude. Thank goodness the proletariat nowadays prefers film to novels or theater and only certain intellectually inclined individuals in the proletariat are turned away from film by the tiny hoof of bourgeois ideology. Film today is already a first-rate propaganda medium, not as much for its material and ideas as for its emotional atmosphere and sheer modernity.

Of course, we wish we could make film into a *powerful weapon of ideas*, that we could thrust into the world "ten thousand films against capitalism" that people would feel compelled to see simply because irresistible film stars play in them, that we could produce "kilometers of film against borders and against the barriers of nationalism" (Mierendorff).[3] However, as long as governments prohibit the presentation of films "that instigate class hatred" (yet not those that instigate national hatred), it is unlikely such films will be approved for presentation anywhere outside of Russia at any time in the foreseeable future. For this reason, many Russian films will have to remain limited to Russia, and in the meantime we must allow for the effects of just those aspects of film that are already taking part in the fight against reactionism and for a new world. A person who sees Chaplin's *Shoulder Arms*[4] is more revolutionized against militarism and poses a greater threat to it than the person who listens to political speeches at mass meetings. Hundreds of thousands of films, written in all languages and jargons of the world, become bridges to all, daily overcoming na-

[3]   Carlo Mierendorff, "Hätte ich das Kino!" [1920], in *Kino-Debatte. Texte zum Verhältnis von Literatur und Film 1909–1929*, ed. Anton Kaes (Tübingen: Max Niemeyer, 1978), 145.

[4]   *Shoulder Arms* (Charlie Chaplin, USA, 1918).

tional borders. The spectator sees all parts of the world flying before him. He sees that people of all countries are delighted and tormented by the very same things. Nations get to know each other better from films than from the falsifying politics of the newspapers and the dry statistics in books. Borders fall and man (particularly proletarian man) enters the consciousness of the masses of all nations of the entire earth. And the film spectator, revolutionized by technology, becomes a devoted and assertive partisan of the new world.

(1924)

Jiří Voskovec
PHOTOGÉNIE AND SUPRAREALITY

1. Photography

Photography is the practical science of the *cinégraphic* art. – It is necessary to recognize that photography provides the only aesthetically valid criterion for film beauty, because it is justified scientifically, i.e., optically.

> *Cinégraphie* is an art that relies first and foremost on the technical application of physical optics. A film director can create a film only by virtue of the light that is harnessed by the lens, made rhythmic by the Maltese cross,[1]
> and chemically processed with hydroquinone and gelatin bromide.
> The first requirement of good filmmaking is the mastery of light, which is achieved through the perfect utilization of the film industry's technical capabilities. All other aspects of filmmaking rely on this.
> Photography is the instrumental substance of *cinégraphie*.
> Photography is the first element of *photogénie*, or film aesthetics.

2. What Photography Presents: SUPRAREALITY

Defined thus, photography is nothing more than instrumental, supportive, and qualitative. What, then, does it reveal to us?

> Optically true photography reveals suprareality.
> It is said that a photograph is the most truthful image of reality, that it is perfect realism. This is a fallacy:
> It is true that the photograph undermined realism in painting, but not because

---

[1] Also known as the Geneva drive, the mechanism in a film projector that translates continuous rotation into intermittent rotary motion, moving each film frame intermittently in front of the aperture for projection of the image.

it stripped painting of its *raison d'être* by creating perfect realism. Rather, this occurred because the photograph introduced a new realism: super-realism.

Because: Despite all arguments to the contrary, realism in painting was subjective.
Of course, the realist painted what he "objectively saw," but during this act his
eye was connected via his nervous system to all of his other sensory organs and
to his entire organism. Therefore the optical characteristics of represented reality were contaminated by all of the other characteristics simultaneously perceived
by the painter.

In contrast: Photo-realism is purely objective, because the representation is created
by a machine and is, moreover, merely optical, based purely on light.

Practical evidence of photographic suprareality:
Our eye never sees the world in the same way as photography.

— No mortal has ever in his or her living experience of reality perceived a snapshot. A snapshot registers a fragment of suprareality, which is an uninterrupted
thread running parallel to reality. Suprareality is something like ultraviolet reality, lost to the naked eye but saved by photography.

The fact that each snapshot surprises our eye is not the result of immobility, for
film, which captures suprareality in motion and takes a strip of snapshots in the
optical rhythm of visual life, does not then present ordinary reality, but rather su-
per-reality. After all, if we observe a landscape through the viewfinder of a camera, we see it differently than with the naked eye. We discover in it a kind of
charm for which we search in vain when we take our eyes from the viewfinder,
simply because with the camera we see it in a concentrated, optically super-satu-
rated version, in a suprarealistic version.

From normal reality film distills the luminous alcohol of suprareality:
1 — it emphasizes the optical qualities of the subject and ignores all other qualities,
2 — it creates an enormously massive, plastic space by means of an objective deformation of perspective, which the naked eye, due to habit, only perceives weakly,
3 — it presents a bold black-and-white caricature of the colorful world,
4 — it leaves silent all sounds, scents, and tastes speechless beneath a dazzling cas-
cade of light.

— And, until film exists in natural colors, things will remain the same:
Reality filtered by a recording apparatus always becomes
suprareality, an optical review of reality.
Suprareality is the objective essence of *cinégraphie*.
Suprareality is the second element of *photogénie*.

3. Photogénie

Photogénie is the aesthetic of *cinégraphie*, or film art.

If we combine two preceding elements, the instrumental and the objective, that is, if we photograph suprareality, we get the basis of *photogénie*.

The aesthetic laws of *photogénie* thus rest on the scientifically legitimate properties of these two elements.

At the beginning, we stated that the fundamental requirement of good cinema is masterful utilization of the technical possibilities of film optics. We also stated that the only valid aesthetic criterion of *cinégraphie* is optical perfection, because it is scientifically justified. This does not mean that an impeccably photographed film will necessarily be artistically correct. It is necessary to understand the criterion of optical perfection as a standard with which we evaluate a film in terms of optics and which we do not abandon even when critiquing the overall rhythm and plot of the film.

– The form of any human product is dictated by the material.

The material with which cinema works is light; light determines what can be filmed and what cannot.

– *Photogénie* is art.

1 – To harmonize these unalterable rules of photography with the artistic *sujet* of a film implies:

2 – to allow the photographic images of suprareality to make purely optical impressions,

3 – to introduce the spectator to a world where optical beauty does not dissolve into theatrical schmaltz,

4 – to avoid destroying the evident and magically primitive language of light with symbolism and romantics quite reprehensibly adapted from hackneyed literary clichés.

– Thus understood, *photogénie* permits two types of *cinégraphie*:

1 – Pure *cinégraphie*, the lyric poetry of light, an unbounded hymn of light, whose only rule is the perfect rhythmic movement of optical realities; a suprarealistic ode, a chain of optical associations whose links are suprarealistic elements. (See also Teige's articles on optical film[2] and the librettos of Teige and Seifert.[3])

---

[2] Teige's articles on film appeared in the years 1922–1925 in the journals *Život*, *Host* and *Pásmo*. They were collected, together with other studies, in Teige's book *Film* (Praha: Václav Petr, 1925) and reprinted by Petr Král in *Karel Teige a film* (Praha: Filmový ústav, 1966).

[3] In *Pásmo* 1, no. 5–6 (1924–1925, 7–8), K. Teige and J. Seifert published the film libretto "Pan Odysseus a různé zprávy" [Mr. Odysseus and various reports], an attempt to realize their ideas about pure cinema, which, in their view, should be an optical drama of things in motion. They published another film libretto in 1925 called "Přístav – Partitura lyrického filmu" [Harbor: a score for a lyrical film]. Together with other film scenarios, these were reprinted by Viktoria Hradská in the collection *Česká avantgarda a film* (Praha: Čs. filmový ústav, 1976).

2 – A perfect optical epic, a film with a plot—which, however, should not be an adaptation of a literary novel or a reworking of a dramatic play—a film whose narrative plot is just as suprarealistic as the filmed objects. Photography itself condenses reality and creates suprareality from it. *Photogénie*, which provides photography with meaning and artistic order, must utilize reality in the formation of appropriately condensed optical drama: the dynamic rhythm of an insanely super-real plot, the language of hypnotic details, the syncopation of rapid changes of setting. From all of this the viewer's emotions arise and excite his entire sensibility, yet only via the direct optical path, without mediation by his literary or theatrical reminiscences.

Examples? Except for Chaplin, who was the first to perfectly understand the essence of cinema and accommodated it to his own personal genius, thus creating an entirely unique type of cinema, we have yet to find in contemporary productions even one film in accordance with this ideal. Yet there are American films that come close to it, and all over the world today film projects are emerging that represent important steps toward reaching it.

— In closing, let us then address that fundamental rule for harmonizing perfect photography with the rhythm of cinema:

The secondary optical qualities of film (direction, rhythm, the course of the plot) must be commensurable with its primary optical qualities (i.e., photographed suprareality); that is, with its photographic conception and the selection of optical *sujets*.

Louis Delluc wrote: *"La photogénie, c'est l'accord de la photo avec le ciné."*[4]

(1925)

---

[4]   *"Photogénie* is the harmony between photography and cinema." Voskovec slightly misquotes the original text: "La photogénie, au contraire, c'est l'accord du cinéma et de la photographie!" (In Louis Delluc, *Photogénie*, Paris: de Brunoff, 1920, later reprinted in Louis Delluc, *Écrits cinématographiques I: Le Cinéma et les Cinéastes*, ed. Pierre Lherminier, Paris: Cinémathèque Française, 1986, 36.)

Vítězslav Nezval
PHOTOGÉNIE

Every art form has its own specific formative elements from which it is composed and which it must respect if it is not to lose its proper function.

Every art form is psychological, both in terms of its genesis and in its effect. With the aid of form and by means of the senses, its goal is to create inside us the same sense of harmony we feel when observing perfect beauty.

In accordance with the senses used to perceive it, art creates appropriate forms of expression.

In this respect, film is a new, purely optical art form. Only ideas that have been perfectly visualized fall within the realm of this new art form created by a century of technical invention.

Therefore, film aesthetics is first and foremost the aesthetics of a new optics.

The image, existing in constant motion, determines the elements of this art form.

Its formative material is everything that is visible and in motion.

Platonic beauty, that is the beauty that we perceive and that ushers us immediately into a state of harmony, without even having any sort of utilitarian relation to it. It is the highest aesthetic ideal.

Yet beauty does not exist as an eternal concept.

It changes from age to age and represents the spiritual sum of ideals of a particular era. There are very few elements of reality that can be considered standard forms of beauty, because they correspond to those elements in humanity that have not changed throughout our development. Otherwise, the idea of beauty changes from generation to generation.

In each era, to perceive this Platonic beauty is a fate afforded to only a small number of individuals who perfectly depersonalized themselves and whose sense of beauty does not presume any sort of indirect benefit, being in and of itself a pure benefit for the soul. This cold, aristocratic beauty requires a man for whom every sense is entirely a spiritual matter, and is, therefore, not a property for the wider public, which is not contemplative.

The thing that links a practical person to beauty is an intimate relationship: human interest. In order for pure visual beauty to achieve its perceptive potential for the masses, it is necessary to place between it and humanity a link through which beauty is transferred and mediated. This link is dramatic action.

A purely formal action, being itself both content and action, does not satisfy common human interest, because it requires cultivated "senses with a brain."

Given this humanized perspective, film aesthetics must be sought in the proper proportion of optical and kinetic elements in action.

Why is dramatic action required to attain and express harmony? For the highly civilized person, form and movement are themselves drama enough and do not require mediating action. The relationship of the straight lines, curved lines, and movements created by reality in motion is sufficient drama for those with a cultivated sensibility. This drama unfolds without regard to its application, entangles and untangles itself, and composes a sublime harmony.

This process of entanglement and disentanglement constant to all forms of life, or, in other words, this pursuit of harmony, must be made manifest to persons with a less mature sensibility—its pure formal qualities must be demonstrated through dramatic action. Thus action functions as an intermediary between pure beauty and human interests. Dramatic action in film is a translation of the formal process in terms of harmony.

The summation of all the intrinsic elements employed by film is called *photogénie*.

As a consequence of what is discussed above, *photogénie* is of a dual character.

Photogénie in the purely formal sense of the word is the constant drama of the relationships of shapes and movements in light and shadow. And *photogénie* in the broader sense is the constant drama of the relationships of shapes and movements in light and shadow as employed by dramatic action.

Film aesthetics thus relies, above all, on these basic questions:

What is artistic visuality in terms of film?

What is movement in terms of film?

What is action in terms of film?

Finally, the fundamental premise for these questions is the answer to the following:

What is the essence of modern beauty?

It is of primary importance to answer this last, complicated question, for only on the basis of this answer is it possible to solve the previous questions.

There are centuries that can be characterized with epithets—heroic, rationalistic, contemplative, romantic, decadent, speculative, energetic, etc.

Without a doubt, these last two epithets are fitting for the twentieth century.

The twentieth century is characterized by the clear desire for harmony and creation, as is manifest primarily in the century's technical inventions, revolutions, and modern culture. Invention, mobility, and maximum work efficiency are compelled by the law of economy, which has imposed on the century an artistic taste that emerges from the most current products and facts. We can call this artistic taste classical in the sense that it relies on relative simplicity in its means and maximal perfection and effectiveness in its form. Being creative in the full sense of the word, the twentieth century does away with any kind of ornamentation or stylization. In those moments where previous centuries sought out embellishment, this century strives for the most elementary and sublime fullness and beauty of essence. Without a doubt, it is the machine, being both mathematical and, in terms of its effects, fantastical, that is the source of this constructive classicism that is gradually appropriating all fields of civilization and culture. This can be seen in normalized factories, constructivist architecture, and in the arts.

Classical beauty always lay in the magnificence of the line. Classical beauty is beauty that arises from the revelation of essence. The essence of a singular existence, represented in a clear composition with all of existence, is the highest form of poetry.

This poetic spirit, this discovery and harmonization of essences, is the spirit of this century. This defines the century's sense of beauty.

Film is the most typical product of the contemporary age; it has existed in no other century. If we look at its history, we find in film the highest realizations of this spirit.

We must, however, return to the more general questions.

Film's visuality differs from that of all other preceding optical arts in that it is dynamic. Through the alteration of its compositional proportions, film ceases to be a picture and becomes kinetic.

As an individual moment, film can learn a great deal from painting, primarily the lesson of composition.

Film as a summation of moments has a composition in motion. In this respect, filmic composition is connected to composition in painting solely in terms of its specific imagined structure, whose anchors are the steadfast, stable components of the scene. Everything else moves within this framework as on a grid. Constant care must be taken so that the fourth dimension created by motion is kept in constant (and, of course, moving) proportion to the basic structure.

Thus far, we have dealt only with the summation of moments that create a homogenous, optical framework, i.e., a scene. Every scene, however, leaves behind a trace in the optical memory; I would say that it persists, and that it is necessary for the following scene to maintain the same spiritual perspective if it is to avoid causing violence to the persistence of vision. Two scenes, here, must correspond optically when one no longer even exists, except in the memory.

Although they are, of course, a necessary starting point, the rules of composition in painting and sculpture are certainly not sufficient for this type of artistic visuality. In terms of composition, the scriptwriter and director must study works of both older and modern visual arts (see the article "The Development of Czech Film" by -ol.-).[1] In doing so, they can find many examples of perfect harmony and can occasionally learn how to avoid fundamental flaws in the composition of scenes.

Under certain conditions of light and color, film can successfully record the entire visible spectrum. Nevertheless, it is never naturalist in the full sense of the word. In film, reality is distorted by the effect of ultraviolet rays on the one hand and by the restricted sensitivity of the emulsion to color and light on the other, such that it never exactly coincides with phenomenal reality. In order for ideal harmony to be realized in film, it is often necessary to deform reality (with lighting, makeup, etc.)

Film is a dictator that embraces everything for which it has a use, and treats everything else with irony. Although it finds thousands of incentives in the phenomena of the contemporary world, it must first revise them all. Otherwise it would function falsely. Its optical heart adheres to all that is in harmony with its own capabilities.

A man has no desire for repetitious forms, wanting instead to constantly discover newer and newer forms. He is not concerned with the imitation of reality, but with the discovery of reality in all of its hidden forms. Therefore, film seeks out forms not only in the present, but also in the past and in utopian visions. From this point of view, a historical film is just as modern as a film that deals with contemporary matters. Of course, it is not necessarily the aim of a historical film to interpret the past (which does not interest us all that much anyway), but to discover everything in the laws of history that appeals to our modern sensibility. According to this interpretation, even the historical film represents the distribution of optical wealth. Appropriately chosen historical clothing, i.e., appropriately fitting to modern taste and visuality, can highlight some movements and contours of the human body that would otherwise remain hidden and unutilized if modern clothing were used.

When interpreted correctly, the action of a film is of a completely different type than that of a novel. In film, the narrative action is subordinated to concerns of visuality and laws of motion; it does not derive from *fabula*, but rather from character, i.e., from sensibility. The actions that emerge from Fairbanks's characters are ones chosen by him and are the pretexts for visually motional situations. This is the case for all films created by a genuine individual. The genuine individual serves as a guarantee of true modernity, which is born only of true individuals. Therefore, film does

---

[1] Nezval refers to a text by Zet Molas (signed as -ol.-): "Vývoj našeho filmu" [The development of Czech film], *Český filmový svět* 3, no. 4 (October 1924), 6.

not require strange or astonishing dramatic actions (viz. Epstein), but even here it is necessary to pay attention to good arrangement and selection. The dramatic action serves to link filmic situations together and to make them more accessible to the spectator. Otherwise, the situations remain simply fragmented segments and are thus flawed in their effects. One must keep this fact in mind whether conceiving an original filmic action or adapting a novel. The choice of sources for dramatic action is determined by convention. Yet how we transfer the action into the language of *photogénie* is a fundamental question that demands its own specific solution.

As a result, *photogénie* is created through the equal efforts of the librettist, the scriptwriter, the director, the actor, and the cameraman. *Photogénie* emerges from the absolute harmony of their collaboration.

(1925)

Vítězslav Nezval
FILM[1]

Down with the two idols! The first one, *ars academia*, was already threatened with extermination by shrapnel from the *mitrailleuse* of dadaism. But now academic art in all of its forms is once again engulfing the shattered remains of dadaistic bohemianism.

We must agree with those who seek to warn film of the Muses.

But there is another idol: the laughable and unintelligent idol of dilettantism, who sneers at art in the same way as a painter of postcards sneers at Monet's *Boulevard des Capuchines*.[2]

The disciples of cultural waste, whose vitality and courage are no greater than that of a blind man who lies down next to a beehive.

They must be expelled from film in the same way that they are expelled from academies.

Film—a speech machine and speech itself.

The abstract arts, blockaded by modern concepts of beauty, mixed up languages in an attempt to create something interesting that was, from the very beginning, as lifeless as Esperanto; the abstract arts—miraculous, but lacking the general faculties of a native language.

Film is a native language without a country, the Sanskrit of a new humanity. Being at home everywhere, it does not have the sorrows of the Wandering Jew. Its face does not resemble the faces of Janus. It is not bound to the past and does not fear the future. Behold this quivering leaf, which, already lost forever in the universe, can yet be brought to life at any time on the cinema screen—one pulse from the rhythm of eternity, which can convince us at any time that the Divine is ageless.

---

[1]   This text, originally published in the journal *Český filmový svět* [Czech film world] 3, no. 10–11 (1925), 6–7, was later included with minor alterations in Nezval's book *Falešný mariáš* [Fake marriage game] (Praha: Odeon, 1925).

[2]   Monet's *Boulevard des Capuchines*: in 1873, French painter Claude Monet (1840–1926) painted this famous view of the Boulevard des Capuchines filled with great movement of people and carriages and a colorful atmosphere in the attempt to capture the "landscape of the city."

There is no need to think up new divinities, heroes, or forms. All is provided in time and light. Old languages: *aqua, l'eau, Wasser, voda*. The modern arts have employed a sort of generalization, an Ido.[3] But how water projected on a cinema screen talks! Speech that is as comprehensible to Papua New Guineans and Frenchmen as it is to poets.

It speaks to all! To old Europe and to territories without history. What use, then, do we still have for dilettantes with their perennial love triangles, detectives, and melancholy prostitute make-up!

Let's turn to the stars: Chaplin, Fairbanks, Mary Pickford, Alla Nazimova, Lillian Gish. We've loved their magical canes, with which they evoked laughter; we've loved their childishness, fragility, and quivers of love. But film is more than just stars.

Film should not concern itself with a drama, novel, heroic or idyllic epic, or a funny or tragic story. These are merely the lingering legacy of an older art form, as is the photographic chiaroscuro created by artistic film directors in imitation of Leonardo. Film should concern itself with clairvoyant arrangement and human variety. And the Broadway competitions that reek of art and business are just as far removed from film as the Olympic Games from Euripides.

We must rejuvenate all of our senses so that they can perceive as a camera lens and have the casual accuracy of Archimedes and the brain of Newton. We must lie down beneath a tree and let our nose be broken by a falling apple so that we can uncover eternal laws for people to use for their benefit. "The imitation of nature" and "the reassessment of nature" ring today like empty slogans. They both put their faith in the Muses. All you painters, poets, and philosophers have, in the process of developing one new form or axiom, ignored the other thousands of forms and rules that occur every second. Farewell, Muses, and farewell, stars! Thanks to inertia, your charm will survive for several decades yet. Farewell, artists, whose slogan is *création*![4] Your story will be told just like the fairy tale about the Tower of Babel. Farewell, adherents of art as imitation! Neither Zola nor Dostoevsky was able to provide us with Paris or with a human being. We are not dealing with *création*, nor *imitation*,[5] not with Muses or with stars. But with film! For the word "naturalism" has been discredited by both idols. And from now on film, which originally sought to capture the gait of a horse and has since been applied to art, will be dedicated to its mission. Science and poetry—isn't it reminiscent of those great epochs of now-extinct religions!

Film. The new Sanskrit. But what to talk about in the first place?

Contemporary perception. A point that has been on the program of all modern aesthetics. On the program. A point justified by a civilization of speed that hammers

---

3   Ido: an artificial international language developed in 1907 as a revised Esperanto.

4   *Création*: Nezval uses the French word for creation instead of the Czech one.

5   *Imitation*: as with *création* (see note 4), Nezval uses the French word here.

things into itself, changing its sense of perspective. Simultaneism and so many other names!

Film alone is able to achieve this without the use of petrified syntax. The sea ripples on the roof of a villa while fireworks explode in a garden nearby, and in the doorway is the dissolving vision of a woman who lived there twenty years ago. Film alone is able to achieve that which structures music—harmony and counterpoint. An optical pipe organ. Its scales define the *photogénie*. With a marching rhythm. The whole tempo is broken down into sixteenth notes. With the addition of syncopations *à la* a jazz band. A matter of psychology and technology. Simultaneity of action and memory in equal intensity. Dreams have gradually achieved superiority and now fill up the screen with a music-hall performance, while all that remains of the dreaming man are enlarged eyes fluttering over a glass of absinthe.

Film technique. This is not a matter of aesthetics. Luckily, film thus far does not have aesthetics and will thus in the future have one unnecessary battle less. Although the sea floor or a landscape filmed from an airplane does indeed pass muster with regard to aesthetics. People without embellishments. A beautiful film does not reproduce forms. It manufactures them firsthand. The point is to recognize in film a machine, endowed with flawless nerves by human ingenuity, devouring matter and creating the afterlife. (Let's call it that.) From a certain distance, the lens devours an anthill. Two hundred pictures a second. A permissible fever. But dangerous! The stomach works away. And then on the cinema screen. The film projector, speaking as if from a dream. Anthill. Yet we have never seen this before. Film does not reproduce forms. It manufactures them firsthand. And yet nothing other than an absolutely precise reproduction, the complete achievement of a task. A matter of technology and spirit.

Mystification in directing. Away with the old showmanship! A definitive separation between theater actors and film stars. It is possible to emulate emotions every night before the sold-out theater boxes. Vocal performance will be determined by temperature.

But who ventures to repeat his smile from yesterday? Repeat! Obviously, film direction will completely break from the habit of such drills. For certain.

The star: a supremely fine-tuned person who is deserving of this crown. Hanging with all his senses on the current second. For the time of exposure is the sole painter of *valeurs*.[6] In the face, while walking. The star: must be so perfect as to emulate the operation of a machine. The chord of C# major. Does this piano have a bad soundboard? Let's test it. A bit out of tune? Everything in luxurious order. A C# major chord.

---

[6] *Valeur*: French for "aesthetic value" or "tonal value of colors."

It is the same for stars: to produce an impeccable C# major chord. But what does this mean? There are no norms here. The production of stars is not standardized or patented. Lillian Gish—a violin, manufactured only once in human history. From now on, instruments will give birth to themselves. The task of the director—to properly strike the C# major chord. But this presumes that he knows his way around the keyboard. To figure out the basic key in which this particular person is tuned. What a task! And to wait until the required C# chord is coaxed out. The star is surprised, but not humbled. An instrument in tense expectation of what will be struck on it. The director in the same tense expectation of the response. The response that will be unexpected and with complete determination.

To achieve the reflection of a father's death in a close-up of his daughter's face. This is the task.

Let's try rehearsing it. The father is completely healthy. Like the healthiest of men. So how shall one find all the possible reasons for the death of the healthiest of men? The analogies are liberating and murderous. For just this moment, you must be a complete and utter tyrant. What's going on in your face, star? Trembling for fear of your father's life? The director likewise believes the mystification of the task at hand. These reasons are probable, after all. He experiences with you the terror at the death of your father, the father of you both, a father in general. Just like you? He experienced terror. But you are a woman. Father, do you want to know how much your daughter loved you today at 10:15? The cameraman was filming. And this momentary drama, which actually took place today at 10:15, will be a component of and a moment in the newest film spectacle.

[1925]

Artuš Černík
THE TASKS OF THE MODERN FILM LIBRETTIST

1. To abandon the complex plotlines
>> that have been already sufficiently toyed with by life,
>>> Dumas,
>>> Conan Doyle.

2. To study the reactivity of the human spirit
>> to various optical phenomena,
>>> combinations,
>>> sequences,
>>> alternations,
>>> durations.

3. To understand the genuine function of the photographic plate and photography,
>> *to discover and apply*
>> *the laws of "l'art pour*
>> *l'artisme" to photography.*

4. By means of a precise screenplay, to wrest impossible realism,
>> naturalism,
>>> hyper-romanticism,
>>> and literary plagiarism
>>> from the hands of the director.

5. To prescribe experiments of a purely visual character to the camera operator.

6. To find a storyline that is in no way dramatic or novelesque, but rather a story of forms,

of nuances, of lights and shadows,
of constant shapes and shapes in motion,
of horizontal and vertical shapes,
of regular or disruptive rhythms.

7. To become familiar with the qualities of the lenses, photo plates, and the effects

of light before learning the rules of purely
external narrative, in which 10,000 extras,
Buenos Aires, and real
Nile crocodiles appear.

8. To be a modern poet, for whom poetry has ceased to play its traditional role

as the shell of a worm-infested walnut.

(1925)

Film as Service:
Functionalism and Ideological Struggle

PART THREE

Vít Obrtel
ARCHITECTURE AND FILM

Architecture is a matter of realization. It is reality endowed with a purpose. Based on this purpose, the form will emerge as a function of the material. In the building trade, form does not exist in and of itself. The blueprints for a room, a house, a city are organized for human existence.

Film is a series of realized unrealities. The duration of a filmic still life does not have the longevity of a material product. Its purpose was achieved with the final turning clicks of the camera. The organization of a scene, its blueprint, is naturally arranged according to human criteria for the assertion of its formal priorities. Even here, of course, form does not cease to be a function of the material.

Film—optical effect. Of all the senses, only sight takes part in it, for film is a pure art of spectacle. Perfect mechanics, perfect direction—perfect film.

To what does film refer? To the whole world. But this relationship is plastic, in the sense that it forms a new reality. The beautiful *reality* of a world that *does not exist.*

In the end, only the most perfect and purest forms of all remain. It is the task of the director to introduce them in a way that is in harmony with the public. It is the work of the set designer to discover or to create these forms.

Dancing girls and the magic of the night, landscapes, snow and skiing competitions, the circus or the still life of a villa or a park, the mechanical lyricism of luminous pictures, all will invariably be a matter of form governed by the will of the director. (Assuming, of course, that he has technical mastery of film.)

In life, an architect is not always able to realize his ideas. Financial concerns and the indecisiveness of the public hamper his work. Yet forms persist in his imagination. Film enables him to acknowledge them, not as the architecture of enduring existence, but as the architecture of temporary formal beauty. It is precisely the temporariness of the medium, the ephemeral quality of the material, that entitles him to this spectacular, perhaps even fantastical, assemblage of components in magical spaces (form is a function of material!!), where a drama of light and shadow unfolds in an artificial milieu.

All the elegance and subtle beauty of the material, optimized to the most extreme static limit. All the stylishness and sophistication of composition. Creative courage and a crafty combination of unexpected and purposeful conjunctions of material. These are the means with which to achieve the purpose—modern film.

(1926)

Jan Kučera
ADVERTISING AND CINEMATIC ART

Advertising and film did not meet by chance. The circumstances of the century and their own specific natures brought them together. You might say that advertising existed prior to film. Yes, but how imperfect it was, barely scraping by and limited in its possibilities. Film is fertile soil for advertising, immeasurably more fruitful than any poster or light mechanism.

For advertising requires movement and the possibility of manifold transformations. It must captivate and astound. That is why static advertising wore out long ago. It had exhausted its possibilities. Nowadays every common merchant strives for advertising that is at least somewhat dynamic. He pays a man to walk through the streets with a placard displaying the company's name, or he frames the name in a box fitted with light bulbs, half of which intermittently turn off and on. Then large businesses began promoting themselves with complex luminous advertising installations that could even present short actions. Yet mechanisms made of light bulbs are extremely cumbersome and expensive, and unsuitable for the growing demand for advertising. They are fixed to one particular location. Film is much cheaper and its internationality is invaluable. Thus I believe that, before long, cinema alone will be capable of fully achieving the tasks of advertising.

I will not expand here further on the goals and practice of advertising, as I am not qualified to do so. In this article, I aim merely to specify the *relationship between advertising and cinematic art*. And here: film advertising as well as film newsreels (for these two fields are not all that different from each other) *influence and fertilize cinematic art*. This relationship, however, is not reciprocal, a fact that is rooted in the low standard of contemporary film art, which is unable to distribute any of its wealth since it does not yet possess sufficient means for itself. This is so because its artists have not yet managed to bring it to the place for which it is truly intended: to realms of movement, light, and form. Advertising, however, beckons filmmakers. It beckons them to a place where, in balmy baths of light, motion molds matter, changes it, endows it with new qualities, and sets it in a different world, where its tasks and capabilities are distinct from its tasks and capabilities in this world. In that world, dead objects come to life and vigorously proliferate. In that world, light is not bound to a finite number of immobile bulbs assembled into a stiff metal construction.

Film art should likewise sink its roots into new, original territory. Like advertising, it should be animated and internationally intelligible. The freedom in handling the visual forms of our world that true film art so demands was first displayed in advertising. The director of advertising films was not afraid to create absolute films, to use nonfigurative editing, and to avoid the use of intertitles.

And the director-artist turns to advertising for training.

We find proof of this primarily in Russia (Pudovkin et al.). Hopefully this will also be the case in our country, if the Elektajournal[1] company, already highly distinguished in advertising, propaganda, and newsreel films, successfully enters the realm of feature films without neglecting to implement the qualities and experiences it acquired in its original field of production.

The film art of the future will therefore be tremendously indebted to advertising films and newsreels.

And where will their relationship go from here? Naturally, their journey together can only proceed within the limits of practicality. The attempt to transform advertising film into artistic film or vice-versa would result in utter kitsch. Advertising is and will always be an entirely technical and commercial system. Its power lies in the pureness of its supremely functional form. This applies to newsreels as well. Art, however, will take a different path. Once it is tamed by the craftsmanship of advertising films, the visual world will be put to use in another place where it will have a different value—just like a tamed animal hitched to the yoke but also trained in the circus. All contemporary arts eschew dilettantism, and the more modern film art becomes, the more it requires skilled craftsmanship. Yet it does not stop at craftsmanship. It amplifies it. It amplifies the practice of the American serial film (which is completely nonartistic), and increases and will continue to increase the returns of the plainly practical and most modern craft: the cinema of advertising.

(1928)

---

[1]   Elektajournal: The most important Czech producer of nonfiction films during the second half of the 1920s, which, between 1925 and 1930, produced *Elektajournal* (the *Elekta* newsreel). Jan Kučera began working with Elektajournal in 1928 as a student. In 1931, when production of the original newsreel was stopped and replaced by *Československý filmový týdeník* [Czechoslovak weekly newsreel], he became its editor, cameraman, and producer. Between 1926 and 1929 the Elektajournal company also produced several silent feature films, but with no major success.

Jan Kučera
FILM AND BUILDING

There is a classic American cartoon that bears the title *Sky Scraping*.[1] The vitality of this animated short derives from the rhythm of image and sound, whose tight and direct order permeate the crazy conception of the film's very modern theme, i.e., the construction of a huge iron building. The skyscraper in this cartoon rises above the immense street of an unnamed big city, up beyond the clouds in a sky that is most definitely not the sky we know. Likewise, the workers below are not simply your everyday laborers, for they bear the likenesses of animals, and yet are strangely engaged in real human activities, in an astonishingly convincing manner. These nimble and wily builders jump along the structure, from line to line, according to the strict tempo set by some kind of mystical foreman; they carry in and assemble the two-dimensional forms that are the building materials in this realm; and, with a suspiciously cavalier attitude to the laws of gravity, they encircle the skeleton of the restless building with a mesh of ever-newer structures. Their movement both at work and at rest is a dance, or perhaps it would be better to say that the dance that is their normal form of vital expression sometimes tends toward work and sometimes tends toward rest. The rhythmicality of these little drawn creatures is so convincing that the entire universe around them—the universe that we peer into through the linear borders of the film screen—is swept up in a collective jig in which objects usually considered to be inanimate, such as bolts, rivets, and girders, are awakened from their rigid slumber like a colony of Sleeping Beauties. Things everywhere start to jump and hop, bend and turn, bow down and rise up; they rumble, hum, and fiddle, but not out of pleasure or in their own groove, but rather as a unified, monolithic whole, in a true and thoughtful community, in the brotherly cementation of all those things that belong together in accordance with the law of purpose and form. The cartoon ends with the rhythmic harmony of the parts and the whole, the harmony of all things in this universe that cinema has discovered.

---

[1]   Dave Fleischer, 1930.

Figures 2–9. Stills from the film *Stavba*, shot by director Jan Kučera with architects Josef Havlíček and Karel Honzík on the building site of the General Pensions Institute in Prague. The film was intended to capture the tempo and character of the modern building process, and was a production of the Elektajournal company [Original caption].

I do not think this comedy should be seen as a model for those who wish to make a film about modern construction, but it could certainly be a great source of inspiration, for it offers the quintessential components, both ideological and visual, that make up such a film. It even has an analytic aspect in which details play the role of the whole, and which leads to a synthesis in which the hierarchy of components within the completed work is legitimized.

The modern reinforced steel construction is one of the most characteristic manifestations of our era. Its persuasive power lies in its precise concretization of the needs of contemporary man, whose interests are met both in the rapid tempo with which the building can be made and in the type of material from which it is made. Its creation is full of a drama that derives from the process by which the building materials are modified. As determined by their chemical and physical structure, these materials add a kernel of pathos to the building's image. On the way to their predetermined form and place, these materials undergo a series of metamorphoses in preliminary stages during which they are modified. The contemporary construction site is a rich world of values that are systematically focused on their anticipated goal, like iron filings toward a magnetic pole, and whose character is transformed in accordance with their purpose. Yet this order tends to remain hidden from the observer during the creation of the work. It seems to me the purpose of the film[2] is precisely to discover the systematic order that the builder is specifying as he realizes his plans. At the same time, however, the depiction of a construction sequence should not lose sight of the moments of seeming confusion and chaos that accompany construction work. It is this very counterpoint between the order that corresponds to the purpose on the one hand and the confusion that arises during the realization process on the other that allows drama to be born on the screen, where each individual picture contains a certain pathos. The life of a building is made manifest in the continuous crystallization of various substances that are connected and fused together until a certain point at which balance is achieved and the work is completed. This wavy trajectory of the building process is penetrated by another line that is straight, sharp, and unswerving: the trail of thought that links the flat architectural design to the three-dimensional, material result.

The temporal and spatial dimensions of the film are filled out by the work process, during which the focus of importance shifts from individual components to ever-growing wholes, from raw and more unsteady forms to forms that are riper and more stable. In representing these shifts, the filmic depiction relativizes space and

---

2   Here, Kučera refers both to films about modern architecture in general as well as to a film project of his own, a documentary called *Stavba* [Building] depicting the construction of a functionalist building in Prague for the General Pension Institute (Všeobecný pensijní ústav). The film was never finished; for further details, see the introduction to this anthology; for stills from the film, see facing page.

time, lending the picture not only an expressivity of content, but also an internal graphic dynamism. At first, the film-image deals with specific components that will become subordinate in the end product, yet at this moment it nevertheless treats these components as primary wholes. Then it shifts to newer and different components, in which entire systems of aesthetic value are revealed. These components include cement production, the bending of iron rods, window production, laboratory experiments testing the qualities of reinforced concrete, etc. Gradually, though, these elements recede from the foreground and the screen is filled with more complicated components. In the end, the camera represents the highest whole—the final result itself as a single, now-unchanging value. All of the iron components, struts, and girders that were at the forefront of interest in the beginning are classified, subordinated, and concealed within the whole, which now reigns supreme over space and time. In reality, the completed building stands before us like a carcass, resembling a coral reef that has been abandoned by its creatures. Film, on the other hand, is able to capture alive that which created the building: the formative labors, the process of crystallization, and the work of the people, in which the most authentic face of the times is reflected. In this sense, while a building itself is more like a monument to the past, a film is a document of the present. At the same time, through its lenses, the film camera discovers new and beautiful faces of substances at rest and in motion; it reveals a new, unified, rhythmic, and law-abiding world beneath the stiff, ordinary façade of present-day reinforced concrete. This is reminiscent of the intentions of the creators of that American cartoon.

Thus, having mastery over time and space, film will express the most fundamental aspects of building. At the same time, the construction process will provide film with rich visual material.

[1933]

Lubomír Linhart
THE PROLETARIAN FILM STRUGGLE
IN CZECHOSLOVAKIA[1]

Half of all cinemas in Czechoslovakia belong to the reactionary, semi-fascist gymnastics organization Sokol, which is also a subdivision of the Social Democratic Party.
Of course, the programs in these cinemas do not vary—bourgeois "commercial" films
are in perpetual rotation, while Soviet films are boycotted. In response to the dumb-
ing down of the masses by the bourgeois film, "*proletarian film criticism*" was established. Its purpose is to enlighten the proletarian public as to the true nature and
hidden political agendas of capitalist film production and to support Soviet film. Of
course, *proletarian film criticism* is carried only by the Communist Party's daily newspaper *Rudý večerník* [Red evening paper], which, every Saturday, runs critiques of
all Prague cinema programs written by proletarian critics. These critiques cover all
films. Our most current mission is to increase the staff of proletarian film critics, particularly from among the ranks of working-class correspondents reporting on film,
with whom the editors of *Rudý večerník* have established connections thanks to the
film column.[2] In February, a special course for proletarian film critics will be organized. The first lessons will be dedicated to general issues of the Marxist sociology of
art and to broader artistic-ideological problems with respect to film. After this course
has ended, the participants will conduct further courses in their own residential areas based on the notes, materials, and information they obtain in the main course.
With this "avalanche" method, it will be possible to eradicate "film illiteracy" and to

---

[1] Translated from the German original by Kevin B. Johnson.

[2] In November 1927, the daily newspaper *Večerník Rudého práva* (published after 1928 as *Rudý večerník*) established a special column titled simply "Film." Initially, the weekly column, which specifically addressed working-class spectators and asked them to contribute their own film reviews, was under
the supervision of Czech communist writer Julius Fučík. Five months after its inception, it was rena-
med "Filmy, které se hrají" [Films that are playing] and was incorporated into the section "Dělník
a kultura" [The worker and culture]. Also at that time, the 20-year-old Communist Party member and
engineering student Lubomír Linhart became editor of the column, and a group of about twenty
young leftist critics came to work for the newspaper.

prepare the ground for widespread Marxist film criticism. It is necessary to *organizationally* utilize the "popularity of the most widespread mass art" and to give this art proper direction, in order to realize—as much as it is possible in a capitalist state—Lenin's slogan: "Of all the arts, the cinema is the most important for us."

The great enemy of Soviet film, the Czechoslovak censorship board, has been joined by a no less serious enemy. More and more often, the cinemas themselves are boycotting Soviet films, even the "revised versions" that the Czechoslovak censor and film exchanges are giving them. As a result, proletarian organizations (Red Help [Rudá pomoc], Workers' Help [Dělnická pomoc], the cells of the Communist Party, the workers' union the Bee [Včela], etc.)[3] have begun arranging screenings of Soviet films in rented cinemas. This campaign has already been extended to the countryside, where it is expanding promisingly and where it has encountered the greatest appreciation of the proletariat. We are also seeing an increasing number of cases in which the proletariat itself *forces* cinemas to program regular screenings of Soviet films.

The public's discontent with American, German, and Czech military films and "weepies" (as these foul bourgeois films are commonly called) is culminating in multiple cases of open resistance and public demonstrations. The mass organization the Workers' Theater Amateurs' Association in Czechoslovakia (Svaz dělnického divadelního ochotnictva československého, DDOČ), is engaged in the organization of film circles that aim to embrace this discontent and give it an organized form. Once these circles have grown large enough, they will be combined to form the proletarian Alliance for the Friends of Good Film,[4] which will publish a weekly film journal, organize screenings, educate proletarian critics, and produce short reportage films depicting demonstrations, strikes, the daily life of the proletariat, etc.

[1931]

---

[3] Rudá pomoc and Dělnická pomoc were the Czechoslovak branches of the organizations Die internationale Arbeiterhilfe (IAH, or International Workers' Relief) and Internationale Rote Hilfe (IRH, or International Red Aid, whose affiliate organization in the United States was called International Labor Defense).

[4] The plans that Linhart describes here follow the communist intelligentsia's organizational strategy in the field of film criticism, which was inspired by the German associations Volks-Film-Bühne and Deutsche Liga für unabhängigen Film. Although the Alliance for the Friends of Good Film was never established under the auspices of the DDOČ, Linhart's ideas were to a certain extent implemented shortly after he published this article in 1931, with the establishment of the Film-Photo Group (Film-foto skupina), a section of the leftist cultural organization Left Front (Levá fronta).

Lubomír Linhart
NEWSREELS SHOW US THE WORLD...

Newsreels. Silent and with sound. American, German, Czech. Maybe some of you even remember the French ones,[1] the ones that regularly featured some French chateau, normally in color photography, but which have almost completely disappeared from the nation's cinemas. One joke declared that this was because the supply of French chateaux had been exhausted. This may not be a bad joke, but it is untrue, because the real cause lies elsewhere. For the most part nowadays, American, German, and Czech newsreels make up the regular program of all premier cinemas and most second-run cinemas.[2] In Prague, there is even one cinema where newsreels comprise the majority of the program and repertoire, and which can thus indirectly provide evidence to those otherwise unable to notice the similarly poor quality of all the newsreels shown in Czechoslovak movie theaters. They could not be otherwise. Just because they are produced in different countries, depict events from different locations, and are filmed by various cameramen of various nationalities does not mean that their essence differs in any way; in the end, the only difference lies in the degree of skill and cinematic quality with which they are made. In terms of content, there is no essential difference between them, and it might seem that this uniformity is accidental were it not for the fact that all of the newsreels that we can see—or, rather, are permitted to see—in this country originate from one and the same international family: from the production of capitalist film entrepreneurs. Their production guidelines serve twofold interests: on the one hand entrepreneurial interests

---

[1] Linhart probably refers to Pathé newsreels (distributed from 1910 in Czechoslovakia under the name *Pathé journal*) and above all to Gaumont newsreels, called *Gaumontův týdenní přehled* [Gaumont's weekly show] in Czech and screened regularly from 1920 through 1931.

[2] In 1932, when Linhart published this article, one Czech, one German, and four American newsreels were regularly exhibited in Czech cinemas: *Československý filmový týdeník* [Czechoslovak weekly newsreel], produced in Prague; Ufa newsreels from Germany; and finally the newsreels of Fox, Paramount, MGM, and PDC from the United States.

and on the other hand the interests of the social class to which they belong. The entrepreneurial interests dictate form; the class interests dictate ideology. For the entrepreneurial interests, the most important thing is profit; for the class interests, the most important thing is to maintain and reinforce the position of power held by the class. As a result, newsreels must be made in such a way that they appeal to audiences and simultaneously fulfill the role appointed to them as an aspect of capitalist film production more broadly. This is the same in America as it is in Germany and Czechoslovakia.

There is no denying that there is public interest in newsreels. This is confirmed not only by the regularity with which they are included in cinema programs but also by cinema audiences who have opted for the newsreel repertoire. This does not mean, however, that the newsreels are good, or that they meet the demand that is rightly put to them: to be a real reflection of the world, with its constant motion and complex process of historical development. Exactly the opposite is the case. Instead of seeing and portraying the whole, newsreels only see their own part. Rather than seeing both faces of the world, they see only one face, and even this face is reflected in a warped mirror. This is a face to which make-up has been applied; the illuminated, clear, and from year to year increasingly radiant face of a world that anxiously denies its own senility, artificially and violently smoothing out its wrinkles, tinting its thinning eyebrows, frantically clinging to life with all its strength.

With the same regularity as those chateaux in French newsreels, every year newsreels of all the producers present floral celebrations on the Riviera with merry, dancing people, impressively filmed maneuvers of maritime behemoths, the astonishing poise of thousands of soldiers lined up in rows, the charm of the Prince of Wales and the energy of Mussolini, traditional sports competitions at English and American universities, the steeplechase in X and Y, the christening of new ships (usually battle cruisers), disarmament conferences, the acrobatics of daring pilots, the wedding of some lofty-looking monarch, the mayor of London's festive motorcade, celebrations of carefree people in traditional costumes, etc., etc. For those viewers who have seen just a few newsreels: who has not seen most of these themes? From those who frequent the cinema: who has not seen these themes five times, ten times, or more? They come in different varieties, with various tints and in various contexts, yet always with the same goal: to obscure that other face, shadowed and deeply scarred, where the wrinkles burrow deeper and deeper, where ever-newer wounds continue to open and grow, becoming more and more difficult to heal for the patient and his doctors, and where splotches of cadaverous decay are starting to spread. In contrast, the world in newsreels lives merrily and carefree.

Monarchs get married, congratulate each other on their birthdays, pay visits to one another, laugh, and, just like their colleagues from exotic monarchies and their relatives in republics both big and small, are turning up in newsreels more and more often. They are even shown as respectable fathers in happy family settings. Their sons and daughters also get married—democratically, but with considerable pomp.

In newsreels, Mussolini pontificates, his appearance ever more pompous and provocative; he celebrates ten years of fascism in Italy, decorates heroes, and consoles the widows and orphans they leave behind. More and more often, the size of his audience is presented—fifty thousand, one hundred thousand, hundreds of thousands. The numbers are enormous and therefore impressive and striking; this is why they are presented. Other statesmen also appear in newsreels with ever-greater frequency, speaking in parliament and at festive occasions, condemning war at the graves of unknown soldiers, tipping their polished top hats with white gloves, and participating in disarmament conferences. Recently, many of them have spoken of crisis and the need for trust in the government, giving advice and providing assurances of their genuine engagement in struggling against this crisis.

No less often do we see the reserved and stern faces of men caring for our earthly well-being, alternating with the beautiful and smiling faces of fashion-show models or with the lovely legs, backs, faces, and entire bodies of beauty-pageant competitors.

Nearly every week we are informed that folk habits and customs have not yet died out, we see historical processions in folk costumes with folk music and allegorical wagons, we learn that the festival of the grape harvest was merrily celebrated on the Rhine, in Hungary, and in Italy. In addition to these "current events in the life of the people" we are told about the celebration of merrily imbibing members of the patriotic-beneficent association of the "Baráčníks" [Property owners] in Prague, an event that would have otherwise certainly escaped our attention. Of course, we are no less carefully informed about the celebrations of members of the upper class here and across the ocean, as well as about religious celebrations, and not only Christian ones, but also those of other religions.

They never fail to show us the police, how they are trained and what weapons they carry, and also the defense forces—which never appear small, even in the case of lesser nations—with their Scottish troops, cavalry, mountaineering, and other regiments. We know that the armies of civilized states "pacify" colonial nations, that the training of American pilot cadets culminates with a parachute jump, that the use of artificial fog has become a common occurrence in naval training, that new cruisers and submarines were launched, that new weapons were tested and a new memorial to fallen soldiers from the last war was unveiled, even that some courageous American captain personally feeds seventy hungry lions from within their cage. We also remain fully informed about the world of sports, since we are shown at least the main highlights from all important baseball games, football games, boxing matches, tennis matches, automobile races, and other contests, including shots of the stands filled with fans. Not even science and art are neglected, and we can be sure that everything that newsreels show us from the worlds of science and art is truly worthwhile. Each case is a first-class sensation, ignorance of which would be truly shameful. It took a team of several sculptors an entire five years to make those four gigantic statues of American presidents, that virtuoso violinist is only nine years old, the American Supreme Court building cost ten million dollars, the organ of the Berlin cathedral has 6,724 pipes, these nightclub singers are known throughout all of Paris, and this man can sing while playing twenty musical instruments at once.

Even reports that show things like a monkey turning the crank of a film camera, riding on roller skates, or playing with an alarm clock, or things like children's roller-skating competitions, a bear drinking milk from a bottle, pageants for beautiful legs or purebred dogs, dancing horses, etc. are included. Quite simply, there is no joyful subject that newsreels would fail to record as a so-called "current event."

In *newsreels*, the world lives merrily and carefree.

In *real life*, the world lives otherwise. Its palette of colors contains more than just those vivid, clear tones of which newsreels speak. Life in its entirety cannot be covered by a few stereotypical snapshots, as the newsreels attempt to do. Caviar and lobster alone cannot satisfy a starving person—he must also have bread. There are other joyful events that newsreels obstinately withhold. There are also other painful matters than those spoken of in newsreels. Newsreels are aware that it is also necessary to speak of painful events—admittedly not at great length, but at least a little bit, just enough and in such a manner that at least something is said that can cause no harm. They also speak of these events in such a way that they remain beyond the reach of human hands and minds. Disasters such as fires, earthquakes, hurricanes, avalanches, volcanic eruptions, storms, train wrecks and other catastrophes are works of fate, misfortune, or other abstract factors that—sometimes truly, sometimes only apparently—lie beyond human control and responsibility. Fate and misfortune—abstract concepts, impossible to pursue and punish like an accountable human offender. This is why newsreels show unemployment, strikes, and famine only sporadically, merely as a sensational variation in an otherwise monotonous newsreel, as "its way to the people," recorded only as isolated snapshots without context or connection to complex contemporary issues and problems. They are not presented as the result of unjust distribution of economic and political power in contemporary society, but rather as the wound of fate that humanity must endure. This is the interpretation provided by newsreels, which act as if they merely present objective and documentary visual material. And how real that objectivity appears to be! Take, for example, a segment depicting a hungry parade of the unemployed in London, from which we see only two musical bands in colorful Scottish costume. From the multitude of banners expressing the demands of the demonstrators, the newsreel carefully selects and photographs only two entirely meaningless ones. A sensation and curiosity to be comfortably and idly observed from even the most expensive loggia seats.

It does not suffice to present viewers with isolated snapshots of a specific event without at least hinting at the links to its causes and context, because average viewers—who make up a good ninety percent of the audience—either do not see the causes and context at all, or they interpret them falsely.

The following is certainly not an isolated case: a woman who happened to be sitting next to me in the cinema was muttering enthusiastic commentary to her neighbor during an artistically and impressively photographed segment featuring a flotilla of bomber aircraft doing maneuvers. Her reaction was probably a response to the aesthetic beauty of the pictures, which probably reminded her of birds in flight. However, if these beautifully photographed pictures of planes were followed by images of an air attack and its consequences—images of a bomb-ravaged city, of burning houses, mutilated bodies, people poisoned by gas, or a massive cemetery—this woman would surely have the complete opposite reaction. *The very same* airplane that was the object of beautiful photography would become a carrier of death. When a newsreel presents a warplane simply as an object of beautiful photography without showing its true purpose, this is not objectivity but rather the concealment and distortion of reality. By analogy, the same applies to other current events featured in newsreels. Here is another example: the Japanese representative to the League of Nations giving a speech in praise of peace. Unless the newsreel immediately follows these images with those of a Manchurian battlefield, it is again distorting reality. Once again it is not objective.

Newsreels do not utilize the effective possibilities of counterpoint at all, neither as the confrontation between two images, which can be used even in silent newsreels, nor as the contrapuntal linking of images and sounds. Let us imagine the image of a bear drinking milk from a bottle edited together with the image of a starving, undernourished child. Or the same image of the bear linked with a voice on the soundtrack announcing the stoppage of the milk campaign due to a lack of financial resources.

Imagine shots of American millionaires and their lifestyles, extravagant parties, and luxurious yachts linked with images of unemployed Americans sleeping in sewer pipes. Newsreels have shown us both of these images, but as isolated items without any connection. Or imagine a shot of a millionaire's party accompanied by a voice-over announcing that the number of unemployed in the United States has reached eleven million.

The image of a starving unemployed man who drowned in a river cut together with the image of grain being dumped into the river in order to avoid a decrease in the market price.

One might object that such a newsreel would be tendentious. Not at all—it would be a *truthful newsreel that presented reality in its true light*. On the contrary, the tendentious and untruthful newsreels are those that present road workers simply as cheerful guys whose hammer blows draw xylophonelike tones from the stones. Tendentious and untruthful are those newsreels that conceal or distort the events and problems that are shaking the entire world these days: economic battles and social conflicts, mass phenomena and rising unemployment rates on the one hand, and overabundance and the destruction of "surplus" economic goods on the other. Tendentious and untruthful are those newsreels that intentionally conceal and ignore the admirable construction of the five-year plan in the USSR, those newsreels that feed the viewers cheap sensations and naïve superfluities, completely ignoring the central questions of our age.

[1932]

Optophonogeny:
The Musicality of Film and the Plasticity
of the Spoken Word

PART FOUR

Emil František Burian
MUSIC IN SOUND FILM

When we consider music in sound film, we must first of all depart from the assumption that we are dealing with a certain number of meters of sound that dynamically and rhythmically organize space on the film strip.

The Meter of Sound

This measurement is turning history upside down. All theories, from Monteverdi all the way to Stravinsky, are herewith liquidated. All the periodicals devoted to decadent, i.e., serious, music are unable to break down this measurement with any musicological formula. Even for me, the first shock of this realization was so strong that I was on the verge of burning all my previous manuscripts—and with my heretical work, I am used to quite a lot! Now all those leitmotifs and jokes of program music will again become fashionable, recitative will be considered once more, although now a specialist with a ruler[1] will measure exactly how many centimeters a word is long and for how many millimeters the flute will whistle.

What to Do With Theory?

Imagine that music has a firmly demarcated evolution, and that genius traverses the centuries, tackling its compositions in firm linkage with that tradition. Even the jazz revolution was firmly linked to the tradition of the Protestant hymn and African tom-toms. If something remarkable happened here, it was only because jazz was really the predecessor of the changes we are now witnessing with the flourishing of mechanical production. And now compare the film tradition with this colossal tradition

---

[1]   Throughout this text, Burian uses the Czech *metr* to signify a tool for measurement.

of the world's Palestrinas, Beethovens, and Smetanas. Can we discover anything commensurate between musical and filmic development? No, the ratio of these two traditions is equal to zero. The content and technical problems of music are fundamentally different from, even directly incongruous to, those of film. Film thinks, feels, and works quite differently than music with its Bach tradition. Film is actually not interested in anything other than measurable and palpable musical space. Film cuts, shortens, and lengthens its musical component according to its own law, i.e., to the law of its own tradition, not the musical tradition.

Structure

If the composer of yesterday's style laments that he is limited by the hegemony of filmic content, if he tears at his hair when asked to once again repeat tacky effects for a scandalous concert or for the theater stage, then he will have no other option than to forget that he ever called himself a composer and to start referring to himself as a sound technician, since this is the only designation that truly fits him. When a film composer begins his work with sound, the best solution for him is to ask for a ruler with which to measure words and instruments, and to transform himself from an insincere genius into a sound engineer, a function we boldly approach with the mere recognition of his profession's name. Then it will make no difference at all if there is a tradition of symphonies and sonatas, nobody will be interested in whether Stravinsky composes as a neoclassicist or impressionist. The entire theory of musical evolution will progress or regress at its leisure—the sound engineer, however, will construct and make blueprints for kilometers of tones in accordance with film structure. Thus the musician will not complain about violence, and film will have its tectonic space.

Functional Sound

Unlike the old music of the silent cinemas, where the bandleaders of screaming salon orchestras invented every manner of mood and stole from musicians all over the world, today music in film finds its purpose only in function. What is the function of music? It is the legitimacy of sound material that does not simply underscore the picture and is not composed in the sense of the old operas (by Gluck, for example), but is itself film, is itself a sequence of film images and their action. The theory of mechanical music shall always have the function of sound, rather than pure musical rules, as its point of departure. Let us not forget that we are not dealing here with an accompaniment to the picture, but with the picture itself. Music in a sound film is not only heard; it is, first and foremost, seen. This is the theoretical foundation that transforms the acoustic aspect of sound into a visual one. Like the image track, the visual character of sound is determined by montage, and some compositions, i.e., purely musical composition in the concert sense, are excluded. If today somebody still thinks about music in sound film from a purely acoustic standpoint, he is nowhere near comprehending this achievement. Only the visual character of sound turns musical work in film into what should properly be called functional sound. However, the sounds of the instruments or voices in the picture are not the only thing that falls under this designation. A shot of people playing and singing is not yet a realization of the filmic function of sound.

Montage

If we proceed from the assumption that film is, above all, governed by the law of montage, then we cannot exempt film music from this law and place it in some special extra-filmic music-historical position. Quite the contrary, in sound film, once we move from exclusively acoustic music to exclusively visual meters, we will realize that only in montage do we find true musical composition, a composition that composers have heretofore attempted to supplant with the composition of moods. And if we, as absolute composers (i.e., composers who have good reasons to believe only in music that is not based on literary content) know that music cannot be anything other than acoustic, and if we add to this view the insight sound film provides into the visual character of this acoustic music, we will have an obvious point of departure for work in film: each musical progression of chords, tones, and halftones, every instrumental expression, every tone of the human voice can become phonogenic only after it has been treated mechanically.[2] What do I call mechanical work in film music? We record certain musically dynamic wholes on rolls x meters long. We record them at various dynamic levels at various lengths within various shots. For this we require some raw musical material written by the composer with the forthcoming montage already in mind. This x number of sound rolls provides us with the same type of working ma-

---

2   *Phonogeny* (from the French *phonogénie*) is a term analogous to *photogeny*; unlike photogeny, however, it virtually disappeared from film practice after the sensitivity of sound recording equipment improved. In the 1930s, the term was popular among sound engineers to refer to the adaptability of certain voices to the limited sensitivity of microphones and to other technical conditions of sound recording and reproduction. The *phonogenic* voices sounded "better" than other voices when recorded and reproduced; they were able to "make up for the absence of the sound's real source by means of another kind of presence specific to the medium," as Michel Chion puts it; see Michel Chion, *Audio-Vision: Sound on Screen* (New York: Columbia University Press, 1994), 101.

terial as the so-called rough cut of the work print that includes individual filmed scenes. What is the next stage of work for the film director? To clarify, complete, and make dynamic the action on the film rolls through cutting and montage. To take the raw, unassembled material and produce a film work that functions on the screen as a unified whole. What is the next stage of work for the composer? The same as for the film director: the proper composition of the work. The composition that was recorded is not a film composition, it is merely rough material of rhythms, chords, melodies, etc. The composition proper begins only at the sound-editing machine, with scissors in hand. Here the composer can finally demonstrate his art, here he finally begins to compose musically. He cuts up his sound meters into elements that, even with the best of intentions, cannot be recorded *in natura*. He separates the composition material into centimeters, into thousandths of a second, and he reassembles it, together with the director in need of an acoustic dimension to his picture. This is a miracle that is waiting for theorists and entrepreneurs to finally—for God's sake!—stop believing in the synchronization of sound and picture and realize the significance of the new film and its technology. Today, montage is the law above all laws for a film theorist. It is such an evident and simple matter, and simultaneously so complicated, that it alone will show whether the film director is that which he purports to be. Musical film montage is still all Greek to the musical theorist, just as twenty years ago photomontage was incomprehensible to film. Film itself is quite old, but film sound is still a child in diapers. This gives rise to contradictions that can have a very embarrassing effect even in films of world renown. The result can be a scandal that reaches the skies, as was the case with the Czechoslovak film *Vražda v Ostrovní ulici*,[3] in which the producers, fascinated with the mixing board (the machine for mixing sound), crammed the entire film full of tasteless music from the old silent cinema, thrown together without rhyme or reason, such that the picture suffered an irreplaceable acoustic loss. Cases also arise in which a composer who is ignorant of film technique is forced to invent "storms," "loves," and "sunrises," while the music's actual filmic character slips through his fingers. Now tell me: in what other art form can one find so much magic as in film, which can poetically link the song of a nightingale with the sweet talk of lovers, or the growling of machines with the protests of workers? And have you ever heard the alarm that sounds at the opening of a gate, or the moon playing the violin as clouds burst into song? Certainly not in Czechoslovak film, because contracts are contracts, business is business, and entrepreneurs are entrepreneurs.

[1933]

---

3   *Murder on Ostrovní Street* (Svatopluk Innemann, Czechoslovakia, 1933).

Alexander Hackenschmied
FILM AND MUSIC[1]

In collaboration with the composer Frantisek Bartoš, I have tried in my experimental film of Prague Castle (now titled *The Music of Architecture*)[2] to find the relationship between architectonic form and music, between an image and a tone, between the movement of a picture and the movement of music, and between the space of a picture and the space of a tone. This all being part of the wider problem of the relation between film image and sound.

Similar problems have already been encountered on the stage, by music itself, and by the silent film accompanied by an orchestra. These problems have been solved only intuitively by practice. On the stage, a scene accompanied by special music can become quite different from the same scene without music, just as in the sound film music can give an emotional, spatial, or rhythmic character to the picture, be it either purposely or by chance.

The fundamental element in the relationship between sound and image is the influence of tones of different pitch, timbre, and force upon the relative spatial formation of the image. There is also to be considered the relationship of tones and colors, and considerable experimental work has been attempted in this direction. The faculty of having visual color impressions upon hearing different tones is possessed by many people, all of whom, however, do not visualize the same color for the same tone. Scriabin, the Russian composer, possessed this faculty, and has recorded on the margins of his musical manuscripts the colors that arose in his mind while composing. When played on Pešánek's "color-piano"—by which it is possible to produce on a screen, simultaneously with the music, colored shapes of varying size[3]—

---

[1]   Originally published in English, reprinted here with minor grammatical and stylistic changes.

[2]   Hackenschmied's second film premiered with the title *Na Pražském hradě* [Prague Castle, Czechoslovakia, 1932].

[3]   The Czech sculptor Zdeněk Pešánek created three different kinds of color piano (*spektrofon*) in 1924–1930—see also Pešánek's texts in this anthology.

Skriabin's theory became clear, even to people who did not have the faculty of see-ing tones in colors. These color compositions have a direct analogy to the sound film I have in mind: the indivisible sound and film composition.

Similar experiments have been made by Hirschfeld-Mack at the Bauhaus School in Dessau in his reflectorial plays (*reflektorische Lichtspiele*). By means of reflectors he threw on the screen colored geometrical shapes capable of moving, each corre-sponding to a certain tone. The spectators' impression was that these shapes sound-ed themselves. They were made to appear, move, disappear or change places in accor-dance with the rhythm of the music, thus introducing a geometrical and moving (almost dancing) component part. In this way [Alexander] László's modernist compo-sitions of color and music were performed.

Skriabin, László, Pešánek, and Hirschfeld-Mack put stress before all upon color, but in the film we are putting stress upon shape, space and movement. There is not, however, a great difference, as in both cases the basis is the simultaneous fusion of musical and visual impressions into one emotional whole. The sound film made the work much easier by introducing an unbreakable mechanical connection of both component parts.

The first film experiments of this sort were made by Oskar Fischinger in Berlin. In his *Dancing Lines* cartoons (*Tanzende Linien, Opus 1.–12.*),[4] Fischinger was not in-terested in color, but in movement and shape as he could feel them in music. He composed, to given music played on gramophone records, abstract and prevailingly lineal images, following uninterruptedly one after the other as well as moving inter-mittently or changing according to the rhythms or dynamics of the music. He pre-ferred predominantly rhythmic music and gave an almost dancing character to the changes and movements of lines. Fischinger's work, a sort of visible lineal transcrip-tion of the music, was impressionist, as, being a painter, he recorded visual impres-sions as they arose while hearing music with closed eyes. Music was the leading force that he obediently accompanied by the dance of his lines.

It has often been said that the best film music is that which we do not hear—that is, which does not intrude upon us but faithfully follows the atmosphere of the film, its chief task being to remove the painful silence and the noise of the projector. This might be valid in the period of the silent film, which had no need of music and was even better without it. But for the sound film this statement would mean the deepest misconception of the new medium. The silent film was better when music was smooth, subserviently followed the action, and brought nothing new to the film, which the spectator could see as the director had made it. But if the musical conduc-

---

4   Hackenschmied's reference is not exact. Fischinger created a series of fourteen experimental anima-ted films titled *Studie* between 1929 and 1934. Only the second film in the series, made in 1930, was titled *Tanzende Linien*.

tor endeavored to create something new, if he endeavored to strengthen the impressions of the film, then he became a violator of the director's work, and always made errors. The music would draw attention to itself through its dynamic and rhythmic incongruities with the film, both as a whole and in parts, and if the spectator had a sense of film rhythm the result was ear-splitting. This was especially the case in the Russian films that stressed montage.

The composer could not subordinate the rhythmic and dynamic changes of music to the changes of the film, because, in doing so, he might violate the laws of music. The director, on the other hand, paid no attention to the future music and its laws. Music always brought forth some new and unforeseen changes in the whole impression of the film. The director expressed with the aid of filmic means all he wanted. Apart from the director's work, the composer wrote music according to the old independent rules, and the film served him only as the raw theme. This gave rise to music that was self-sufficient in its form and could be played even without the film. Film and music ran side by side, both endeavoring to express the same thing in different ways. They illustrated each other mutually, and in some places the impressions accidentally supplemented each other, thus creating some new impression unforeseen either by the director or by the composer. For a space there was something new—a sound film; but a sound film only by accident, and therefore bad on principle.

The musical film is a new medium consisting of two component parts—music and film, both of which must be created simultaneously. Neither music nor film can be divided and performed separately, because one part without the other would be unintelligible. It is possible that music already composed, or a silent film already made, may be used as part of a requisite whole. Such cases, however, are rare, for the actual work often involves some violation of the original, and it is therefore a responsible task to choose the parts. As a matter of course, it is much easier to make a new film with music already composed than to compose new music for a film already made, the laws of film composition being more flexible than the laws of music. But primarily it will always be the formal, syntactic relation that will condition the cohesion of both component parts, the content or motive relation remaining secondary and unnecessary. The possibilities are far-reaching and await application as well as theory. Sound gives to a picture a new coloring; it determines its space and depth. The cohesion of music and film may result in counterpoint of rhythm; by contrast it may give to each a new inner significance.

Here are a few examples to illustrate what a musical film really is:

Films made to music already composed: *Sentimental Romance* by Eisenstein, to the old Russian music; *In der Nacht*, by Ruttmann, to Schumann's music; Tsekhanovsky's *Pacific 213*, to Honegger's music; Fischinger's *Dancing Lines*; the opera air in René Clair's *Le Million*; the gypsy dance in Otsep's *Karamasoff*, with music by Rathaus.

Music composed to a finished film: Honegger's music for *L'Idée*, made by F. Masereel; Dessau's music for *Storm over Mont-Blanc*, made by A. Fanck (simultaneously with the picture of a planet enlarged by a telescope we hear a single long-drawn tone that gives the effect of space: one feels the surrounding universe); the music of Rathaus, Eisler, Auric, Lou Lichtveld (*Phillips Radio* by J. Ivens), and Hollaender—composed for different pictures.

Film and music composed at the same time: *The Song of Life* by A. Granowsky, with Hollaender's music (close-ups of a rich wedding feast alternating in a slow funeral-march rhythm, so that with every time-measure there appears a new image; René Clair's *À nous la liberté* with Auric's music (simultaneously with the view of a big gramophone factory with open windows there sounds music as if of thousands of gramophones—this picture has the effect of great spaciousness and is very convincing: this is really a gramophone factory); many other places in the films of René Clair; in King Vidor's *Hallelujah!*; in the new Russian pictures; and my short experiment, *The Music of Architecture* (*Prague Castle*), with music by F. Bartoš.[5]

(1933)

---

[5]   The films mentioned in the last three paragraphs are: *In der Nacht. Eine musikalische Bildphantasie* (Walter Ruttmann, Germany, 1931), *Romance sentimentale* (Grigori Aleksandrov and Sergei Eisenstein, France, 1930), *Pasifik 231* (Mikhail Tsekhanovsky, USSR, 1931), *Le Million* (*The Million*, René Clair, France, 1931), *Der Mörder Dimitri Karamasoff* (Fyodor Otsep, Germany, 1931), *The Idea* (*L'Idée*, Frans Masereel, France, 1932), *Stürme über dem Montblanc* (Arnold Fanck, Germany, 1930), *Philips Radio* (Joris Ivens, Netherlands, 1931), *Das Lied vom Leben* (Alexis Granowsky, Germany, 1931), *À nous la liberté* (René Clair, France, 1931), *Hallelujah!* (King Vidor, USA, 1929), *Na Pražském hradě* (Alexander Hackenschmied, Czechoslovakia, 1932).

Jindřich Honzl
CONTRIBUTION TO THE DISCUSSION
OF SPEECH IN FILM[1]

In terms of the spoken word, film has one great advantage over theater: it works with the photographic *image* of sound.

The human voice and natural sounds are deformed by filmic reproduction, because film does not capture tones at frequencies for which the sound apparatus is not tuned or that escape the photographic possibilities of the sound track. Therefore, sounds sometimes lose their color [timbre], just as photographs lose color. Sound is dependent on the "focus" of the recording equipment, especially old ones, whose range is sometimes only several hundred frequencies, whereas our hearing is "tuned" to frequencies from 60 to 10,000. The timbre of voices or other sounds, however, lies precisely in those tones and sounds that are "too high" or "too low," in sounds that escape the standard tuning of sound recording or sound reproduction apparatuses.

For this reason, in a sound film, we do not recognize an actor's voice by its timbre, but rather by its movement: the melody and rhythm of the sentence, the division of syllables and words, and the actor's individual method of expression. Thus, film *photographically represents* words and sentences by utilizing their most prominent features.

The intensity of voice reproduction in film is determined by the sound track, which records the intensity of sound as a variable density of black and gray. We can imagine that the limited scale of photographic gray is very narrow considering the unlimited scope of intensity in natural sounds. On the other hand, we can arbitrarily alter and magnify the *intensity of the reproduced voice*. So, a sound image of a quiet sigh or whisper can deafen the listener without ceasing to be an "image" of the most subdued vocal manifestation.

Another transformational precondition is the complete separation of sound and image reproduction, which are bound together through the *simultaneity* of two inde-

---

[1]   This text was published, together with one written by Vladislav Vančura, under the common title "Contribution to the Discussion of Speech in Film" (see the following text in this volume).

pendently running machines. Of course, even this simultaneity is very loose and the index of its precision is small.

These preconditions could lead to extraordinary and miraculous sound synecdoches, metonymies, and metaphors. But in contemporary film they lead only to the most naïve illusionism.

Film had and still has great potential for technical invention as opposed to theater, which works only with the actual voice of the actor. In film, the transformational process had an extraordinarily open path, because the precondition for film work contained a conflict between two levels: the "sound" and the "image," which had nearly complete freedom and independence from each other. In addition to this freedom, there is a permanent conflict between the sound "image" and the reality that the sound "image" represents. There is the possibility here for a dialectical relationship between a word and its image, the possibility to repeatedly and with ever-newer means rip the word from its ordinary context and bring it into a state of sonic superreality. All of the advantages and flaws of "lighting," all inventions or conventions of the "shot," all the accuracies or insufficiencies of photography (of the negative and positive process) can also work together in photographing the image of the word.

In order to utilize the transformative means of the photographed word—and to even recognize them in the first place—film must risk that which theater seldom risks, or is unable to—disruption of and liberation from organic contexts, which are then transformed by sound film into mechanical contexts. Only their separation permits them to be fully known and knowingly mastered. This entails separating out and making independent the formative elements that create the sound film complex, i.e., the spoken word.

I think we are still far from achieving the liberation of the word in film and from realizing a new speech composition. In fact, we are descending into naïve illusionism, which is obsessed with the flawless synchronization of image and sound and with the fidelity of the photographed word. Speech in contemporary film strives to represent the words of a speaking person without leaving room for anything else. Filmmakers are completely ruled by this most naïve illusion and they have, in turn, imposed it upon spectators and listeners. We are not aware of the components that compose a sound image, and rather than trying to experiment with them, we continually strive, using all possible and impossible means, to conceal and obscure any conflict. (The attempts to add synchronized sounds to silent images have been wretched, and the results of dubbing—of converting a sound film into a version in a foreign language—are completely hopeless.) Conversely, there is no experimental or laboratory work being conducted that goes beyond this illusionism.

With the theatricalization of film plots, we have reached a state in which films always opt for the shortest and most comfortable path to communicate something to the film spectator and listener. Sound film is killing the photogeneity of eyes, faces, and lips. The silent image "communicated" with the spectator by indirect, yet there-by all the more expressive means, for these indirect paths, full of detours and mazes, are paths of discovery full of miraculous finds—they are paths of emotivity and poetry.

In watching a film and hearing speech that we could not understand, we hap-pened to learn that "understanding" is sometimes an obstacle to "feeling." The film *Amok*[2] lost all of its emotivity because the words spoken by exotics and foreigners were translated into Czech via dubbing. I remember the impression I had from a documentary film that showed a Subcarpathian rabbi pontificating with the raised fingers of his right and left hands. I recall the thrill of the dancing song in the film *Insel der Dämonen (Black Magic)*.[3] In contrast to this, a contemporary director would not even dare to convey the sense of love between two beings using the words "I love you," because of the risk that the audience will burst into laughter. This word scheme and others like it have lost any sense of emotionality and have assumed the opposite of their original meaning.

Filmmakers do not undertake and indeed are unable to undertake an investiga-tion into the means of expression in the way that cubist painting and constructivist theater did. This is because they do not have the opportunities or the resources to do so, and also because there is a fundamental skepticism toward film. Salvador Dalí, who collaborated on the films *Un chien andalou (An Andalusian Dog)*[4] and *L'Âge d'or (The Golden Age)*[5], has proclaimed,

> Contrary to the common opinion, I assume that film is infinitely poorer and more lim-ited than the written word, painting, sculpture, and architecture in its ability to achieve an expression of the true activity of human thought. The only thing lower is music, whose intellectual value is nearly zero, as everyone knows.[6]

For Dalí, this skepticism is justified by the fact that film does not contribute any-thing toward realizing individual creative spontaneity. This is because the conditions of its production bind it to machinery and to a lot of foreign interferences that aim to divert individual creative spontaneity into the realm of rationalized schemes and conventional means of expression. However, film could be an invaluable means for realizing and investigating the spontaneity of *perception*, for experimentation with the spectator and listener. Yet in our social structure this is completely impossible. If

---

[2]   Fyodor Otsep, France, 1934.

[3]   Friedrich Dalsheim, Germany, 1933.

[4]   Luis Buñuel, France, 1929.

[5]   Luis Buñuel, France, 1930.

[6]   Salvador Dalí, "Stručná kritická přehlídka filmové tvorby," *Doba* 1, no. 17–18 (1935), 253.

not even the individual artist has liberated himself enough to fulfill his human and artistic function through the spontaneity of poetic expression, how could this then be demanded of the public, which suffers from class contradictions and prejudices, and which attempts to mystically affirm these class contradictions in religion, in art, and in prejudice (racial, national, moral, etc.)

Contemporary film can proceed only from those assumptions and with those artistic methods that are appropriate for this social structure and for an idealist aesthetic that relies on the complete ignorance of dialectics and on the ignorance of any *realistic* solution to the inner conflicts of material and method.

Film production and its aesthetic do not recognize the real causes of emotion and they artificially obstruct the paths that could lead to this recognition. They do this by artificially covering up all conflicts and contradictions, be they of a general nature or specific to film material and method.

What is to be done?—Materialist film!

(1935)

Vladislav Vančura
CONTRIBUTION TO THE DISCUSSION
OF SPEECH IN FILM

In talking film, photographed speech is just as much a mechanical product as it is a human product and human expression.

Which is predominant?

This is a matter of applied speech as art; that is to say, a matter of the specific manner of verbal expression as well as of the intentionality of physical-chemical processes.

The intended effect is dependent on both components, which form a new whole.

In talking film, what is the nature of the dependence of artistic expression on physical-chemical processes?

The intended effect (assuming, of course, that received sounds correspond with the intentions of the maker of a sound film) is roughly dependent on the following: on the sensitivity of the recording apparatus; on the distance of the microphone from the source of the sound; on the pitch of the recorded sound phenomena, on their intensity, their timbre, the conditions of their production and recording, etc.; and, finally, on the manner of sound processing and on the quality of the material used. Just as important are, of course, the sound reproduction system and, lastly, projection speed.

Is such a multitude of dependencies an advantage or a disadvantage?

Most of the components enumerated here are able to alter and intensify sound expression. These possibilities enrich talking film's creative means.

This all points to deformation.

Mechanical recording and mechanical reproduction inevitably distort the original sound. In talking film there can be no other concern than that sound, as a component of actors' performances, be incorporated into the *order* of the film drama. It is no longer a matter of speech as heard from the stage or even in conversation. Talking film seeks the veracity of its own order. It would be foolish for it to strive for the imitation of sound in profilmic reality at the cost of losing its own expressive means, which have (or could have) an emotional effect.

What does this mean, in a practical sense?

Sound superimpositions, sound grotesque, symphonies of detonations, etc.

Let's get back to speech in film drama!

So far, film production cannot give rise to any work that would be perfect in this regard. Talking film as a specific form of art is only now emerging.

From what background is it emerging and what are the preconditions?

The rules of talking film derive from contemporary artistic film praxis, from sound newsreels, from radio speakers, perhaps even from the reproduction of gramophone discs; in short, from the order of things as governed by the nature of sound photography or voice recordings.

According to this conception, it would be necessary to categorize speech in film dramas as distinct from speech in newsreels, but is the spoken word in the newsreels we see really communicative? Is it not here a matter of speech under special circumstances, of affect, of a certain pathos, even in those trivial pictures that promote some kind of product?

Film always speaks to the public. Whether it is a matter of art, sensation, or advertisement, that which is said should not be misheard under any circumstances. To this end, newsreels adopt a certain urgency; however, this does not mean that this special mode of address is of lesser value than normal communicative speech for the creation of poetic film speech.

If realizing a drama, film, or at least the most prominent portion of film production takes account of factual reality just as it is, why should this be otherwise with the spoken word?

Film does not take into account only reality, but also the effect of reality. It is always focused on this goal. The role of the public cannot be overlooked.

So it's an artistic matter, but film aesthetics is first and foremost the aesthetics of things in motion! The spoken word cannot stand in the foreground of this discipline.

Things in motion and motion itself presume a temporal measure. Time is just as much a principle of sound as of movement. The most expressive hallmark of talking film is the spoken word, which determines, or should determine, the rhythm of dramatic motion as the rhythm of alternating images.

What is the reason for this?

The means bestowed upon talking film. If there is talking during some dramatic action, then the spoken word is the most important.

Is talking film, therefore, a form in which the action focuses on the spoken word?

Talking film is not talked film. What is the difference here? Talking film realizes its dramatic intention according to its own rules and its own means (primarily speech). Talked film imitates theater. The number of words used speaks neither for nor against specific filmic quality. This is matter of economy derived from a plan to achieve an intended effect.

Is it possible to predict the course of this development?

Being the most prominent hallmark of talking film, the spoken word will determine the formation of all other aspects of film. The spoken word will become the dominant feature of talking film.

(1935)

Creative Alternatives: Independent Film and Visions of New Artistic Synthesis

PART FIVE

Alexander Hackenschmied
INDEPENDENT FILM—A WORLD MOVEMENT

The film industry has pledged itself to the production of popular entertainment.

Independent film intends be an expression of the free spirit in every area whose activity can be successfully recorded on film, as well as in those areas where film is used directly as visual material. Thus, the concept of independent film includes far more than the concept of film *avant-garde*, which has, until now, been considered the newest and freest branch of film creation. With the exception of film professionals, conservatives, and the ignorant general public, who see it as mad extremism, the film avant-garde has been understood as pure film art in contrast to the rotund, painted up, and softly photographed commercial film art.

Where else should these attempts at pure film art be classified if not together with the perfect scientific film, the perfect travel film, or the perfect propaganda film? Should any of these attempts be indeed fashioned with an understanding of the technical needs and possibilities of film technology such that they could be fully utilized to satisfy the film's objective without limiting the artistic will of the author, the result would be a *good film*.

The independent film movement demands and defends *good films*. There have been examples of all-around good films, for their time, even among the productions of the film industry. Apparently, the conditions of production in such cases completely satisfied the needs of the creator without restricting him in any way. In this respect, these films were produced independently.

A complete list of such good films and their history has not yet been written. Certainly the list would include all initial experiments made by the inventors and pioneers of the cinematograph, be they scientists (Marey), technicians (the Lumières, Reynaud), or the first artists (Méliès, Houdin).[1] A deeper investigation would be diffi-

---

[1]   Beyond the well-known Lumières and Georges Méliès, Hackenschmied refers here to Étienne-Jules Marey (1830–1904), one of the founders of chronophotography, which in this case meant recording sequenced phases of movement as overlapping images on a single photographic plate; Charles-Émile Reynaud (1844–1918), creator of the Praxinoscope and Théâtre Optique, key forerunners of

cult, as there is no precise history of film whatsoever, not to mention a history of "film art" or something similar. If someone nowadays intended to provide a thorough account, he would have to view all of the (at least somewhat) important films, which is impossible, because they no longer exist or are inaccessible.

It seems that, after film's first unfortunate decline, which resulted after 1900 from attempts to imitate theater, the first noteworthy period was that between 1910 and 1914, when the film industry and its products began working toward specific rules and a sense of style. This was accomplished through the efforts of the Frenchmen Abel Gance and Louis Feuillade, and of some Italians. But the main impetus came from the creators and contemporaries of the golden age of American film (1910–1920): D. W. Griffith, Allen Holubar, Thomas H. Ince, Cecil B. DeMille, and a few others, whose works were indeed spontaneous and the pinnacles of perfection at that time. People will admire these works forever. They had a tremendous effect—DeMille's film *The Cheat*[2] prompted a full-scale (but unfortunately not very fruitful) revolution in French cinema in 1915—and their power was certainly the catalyst for all the unforgettable (to those who saw them) works that came from Scandinavia after 1914 and later from Germany.

The first tangible dissentions between commerce and ideas did not come about until the years around 1920, which saw the release of the first and best works of Lupu Pick, F. W. Murnau and Fritz Lang in Germany, and L'Herbier, Dulac, Gance, Baroncelli, and Hervil in France, as well as the works of others who would later become victims of the film industry and commerce. This was European film's best era, the era of Delluc, who was the first to clearly formulate film's potential as a new creative material and the first to accuse commerce of abusing film.

The first works of the French avant-garde were still produced by the graces of commercial production, which exploited the avant-garde for its numerous technical innovations and later appropriated its artists in order to treat paltry themes in an "avant-garde" manner. The real avant-garde was bequeathed to smaller entrepreneurs; they were won over by young enthusiasts for a good cause. The shortcomings of technology and high costs impeded the creation of amateur films financed by an individual author.

It is not until the years 1923 to 1925 that short film experiments with absolutely no connection to any part of industrialized cinema appear. These works include the first abstract films of Chomette (produced with the support of the Count de

---

the cinematograph; and to French conjurer Jean Eugène Robert-Houdin (1805–1871), the "father of modern magic," whose theater was sold after his death to Georges Méliès, who then started to incorporate his trick films into its repertory.

[2] USA, 1915.

Beaumont),[3] the surrealist grotesques of René Clair and the two-dimensional motion studies by the Dane Viking Eggeling[4] and by the Germans Hans Richter and Walter Ruttmann. Since then, there has been (thanks to technology) a constant and ever-stronger stream of independently produced avant-garde films.

It is not possible to group these young enthusiastic pioneers of new film into specific schools or movements. They had such a sense of independence (even from each other) and their fields were so open and seductively spacious that it was only natural for nearly all of them to set off in unique directions. It is only possible to distinguish certain spheres of inclination. After the abstract films there appeared a series of "big city" films with social commentary (Cavalcanti, Ruttmann, Guyot, Birdwell; Quarberg in Los Angeles; and Florey and Flaherty in New York).[5] In addition to these, there has been an immensely diverse array of both experimental and perfect works.

Many of these young directors had their fill of independence, and consequently the industry was enriched with new energy, as an increasing number of Griffiths and Murnaus were lost to its ranks. Without a doubt, were it not for the gigantic boom within the film industry, film technology would probably not be half as accomplished as it is today. But there is also no doubt that it was only in response to the requests and initiatives of those who sacrificed their ideals for the promises of commerce that producers strove to realize their (at least outwardly) broad-minded and admirable projects as a means to show off their power, to offer something new to the public, and to outshine the competition.

Dozens of fresh attempts are being born, either charged with ideas or astonishing with delicate faeries of lights, shapes, and rhythms. France leads the way in terms of number and imagination: Cavalcanti, Man Ray, Dulac, Allégret, Heymann, Dréville, Lambert, Grémillon, Silka, Landau, etc.[6] In Germany, filmmakers such as

---

3   In 1924, Chomette, together with Man Ray, completed the film *À quoi rêvent les jeunes films?* (*What do Young Films Dream About?*, France, 1924) commissioned by Count Étienne de Beaumont.

4   Actually, Eggeling was born in Sweden.

5   Hackenschmied probably refers to the following city films: *Rien que les heures* (*Nothing but Time*, Alberto Cavalcanti, France, 1926), *Berlin: Die Sinfonie der Grosstadt* (*Berlin: Symphony of a Big City*, Walter Ruttmann, Germany, 1927), *Mon Paris* (Albert Guyot, France, 1927), *Street Corner* (Russell Birdwell, USA, 1929), *Hello New York!* (Robert Florey, USA, 1928), *The Twenty-Four-Dollar Island* (Robert Flaherty, USA, 1927). It is possible that the name Quarberg here refers to the publicist and press agent Lincoln Quarberg, known for his collaboration with Howard Hughes.

6   Among these names, Lambert, Landau, and Silka are unknown today. Hackenschmied likely refers to the following avant-garde films: *Un Film sur Paris* (Claude Lambert, France, year unknown), *So This Is Marseille* (Claude Lambert, France, 1928), *Rythmes d'une cathédrale* (Raphäel Landau, France, 1928 [?]), and *La Malemort du canard* (a.k.a. *La Ballade du canard*, A. Silka, France, 1929). See Noureddine Ghali, *L'avant-garde cinématographique en France dans les années vingt: Idées, conceptions, théories* (Paris: Experimental, 1995), 367 and 369.

Erno Metzner, Piel Jutzi, Viktor Blum, Moritz Seeler, and others are involved in social topics while Moholy-Nagy, Casparius, Stella Simon, Reiniger, Strasser, etc. pursue other themes. Working in Belgium are Charles Dekeukeleire, Gussy Lauwson, and Carlo Queeckers; in Holland Joris Ivens, M. Franken, Dick Laan, and van Canstein; in England Oswell Blakeston, Kenneth MacPherson, Len Lye, Brugiere, and others; in the United States Ralph Steiner, Melville Webber, Watson, and others; Suzuki in Japan; Luis Buñuel and Salvador Dalí in Spain; Dziga Vertov, M. Kaufman, etc. in Russia; and many more, as yet unknown, throughout the world.

***

This is all just part of the avant-garde's "search for paths toward art," yet it would be much more difficult to gather examples of good *science* and *culture films*. Everyone knows how much dead weight there is in that field. There are the good microscope films of Jean Painlevé and the Dutchman J. C. Mola. There are the French medical films (dating as far back as 1900) and numerous Russian scientific and instructional films. There are the beautiful documentary pictures of Poirier, Allégret, Ivens, Flaherty, and the Englishman Grierson. But there are also so many wretched examples that torment the public in cinemas and the children in schools, undermining their good judgment about film!

There is a great unknown here: why should we only read about the efforts of these filmmakers? Why doesn't anyone with an interest have the chance to decide on his own whether the praises heaped upon a certain Man Ray have any validity? Why shouldn't the general public find out more about the other things going on in the film world beside the amorous intrigues of Pola Negri?

Around the world there are numerous *film clubs* that present interesting works and discuss them at their meetings. Such clubs already have a long tradition in France. There are Amis du Cinéma in all of France's major cities. There are several in Paris alone (e. g., Film-Club with its journal *Du Cinéma*, Tribune libre du Cinéma, Club de l'Écran, Ciné Club de France). They are also in other countries: in Brussels (the Brussels Ciné-Club has its representative residence in the new Palais des Beaux-Arts), in Ostende, in Geneva, in Buenos Aires (a film paradise without censorship), the Guild Art Cinema in Boston (whereas the Film Arts Guild in New York is not entirely independent). Some of these clubs also unite filmmakers, bring them closer to the public, distribute good films, and thereby provide an important cultural service (the Film Guild and Film Society in London, Filmliga in Holland, Volksfilmverband in Germany, et al). This is especially the case in Russia, where there is no independent film per se, since there is, after all, no commercial film in the sense with which we are unfortunately familiar.

This discussion should also include the *teams of amateur filmmakers* at work on

16mm film. Thus far, their organizations (predominantly in Germany, England, and the United States) have been affiliated with societies of amateur photographers and thus subject to their altogether conservative spirit. Regardless, there are a number of noteworthy mature works on narrow-gauge film (e.g., from the amateur group "Cinimpressionists" in London). Amateur filmmakers will be a very important element in the independent film movement. Their good organizations, necessary for the mutual recognition of their works and for technical advancement, will become the schools and recruitment facilities for new independent filmmakers.

The most recent developments within the Independent film movement are the convention of its representatives held this year in La Sarraz in Switzerland (about which much has been written)[7] and the organizations created at this convention: *The League of Film Clubs* (Ligue des Ciné-Clubs) with its headquarters in Geneva, and *International Cooperative of Independent Film* (Coopérative Internationale du Film Indépendant) with headquarters in Paris, whose purpose is to mediate film exchange and sales and to facilitate the production of good films. Surely the somewhat older International Educational Cinematographic Institute in Rome will also choose to join in cooperation with these new organizations.

Independent film is not calling for a struggle against the film industry. Independent film intends to work in all the fields that have been abandoned by the industry, thereby complementing the industry. Independent film should present the industry with a new and better manner of working. The highest goal of the work done by independent film is the social and ideological reformation of the film industry.

(1930)

ALEXANDER HACKENSCHMIED / Independent Film—A World Movement

---

[7] The International Congress of Independent Cinema (Le 1er Congrès international du cinéma indépendant) was held in September 1929 at the La Sarraz Castle near Lausanne.

Zdeněk Pešánek
POSTSCRIPT TO
LIGHT AND THE VISUAL ARTS

The editors of this booklet[1] have returned this article to me three times because of its length.

Despite its present shortness, however, the text is intended to acquaint the reader not only with the general *development and principles* of light in the visual arts, but also specifically with the *sculpture* on Edison's transformer,[2] which was the first attempt to apply one of the several artistic disciplines that allow light to become a new, mostly kinetic, plastic element.

I hope that it is not necessary to demonstrate that light and the light spectrum can be employed as a plastic element.

This has already been demonstrated by theater and its set design.

Furthermore, this has been demonstrated by light advertising, among other things. On a theoretical level, I am close to futurism. I contend that cubism and all that followed it has led and must necessarily lead to a dead end, due to their primitivity and to the dearth of options the paintbrush or the palette knife offer compared with the instruments of modern technology.

I consider such older instruments (e.g., the paintbrush and palette knife) to be merely auxiliary instruments.

I consider the film camera and projector to be the most refined instruments of the day in the service of absolute visual expression. The significance of their black-gray-white spectrum will decline proportionately with the increasing technical per-

---

[1] Pešánek refers here to the brochure *Světlo a výtvarné umění v díle Zdeňka a Jöny Pešánkových* [Light and the visual arts in the work of Zdeněk and Jöna Pešánek] (Praha: Elektrické podniky hlavního města Prahy, 1930).

[2] Pešánek refers here to his "Kinetic-Light Sculpture" (1930), which was commissioned by the Prague Municipal Electricity Corporation and placed on the façade of the Edison Transformer Station in Prague. Otakar Vávra and František Pilát later made the short abstract film *Světlo proniká tmou* [Light penetrates the darkness, Czechoslovakia, 1930], a rhythmic ode to electrical light featuring the sculpture.

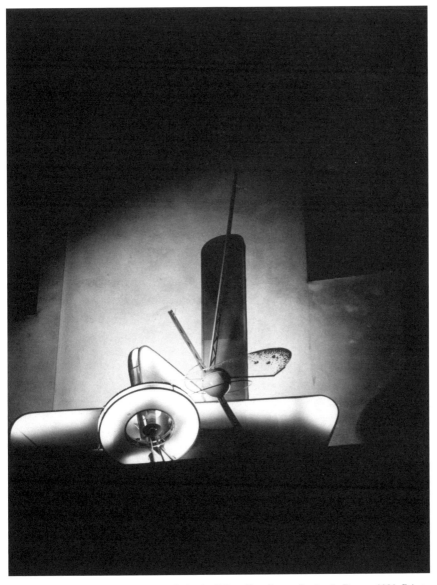

Figure 10. "Kinetic-Light Sculpture" made for the Edison Transformer Station in Prague, 1930. Private collection.

Figure 11. "Kinetic-Light Sculpture," made for the Edison Transformer Station in Prague, 1930. Private collection.

fection of color film and the increased use of genuinely visual filmic qualities (as opposed to dramatic qualities).

The great advantages of film, which enables a particularly complete mastery over forms (of drawing rather than of color), will become a hindrance at the stage in its development when it begins to move toward absolute qualities. The ease of "producing" film by merely photographing reality will constantly detract from the artistic values of absolute formal expression and abstract colors.

Action—a display of colorful light bulbs or simply luminous patches of color, whether three-dimensional or on a flat surface, whether *of its own accord as a single tone* or *clustered together as harmony*, or *lined up temporally as a melody*—action remains the foundation for the existence of kinetic and colorful visual sensation.

The emotive potential of the light spectrum grows in proportion to the perfection of light technology.

The visually expressive potential of *light* in the form of fire is probably just as old as the expressive potential of music discovered in sonorous strikes to a hollow tree— the first drum.

There are two main differences between these two expressions: first, they are perceived with different sensory organs, and, second, musical expression is richer in terms of *time*.

This essential difference derives from the technical characteristics of instruments and is continually increasing. The inventive construction of musical instruments facilitates this escalation.

Time became a concern in the visual arts at a very late stage. The first instance where we can speak of a certain level of sophistication is with baroque fireworks.

Film, on the other hand, already has perfect control over time.

Time is controlled with equal perfection by a light-advertising machine. This machine enables the technically perfect performance of a color melody. It was not until the technician reached this level of development that the artist understood the significance of light for art.

Until this point, light served everyday needs almost exclusively.

In the course of several years, light has commanded utilization in several directions.

Each of these directions defines an individual discipline.

Light signals and such functional things aside (although even these can be beautiful or as ugly as an automobile horn), I dispute the notion that any luminous display in existence was created without regard to aesthetic concerns, even if nowadays such concerns are mostly dependent on technical innovation.

The more we bestow poetry upon light technology, the more it becomes art, or at least an attempt at art.

The main elements in the architecture of light technology are:
1. The lighting of cities and streets as a whole
2. The lighting of interiors
3. Illumination
4. Light advertisement
5. Fireworks (in their capacity to demarcate space)

The elements of light kinetics are:
All light phenomena, for which time is just as important a creative element as form and color.
This includes:
1. The kinetic film picture
2. Reflectorial color play
3. Illumination in motion
4. The articulation of the color piano and its application to a plastic body
5. Illuminated fountain in motion
6. Variable lighting of interiors
7. Fireworks[3]

My sculpture[4] didn't grow tectonically out of direct necessity. After several years of experimental works, I simply seized the opportunity to make a first attempt at a three-dimensional shape with light-color kinetics. The sculpture was to be placed on a building.

Rather than positioning my sculpture in the direction of the street, I placed it facing the park. The benches and the relative tranquility of the park's intimate seclusion provide the possibility for meditation.

Today's observer, who does not yet possess the cultivation necessary to visually comprehend a musical opus *composed* of color, must observe it several times in tranquility.

The street is bright; it is not the purpose of light in sculpture to "outroar" the light of the street. The light's gradual fading from "forte" to "piano" cannot be comprehended if one is disturbed by the headlights of cars on the street.

The sculpture is constructed so that in given moments the horizontal line, the

---

[3] Pešánek's list is similar to the taxonomy of kinetic-light architecture proposed by László Moholy-Nagy in 1936. In his letter to the Czech avant-garde film critic František Kalivoda, Moholy-Nagy defines reflectorial plays (*reflektorisches Lichtspiel*) as light plays in closed spaces, realized with colorful projectors and stencils or with color piano. See László Moholy-Nagy, "Lieber Kalivoda," *Telehor* 1, no. 1–2 (1936), 116.

[4] Once again, the reference here is to the "Kinetic-Light Sculpture," on the façade of the Edison Transformer Station.

vertical line, or the circle can function either individually as fundamental forms unto themselves, or together in formal alignment with each other.

The apparatus's mechanism allows me to compose a harmony of my choice from a spectrum of 424 color tones, and to arrange (in a temporal alignment) individual tones into a melody of my choice.

The first step was completed with the realization of the sculpture, an apparatus for executing color kinetics. The second step is determined by the composer's contribution. It is only then that a true relationship with the observer is created.

I was already composing the first experimental notes when I constructed the mechanism according to the principles of form and color and the relationship of these principles with the setting and its surroundings, and vice-versa, when I constructed the principles of form and color according to the associated technical difficulties that accompany every first attempt.

In the future, I shall periodically attempt to offer new compositions that will allow the assessment of the expressive potential of color kinetics.

(1930)

Zdeněk Pešánek
KINETIC ART: FILM[1]

With film, it is possible to demonstrate everything necessary to understand kinetic art. Film is also a visual technology with kinetic-light properties. The light bulb, the transparent strip of film, the projection screen, the projection apparatus, and before this the camera and chemical processing—these are the tools with which a great number of technicians and artists work.

Overall, film is frequently considered only an art of acting. However, film is not solely a dramatic art. It can be a purely visual art. It suffices to present a static image or photograph of a waterfall next to a film image of the same waterfall for everyone to realize that the second image is also a visual work, even though it is kinetic.

The significance of kinetics for visual art can be seen if we remember how the director of *The King of Kings*[2] employed film's kinetic technology to plagiarize old "static" images from the Bible. These images gained quite a lot from kinetics.

We also know that a simple *filmic image* of pounding waves, a windstorm, or the movement of clouds is more pleasing than most acted films. How many films have had sufficient success based only on their beautiful photography? Furthermore, is it not true that a great number of subjects are no longer seen in the painted image simply because the moving filmic image has taken over these subjects? Isn't it the case that painted pictures of sailboats on rough seas are giving way to filmic images with just the same inevitability as they gave way to photography?

If we consider all the points of intersection between film and traditional painting, we cannot fail to notice how painting has wholly surrendered to film the representation of the movement of airplanes, motorboats, automobiles, motorcycles, etc., and how poor painting's expressive abilities are in *these instances*.

Let's consider another example: a typical affluent citizen commissions a family portrait. (In the nonaffluent classes, the painted miniature would be substituted with a cheap photograph.) These days, when deliberating about the portrait of an old fa-

---

[1]   "Film" is the third section of Pešánek's book *Kinetismus* (Praha: Česká grafická unie, 1941), 20–29.

[2]   Cecil B. DeMille, USA, 1927.

ther or a child we encounter two possibilities: we can have either a painted or sculpted portrait for at least five thousand Czechoslovak crowns, or a film portrait, together with the projector, for two thousand crowns, plus a film camera for two thousand crowns, accessories for one thousand crowns, and training on how to film—for free. Let's look at how many prospective buyers finally decide for the picture and how many for film, the film apparatus, and the chance to create on their own. The statistics show that "film" wins by a ratio of 1:114.[3]

I have not yet even attempted to calculate statistics relating to landscape pictures. The ease with which it is possible to photograph landscape objects and the great number of photographic amateurs discouraged me from undertaking such an endeavor.

With this example, I do not wish to contend that painted portraits, and maybe even landscapes, will meet the same fate as the now-extinct portrait miniature. On the contrary, the reality of the statistics compels me to reflect on the points of intersection between traditional and new techniques as well as on the probable development and planning of the art of tomorrow. In this consideration, it is also necessary to register answers to the questions of whether kinetics and its techniques are important for the visual arts and whether the visual arts have any influence on them, and, if so, what kind.

The wealth of art consumers has always had as much influence on the development of art as their predilections. It is therefore impossible for us to constantly tiptoe around these matters, since we know that film can also be used to create visual art. Although this is a purely economic matter, it cannot be overlooked. Naturally, the market has an influence on production.

In larger markets, we can reckon with a greater number of artists, more variety, and greater productive potential. In the current market, by contrast, we must reckon with the daily desertion of visual artists to the newer, more marketable form of art—that is, to film—and this even though film lies in a different field of visual production that contains dramatic elements.

This example demonstrates the connection between film and the visual arts in economic terms as well; the interconnections between intrinsic modes of visual production have been shown above.

Of course, film is a kinetic method that does not only work with the abstract creative elements that surely come to the reader's mind in connection with the contents of the previous pages.[4]

---

[3]   It is possible that the socialist society of the future will have a different attitude, but there is no reason it must be so. [Original footnote]

[4]   In the previous chapter of his book, "From Impressionism to Kinetic Art," Pešánek describes how modern art, under the influence of new technologies, has moved toward abstraction and kinetics.

On the contrary, for the most part, film works with reality. Of course, in this respect we must also accept as reality those photographed images that show actuality in a manner such as the human eye in its natural state has never seen nor will ever see. It is also necessary to accept actors' performances as reality, even if presented in film montage, although in fact this contradicts the concepts of those film artists who view film with the eyes of someone like Pudovkin.

It has been shown here that film not only makes pictures, but also moving pictures, and that it is a visual art even in cases where reality is photographed.

In some respects, film is a visual art even in cases where the pictures are assembled into the plot of a filmed theatrical play.

According to Pudovkin, however, even in normal films, the matter of reality is somewhat different than this. To use his example, if we film a waterfall not just as a whole but also insert various close-ups into the picture (i.e., a stone whose stability is slowly undercut by the impact of water until it becomes dislodged, falls, and eventually shatters into pieces), this no longer has anything to do with reality, because the action did not occur before the camera as a random natural phenomenon, but was instead artificially constructed in the act of waiting to film this specific moment. Furthermore, this is no longer reality because the inserted portion could have been filmed in another location, perhaps even using a model, and maybe it was even filmed by someone entirely other than the filmmaker who built this detail into his picture.

And so we arrive at the question of whether abstraction has any significance for a visual work created from "realities."

In fact, there is an incomparably better example in which film displays the use of completely abstract visual phenomena, namely in the expression of rhythm.

In the case that a company commander would quickly exit a room to give an order to be carried out, we could insert an image of a door swiftly crashing shut and then an object tipping over and falling from a shelf touching the door, now rattling in its frame. If the same commander would leave the morgue where he has just said his farewells to a dead comrade, the doors would close behind him slowly. These could both even be the very same doors on the film set. The creative elements here are not color and form, *but rather expression aided by "time,"* an abstract concept. This is something that need not be restricted only to a shot that is part of a filmed theatrical play, but that can also appear as part of an entirely independent image filmed with a wholly visual motivation. That is to say, in this way a visual artist can express himself with film in a truly abstract manner.

We could certainly use other examples to demonstrate this phenomenon.

In this case, only time was abstract, not the object itself. This could, in fact, be an argument against the evidence presented for the existence of abstract elements in visual kinetics. We shall therefore consider another example: in a film image, we have water dripping into a puddle in a decreasing tempo in order to achieve an image of rhythm. The actuality of the drops of water, the puddle, the rings in the water, indeed even the image reflected in the surface of the puddle, divert attention from the specific purpose of the picture, which in this case is simply to evoke a rhythmic effect. For this reason, we would not film the falling drops and the concentric waves with the lens in focus, but rather so much out of focus that the object's reality completely disappears. The rhythm does not suffer with this treatment. On the contrary, it stands out even more. In the picture there remains only an apparition that moves vertically downwards and at a specific moment falls apart along diagonal lines, breaks to pieces and transforms into concentric waves, *not waves of water, but waves of color: black, gray, and white.*

The picture is thus fashioned from independent elements that no longer imitate a specific object. Indeed, we are convinced that such imitation would in fact be a hindrance to achieving the desired goal.

This is a phenomenon whose significance cannot be ignored, a phenomenon afforded to the visual arts by technology whose significance will stand out even more markedly if we now digress to a brief analysis of a similar development and its significance in the realm of music.

In the beginning, music also lacked independent elements in the form of today's normalized sounds, or tones, as determined by the musical scale. In the beginning, it also lacked instruments to produce such normalized sounds, or tones. These came only later as the result of man-made technology. Sound as a natural phenomenon (for example, the screech of a bird) and its human imitation were the first steps toward musical "creation."

In order to connect this back to the paragraph dealing with the discovery of true rhythm in the visual arts, we must realize that even music lacked rhythm during the time when it merely imitated nature. To create a musical work analogous to the film that uses realistic images of drops and water, a musical composer would have to use gramophone discs upon which natural sounds were recorded. It is overly evident to the contemporary composer that he is using tones that are independent elements unconnected with any sound other than that which arises wholly and entirely in the artist's imagination. His imagination is either tied by means of an illusion to something heard in reality somewhere at some time, or is tied to a sound idea. (It lies beyond the scope of this book for us to concern ourselves with the retrograde development permitted by modern technology, by that very gramophone disc that enables a musician to capture sound actuality and subject it to a process of musical creation.)

If we were to also analyze dance, we would arrive at the conclusion that the movement in dance is just an illusion, an abstraction, a conception of a specific animated action; we would conclude that a war dance, for example, is only an imaginary phenomenon.

The preceding explanations might very likely seem forced, because we have thus far clarified neither the need to transform reality into abstract phenomena nor the necessity of a psychological connection. Furthermore, it is not fitting to the task at hand to explain the causes of the desire to create. Every day we are witnesses to the transformation of reality into play, of play into an abstract phenomenon, and to how the elaboration of this phenomenon then leads to the compulsion to create. From the children's game of hopscotch, where one hops with feet together and feet apart among squares drawn on the ground with chalk, it is only a short step to the act of hopping with no thought as to the rules of a game, and from these hops to dance movements.

The existence of abstractness (not only internal but also external) alongside reality and beyond reality creates new fields of possibility for the visual arts: it affords mastery over subjects other than those that are seen "tangibly." This is similar to how music can create from subjects that are not only heard, but also felt, indeed even from the idea of a visualized subject.

With thoughts of this kind in our mind, we are surely not far from the inverse process, in which sound reality is poured into a visual artist's creative mold and re-cast as a visual illusion. We will address this point later. Our concern right now is with film, not with such broad matters.

Before enumerating the kinetic methods, I wrote that they are ranked according to how well they are able to master form and color. I stated that film stands in the first place.[5] For that reason, I will attempt to demonstrate all that is made possible by film technology.

First and foremost, it is known that, by photographing reality, film enables the presentation of all movements, in every form and every color. Similarly, it makes possible every movement and every visually independent form and color that do not imitate reality, which we are here labeling as abstract.

Let us once again refer to the diagram of a point, a rectangle, a horizontal line, and a vertical line.[6]

In the previous chapter, in the attempt to explain kinetic visual phenomena, we considered the example of graphic forms that disappear and appear on the composition in various colors. During this process, the position of the graphic elements in

---

[5] In the previous chapter, Pešánek enumerates twelve "methods of realizing light kinetics" in two-dimensional and three-dimensional space; first among the two-dimensional methods he mentions film. A similar list of techniques, though in a different order, is included in Pešánek's "Postscript to *Light and the Visual Arts*" (1930), also included in this anthology.

[6] In the previous chapter, Pešánek uses examples of two-dimensional compositions of four "chords" of colorful forms to illustrate how the kinetic process can be visually constructed and represented as a "melody."

the framed surface remained constant, without the elements growing larger or smaller or changing their form. We know that this is all made possible by film technology.

We know that film technology makes movement possible at all kinds of speeds and in all directions.

The surface of a traditional picture is subject to a certain order. Sometimes the accent is more on form, sometimes on color, and sometimes form and color are equally balanced. *As a picture, film is able to incorporate the law of time as an element of equal value to the already existing laws of form and color.* Indeed, in some cases, the law of time is even more important than those of form and color. In addition, film is able to exploit this element in a manner that is more conscious, more refined, more rigorously based on the study of visual kinetics, and more scientific than ever before. Such is the case when movement in film is neither too derivative of drama and its theatricality, nor of the need to create inner emotional tension.

In a traditional picture, a patch and the respective constellation of patches and their color tonality are subject to the compositional law. In a kinetic picture, these elements are subject to the compositional law not only when in a state of stasis, but also when they are presented in motion.

The *velocities of movement* are also subject to the law of composition. The *shapes of the trajectories* are subject to the law. The *respective formal relationship of the trajectories* is also subject to the law, and likewise the respective *relationship of the velocities performed along the chosen trajectories.* Also subject to the law are the *directions of the movements* and the relationship of the changing sizes and colors of the elements to all of the processes under discussion.

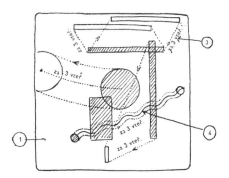

Figure 12. The point, rectangle, circle, etc. here should be, but are not, marked with the number 2. It was also impossible to mark the trajectories' respective formal relationship with the number 5, as should have been done. [Original caption]

Hopefully picture 12 can shed at least some light on the preceding paragraph of text.

1 = The surface of the picture.

2. A point, a rectangle, a circle, etc. (referred to as elements).

3 = Velocity of movement.

4 = The shape of the trajectory taken by the point.

5. The respective formal relationship of the trajectories. On the picture, the trajectories illustrated with dotted lines represent just one example of the infinite number of possibilities. The trajectories of the forms can be either random or composed (and this is the point of the matter).

6. The time needed to complete a certain trajectory is recorded along the dotted lines. So, we see that, in the span of three seconds, the "point" completed the longest trajectory while the horizontal line completed the shortest. Each element, therefore, moved with a different velocity. These velocities can be random or planned so as to create inner tension.

7. The arrows along the dotted lines indicate the directions of the movements, which can be determined either on their own accord or as part of the respective arrangement.

8. The elements may change their size but are not obliged to do so. Consider the vertical line, which gets smaller during its movement to the left. Likewise, such changes can, but need not, be random.

9. The case is similar with changes in the color of the elements or of the background. They can be random or bound by the harmony of colors, or determined with regard to the velocity and trajectory of the shapes and to the relative proportions of the trajectories, etc.

So, with this basic discussion of many characteristics and elements of kinetic and filmic visual creation, the importance of kinetics for the future of visual art should now be evident.

It is still necessary to point out two fundamental differences that such a creation can demonstrate.

I have already shown how movements and changes in form or color may be planned individually or with respect to and in relation to the trajectories, etc.

Even when they are bound to a planned structure (a composition), movements, colors, forms, etc., never return to positions or constellations that they previously occupied, in terms of direction, form, or color.

Here we witness the kinetic prose of which I spoke earlier.

Let's imagine, though, that, within specifically designated intervals, the elements of color and form return to their original position or some similar position and always carry out the same or similar movements in the same or similar colors.

Thus, we now encounter the second primary kinetic trend: a poetry that is tied to kinetics—a sort of kinetic poetry.

As we see, film is a nearly universal technology with unlimited possibilities.

In considering contemporary film creation, we find that it has thus far allowed itself little self-reflection and is developing in this direction more by accident than consciously.

Film as an artistic discipline is still so young that it can astound and amaze even with unplanned kinetic phenomena, and for the vast majority of "consumers" this is sufficient. However, there can be no doubt that sooner or later it will have to increase the number of creative elements it employs. The elements described above will occupy a most important position in this process.

We cannot deny, of course, that it is dramatic action that creates inner tension with which, thus far, formal solutions for individual pictures have complied and that the use of theater as the substance that fills the pictures created by film technology has been an impediment to the development of film's visual and formal aspects.

Certainly this does not bespeak the innovation or the "prerogative" of the film picture.

It was not by chance that artists fell back on subjects such as still lifes in moments when they were coming to terms with a style that was growing exhausted, and were seeking a new style.

The so-called absolute film will have the same type of importance for the film picture as the still life study had in painting. Absolute film must occupy itself with the theories introduced above, for only in them will it discover the fundamentals of the constructions that evoke emotions. It must be art while simultaneously creating principles that can also be used in common film creation.

Film does, however, have one disadvantage. The filmic phenomenon must out of necessity be tied to a fixed pictorial surface. This surface is relatively small and all but prevents monumental creation, thus remaining a kind of kinetic technology fit only for the bourgeois salon. For the time being, film is condemned to be nonmonumental and fixed to a surface. Film technology is condemned to remain in fact just a picture to be perceived only from an acute frontal angle. It will remain so as long as the picture is unable to surround the viewer and to create an atmosphere (if we can call it that) that, in the true sense of the word, surrounds the viewer, envelops the viewer, creating an effect such as that produced by the interior architecture of a church.

Indeed, even in this case, we are only able to observe the tiny segment in front of us, yet, at the same time, we also subconsciously perceive our unobserved surroundings as a whole entity.

In describing fireworks, waterworks, or illumination, we strike once again upon the issue of film's deficiencies. With these phenomena, the observer can be placed somehow in the center of things, and the utmost monumentality of external expression can be achieved.[7]

[1941]

---

[7]   Here, Pešánek points to the following chapters of the same book.

Arne Hošek
NOTES ON THE AESTHETICS OF FILM

When evaluating the development of film into a form of artistic expression, we still encounter one large impediment. Since film is intended for a wide and diverse public spectrum, the standards for judging its value are completely different than those used for the other branches of art, which are able to assert themselves with economic independence and do not require the spectacular public successes that film does in order to prosper. The great amount of work and high sums expended in the production of a film are intended to ensure its success among the broad public. Thus far, such success is not generally founded on artistic values alone. The simple fact that films with such values have been produced does not mean there is a balance between their technological, economic, and artistic success.

In order for artistic success to have greater legitimacy, it will be necessary to educate the public to look at film in a more active fashion. This can be achieved by ceasing to continually provide the public with prepared summaries of filmic works. Thus they will be forced to familiarize themselves with the preconditions for a good film on their own. *Why couldn't film aesthetics itself be filmed?* In order for a film to have artistic success, the most important requirement is that it be, to some extent, timeless. As long as film technology continues to develop, film will not have the lasting vital value that it needs. Technology must become self-evident and should not be permitted to affect film's artistic design. Film technology should be perfected to the point at which it overcomes itself. It will assert itself the most at the point when it is no longer noticed.

Film and Theater

If we pay close attention to how film and theater are realized, we see that the similarity between their approaches is merely an illusion and that there are striking antitheses between them.

Whether to its advantage or disadvantage, theater has forever been an *art* that is subject to changes in style. In its beginnings, film was merely a *technological invention*, only entering the realm of art later and in gradual steps.

The real antithesis between theater and film is the result of precisely these divergent paths of development; it does not lie, as is often claimed, in the distinction between realizing three- and two-dimensional space. As a result of advancements in photographic technology, film often has greater spatial possibilities than theater. In this respect, film works toward becoming entirely plastic, and the distinction between three-dimensional and two-dimensional space is thereby subsiding.

Not even the oft-cited economic reasons are as critical for the distinction between film and theater as is commonly believed. Live theater, in merging all of the other artistic branches, preserves for itself an inviolable independence and will always be supported by the healthy instincts of the public.

Film has a more intimate function than theater, regardless of external motives and of content. This intimacy naturally derives from the fact that film itself is a *permanent reproduction*, always the same for each person. It should become a *document* that draws attention to its own content without relying on the festive mood of the public.

Film can be likened to a book: it is duplicated according to demand from an original negative, just as a book is from a manuscript. Just as the absolute value of a book is constituted by the richness of its ideas and moods, so the artistic value of a film is determined by its *permanently captured internal excitement*, founded on positive psychological and physiological effects.

A theatrical performance is subject to changes resulting from specific and diverse conceptions, interpretations, moods, and repetitions. These all merge to form the overall expression of the poetic work, and only thereby does the work become spatial and plastic. A theatrical performance is always *unique*, each time translating the enduring expression of the dramatic play differently.

In its beginnings, film recorded only simple actions and natural phenomena. These recordings fulfilled film's original purpose as a technological invention and therefore should not yet be thought of as works of art with lasting effectiveness. Yet storytelling alone does not bestow artistic value on a film. Groups of individual filmic views must be linked according to the same rules used to link the individual parts of a musical composition. A film with musical sensibility transports the spectator away from the flat screen into a sort of abstract space. The spectator can be freed from his fixed place in the cinema only when the points of view from which the subject was filmed are linked contrapuntally. Should some of the points of view be particularly emphasized or frequently repeated, we can speak of a filmic drone.

We can find an abundance of such parallels, particularly among the good Russian films that, in a subconscious way, are created musically. Of the arts, perhaps film alone is as flexible and moveable as music, and if film is to become *visual music*, it needs to deal much more diligently with the problems associated with the linkage of visual and audio sensations. The linking of these elements should become the source of internal coherence in the filmic action. Of course, these problems cannot be solved by technology alone and without a musical sensibility. It is not by chance that certain psychological problems emerge along with new technological inventions, which, in turn, later enable solutions to these very problems. Thus is the invention of sound film linked to the investigation of the connection between visual and audio sensations. Synesthesia, supported by examples, should illuminate the conflicting ways in which film and theater conceive the same material.[1] This could also help determine the cases in which one mode of presentation can be substituted by another mode. Finally, one would have to consider the situations in which it might be possible to speak of cooperation between theater and film.

In opera, it is possible for the action to be nothing more than an image that accompanies the music, since music is the most important aspect of the opera. In film, precisely the inverse is true. Music is always accompaniment to the film image. When absolute music, e.g., a symphonic composition, accompanies a film that lacks pictorial value, the music can provide support, but it will not gain anything in the process. The music's spatial quality only accentuates the flatness, lifelessness, and feebleness of such a film. A spoken or musical accompaniment should only supplement a film in those places where the image itself is not sufficient. *The film image and the music and words that accompany it are not concurrent; they merely complement one another.* Therefore, it is necessary to consider when the visual component should have dominance over the audio component and vice versa.

In contrast to film, visual and auditory perceptions have equal shares in theater. The spatial and material qualities of the words and music operate together with the material and spatial qualities of the live acting. Since all sensations in theater are more or less concurrent and concordant, the spectator's complete experience is constituted by their end result, the *sum* total of all sensations.

In film, the end result of all impressions is in fact constituted by the difference between individual sensations. Here, it is rather a matter of *subtraction. In contemporary film, the dominant component diminishes the materiality of the subordinated component. This principle applies to all film production in general.*

It would be a mistake to presume that the concurrence of sound and image amplifies the film's impression. On the contrary, sound and image reach their greatest effect when they achieve a sort of antithetical equilibrium. This principle is perhaps

---

[1]   Synesthesia = multiple perception; synopses = ideas of color and forms through music, recitation, etc.; photisms = the reproductions of these ideas; phonisms = musical feelings produced by viewing colors and shapes (these are more rare than synopses). [Original footnote]

best illuminated with an example: the scene featuring a mass of people assembled for an unofficial trial in the German film M[2] has such a powerful impact precisely because it has neither sound accompaniment nor mimetic gesture. The movement of the image is achieved by turning the camera. Sound would be unable to amplify the scene's impression of terror and is rather likely to weaken it. Perhaps in another film a similarly powerful effect could be achieved by projecting a mixture of sounds without an image.

The concurrence of image and spoken word contributes to the intelligibility of certain nonessential film scenes that function as a sort of "pause," but it can never contribute to the film's dramatic character. On the contrary, a pause in theater is a true pause, with a great dramatic effect.

Whereas the final effect in film depends on the antithesis of its individual sensations (simple synesthesia), precisely the opposite is true for theater, where the effect depends on their sum total (manifold synesthesia). In theater, the concurrence of audio and visual sensations relies primarily on cultivated dramatic speech, operatic music, singing, and set design. A dramatic play should operate within a realm of suprareality; film can stray into pure abstraction and back into reality, even banal reality, without losing any of its value. The music that accompanies a film should, on the other hand, be far removed from reality. The more immaterial it is, the more effective it will be. Such music can be created by sounds that do not exist in nature, for example sounds without aliquot or accessory tones, or hand-drawn sounds.[3] In other cases, dynamic noise could be used instead of immaterial music. Noise, being composed of all kinds of competing sounds, does not have a fixed center like a pure tone does. In terms of synesthesia, it does not evoke the same ideas that actual music does. For the most part, visual ideas that arise from listening to noise are limited to the mere contours of forms that are not filled in with color. Therefore, noise can be used in film differently than actual music can. Noise can be spread around the film image like a kind of frame within which the image can appropriately thrive, whereas actual music might obscure the image. This abstract frame can be modified as needed by the dynamic quality of the noise to enhance the psychological impact of the film images. The contracting and expanding of sound alters the efficacy of images that persist for a longer period of time. The human voice, which in comparison with the film image is highly material, also passes through various membranes and filters until it

---

2   M (Fritz Lang, Germany, 1931).

3   Hošek refers to the avant-garde technique of drawing artificial sounds directly onto the optical soundtrack of a film. In another text from the same period, he mentions Oskar Fischinger and Rudolf Pfenninger in connection with this practice; see Arne Hošek, "Hudba a stavební akustika," *Architektura* 1 (1939), 158.

arrives on the soundtrack as a congruous accompaniment to the film image. All of the components mentioned here can be mutually combined in the composition of an artistic film. Through this, the possibility arises of crossing over from a pictorial idea to a material realization, as well as the possibility of uniting theater and film.

Technology and Art

Technology is condemned to become more and more narrowly specialized, because it is founded on inventions within highly restricted fields. The faster a technological invention expands and becomes generalized, the faster its original idea falls into oblivion so that only its practical function remains. When an invention does not possess broad *ethical* values corresponding to its general purpose, its influence can actually be disastrous.

Art, in contrast with technology, is rooted in an artistic idea sustained by an internal law. There are different ways to materialize this thought and since it is connected to the whole of life, it is not bound by a limited system like an invention is. There are, of course, exact laws that apply to technology, such as rhythm and dynamics, but, for the most part, technology itself is *speculative*, whereas in art the *emotional* component is dominant. Technology gives direction to natural forces; it separates and classifies them to make them useful. Artistic creative power must remain unrestricted and undivided for it to attain internal law by means of subjective discharging.

If technology were to impinge upon creative artistic operation, if art were to become speculative, humanity would gradually lose all of its creative abilities. Already today we are witnessing how the one-sided use of technological inventions has caused a partial regression in artistic culture. It thus appears paradoxical that technology should have the task of retrieving art from the very regression into which it drove it. Nevertheless, by creating modern miracles, technology also inspires faith in them and thereby displaces the faith in the miracles of the old religions.

For this reason, the *ethical* side of technology is found in the *undemanding servitude* with which it supports art. Before technology's great expansion, an artist's aesthetic expression was governed by righteous individualism in all matters. Today, creative individualism manifests itself only in those cases that are truly a matter of artistic expression. In other cases, the artist thrives in the full comfort with which modern technology provides him, and is content to produce artless kitsch rather than things of true aesthetic value.

If technology were to assert itself ethically in film, it could enrich film's expressive capabilities by providing new means of expression and abstract concepts.

When advantageously exploited by technology, elements such as water and fire can have a far greater aesthetic effect when shown on the film screen than a mere verbal accompaniment or the performance of the actors. If a torrent of water is used to illustrate hate and fire to depict some sort of passion, then the morality of regulated water and technologically exploited flames become even more acceptable.

The Elements of Film Production

I have already compared film as a document to a book, because, like a book, it can be reproduced countless times. There are, however, differences between a film and a book. Film always addresses a large number of people, while a book speaks, as a rule, only to an individual.

Therefore, since films and books have different purposes, it follows that a film must be composed differently than a book. Popular subjects for novels are never suitable material for a film of high artistic value.

Because a film is intended to address a large number of people simultaneously, it must possess *broader communicative possibilities* than a book. Sometimes film must reproduce one thing in several different ways, so that it can be understood by spectators of varying dispositions. In this way, the ideas in a film acquire a certain universality. For example, rhythm can be depicted in a number of ways. Take, for example, the movement of a pendulum supplemented by music. Or trotting horses—the movement of a Russian troika itself presents a variously interlaced rhythm—rhythm can also be personified, and so on. These various depictions of rhythm not only contribute to greater intelligibility, but also to the *plasticity* of the whole concept.

That which has been said about rhythm also holds true for different concepts and feelings. Film creates an *abstract space* for them.

Film production is primarily contingent upon two types of movement: that of the filmed subject and that of the film camera. The relative relationship between these two movements determines the various *intervals of motion* and thereby also film's various expressive possibilities.

1. The filmed subject moves around a fixed camera
2. Or the inverse
3. The camera and the filmed subject are in parallel motion
4. Or in contrary motion, etc.

In the first case, the filmed subject acquires a quality that is more spatial, and, in the second case, a quality that is more plastic. In the third case, the subject's linearity is emphasized, and, in the fourth, the expression of motion is the most powerful, because it puts the spectator in the middle of the filmic action itself.

For the depiction of rhythm, the third case is the most advantageous, for it combines the movement of the camera with that of the subject. Since rhythm itself is linear, it is amplified by additional linearity. If a movement were to be photographed not by a moving camera but by a firmly fixed camera, the perspective would disturb the linearity of the movement and thereby its original expression.

Through the succession of various particular details in a film, the spectator is guided to a comprehension of the whole as a consequence of the film's *diversity of expression*. In all the other arts, this process is reversed. Sculpture, architecture, painting, even theater are perceived primarily as a whole, and the examination of details commonly disturbs the perception of the whole. Because of its ability to express one thing in several different ways, film alters the demands that have, thus far, been put to the film director. In the future, films will depend less and less on the simple characterization of human qualities and will instead strive to express various abstract concepts and feelings.

Sound and Image

With silent film, the goal of technology was to faithfully record nature. With sound film, its goal is to precisely synchronize sound and image. In later stages of development, it will be necessary to introduce greater differentiation to this primitive concurrence in order to achieve a more artistic form of expression. It is possible to supplement the spoken word with an image, and the image with music. Music can draw out an image even after it has been replaced on the screen by a different image. In other cases, music sets up the mood for the image much better than the written or spoken word can. We can increase the expressive possibilities of film if we proceed with the demand that musical accompaniment in film have the utmost freedom.

A filmed opera that preserves the reality of the action will undoubtedly end in failure. In contrast to this, even church music would provide a better guideline for the whole filmic composition than opera can.

Seriousness, Cheerfulness, and Grotesque

It has always been the prerogative of mimetic acting to make a distinction between seriousness and cheerfulness. Silent film in particular was afforded its most effective form of expression by such acting.

The films of Chaplin are prototypical examples of films rooted in mimetic acting. But, in the era of sound film, such acting does not have the same effect it once did. Simple mimetic acting, even if it is highly virtuosic, is not sufficient for contemporary films. Contemporary film is subject to internal laws similar to those of musical composition. For this reason, seriousness, cheerfulness, etc. must be expressed in such a way that the connection between film and music is more convincingly manifested.

The most primitive, almost childish, way to make a melody more cheerful is to transpose it to a higher octave. In a similar fashion, a serious film can be made cheerful. For example, when solemnly marching feet are instantly replaced by waving hands. Such a move is an entirely external imitation of musical transposition and it will lose its effect if it is not internally convincing. It is common practice for film to translate musical elements into visual elements like this. Of course, it is important that such translations be dictated by the *internal necessity* of the filmic action.

The cheerful or serious manner of film can easily fill up the entire action. The same cannot be said for film grotesque. Film grotesque can provide a more suitable supplement to a serious than to a cheerful film, but it cannot exist in and for itself alone, because it originates from unreal impossibilities. In contrast, a cheerful film operates entirely within the framework of possible situations, even though they might be exaggerated—for example, when a glass chandelier begins to vibrate with the tremolo of a singing tenor, or when an audible voice of conscience starts to speak during a moment of indecision. Although these are exaggerations, they do not deviate from the realm of possibility. In musical terms, this is comparable to the harmonic resonances in the upper registers of a tone.

The cheerfulness of grotesque is actually linked to seriousness, and therefore it is not entirely free in manifesting itself. Compared with grotesque in film, grotesque in the theater has the disadvantage that it can only express *impossibility* in psychological relationships. With the aid of technology, however, film is able to express external impossibilities, for example by reversing the direction of the film reel, using negative exposure instead of positive, decreasing or increasing the speed of movement, using red-green stereoscopic film, etc.[4]

From such technological grotesques, film also crosses over to the famous cartoon grotesques. Even though grotesque is suitable to liven up a serious film, it must be kept in mind that the effect fades rapidly with the repetition of patterns and stereotypes.

Motion and Absolute Film

An absolute film has an advantage over an absolute painting (which has increasingly become the preoccupation of new painting movements) in that it can also express motion. But, like grotesque, it cannot exist independently. Even an absolute film that arouses *predominantly visual and acoustic ideas* cannot be independent. Unless an absolute film thrusts the spectator into a whirl of motion, the absolute film is not ev-

---

4   Hošek refers to the red/green anaglyph format of early stereoscopic films.

erything that it should be. Film should realize that the inspiration for motion must flow from the art of motion. The perception of motion depends neither on natural perspective nor on the principles upon which the science of musical intervals is founded.

Perspective and musical intervals support visual and acoustic ideas rather than the expression of motion.

A spectator viewing a dance may translate the acoustic concepts into visual ideas, but if *absolute film* were to proceed in this way (i.e., translating acoustic concepts into visual ideas) it would fail in its effect.

The motion art created by a dancer who does not see himself or herself does not flow from acoustic or visual concepts, but from an entirely different source of inspiration.

When dance and mimetic gesture are inferred from music, they are not actually expressions of *absolute motion, which is born only of motion itself.*

Realistic film can only express the inspiration of motion imperfectly, because it is more closely tied to the reality of the image than to motion. Even when the camera moves together with the filmed subject, the filmed motion remains merely a visual idea.

The purpose of absolute film is to evoke a true idea of motion without dependence on the reality of the image.

(1939)

**Structure and Sign:
The Prague Linguistic Circle's
Approach to Film**

PART SIX

Jan Mukařovský
AN ATTEMPT AT A STRUCTURAL ANALYSIS OF AN ACTOR'S FIGURE (CHAPLIN IN *CITY LIGHTS*)

Today, the conception of a work of art as a structure—that is, a system of components aesthetically deautomatized and organized into a complex hierarchy that is unified by the prevalence of one component over the others—is accepted in the theory of several arts. It is clear to theorists and historians of music and the visual arts that, in the analysis of a certain work, or even in the history of a given art, we cannot either substitute the psychology of the artist's personality for a structural analysis or confuse the development of a given art with the history of culture or with that of ideology alone. Much of this is clear in the theory of literature as well, though certainly not everywhere nor for everyone. Nevertheless, it is quite risky to use the method of structural analysis for the art of acting, especially if it concerns a film actor who uses his real name for his performances and even goes through all of his roles in the same typical mask. The theorist who tries to separate the appearance from the man and to study the structural organization of the acting figure regardless of the actor's psyche and ethos is in danger of being considered a scandalous cynic who denies the artist his human value. Permit him, therefore, for the sake of his defense and a lucid explanation, to appeal to a recent photo-montage in the *Prager Presse*[1] that juxtaposed a gray-haired man with an intelligent physiognomy, and the simple-minded face of a black-haired young man in a derby hat... Despite its disadvantages, a structural analysis of the dramatic figure has a certain small advantage: the equality of even quite different aesthetic canons is generally admitted in the dramatic arts more than in other arts. The Hamlets of Kvapil and Hilar, Vojan, and Kohout are evaluated in historical perspective without depreciating one another.[2] Perhaps even this study, therefore, will not be criticized for lacking an evaluative perspective.

---

[1]   *Prager Presse* (1921–1939): a German-language Prague daily that voiced official government politics.

[2]   Jaroslav Kvapil (1868–1950) and Karel Hugo Hilar (1885–1935) were progressive theater directors, the former a neoromantic symbolist, the latter an expressionist and civilist; Eduard Vojan (1853–1920) was an actor of the psychological-realist style, while the acting of his colleague Eduard Kohout (1889–1976) developed from impressionism and expressionism toward civilism. All of them worked in the Prague National Theater.

We must first draw attention to the fact that the structure of the actor's figure is merely a partial structure that acquires unambiguity only in the overall structure of the dramatic work. Here it appears in multiple relations; for example, the actor and the stage space, the actor and the dramatic text, the actor and the other actors. We shall consider only one of these relations: the hierarchy of characters in the dramatic work. This hierarchy differs according to period and milieu and, in part, in relation to the dramatic text. Sometimes actors create a structurally bound whole in which no one has a dominant position and no one is the focal point of all the relations among the characters of the work. Sometimes one character (or several) becomes a focal point, dominating the others, who seem to be there only to provide a background or retinue for the dominant figure (or figures). Sometimes all the characters appear equal and lacking structural relations. Their relationship is merely ornamentally compositional. In other words, the tasks and rights of stage direction are evaluated differently in different periods and different milieux. Chaplin's case obviously belongs in the second category. Chaplin is an axis around which the other characters gather, for which they are there. They emerge from the shadows only insofar as they are necessary for the dominant character. This assertion will be developed and proven later.

Let us now turn our attention to the internal structure of the acting figure itself. The components of this structure are many and varied; nevertheless, we can arrange them into three distinct groups. First, there is the set of vocal components. This group is quite complex (the pitch of the voice and its melodic undulation, the intensity and timbre of the voice, tempo, etc.), but, in the given case, it has no importance. Chaplin's films are "pantomimes" (Chaplin uses this term himself to distinguish his latest movie from sound film). Later, we shall explain why his movies cannot but be silent. The second group cannot be identified other than with a triple designation: facial expressions, gestures, poses. These are three different components both from an objective and a structural standpoint. They can parallel one another, but they can also diverge so that their interrelation is felt to be an interference (an effective comic means). Moreover, one of them can subordinate the others to itself or, conversely, all of them can be in equilibrium. What is common to all three of these components, however, is the fact that they are felt to be expressive, to be an expression of the character's mental state, especially his emotions. This property binds them into a unified group. The third group is composed of those movements of the body by which the actor's relation to the stage space is expressed and carried.[3] Frequently the components

---

[3] Even in Chaplin, though he is a typical film actor, we can speak about the stage in the theatrical sense, that is, a static stage, because here the camera is almost passive. Even if it moves, it has only an auxiliary role—for the purpose of close-ups. To prove and elucidate this assertion, let me recall the active role of the camera in Russian films where the changeability of standpoints and perspectives plays the dominant role in the structure of the work, whereas the actor's figure is structurally subordinated. [Original footnote]

of this group cannot be objectively distinguished from those of the preceding group (e.g., the actor's walk can simultaneously be a gesture, i.e., an expression of a mental state, and can cause a change in his relation to the stage space); functionally, as we have suggested, they are quite distinct from the previous group and conjoin into an independent category.

There is certainly no need to provide extensive proof to propound the thesis that, in Chaplin, the components of the second group have the dominant position. For the sake of expediency I shall simply call these gestures and thus extend this term to facial expressions and poses, without undue distortion. As I have already said, the first group (vocal components) is completely suppressed in Chaplin, while the third group (movements) occupies a distinctly subordinate position. Even though movements that change the actor's relation to space do occur, they are charged to the utmost with the function of gestures (Chaplin's walk sensitively reflects every change in his mental state). Hence the dominant position falls to gestures (expressive elements), constituting an uninterrupted series full of interferences and unexpected *pointes* that carries the entire dynamics not only of Chaplin's performance but also of the whole film. Chaplin's gestures are not subordinated to any other component; on the contrary, they subordinate all the other components. In this way, Chaplin's acting distinctly differs from the usual cases. Even if an actor differentiates and emphasizes gestures, they usually serve a word, a movement, or the action. They are passive series whose peripety is motivated by other series.

For Chaplin, the word, which is most capable of influencing gestures, must be completely suppressed if the gestures are to be the dominant component. In a Chaplin film, every distinct word would be a blotch: it would turn the hierarchy of components upside down. For this reason, neither Chaplin himself nor the other characters speak. Typical in this respect is the introductory scene of *City Lights*, the unveiling of a monument, in which distinct words are replaced by sounds having only intonation and timbre in common with words. As far as movements in the stage space are concerned, I have said that they are charged with the function of gestures; as a matter of fact, they are gestures. Moreover, Chaplin's acting figure is rather immobile (his immobility is even stressed by an organic defect in his feet).

And now for the plot. The plot lacks any dynamism of its own: it is merely a series of events linked by a weak thread. Its function is to be the substratum of the dynamic sequence of gestures. The divisions between individual events serve only to provide pauses in the sequence of gestures and to render it coherent through this articulation. Even the incompleteness of the plot is an expression of its atomization. Chaplin's film does not end in a plot conclusion but in a gesture-*pointe*, indeed one of Chaplin's gestures (a look and a smile). This holds only for the European version of the film, but it is characteristic that such a way of concluding the movie is possible.

If we posit the line of gestures as the dominant component of Chaplin's acting figure, we must now define the character of this line. In a negative sense, we can say that none of the three elements (facial expressions, gestures, poses) prevails over the others but that they assert themselves equally. A positive definition of the very essence of this line is: its dynamics are carried by the interference (whether simultaneous or successive) of two types of gestures: gesture-signs and gesture-expressions. Here we must engage in a brief discussion of the function of gestures in general. We have already said that this function is essentially expressive in *all* gestures. But this expressiveness has its nuances. It can be immediate and individual; yet it can also acquire supra-individual validity. In such a case the gesture becomes a conventional sign, universally comprehensible (either in general or in a certain milieu). This is true, for example, of ritual gestures (a typical case: the gestures of a religious cult) and especially social gestures. Social gestures are signs that, in a conventional way—just like words—signal certain emotions or mental states; for instance sincere emotional involvement, willingness, or respect. But there is no guarantee that the mental state of the person who uses the gesture corresponds to the mood of which the gesture is a sign. That is why all the Alcestes[4] of the world are so angry at the insincerity of social conventions. The individual expressiveness ("sincerity") of a social gesture can be reliably recognized only if it is involuntarily accompanied by some nuance that alters its conventional course. It can happen that the particular emotion coincides with the mental state of which the gesture is the sign. In such a case, the gesture-sign will be exaggerated beyond the conventional degree of its intensity (too deep a bow or too broad a smile). But the opposite can also occur: the particular mental state is different from the mood that is supposed to be feigned by the gesture-sign. In this case an interference will occur, either *successive*, i.e., such that the coordination of the series of gestures unfolding in time will be disturbed (the sudden invasion of an individually expressive, involuntary gesture into the series of gesture-signs), or *simultaneous*, i.e., such that the gesture-sign provided, for example, by a facial expression will at the same time be negated by a contradictory gesticulation of the hand based on individual expression, or vice versa.

Chaplin's case is typical of the interference of social gesture-signs with individually expressive gestures. Everything in Chaplin's acting is aimed at heightening and sharpening this interference, even his special costume: ragged formal attire, gloves without fingers, a cane and a black derby. In particular, however, the social paradox of Chaplin that is encapsulated by the very theme of the beggar with social aspirations serves to sharpen the interference of gestures. This provides the basis for the interference. The integrating emotional feature of social gestures is the feeling of

4   Alceste: a character in *Le Misanthrope* by Molière.

self-assurance and superiority, whereas the expressive gestures of Chaplin-the-beggar revolve around the emotional complex of inferiority. These two planes of gestures interweave through the entire performance in constant catachreses. To characterize this interweaving in detail would require an endless enumeration of verbal paraphrases of the individual moments of the performance, which would be monotonous and useless. Much more interesting is the fact that the duality of the plane of gestures is also reflected in the distribution of the supporting characters in Chaplin's performance. There are two supporting characters: the blind flower girl and the drunk millionaire. All the others are demoted to the level of extras, either partially (the old woman) or completely (all the others). Each of the two supporting characters is modified so that he or she can perceive only one plane, one of the interfering series of Chaplin's gestures. Such a one-sided perception is motivated by blindness in the girl, and by intoxication in the millionaire.

The girl perceives only the social gesture-signs. The deformed image she gets of Chaplin is furnished toward the end of the film through a remarkable process of realization. A man, a nondescript social type, comes to the now-seeing girl's shop to buy some flowers. His departure is accompanied by the caption "I thought that it was *him.*" All the scenes in which Chaplin meets the girl—they are always alone so that the presence of a third, seeing person may not shatter the girl's illusion—are founded upon the polar oscillation between the two planes of Chaplin's gestures: social and individually expressive gestures. Whenever Chaplin draws close to the girl in these scenes, the social gestures gain the upper hand, but as soon as he takes a few steps away from her, the expressive gestures suddenly prevail. This is especially evident in the scene in which Chaplin brings gifts to the girl and moves back and forth from the table where the bag of presents is lying to the chair on which the girl is sitting. Here the sudden changes in gestures, the transition from plane to plane, function almost like the *pointes* of epigrams. In this connection we shall also understand why Chaplin's film cannot have the usual "happy ending." A happy ending would entail the complete negation of the dramatic contradiction between the two levels of gestures upon which the film is based, rather than its resolution. If concluded by the beggar's marrying the girl, the film would appear trivial in retrospect, because its dramatic contradiction would be impaired.

Now to the relationship between the beggar and the millionaire. The millionaire, as we have said, also has access to only one of the two interfering series of gestures, the individually expressive ones. He must, of course, be drunk for this deformation of vision to be operative. As soon as he becomes sober, he sees, as all the other people do, the comical interference of the two series, and he behaves toward Chaplin with the same disdain as all the others. But whereas the girl's deformation of perception (her ability to see only one series of gestures) is permanent, and the solution occurs only at the very end of the film, the millionaire's state of deformed vision alternates with states of normal vision. This, of course, provides the hierarchy of the two supporting characters. The girl comes more to the fore, because her permanent deformation of perception provides a broader and stronger basis for the interference of the two planes of gestures than does the millionaire's intermittent intoxication. The millionaire is, however, necessary as the girl's opposite. From the first meeting with Chaplin, when, by means of his expressive gestures, the beggar sings a pathetic hymn to the beauty of life ("Tomorrow the birds will sing")[5] in front of the millionaire, their relationship is full of outpourings of friendship, from one embrace to another. And thus we have quite imperceptibly proceeded from the structural analysis of the actor's figure to the structure of the entire film. This is another proof of the extent to which the interference of the two levels of gestures is the axis of Chaplin's acting.

I will end here, for everything of substance has probably been said. In conclusion, though, let me make a few evaluative comments. What astonishes the spectator in Chaplin's figure is the immense span between the intensity of the effect that he achieves and the simplicity of his devices. He takes as the dominant of his structure a component that occupies usually (in film) an ancillary position: gestures in the broad sense of the term (facial expressions, gestures proper, poses). And to this fragile dominant of limited capacity he manages to subordinate not only the structure of his own figure as actor but even that of the entire film. This presupposes an almost unbelievable economy in all the other components. If any one of them became only a little more emphatic, called only a little more attention to itself, the entire structure would collapse. The structure of Chaplin's acting resembles a three-dimensional shape that rests on the sharpest of its edges but is in perfect equilibrium. Hence the illusion of immateriality: the pure lyrics of gestures freed from dependence upon a corporeal substratum.

(1931)

---

[5]   An intertitle from *City Lights* (USA, 1931).

Jan Mukařovský
A NOTE ON THE AESTHETICS OF FILM

I

It is no longer necessary, as it was only a few years ago, to begin a study of the aesthetics of film with the argument that film is an art. Nevertheless, the question of the relation between aesthetics and film has not yet lost its immediacy, for this young art, whose development is still disturbed by changes in its technological ("mechanical") basis, has a much stronger need than traditional arts for a norm, both in a positive sense (something to observe) and in a negative sense (something to violate). Film artists are at a disadvantage because they face possibilities in their work that are too broad and undiversified. Arts with a long tradition always have at hand a wide range of devices that have gained a definite, stabilized form and conventional meanings through a lengthy development. For example, comparative studies of literary topics show that there are in fact no new themes in literature: the development of almost any theme can be traced back thousands of years. In *The Theory of Prose*, Shklovsky cites the example of Maupassant's story "Le Retour," which is based on an adaptation of the very old theme "a man at the wedding of his own wife," and counts on the reader knowing it from elsewhere. The same holds true for poetry, for example with metrical patterns. Every poetry has a certain repertoire of traditional verse patterns that have acquired, through long years of use, a fixed rhythmical (not only metrical) organization and semantic nuances under the influence of the genres in which they have been used. The poetic genres themselves can be characterized as mere canonized sets of particular devices. This does not, however, mean that the artist cannot alter traditional norms and conventions; on the contrary, they are frequently violated (the contemporary theory of genres is based on the knowledge that the development of genres results from the constant violation of generic norms), and this violation is experienced as an intentional artistic method.

What seems to be a limitation is thus, in essence, an enrichment of artistic possibilities, and until recently film had almost no truly distinct norms and conventions; even now there are only a few. Film artists therefore seek norms. The word "norm," however, brings to mind aesthetics, which used to be, and sometimes still is, considered a normative discipline. But modern aesthetics, which has given up the metaphysical notion of beauty in any form and views artistic structure as a developmental fact, should not be expected to prescribe what should be. A norm can only be the product of the development of art itself, a petrified impression of the developmental process. If aesthetics cannot be the logic of art judging what is correct and what is not, it can nevertheless be something else: the epistemology of art. Every art has certain basic possibilities provided by the character of its material and the way in which the given art masters it. These possibilities imply a limitation, although not a normative one in the sense, for example, of Lessing and Semper, who presumed that art does not have the right to overstep its boundaries, but a factual limitation, in that a particular art does not cease to be itself even if it extends into the territory of another art. *Si duo faciunt idem, non est idem*; sped-up motion in film is thus understood as a deformation of temporal duration, whereas the acceleration of the actor's gestures in theater would be perceived as a deformation of his personality, for dramatic time and film time are epistemologically different.

The transgression of boundaries between the arts is a very frequent phenomenon in the history of art. For example, literary symbolism has often characterized itself as the *music* of the word, while surrealist painting, which works with poetic tropes (with the "transfer" of meaning), claims for itself the name of *poetry*. After all, this is just a return visit of the kind poetry made to painting in the period of so-called *descriptive poetry* (eighteenth century) and during the period of parnassianism (nineteenth century). The developmental significance of such transgressions of boundaries lies in the fact that art learns to experience its constructive devices in a new way and to see its material from an unusual perspective. At the same time, the given art remains itself, does not merge with the adjacent art, but attains different effects through the same device or attains the same effect through different devices. If, however, the approximation of another art is to be incorporated into the developmental order of the art that is striving for this approximation, one condition must be fulfilled: the developmental order and tradition must already exist. The basic condition for this is certainty in handling the material (which does not mean a blind subordination to the material).

Film has already been in close contact with several arts: drama, narrative literature, painting, and music. However, this was in the days when film had not yet mastered its material and it was more a matter of seeking support than a matter of regular development. The effort to master the material is connected with the tendency toward the purely filmic. This is the beginning of regular development. New approximations to other arts will surely come with time, but only as developmental stages. The striving for pure film is paralleled in film theory by an epistemological inquiry into the conditions provided by the material of film. This is the task of the aesthetics of film. It is not supposed to determine the norm but to reinforce the intentionality of this development by exposing its latent preconditions. This paper is an outline of a particular chapter in the epistemology of film: the epistemology of film space.

II

Film space used to be confused with theatrical space, especially in the beginning. However, this confusion does not correspond with reality, even if the camera simply photographed events on a theatrical stage without changing its position, as the nature of theatrical space requires.[1] Theatrical space is three-dimensional, and three-dimensional people move within it. This does not apply in film, which has the possibility of movement, albeit movement projected onto a two-dimensional plane and into illusory space. The actor's attitude toward space is also quite different in film than in theater. The theater actor is a living and integral person clearly distinguished from the inanimate surroundings (the stage and its contents), whereas the consecutive images of the actor (sometimes only partial ones) on the screen are mere components of the total projected picture, just as in painting, for example. The term "naturshchik," or "model," coined by Russian theorists of film for the film actor, expresses the analogy between the position of the actor and that of the model in painting.[2]

Now, what about the relationship between film space and illusory pictorial space? It is clear that pictorial space does exist in film, and with all the means of painterly illusoriness (if we disregard the more profound basic differences between perspective as a device in painting and perspective in photography). This illusoriness can be enhanced by certain means, but these means are mostly also available to painting. One of them consists in a reversal of the usual conception of depth in illusory pictorial space: the viewer's attention, which is usually directed toward the background, is instead drawn outward from the picture. This device was often used in Baroque painting. The direction of a gesture (the person standing in the foreground of the picture aims a revolver at the audience) or the direction of movement (a train goes off as if at a right angle to the pictorial plane) accomplishes this in film. Another means of intensifying spatial illusion is the high-angle and low-angle shot; for example, looking from a high floor of a building into a deep courtyard. In such cases, the illusion is strengthened by the change in the position of the axis of the perceiver's eyes. In reality this position is horizontal (for the perceiver viewing the picture); however, the po-

---

[1]   Otakar Zich, *Estetika dramatického umění* (Praha: Melantrich, 1931).

[2]   There are, however, nuances in filmic practice; the actor's individuality can be emphasized in film, or, on the other hand, it can be suppressed. Contrast the differences between Chaplin's films and Russian films. [Original footnote]

sition presupposed by the picture is almost vertical. Film has both of these means in common with painting.

Another possibility is the following. The camera is mounted on a moving vehicle, with the lens aimed forward. The movement then takes place in a street or an alley, in other words, along a path lined on both sides by a continuous series of objects. We do not see the vehicle in the picture; we see only the street (the path) leading into the background of the picture but quickly running in the opposite direction, outward from the picture. Because of the motion, it might seem that this is a specifically filmic device, but in fact it is only a modification of the aforementioned case (the reversal of the conception of spatial depth), which is wholly accessible, in some of its variants, to painting.

The basis for film space is thus illusory pictorial space. In addition, the art of film has at its disposal another form of space unavailable to other arts. This is the space provided by the technique of the shot. Whenever a change from one shot to another occurs, whether smoothly or abruptly, the angle of the lens or the placement of the entire camera in space changes, too. This spatial shift is reflected in the spectator's consciousness through a peculiar feeling that has often been described as the illusory displacement of the spectator himself. René Clair explains: "Thus the spectator who sees some faraway automobile race on the screen is suddenly thrown under the huge wheels of one of the cars, scans the speedometer, takes the steering wheel in hand. He becomes an actor and sees, in the turns of the road, rushing trees swallowed up before his eyes."[3] This presentation of space from "inside" is a specifically filmic device; it was only with the discovery of the shot that film was permitted to cease being an animated picture.

The technique of the shot, moreover, has had a reverse influence upon the technique of photography itself. It has called attention to the interesting possibilities of the high-angle and low-angle shot obtained by circling the object from all sides; still more importantly, it has created the technique of the close-up. The pictorial effectiveness of the close-up consists in the unusual way in which an object is brought near (Epstein says: "I was turning my head, and on the right side I saw a gesture reduced to its mere square root, but on the left side this gesture had already been magnified to the eighth power.");[4] the close-up's spatial effectiveness is achieved by the impression of the incompleteness of the picture that appears to us as a section of

[3] René Clair, "Rythme," in *French Film Theory and Criticism: A History/Anthology 1907–1939*, vol. 1, ed. Richard Abel (Princeton: Princeton University Press, 1993), 369. Originally published in *Les Cahiers du mois*, no. 16–17 (special issue "Cinéma," October 1925), 13–16.

[4] "Je déplaçais la tête et je ne voyais à droite qu'une racine de ce geste, mais à gauche ce geste était élevé à sa huitième puissance." Jean Epstein, "Le Cinématographe vu de l'Etna" (1925), in his *Écrits sur le cinéma, 1921–1953. Tome 1: 1921–1947* (Paris: Seghers, 1974), 136.

three-dimensional space felt to exist in front of the picture and on its sides. Let us imagine, for example, a hand in a close-up. Where is the person to whom this hand belongs? In the space outside the picture. Or let us assume a picture of a revolver lying on a table. It arouses the expectation that at any time a hand will appear and pick up the revolver, and this hand will emerge from the space lying outside the picture where we place its anticipated existence. Here is yet another example. Two people are fighting and rolling on the floor; a knife lies near them. The scene is presented in such a way that we alternately see the fighting pair and the knife in close-ups. Every time the knife appears, there is suspense. When will the hand that will grab it finally appear? When the hand finally appears in a close-up, there is new suspense. Which one of the pair has taken hold of the knife? Only where we have an intense awareness of the space outside the picture may we speak of a dynamic close-up. Otherwise it would be a matter of a static section of a normal visual field. It should be noted, however, that the awareness of its "pictorialness" does not disappear during the close-up; we do not transfer the size of the close-up into off-screen space, and the magnified hand is not the hand of a giant for us.

In shots, film space is presented successively through a series of images; we feel it in passing from one image to another. Sound film has introduced the additional possibility of the simultaneous presence of film space. Let us imagine a situation quite common in film today. We see an image, and at the same time we hear a sound whose source must be placed somewhere outside the picture rather than inside it. For example, we see a person's face and hear speech that is not uttered by the person in the image; or we see the legs of dancing people and hear their words; or we see a street from a moving vehicle that itself remains hidden, while we hear the hoofbeats of horses drawing a carriage; and so on. This produces an awareness of a space "between" the image and the sound.

Let us now pose the question of the essence of this specifically filmic space and its relation to pictorial space. I have named three means through which filmic space can be achieved: a change in shot, the close-up, and the off-screen localization of sound. I will proceed from the one that is fundamental to all of them, the one without which film space would not exist at all: the shot. Let us imagine any scene occurring in a particular space (like a room). This space does not have to be shown in a full shot; it can be presented by means of hints, a sequence of partial shots. Even then we will experience its unity; i.e., we shall perceive the individual pictorial (illusory) spaces shown consecutively on the screen as images of separate sections of a unified three-dimensional space. How will this total unity of space be presented to us? To answer this question, let us remind ourselves of the *sentence* as a semantic whole in language. The sentence is composed of words, none of which contains its total meaning. That meaning becomes fully known to us only when we have heard the entire sentence. Nevertheless, as soon as we hear the first word we evaluate it in accordance with the potential meaning of the sentence, a component of which it will be. The sense or meaning of the whole sentence is thus not contained in any of its words but exists potentially in the speaker's and the listener's consciousness in every word from first to last, and we can observe the successive unfolding of meaning from the beginning of the sentence to its end. All of this can also be said about film space. It is not fully given in any of the images, but each image is accompanied by an awareness of the unity of the total space, and the notion of this space gains definition with the progression of the sequence of pictures. Thus we may suppose that specifically filmic space, which is neither a real nor an illusory space, is space-as-meaning. Illusory spatial segments presented in consecutive pictures are partial signs of this space-as-meaning, the entirety of which "signifies" the total space.

We can deduce the semantic nature of film space from a concrete example. In a study on the poetics of film, Tynyanov cites this pair of shots: (1) a meadow where a herd of pigs runs around; (2) the same meadow, trampled down, but now without the herd, where a man is walking.[5] Here Tynyanov sees an example of filmic simile: man – pig. But if we imagine these two scenes in one shot (whereby the interference of specifically filmic space would be eliminated), we discover that the awareness of the semantic link between the two phenomena yields to an awareness of the mere temporal successiveness of the two scenes. Film space thus operates only through a change in shot and does so as a semantic factor. The semantic energy of the close-up, one of the means of creating filmic space, is also well known. Epstein says: "Another power of the cinematograph is its animism. An inanimate object, for example, a revolver, is merely a prop in the theater. In film, however, it can be magnified. That Browning which a hand pulls slowly from a half-open drawer ... suddenly becomes alive. It becomes a symbol of a thousand possibilities."[6] This polysemic quality of the close-up is facilitated by the very fact that the space into which the revolver will be aimed and into which it will disgorge its bullet is at the moment of the projection of this close-up merely an intuitive space-as-meaning, concealing precisely these "thousand possibilities."

Because of its semantic character, film space is much closer to space in literature than to theatrical space. In literature, too, space is meaning. What else could it be if

---

5   Yuri Tynyanov, "Ob osnovakh kino," in *Poetika kino*, ed. Boris Eikhenbaum (Moskva: Kinopechaťٰ, 1927), 67. [Footnote by John Burbank and Peter Steiner]

6   The passage is a very loose quotation from Epstein's "Le Cinématographe vu de l'Etna" (Epstein, *Écrits sur le cinéma*, 134): "L'une des plus grandes puissances du cinéma est son animisme [...] Les décors se morcellent et chacune de leurs fractions prend une expression particulière [...] Il fut temps, encore peu éloigné, où il n'y avait pas de drames américaines sans la scène du revolver qu'on sortait lentement d'un tiroir à moitié ouvert. J'aimais ce revolver. Il apparaissait comme le symbole de mille possibilités."

it is rendered by the word? Many narrative sentences can be transcribed into filmic space without a change in their structure. Let us take this one as an example: "They embrace slowly, then abruptly break apart, savagely snatch up their knives and throw themselves forward, weapons raised." This is a sentence that could serve, with its present tense, as an expression of a moment of suspense in a novel; in reality it has been excerpted from Delluc's screenplay *La Fête espagnole* (*Spanish Fiesta*)[7] and broken down into shots as follows:

shot 175 – It's a deal. They embrace slowly, then abruptly break apart, savagely snatch up
shot 176 – their knives
shot 177 – and throw themselves forward, weapons raised....[8]

It should also be remembered that narrative has at its disposal, and has had for a long time, a means of presenting space similar to that of film, especially the close-up and panning (a smooth transition between one camera position and another). As proof let me cite a few traditional stylistic clichés: "I lowered my gaze toward...," "his eyes were riveted upon..."—close-ups; "X. looked around the room: On the right side of the door stood an étagère, next to it a closet..."—panning; "here two people were standing in animated conversation, over there a whole group of people who ... elsewhere a small crowd was hurrying somewhere..."—sudden change in shot.

The resemblance between film and book illustration is instructive for the proximity between the filmic and the literary treatments of space. Let me mention only one instance. Certain movements in the art of illustration specializing in marginalia to the text frequently work with the close-up. There is, for example, Čech's illustrator, Oliva;[9] when Čech's text speaks about Mr. Brouček lighting one match after another, there is a marginal illustration next to the type—a half-open box out of which a few matches have fallen. This is a close-up; however, it is not quite the same as in film, because the standard frame size is not maintained; that is, the real film close-up takes in the same expanse of screen as, for example, the long shot. Therefore we could only speak of the equivalence of illustration and film (with the exception of movement) if all the illustrations in a given work, close-ups as well as long shots, took up whole pages. However, Oliva consistently avoids any scale in his illustrations, letting the pictures without a frame diffuse themselves in projections over the plane of

7   Germaine Dulac, France, 1920.

8   Louis Delluc, *Drames de cinéma* (Paris: Éditions du Monde Nouveau, 1923), 14. [Footnote by J. Burbank and P. Steiner]

9   The painter Viktor Oliva (1861–1928) illustrated *Pravý výlet pana Broučka do měsíce* [Mr. Brouček's genuine trip to the moon, 1889], the famous satirical novel by Svatopluk Čech about a petit-bourgeois philistine undertaking an imaginary journey to the moon.

the pages. Therefore his technique is precisely a reflection of literary space, which means to the extent that it has no dimension; this is because the sign of literary space is the word, whereas the sign of film space is the shot. Film space thus has dimension, at least in its signs (proper filmic space-as-meaning does not, of course, have dimension, as we saw when we dealt with the close-up). A higher degree of sheer semantic quality thus distinguishes literary space from filmic space, despite their considerable similarities. This is related to the fact that we may abstract from space in literature, whereas space is always inevitably present in film. Moreover, literary space has all the summarizing power of the word. Hence the impossibility of a mechanical transposition of a literary description into film. G. Bofa has vividly illustrated this fact: "The poet wrote that a cab galloped by. The director will show it to us; it is an authentic cab, decked out with a coachman in a white hat whose horse, over the course of a few meters of film, is galloping. You are not given the option to imagine it; this is a reward for the spectator's laziness."[10]

So far I have treated the subject as if the overall space that is gradually provided by the context was unique and unchangeable in every film. However, we must also take into account that space can change in the course of the same film; it can even do so several times. Considering the semantic character of this space, such a change involves a transition from one semantic context to another. A change in scene is something quite different from the transition from shot to shot in the same space. Even if there is a large span between shots, this transition is not an interruption of the continuous succession, whereas a change in scene (a change in the overall space) does constitute such an interruption. We must therefore examine changes in scene.

These changes in scene can occur in several ways: by means of a jump, a gradual shift, or bridging. In the first case (a jump), the last shot of the preceding scene and the first shot of the following one are simply juxtaposed. This is a considerable interruption of the spatial context, the extreme limit of which is complete disorientation. Naturally this kind of transition is charged with meaning (is semanticized); for example, it can mean a condensed summation of the action. In the second case (a shift) a sudden fade-out and fade-in are inserted between the two scenes, or the last shot of the first scene is dissolved into the first shot of the second. Each of these devices has its specific meanings. The fade-out can signify, for example, the temporal distancing of consecutive sequences; the dissolve can mean a dream, a vision, a memory; in both cases, of course, many other meanings are possible. In the third case (bridging), the transition is accomplished through a purely semantic process, for instance,

---

[10] Gus Bofa (Gustave Blanchot, 1883–1968), a French caricaturist and book illustrator; see Gus Bofa, "Du dessin animé, et plus généralement du cinéma envisagé comme une mobilisation de l'absurde," in *Les Cahiers du mois*, no. 16–17 (special issue "Cinéma," October 1925), 53.

a filmic metaphor (a motion occurring in one scene is repeated with a different meaning in the following one: we see young men tossing up their leader, whom they like—then a change in scene—and a quite analogous motion which is, however, shoveling up broken soil), or an anacoluthon ("a dislocation in syntactic construction": a policeman's gesture meaning "the way is clear"—then a change in scene—we see the iron grating of a shop flying up as if at the sign given by the policeman).

We should add that sound film has multiplied the possibilities of transition. On the one hand, it has made possible new variations in transition by bridging (a sound occurring in one scene is repeated in another with a different meaning); on the other, it has provided the possibility of linking by means of speech (it is hinted in one scene that the characters will go to the theater; in the following sequence, presented without optical transition, we see a theater hall). Each of the methods of transition has a specific character that is exploited variously according to the structure of the given film. In general, we can only say that, as film gets closer to its very essence, the gradual shift or bridging becomes increasingly its basic mode of transition. The introduction of sound film in particular has begun a new stage. As long as film worked with intertitles, transition by means of a jump was always possible, so that it was not felt as something exceptional, even in sequences with no intertitles. Since intertitles have disappeared, the feeling of the continuity of space has become increasingly stronger. And thus even the transition from scene to scene is not exempt from the general character of filmic space: its successive unfolding is oriented toward continuity.

The successiveness of film space, whether it concerns a change in shot or a change in scene, does not automatically entail a smooth flow; on the contrary, the tension arising from these changes creates the dynamics of this unfolding of space. It is precisely at these places in a film that the spectator must make some effort to understand the spatially semantic relation between contiguous shots. The degree of this tension varies, but it can be stepped up to such an intensity that it alone suffices to carry the dynamics of the whole film, especially if frequent transitions from scene to scene are used, since they are more dynamic and conspicuous than transitions between shots. As an example of a film constructed solely upon this specifically filmic tension, let me mention Vertov's *The Man with a Movie Camera*,[11] in which the theme is almost entirely suppressed and can be expressed by a single caption: a day in the city streets. This case is exceptional. Usually a film has a theme that takes the shape of a story. If we ask about the essence of this theme, we will discover that a specific meaning is involved here, just as in the case of filmic space. Despite the fact that the "models" of film are concrete people and objectively real things (the actors and the

---

[11] *Chelovek s kino-apparatom* (Dziga Vertov, USSR, 1929).

scenery), the story itself is nevertheless provided by someone (the scriptwriter) and is constructed during the shooting and montage (by the director) so that the audience will understand it, will conceive it in a specific way. These circumstances convert the story into meaning. But the similarity between filmic story and filmic space-as-meaning goes even further. Filmic story (just like literary story) is successively realized meaning: in other words, it is provided not only by the quality of the motifs but also by their succession; if the succession of motifs is changed, the story changes, too. As evidence, let me quote from a daily newspaper:

> It happened some time ago in Sweden. The censor did not pass ... the Russian movie *The Battleship Potemkin*.[12] As is well known, the film begins with a sequence depicting the maltreatment of sailors, after which the dissidents are to be shot, but a revolt and uprising take place on the ship. There is also fighting in the city. Odessa in the year 1905! A fleet of battleships appears, but lets the mutineers sail away. This plot was too revolutionary for the [Czechoslovak] censor. The distributing company presented the film to the censor once more. There were no changes in the pictures and captions. The film was simply "recut" and the scenes scrambled. The result: the film edited in this way begins with the middle part. With the mutiny! (thus after the scene of the interrupted execution). Odessa 1905! The Russian fleet, with which the original version ends, appears, but the first part of the film follows immediately thereafter. Now after the mutiny the sailors stand in a row; they are bound and put it front of the muzzles of guns. The film ends![13]

If, however, story is meaning and moreover successively realized meaning, then in a film with a story line there are two successive semantic series that run simultaneously, but not parallel, through the whole film: space and story. Their interrelation is felt regardless of whether the director takes them into account. If this relationship is treated as a definite value, its artistic exploitation is guided in every concrete case by the structure of the film in question. In general, one can only say that the story is felt to be the basic semantic series, whereas successively realized space appears as a differentiating factor. This is because space is, after all, predetermined by action. This does not mean that this hierarchy could not be reversed by subordinating story to space, but only that its reversal is felt as an intentional deformation. The absolute realization of such a reversal is quite possible in film because it does not violate its specific character but rather enhances it. Proof of this could be the aforemen-

---

[12]   *Bronenosets Potyomkin* (Sergei M. Eisenstein, USSR, 1925).

[13]   We were unable to identify this quote. A similar event is described in almost the same way by Béla Balázs in *Der Geist des Films* (Halle: Wilhelm Knapp, 1930), 48–49.

tioned film *The Man with a Movie Camera*. The opposite extreme is the suppression of successive space in favor of the action; however, to achieve this completely would mean to nullify the specifically filmic space by immobilizing the camera during shooting. What would remain would be only pictorial space as a shadow of the real space in which the action took place during shooting. Therefore, cases of such a radical "defilmization" of film could be found in the initial stage of development of this art.

Between these two extremes, there is a wide range of possibilities. General rules for the actual selection cannot be found theoretically because selection is determined not only by the character of the chosen story but also by the director's intention. Without risk of dogmatism we can only say that the more weakly the plot is connected through motivation (that is, the more it works with mere temporal and causal continuity), the more easily the dynamics of space can assert themselves in the plot, although this does not mean that one could not attempt to link strong motivation with strong dynamization of space. After all, the dynamization of space in film is not a simple concept, as has been shown: shots function in the structure of film in one way; changes of scene in another way. We can therefore distinguish between story lines that yield easily to a great span between individual shots (those in which motivation is transferred primarily into the interior of the acting characters so that unusual transitions between shots can be conceived as shifts in the fields of vision of the characters themselves) and story lines easily reconciled with frequent changes in scene (those based on the external acts of the characters). Again, I am not expressing a rule but simply describing the path of least resistance. The path of greatest resistance can undoubtedly also be taken in a concrete case.

All that has been said in this article about the epistemological conditions of film space claims only a very limited validity. As early as tomorrow, a revolutionary change in the technology of this art may provide it with new, quite unexpected conditions.

[1933]

Jan Mukařovský
TIME IN FILM

Film is an art with multiple relations. There are threads connecting it to literature (both the narrative and the lyric), drama, painting, and music. Film has specific constructive devices in common with every one of these arts, and every one of them has influenced film in the course of its development. The strongest ties, however, link film to the narrative and the drama; this is evident from the number of filmed novels and plays. We can say even more: the epistemological conditions provided by its material place film *between* the narrative and the drama so that it has some basic characteristics in common with each of them. All three arts are related by the fact that they are arts founded on action, whose subject is a series of facts connected by temporal succession and a causal bond (in the broadest sense of the word). This has its significance both for their practice and for their theory. In practice, this affinity facilitates the transposition of subjects from one to another and increases the possibility of mutual influence. At the start of its development, film was under the influence of the narrative and the drama; now it is beginning to reciprocate by means of a reverse influence (for example, the influence of the filmic techniques of the shot and panning on the presentation of space in modern narrative prose). For theory, the closeness of film to the narrative and the drama makes their comparison possible. To this closely bound triad of arts we can appropriately apply the general methodological rule that the comparison of materials with many common features is scientifically interesting because, on the one hand, latent differences come sharply to the fore against a background of multiple coincidences and, on the other hand, we can arrive at reliable general conclusions without the risk of hasty generalizations. In this outline I wish to attempt a comparison of filmic time with dramatic and narrative time in order to elucidate film itself through a comparison with arts that have been better theorized, and possibly to arrive, with the help of film, at a more precise characterization of time in the arts of action in general than has been possible up to now.

As I have said, the most basic common feature of the film, the narrative, and the drama is that their subject matter is founded on action. Action can be defined in the most elementary way as a series of facts connected by temporal succession; it is thus inevitably bound to time. Time is therefore an important structural component in all three of these arts, though each has different temporal possibilities and requirements. The drama, for example, has a very limited potential to present simultaneous actions or even displace segments of a temporal series (perform what happened earlier after what happened later), whereas the exploitation of simultaneity and temporal shifts are normal in narrative. In this respect, as we shall see, film stands between the temporal possibilities of drama and narrative.

If we wish to understand the differences among the temporal constructions of the three contiguous arts, we must realize that there are two temporal levels to each of them: one provided by the action, the other by the time experienced by the perceiving subject (the spectator, the reader). In the drama these two times elapse parallel to one another. When the curtain is up, the flow of time is the same on stage as in the audience (if we disregard subtle discrepancies that do not disturb the subjective impression of sameness; for example, acts whose course does not have significance for the action, such as writing a letter, are abbreviated on stage; the flow of the audience's real time can also be projected into a much larger scope if the parallelism of temporal proportions is preserved). The time of the perceiving subject and that of the action thus elapse side by side in the drama; therefore the action of a drama takes place in the spectator's *present*, even if the subject of the drama is temporally located in the past (a historical drama). Hence the feature of dramatic time that Zich designates as its transitoriness,[1] which consists in the fact that only that section of the action immediately before our eyes appears to us as present, whereas what has preceded is at the given moment already swallowed up by the past; the present then is in constant movement toward the future.

Let us now confront the drama with the narrative. In narrative, action is also presented as a temporal sequence. The relation of this action-time to the temporal flow experienced by the perceiving subject (the reader) is, however, quite different, or, more precisely, there is no relation between them. Whereas the flow of action-time in the drama is connected to the elapsing of the spectator's time to the extent that even the duration of the drama is limited by the normal ability of the spectator's concentrated attention, it does not matter how much time we spend reading; we can read a novel continuously or intermittently, in a week or in two hours. The time in which the narrative action takes place is completely detached from the real time in which the reader lives. In the narrative, the perceiving subject's temporal localization is felt as an indefinite present without temporal flow reflecting itself against the background of the elapsing past in which the action takes place. Through the separation

---

[1]   Otakar Zich, *Estetika dramatického umění* (Praha: Melantrich, 1931), 219.

of action-time from the reader's real time, the narrative has a theoretically infinite potential to condense the story. A story covering many years, which would require an entire evening in a dramatic performance, even with great temporal omissions between single acts, can be summed up in one sentence in a narrative: "A certain rich gentleman married a beautiful young girl who, however, soon died and left him a little daughter, Helen."[2]

If we now compare film with these two types of temporal constructions, that is, the drama and the narrative, we see that here again it is a matter of a different exploitation of time. At first glance it might seem that film is temporally so close to the drama that the temporal construction is the same. A more detailed examination, however, will show that filmic time also has many characteristics that distinguish film from the drama and bring it closer to the narrative. In particular, film has an ability to condense a story that is quite similar to narrative condensation. Here are a few examples. Consider a long journey by train, which has no significance for the story since it elapses "uneventfully." The narrative writer would sum this up in one sentence. The film director shows us a railroad station before the departure of the train, the train going through the countryside, a person sitting in a compartment, and perhaps the arrival of the train at the destination; thus in a few meters of film and in a few minutes he "depicts" synecdochically the action of many hours or even days. An even more illustrative example is Shklovsky's film *House of Death*,[3] where the march of a column of convicts from Petersburg to Siberia is presented in the following way: We see the legs of the convicts and their guards tramping over the frozen snow while we hear a song that they are singing; the song continues and the shots change; we catch sight of a winter landscape, then the procession itself, again close-ups of legs, and so on; suddenly we realize that the landscape through which the procession is passing is no longer wintry but springlike; summer and autumn landscapes flash by in the same manner; the song goes on uninterruptedly, and, when it is finished, we see the convicts at their destination. In this way, a journey of many months has been summed up in a few minutes. The departure of the action-time from the spectator's real time is obvious in these cases. In the same way that a narrative writer could abbreviate the long period of the journey by omitting all the detailed events in a short span of several sentences, the scriptwriter summarizes it into a few shots.

Another characteristic that filmic time shares with narrative time is the possibility of transition from one temporal level to another, that is, the possibility of succes-

---

[2] Josef and Karel Čapek, "Mezi dvěma polibky," in J. and K. Čapek, *Zářivé hlubiny a jiné prosy* 2nd ed. (Praha: Ot. Štorch-Marien, 1924), 46.

[3] The film *Myortvyy dom* (Vasili Fyodorov, USSR, 1932) was based on Viktor Shklovsky's adaptation of Fyodor Dostoyevsky's novel *Zapiski iz mertvogo doma* (*House of the Dead*).

sively presenting simultaneous actions on the one hand, and the capability of returning in time (flashback) on the other. Here, however, the analogy of film with the narrative is not so unconditional as in the previous case. Jakobson has recently pointed out that simultaneous actions are applicable only to film with intertitles, that is to say, a kind of film with a narrative component (the verbal presentation of action), since a caption of the type "Meanwhile," conjoining simultaneous actions, is a narrative device.[4] Flashback also has more limited possibilities in film than in the narrative, though it is not as impossible as in the drama. As an example, let me cite an excerpt from Delluc's screenplay "Le Silence":

52 Pierre's drawn face; he is remembering.
53 Pierre seen from afar in the middle of the apartment. He is searching his memory. Slowly. But for us the shots follow one another very quickly.
54 Aimée, in an evening grown, falls forward in the middle of the drawing room.
55 Smoke.
56 A revolver.
57 Pierre's hand (the same rings) is holding the revolver.
58 Aimée stretched out on the rug.
59 Pierre standing in front of her. He throws the revolver down.
60 Pierre is bending over and is going to lift Aimée.
61 The servants are coming. Pierre instinctively steps back.
62 Pierre's face after the murder.
63 Pierre's face, now remembering the scene.
64 A shot of Pierre in the past, at his desk. He is writing. Aimée sits on the arm of his easy chair and tenderly kisses him. A visitor enters. It is Jean, an elegant young man. Aimée leaves, annoyed. Jean follows her intently with his eyes. Pierre notices this and becomes worried.
65 A dinner. Suzie, next to Pierre, is speaking to him with as much emotion as circumstances permit. Jean, next to Aimée, is passionately courting her. Aimée's embarrassment; she is compelled to remain courteous. Pierre watches them anxiously.
66 The same evening. A corner of the drawing room. Suzie is bothering Pierre (who is no longer thinking about his jealousy). But Pierre is either cautious or faithful. He gracefully slips away from her.
67 Another corner of the drawing room. Jean is harassing Aimée with his amorous insinuations; she doesn't know how to get rid of him.
68 Pierre notices them and again becomes furious. Suzie comes up to him, all smiles, but he coolly spurns her.

---

[4]   Mukařovský refers to Roman Jakobson's 1933 article "Is the Film in Decline?" See this anthology.

69 Suzie's face. She is insulted, and her pride has been terribly wounded.

70 Pierre in his smoking room. One morning. He is opening his mail.

71 An anonymous letter: "If you do not want to be intentionally blind, you will defend your honor. Keep a close eye on your wife."

72 Pierre, nervous and grim. He goes out. He hides behind a door opening onto the street.

73 Jean, very elegant, dressed for a visit, in the street. He goes into Pierre's house. Pierre goes after him.

74 Jean in the drawing room. Aimée comes in. She reproaches him, begs him to leave her in peace, etc... He laughs, doesn't want to know anything, cries out that he is in love, etc. ... etc.

75 Pierre behind the door.

76 Jean grabs Aimée. She defends herself. He kisses her against her will. Smoke. Aimée falls. Jean flees.

77 Aimée stretched out on the rug.

78 Pierre standing in front of her, the revolver in his hand.[5]

Here we have an obvious flashback: a murder and only afterwards a depiction of how it took place. The flashback is presented here in a loose temporal sequence, that is, it is motivated by the free association of a recollecting individual. In the drama, such displacement of story segments would necessarily be understood as a miracle (the resurrection of a dead person) or as a surrealist disruption of the unity of theme but never as a return to the past. This is because dramatic time is strictly irreversible due to the close bond between action-time and the perceiving subject's time. Even in sound film we could hardly imagine such a transition from a closer temporal level to a more remote one, even though it is motivated by recollection, for sound (in the above case, a shot and the characters' utterances), added to the optical impression, would make the break between temporal levels impossible. It would not be very plausible, for example, for the person whom we see as dead to appear and even speak in the following scene. In the progression from silent film with captions to silent film without captions to sound film the possibility of a temporal shift thus decreases. Nevertheless, the possibility of such a shift is not totally suppressed, even in sound film. For instance, in a flashback motivated by a recollection, the recalled scene can be rendered only acoustically (a reproduction of a past conversation that the spectator has already heard) while the recollecting person is shown on the screen.

How can we explain these characteristics of temporal construction in film? Let us first note the relationship between the time of the perceiving subject and the time of the image projected on the screen. It is obvious that the temporal flow experienced

5   Louis Delluc, *Drames de cinéma* (Paris: Éditions du Monde Nouveau, 1923), 24–27. [Footnote by John Burbank and Peter Steiner]

by the spectator is actualized in film similarly to the way it is in the drama: the time of the film image flows parallel to the spectator's time. This is the resemblance of film to the drama, which explains why film stood so close to the drama in its beginnings and again upon the introduction of sound. We must, however, consider another question. Is what we see on the screen actually the action itself? Can we identify the time of the filmic image with the time of the filmic action? The above examples provide the answer. If a march of many months from Petersburg to Siberia can be presented in a film without interruption and without any obvious temporal leaps in a few minutes, it is apparent that the presupposed action (which in fact did not actually have to be performed continuously) elapses in a *different* time than the picture. Its temporal localization is also different. We are aware that the action itself belongs to the past, whereas what we see on the screen is interpreted as an optical (or optical-acoustic) *report* about this past action. Only this report takes place in our present.

Thus filmic time is a more complex construction than narrative and dramatic time. In narrative time, we must take into account only one temporal flow (the elapsing of the action), and in dramatic time a dual flow (the action line and the elapsing of the spectator's time, the two lines necessarily parallel); in film, there is a triple temporal flow: the action elapsing in the past, the time of the image flowing in the present, and the perceiving subject's time parallel to the latter. Film gains ample possibilities for temporal differentiation through this complex construction. The exploitation of the spectator's own experience of temporal flow provides film with a vitality similar to the vitality of dramatic action (rendering it present), while the sequence of the time of the image inserted between the action and the spectator prevents the automatic linking of the flow of the action with the real time in which the spectator lives. This makes possible a free play with action-time in a way similar to that in the narrative. I have already cited examples; let me add one more concerning the halt of the flow of action in film. It is well known in narrative that beside dynamically ordered motifs (those bound by temporal succession) there are statically clustered groups of motifs as well; that is to say, besides a temporally progressive narration, the narrative has the possibility of temporally static description. Tynyanov has shown that descriptions cut off from the temporal sequence of the action also occur in film. He attributes descriptive power to the close-up, citing a scene in which robbers leaving a burglarized house are described. The description is achieved by means of close-ups of their weapons, and so forth. At this moment, time has stopped. Tynyanov extends this finding to the close-up in general, declaring it excluded from temporal flow,[6] but we could also cite examples of close-ups strikingly incorporated into tem-

6   Yuri Tynyanov, "Ob osnovakh kino," in *Poetika kino*, ed. Boris Eikhenbaum (Moskva: Kinopechat', 1927), 66. The scene Tynyanov describes here comes from the film *Chyortovo koleso* (Grigori Kozintsev and Leonid Trauberg, USSR, 1926).

poral sequences. The fact that Tynyanov's generalization is erroneous does not, however, mean that his observation about the case in point is unimportant. Here it is, indeed, a matter of the suspension of temporal flow, a matter of filmic description made possible only by the fact that the flow of the "image-time" mediates between the spectator's time and that of the action. The action-time can stop because even during its suspension, "image-time" flows parallel to the spectator's time (which, in contrast to the narrative, is actualized).

There are other possibilities for playing with time in film at the boundary between "image-time," which corresponds in its course to the spectator's time, and action-time, which is loose. These are slow-motion and fast-motion film, as well as "reversed" film. In fast- or slow-motion film, the ratio of the speed of action-time to "image-time" is deformed. A much larger (or much smaller) segment of action-time than usual is assigned to a specific segment of image-time. In reversed film, the plot sequence elapses regressively, whereas the flow of "image-time" bound to the spectator's real time is naturally felt as progressive.

In conclusion, let us return to the problem of time in general in the arts founded on action, in order to attempt, on the basis of the experience gained through the analysis of film, a more precise solution than we were able to suggest at the beginning of this article. In analyzing film, we have detected three kinds of temporal sequences: one created by the flow of the plot, another given by the movement of image (objectively we could say by the movement of the film strip in the projector), and another one based on the actualization of the real time experienced by the spectator. However, traces of this triple temporal stratification can also be detected in the narrative and the drama. In the drama, the existence of two extreme temporal streams—action-time and the perceiving subject's time—is not in doubt. As for the narrative, there is, to be sure, only one distinct temporal flow, that of the action, but, as I have already remarked, the spectator's time is given at least as a static present. In both cases, the existence of two temporal levels is thus discernible. What is seemingly missing is the third level, which mediates between these two extremes in film; it is what I have called, in view of the material of film, image-time. What, in fact, constitutes this time? It is the temporal extent of the very work of art as a sign, whereas the other two times are defined with respect to things outside of the work itself. Action-time is related to the flow of a "real" event that is the content (story) of the work; the perceiving subject's time is, as I have remarked, merely a projection of the spectator's (or reader's) real time into the temporal construction of the work. However, if "image-time," which we could perhaps designate more generally as "sign time," corresponds to the temporal extent of the work, it is obvious that its preconditions are also present in the narrative and the drama, whose works also unfold in time.

If we now look at the narrative and the drama, we will find that, here, the duration of the work itself is also reflected in its temporal construction, through the so-called tempo, a term meaning the rhythm of the narration in the individual parts of narrative prose and the overall pace of a stage work (determined by the director). In both cases the tempo appears much more as a quality than as a measurable temporal quantity; however, in film, where the temporal extent of the work is based on the mechanically regular motion of the projector, a quantity also manifests itself in sign time, and this time comes to the fore as a distinct component of the temporal construction. If we thus accept as a necessary epistemological precondition three kinds of temporal levels in all arts founded on action, we can say that film is the art where all three levels have equal status, whereas in the narrative, the level of action-time comes to the fore, and, in the drama, it is the level of the perceiving subject's time (while the level of action-time is passively bound to this).

If we asked—and not only for the sake of symmetry—whether there is an art in which sign time prevails, we would have to turn to the lyric, where we would find a complete suppression of the perceiving subject's time (a present without signs of temporal flow) and of action-time (motifs are not connected through temporal succession). Proof of the full significance of sign time in the lyric is the importance of rhythm, a phenomenon linked to sign time, which it converts into a measurable magnitude.

[1933]

Roman Jakobson
IS THE FILM IN DECLINE?

"We are lazy and uninquisitive." The poet's pronouncement still holds.[1]

We are witnessing the rise of a new art. It is growing by leaps and bounds, detaching itself from the influence of the older arts, and even beginning to influence them itself. It creates its own norms, its own laws, and then confidently rejects them. It is becoming a powerful instrument of propaganda and education, a daily and omnipresent social fact; in this respect, it is leaving all the other arts behind.

Art studies, however, appear completely unaware of the emergence of this new art. The collector of paintings and other rare objects is interested only in the old masters. Why preoccupy oneself with the rise and self-determination of the cinema when one can simply remain content with dreamy hypotheses about the origin of the theater or about the syncretic nature of prehistoric art? The fewer the traces preserved, the more thrilling the reconstruction of the development of aesthetic forms. The scholar finds the history of cinema too banal; it is virtually vivisection, whereas his hobby is hunting for antiques. Still, it is clear that searching among the early heritage of film will soon be a task worthy of the archaeologist. The first decades of the cinema have already become an "age of fragments." For example, there remains almost nothing of French films prior to 1907 except the Lumière brothers' first productions, as the specialists report.

However, is cinema an autonomous art? Where is its specific hero to be found? What kind of material does this art transform? The creator of the Soviet film, Lev Kuleshov, correctly states that it is real things that serve as film material.[2] And the creator of the French film, Louis Delluc, has perfectly grasped that in film even man is "a mere detail, a mere bit *de la matière du monde.*"[3] But, on the other hand, signs are the material of every art. The semiotic essence of cinematic elements is clear to

---

[1]   Alexander Pushkin, *Puteshestvie v Arzrum (Journey to Arzrum),* 1835. [Original footnote]

[2]   See Lev Kuleshov, *Iskusstvo kino* (Leningrad: Tea-kino-pechat', 1929), 34.

[3]   See Louis Delluc, *Photogénie* (Paris: Editions de Brunoff, 1920). [Original footnote]

filmmakers. "The shot must operate as a sign, a kind of letter," emphasizes Kuleshov.[4] For this reason, essays on cinema always speak in a metaphorical way about the language of film and even introduce the notion of film sentences, with subject and predicate, and of film subordinate clauses (Boris Eikhenbaum),[5] or look for verbal and nominal elements in film (André Beucler).[6] Is there a conflict between these two theses? According to one of them, film operates with things; according to the other, with signs. There are observers who answer this question affirmatively: rejecting the second thesis and bearing in mind the semiotic nature of art, they refuse to recognize cinema as art. However, the incompatibility of the two above-mentioned theses was actually already eliminated by St. Augustine. This great thinker of the fifth century who aptly distinguished between the intended object (*res*) and the sign (*signum*), taught, that alongside signs, whose essential task is to signify something, there exist objects that may be used in the function of signs. It is precisely things (visual and auditory), transformed into signs that are the specific material of cinematic art.

We can say about the same person: "hunchback," "big-nose," or "big-nosed hunchback." In all three cases, the object of our words is identical, whereas the signs are different. Likewise, in a film we can shoot such a person from behind—his hump will be seen; then *en face*—his nose will be shown; or in profile, so that both will be seen. In these three shots we have three things functioning as signs of the same object. Now let us demonstrate the synecdochic nature of language by referring to our ugly fellow simply as "the hump" or "the nose." The analogous method in cinema: the camera sees only the hump, or only the nose. *Pars pro toto* is a fundamental method of filmic conversion of things into signs. Scenario terminology with its "medium long shots," "close-ups," and "medium close-ups" is sufficiently instructive in this respect. Film works with manifold fragments of objects that differ in magnitude, and also with fragments of time and space that are likewise varied. It changes their proportions and juxtaposes them in terms of contiguity, or similarity and contrast; that is, it takes the path of *metonymy* or *metaphor* (two fundamental kinds of cinematic structure). The treatment of the functions of light in Delluc's *Photogénie*[7] and the analysis of filmic time and motion in Yuri Tynyanov's penetrating study[8] clearly

4   Lev Kuleshov, *Iskusstvo kino* (Leningrad: Tea-kino-pechat', 1929), 44.

5   See Boris Eikhenbaum, *Problemy kino-stilistiki*, in *Poetika kino*, ed. Boris Eikhenbaum (Moskva: Kinopechat', 1927), 11–52. [Original footnote]

6   André Beucler (1898–1985): French writer, author of film scripts, film critic for numerous interwar journals.

7   See note 3.

8   Yuri Tynyanov, *Ob osnovakh kino*, in *Poetika kino*, ed. Boris Eikhenbaum (Moskva: Kinopechat', 1927), 53–86. [Original footnote]

show that each phenomenon of the exterior world changes into a *sign* on the screen.

A dog does not recognize a painted dog, since a painting is wholly a sign—the painter's perspective is a conventional device. A dog barks at dogs on film because the material of cinema is a real thing, but he remains blind to the montage, to the semiotic interrelation of things he sees on the screen. The theoretician who denies that cinema is art perceives a film as a mere moving photograph; he does not notice the montage, nor does he want to acknowledge the fact that, here, a specific sign system is involved—the attitude of a reader of poetry for whom the words of the poem make no sense.

The number of those who absolutely reject cinema is steadily declining. They are being replaced by critics of sound film. Current slogans state: "Sound film marks the decline of cinema," "it considerably limits the artistic potential of cinema," "the style of the film is in inherent contradiction to speech,"[9] and so on.

Criticism of sound film is particularly rich in premature generalizations. It does not take into consideration the temporarily limited history and narrow character of certain phenomena in cinema. Theorists have hastily assumed that silence is one of cinema's structural properties, and now they are offended that its venture into sound makes it deviate from their biased formulae. Instead of throwing out their theory, they throw out the facts.

They have hurriedly assumed that the features of today's films are the only ones that cinema will devise. They forget that the first of the sound films cannot be compared with the last of the silent ones. The sound film is absorbed today with new technological achievements (it's good enough if one can hear well..., etc.) and preoccupied with the search for new forms to utilize them. We are in a period analogous to that of prewar silent film, whereas the most recent silent films have already achieved a standard, have created classical works, and perhaps just this realization of a classical canon contained its own demise and the necessity of a fundamental reform.

It has been stated that sound film has brought cinema dangerously close to the theater. It has certainly brought the two closer together again, as they were at the dawn of the century, during the years of the "electric theaters"; and it was their being brought together that prepared the way for a new liberation. For, in principle, speech on the screen and speech on stage are two profoundly different phenomena. As long as film was silent, its only material was the visual object; today it is both the visual and the auditory object. Human behavior is the material of the theater. Speech in film is a special kind of auditory object, along with the buzzing of a fly or the babbling of a brook, the clamor of machines, and so forth. Speech on the stage is simply

---

[9]   In the Czech original, Jakobson uses German: "die Stilwidrigkeit des Sprechfilms."

one of the manifestations of human behavior. Speaking about theater and cinema, Jean Epstein once said that the very essence of their respective expressive methods is different.[10] This thesis remains valid for the sound film as well. Why are "asides" and soliloquies possible on the stage, yet not on the screen? Precisely because inner speech is an instance of human behavior and not an auditory object. On the same grounds that film speech is an auditory object, the "stage whisper," which is heard by the audience in a theater but by none of the dramatis personae, is impossible in film.

A characteristic peculiarity of speech on screen, as opposed to speech on stage, is also its optional nature. The critic Emile Vuillermoz condemns this freedom of selection: "The convulsive and irregular way in which speech is sometimes imposed upon and sometimes eliminated from an art consistently silent in the past has destroyed the laws of the spectacle and assigned an arbitrariness to the silent segments."[11] This rebuke is erroneous.

If on the screen we *see* people speaking, we simultaneously *hear* either their words or music. Music, but not silence. Silence in the cinema is valued as an actual absence of sounds; consequently, it becomes an auditory object, just like speech, like a cough, or street noises. In a sound film, we perceive silence as a sign of real silence. It is sufficient to recall how the classroom grows quiet in a scene of Vančura's film *Před maturitou* [Before graduation].[12] In cinema, it is not silence but music that announces the exclusion of the auditory object. Music in cinema serves this end because musical art operates with signs that do not relate to any objects. Auditorily a silent film is entirely "nonrepresentational," and for that very reason demands continual musical accompaniment. Observers unwittingly struck upon this neutralizing function of music in the cinema when they remarked that "we instantly notice the absence of music, but we pay no attention to its presence, so that any music whatsoever is appropriate for virtually any scene" (Béla Balázs),[13] "music in cinema is destined not to be listened to" (Paul Ramain),[14] "its only aim is that one's ears be occupied while complete attention is concentrated on seeing" (Frank Martin).[15]

---

10   See Jean Epstein, *Bonjour cinéma* (Paris: La Sirène, 1921). [Original footnote]

11   Emile Vuillermoz, "La Musique des images," *L'Art cinématographique*, vol. 3 (Paris: Félix Alcan, 1927), 41–66. [Original footnote]

12   Svatopluk Innemann and Vladislav Vančura, Czechoslovakia, 1932.

13   Béla Balázs, *Der sichtbare Mensch, oder die Kultur des Films* (Vienna: Deutsch-Österreichischer Verlag, 1924), 143. [Original footnote]

14   Paul Ramain, "Sur le rôle exact de la musique au cinéma: la musique est-elle utile? – improvisations, partitions cinématographiques, adaptations? – musique ou silence?" *Cinémagazine*, no. 39 (September 25, 1925), 515–518.

15   Frank Martin, "Musique et cinéma," in "Cinéma," special issue, *Les Cahiers du mois*, no. 16–17 (October 1925), 116–119.

The frequent alternation of speech with music in the sound film must not be seen as nonartistic chaos. Just as the innovation of Edwin Porter, and later D. W. Griffith, involved rejecting the use of an immobile camera in relation to the object and brought a variety of shots into film (the alternation of long shots, medium shots, close-ups, and so on), similarly the sound film, with its new diversity, replaces the inertness of the previous approach, which consistently discarded sound from the realm of film objects. In a sound film, visual and auditory reality can be given either jointly or, on the contrary, separately from one another: the visual object is shown without the particular sound to which it is normally connected, or else the sound is severed from the visual object (we still hear a man speaking, but instead of his mouth we see other details of the given scene, or perhaps an entirely different scene). Thus there arise new possibilities for filmic synecdoche. At the same time, the number of methods for joining shots increases (a purely auditory or verbal transition, a clash between sound and image, and so forth).

Intertitles in silent films were an important means of montage, frequently functioning as a link between shots. Semyon Timoshenko even sees this as their primary function.[16] Thus film maintained elements of purely literary composition. For this reason, some silent film directors made attempts to rid film of titles, but these attempts either necessitated the simplification of the plot or considerably retarded the film's tempo. Only in the sound film has the elimination of titles actually been accomplished. Between today's uninterrupted film and yesterday's film interlaced with titles, there is essentially the same difference as between opera and musical vaudeville. Laws of purely cinematic shot linkage are, at present, gaining a monopoly.

If someone in a film shows up in one place and then we see him in another place noncontiguous to the first, a time segment—during which the person is absent from the screen—must have elapsed between the two situations. In the process we are shown either the first place after the person has already departed, or the other place before his arrival, or, finally, a "cutaway": some other scene in which the person doesn't take part. This principle already occurred in silent films, but there, of course, it was enough to connect such scenes with titles in the vein of: "And when he came home..." Only now is the above-mentioned law consistently realized. It can be dispensed with only when two scenes are not joined by contiguity but by similarity or contrast (the person occupies the same position in both scenes), as well as when the intent is especially to stress the rapidity of the jump from one situation to another, or the interruption, the break between the two scenes. Similarly unacceptable within a scene are unmotivated jumps of the camera from one object to another, noncon-

---

[16] Semyon Timoshenko, *Iskusstvo kino i montazh fil'ma: Opyt vvedenyia v teoriu i estetiku kino* (Leningrad: Academia, 1926), 71. [Original footnote]

tiguous one. If such a jump nevertheless occurs, it cannot but emphasize and semantically overload the second object and its sudden interference in the action.

In films of today, following an event, only a succeeding, not a preceding or simultaneous event, can be shown. A return to the past can be performed only as a reminiscence or a story narrated by one of the participants. This principle has an exact analogy in Homeric poetics (in the same way that filmic cutaways correspond to Homeric "horror vacui"). As Tadeusz Zieliński points out, simultaneous actions are presented in Homer either as if they were consecutive events or by the omission of one of the two parallel events, and a palpable gap results if an event is not delineated in advance so that we may anticipate its course.[17] Surprisingly enough, the montage of sound film coincides exactly with these principles of ancient epic poetics. An obvious tendency toward the "linear" character of cinematic time was already present in silent film, but titles allowed for exceptions. On the one hand, captions such as "And meanwhile..." introduced simultaneous actions, and, on the other hand, titles like "He spent his youth in the village" made jumps into the past possible.

Just as the above-mentioned "law of chronological incompatibility" belongs to the Homeric age, not to narrative poetry in general, so, in turn, we do not want to hastily generalize upon the laws of contemporary cinema. The theorist of art who attempts to include the future development of art in his formulae too often resembles Baron Munchausen lifting himself by his own hair. But perhaps one can pick out certain points of departure from which more definite tendencies might develop.

As soon as an inventory of poetic devices takes root and a model canon is established so thoroughly that the literacy of epigones can be taken for granted, then, as a rule, a striving toward prosification usually develops. The *pictorial* aspect of film is minutely elaborated today. And, just for this reason, filmmakers are suddenly calling for sober, epically oriented reportage and there is an increasing aversion to filmic metaphor, to self-contained play with details. In a parallel way, interest in plot construction, which until recently was almost ostentatiously neglected, is increasing. Let us recollect, for instance, Eisenstein's famous, almost plotless films; or Chaplin's *City Lights*, which in fact echoes the scenario of *A Doctor's Love*,[18] a primitive film by Gaumont from the beginning of the century: a blind woman is treated by an ugly hunchbacked doctor, who falls in love with her but does not dare tell her; he says that

---

[17] Tadeusz Zieliński, "Die Behandlung gleichzeitiger Ereignisse im Antiken Epos," *Philologus* 8, no. 3 (1901), 422. [Original footnote]

[18] Despite extensive research into period Czech sources, Gaumont's catalogues and various filmographies, we were unable to identify this film. It is possible that Jakobson is mistakenly ascribing it to Gaumont or translating the distribution title loosely from Russian. We thank Dr. Karel Tabery, an expert on identifying French distribution titles in Czech, for help with this issue.

she can remove the bandage from her eyes the next day because the treatment is over and she will see. He leaves, suffers, convinced that she will despise him for his ugliness; however, she throws herself upon his neck: "I love you, for you cured me." A kiss. The end.

As a reaction against overdone sophistication, against a technique reeking of ornamentation, there arises a purposeful looseness, an intentional rawness, sketchiness as a device (*L'Âge d'or* of the cinematic genius Buñuel[19]). Dilettantism is beginning to delight. In the current vocabulary, the words "dilettantism" and "illiteracy" sound despairingly pejorative. Yet there are periods not only in the history of art but even in the history of culture in which these factors have undoubtedly had a positive, dynamic role. Examples? Rousseau—Henri or Jean-Jacques.

After an abundant harvest a field needs to lie fallow. The center of film culture has already changed several times. Where the tradition of silent film is strong, sound film has had particular difficulties in finding new paths. Only now is Czech film going through a period similar to the modest Czech debuts at the threshold of the eighteenth and nineteenth centuries for a new national literature. In Czech silent film, little of significant interest was done. Now, since speech has penetrated the cinema, Czech films worth seeing have appeared. It is highly probable that precisely the lack of a burdensome tradition facilitates experimentation. Real virtue arises from necessity. The ability of Czech artists to profit from the weakness of their native tradition is almost traditional in the history of Czech culture. The fresh, provincial originality of Karel Hynek Mácha's romanticism would hardly have been possible if Czech poetry had been burdened with a mature classical norm. And is there a more difficult task for contemporary literature than the discovery of new forms of humor? Soviet humorists imitate Gogol, Chekhov, and so on; Kästner's poems echo the sarcasm of Heine; present-day French and English humoresques largely recall centos (poems composed from quotations). *The Good Soldier Švejk* could emerge only because the Czech nineteenth century did not generate a canonical humor.

[1933]

---

[19]   *The Golden Age*, Luis Buñuel, France, 1930.

Petr Bogatyrev
DISNEY'S *SNOW WHITE*

The signs of each art have their own unique development, their effect being quite distinct from the signs of any other art. This does not mean, however, that we cannot transfer the signs of one art to those of another art. We know of many examples in which poetry was the inspiration for great paintings or sculptures and, vice versa, where paintings or statues inspired poetic works.[1] Whereas slavish imitation of the signs and creative means of one art in another is openly dangerous because the material and its structure are violated by an alien material and an alien structure, the creative treatment and adoption of signs from the sphere of one art to another can be fruitful if the structure of the material is respected.

The arts of theater and of film are closely related both in form and in some points of their historical development. Until now it has only been possible to speak about the influence exerted by the old theatrical art on the young film art. Alas, film often adopted theater's creative means, so foreign to its own artistic technique, in a merely mechanical manner. A long and courageous struggle was necessary for film to achieve the right to the development and existence of independent forms and expressive means, for the liberation of film art from alien theatrical elements. Currently, a reverse phenomenon can be observed: the influence of the young film art on theater. It will therefore, in my view, be appropriate to point out a number of the film techniques in the marvelous Walt Disney film *Snow White* that, if creatively treated, can be valid for the theatrical art as well, and that can be quite illuminating for our theoretical analysis of the theater.

In the film *Snow White*, there is a strikingly careful economy of expressive means for all the figures that appear in it. Each trait of Snow White herself, of every dwarf and animal, has its own specific function for this or that filmic expression. The fig-

---

[1] See Roman Jakobson, "The Statue in Pushkin's Poetic Mythology," *Slovo a slovesnost* 3, 1937, 2–24 [Original footnote]. The article is available in English in Roman Jakobson's *Selected Writings*, vol. 5 (The Hague: Mouton, 1979), 237–80, and in his *Language in Literature* (Cambridge: Harvard University Press, 1987), 318–368.

ures are endowed only with such traits as are useful for their roles, while all that would have impeded or been useless to the filmic expression was simply excluded by the cartoon animators—they did not draw them. Snow White has all the signs of fairy-tale beauty: red lips, red cheeks, big eyes, but in some facial positions her nose is practically invisible, being here (as in children's drawings) considered redundant. Each little animal has strikingly drawn details, but only those that are necessary for its typical movements and for its characterization.

A live actor creates theatrical signs with his posture, eyes, hands, legs, the register and color of his voice, etc. The individual traits of the actor's appearance not only contribute little to theatrical expression, but often weaken the signs created by other traits. The strong and powerful voice of an actor playing a giant will thus lose its effectiveness if the actor is small in physical stature. Obviously, the actor's physical properties do not allow for the elimination of all that is unnecessary for a specific theatrical expression, as is possible with a drawn figure. There is a fundamental difference between a cartoon and a live actor. The creative processes of these two cases develop in completely opposite directions. In the Walt Disney cartoon, the individual signs of the figures are created with a specific intention that takes both the figure as a whole and the expressive possibilities of the film medium into consideration. Let me offer some concrete examples. Every detail in each drawing of an animal in the *Snow White* film was created by the cartoon animator in such a way that it can be used in the scene in which the animals are cleaning up. And how well each of the reindeer's limbs was utilized in carrying the laundry, and the belly of the turtle during the washing! In a cartoon, the course of the creative process is such that individual signs are drawn first. Their grouping creates the figure, which then begins to move and live. This approach, from individual signs to a group of signs and then to the complete figure, presupposes the perfect functionality of each single trait for each figure and guarantees that the filmic expression will not be weakened by anything that lacks use or function. We have already mentioned that the face of Snow White is outfitted with everything typical of fairy-tale beauty. The same can be said of her body: half girl, half woman, a body that every movement characterizes as belonging to an ethereal fairy-tale being, neither a child nor a mature woman.

In the entire film *Snow White*, there is not a single useless gesture, not even a single useless fold or detail on any of the figures' costumes. The black satin cape of the Queen is drawn and used for filmic expression in such a way that it is more effective for the characterization of its wearer than a drawn-out monologue about her mental state. With a live actor, the process of creating theatrical signs proceeds in exactly the opposite direction. At the beginning of the acting performance there is a living human being who has very many means of expression at its disposal, from which it chooses, in the creation of a role, only those elements suitable as signs of the specific theatrical figure. There is a danger that the actor will fail to sufficiently suppress the physical attributes he has in his civilian life and that they will uselessly burden him, or even obstruct him in the creation of the stage figure.

So, for example, the vigorous movements of a young actor playing the role of an old man weaken the impression that the makeup of an old man is intended to generate in the audience. In this case, his movements are in opposition to the makeup. It is up to the actor to suggest to the audience the veracity of his theatrical expression so that his body, his voice, etc., as well as his movements aid his theatrical performance.

In his book *My Life in Art*, Stanislavsky recalls the famous Italian tragedian Rossi, a small man with a pot belly who, despite his physical disposition, could create an ideal artistic expression in the role of the young prince of Denmark through his marvelous playacting.[2]

We cannot analyze in detail all the artistic techniques of the film *Snow White* in this single article. We should, however, offer a few remarks about some of them. When artistic techniques are repeated frequently, they lose their emotional impact, and like a tune played too often, can sometimes produce the impression of banality. In order to prevent this and to re-invigorate the old creative means, the artist resorts to an ironic mode. If he succeeds in bringing a gentle irony to the old, "worn out" technique, he creates an impression that is half serious and half ironic. And so, for some viewers, the dominant element is the ironic one, while for others it is the serious one. The film *Snow White* takes full advantage of this circumstance. Here, the completely banal rendition of a song with an echo is endowed with a comic element when we hear the individual tones reverberating off the surface of the water in a well, and the sentimentality of Snow White's song is emphasized by the cooing of a little bird that accompanies her.... The parents of the little bird behave exactly like a father and mother overcome with joy at the success of their child. The comic element of this accompaniment is further underscored when the little bird that accompanies Snow White's song ultimately fails and sings off-tune, whereby the parents are enormously embarrassed.

One of the most complex problems in aesthetics is the issue of the tragic versus the comic impressions of various artistic techniques. The history of art teaches us that the same artistic technique was perceived tragically in one period and comically in another. The songs of uncivilized nations that originally had a serious, e.g., religious, function can have a comic effect on a European. It is extremely difficult and perhaps even impossible to determine which techniques are unequivocally tragic or comic for all fields of art.

---

[2] See Konstantin Stanislavsky, *My Life in Art* (New York: Theatre Arts Books, 1948), 77–79. In fact, the Shakespearean role that Stanislavsky describes here as discordant with Ernesto Rossi's "stumpy" and "wrinkled" body is not Hamlet, but rather Romeo.

The very interesting experiments by Bergson, which attempt to define the comic, specifically in the theater, are only partially correct. All the techniques that Bergson characterizes as comic can be perceived as tragic in another structure.

In the film *Snow White*, Disney very successfully exploited the circumstance whereby similar techniques in different contexts can have either a tragic or comic effect. At the moment of tragic suspense during Snow White's nocturnal escape, the natural landscape, trees, and birds create a terrifying impression. During the day, when Snow White is in a good mood, the very same landscape, trees, and birds are her best friends and arouse joy in the spectator. Here we can see how the same detail induces a totally different impression. At the end of the nocturnal travails, a row of threateningly luminescent eyes appears. After a while we see that they are the eyes of cute, friendly little hares. Every art must confront the crucial problem whereby a created work should have the broadest possible resonance among all strata of the audience without its artistic value being diminished; this means that a created work should be avant-garde, i.e., its form and content should bring much that is new, it should discover and forge new artistic paths without being art-for-art's-sake to only a select few. Such works of art have existed and continue to exist: folk art, for example, which was successful amongst the widest of circles that included demanding spectators, specialized connoisseurs and even artists themselves, who found in it inspiration for their own creative work. In film it is Charlie Chaplin who is enthusiastically received by the widest strata of the public as well as by avant-garde critics and filmmakers.

It is even more difficult to create a work of art that can be understood equally well by adults and children. To write a children's book, to draw pictures or compose music for children, or to stage a performance for children is extremely difficult, yet gratifying, work, since through it we are raising the next generation of active and passive workers and consumers of creative artistic work. A child's artistic impressions influence its life and shape its capacity to perceive artistic forms. Let us just consider the influence that children's fairy tales had on many great writers (e.g., Pushkin, Němcová). Alas, artistic work for children is not considered worthy of the best artists and the attitude toward this difficult task is not adequately serious. The film *Snow White* is proof that a work of art intended for children can be just as exciting for adults if it is created with the level of seriousness that it requires. Obviously, a seven- or eight-year-old child and an adult perceive the same scene in the film *Snow White* differently, yet they are both equally fascinated. It would be very interesting to gather material based on interviews with spectators of different ages as to which scenes of *Snow White* they liked most and why. The answers of the children and those of the adults would surely be very different. I believe that such interviews would prove to be very instructive for artists who create for adults as well as for children.

(1938)

SHORT BIOGRAPHIES OF THE AUTHORS

Bogatyrev, Petr Grigorievich (1893–1971) – Russian ethnographer, art historian, and pioneer of structural ethnography. From 1921 to 1939, Bogatyrev lived and worked in Prague, where, in 1926, he co-founded the Prague Linguistic Circle. His articles on film are closely connected to his interest in folk theater, which culminated in the 1940 publication of his monograph *Lidové divadlo české a slovenské* [Czech and Slovak folk theater]. In the late 1930s, he worked with E. F. Burian's theater group, in whose journal he published the article "Disney's *Snow White*."

Burian, Emil František (1904–1959) – theater and film director, dramatist, composer, writer, film and theater theorist, actor, and singer. Educated in musical composition, he was a member of the artist group Devětsil and active in the avantgarde theater groups Liberated Theater (Osvobozené divadlo), Dada, and Modern Studio (Moderní studio). He founded the recitation group Voice Band in 1927 and his own professional theater, called "D," in 1933. During the Nazi occupation of Czechoslovakia, German authorities closed his theater in 1941, and Burian was deported. He survived a series of concentration camps, to reopen his theater after Czechoslovakia's liberation in 1945. After the Communist Party seized power in 1948, Burian publicly subscribed to the tenets of socialist realism and staged productions in support of the regime. In his work for the stage, he strove to create a synthetic theater that combined political elements with directorial and visual innovations. He undertook the dramatization and staging of a number of poetic and prose texts, most importantly Karel Hynek Mácha's *Máj* [May, 1935], Božena Benešová's *Věra Lukášová* (1938), Alexander Pushkin's *Eugene Onegin* (1937) and Viktor Dyk's *Krysař* [The pied piper, 1940], and was the author of operas such as *Maryša* (1938), films such as *Věra Lukášová* (1939), and theoretical books such as *Polydynamika* [Polydynamics, 1926] *Jazz* (1928), *Zamette jeviště* [Sweep the stage, 1936] and *O nové divadlo* [Toward a new theater, 1946]. He also initiated a number of new theatrical genres and techniques such as, with Miroslav Kouřil, the "Theatergraph," which juxtaposed actors' performances on the stage with images on a transparent projection screen. His musical compositions consisted of vocal and musical-dramatic works. He was one of the first Czech musicians to be inspired by jazz. He also wrote music for films, and the function of film music was the primary subject of his theoretical studies of film.

Čapek, Josef (1887–1945) – painter, graphic artist, stage designer, writer, art critic, and brother of Karel Čapek. Čapek co-founded the Group of Creative Artists (Skupina výtvarných umělců) in 1911. He left Skupina in 1912 and joined the the Mánes Association of Fine Artists (Spolek výtvarných umělců Mánes), from which he was expelled in 1914. In 1918, he became one of the main initiators of the art group The Obstinates (Tvrdošíjní). From 1921 to 1939, he worked as an editor of *Lidové noviny* [People's news] and was active as a stage designer, working on his brother Karel's theatrical productions, among others. In the 1930s, he joined the anti-Nazi front, for which he was arrested in 1939, and was imprisoned in a number of concentration camps, dying on a death march in 1945. His earlier artistic works represent his own distinct version of cubism; his more mature works are characterized by their condensed form and their focus on socially sensitive urban subjects, landscapes, and children's themes. He also drew political caricatures for newspapers, worked as a graphic designer and book illustrator, wrote prose works (e.g., *Stín kapradiny* [Shade of a fern, 1930], *Kulhavý poutník* [The limping pilgrim, 1936]), children's books such as *Povídání o pejskovi a kočičce* [*All about doggie and pussycat*, 1929], and, with his brother Karel, stage plays (*Ze života hmyzu* [*The insect play*, 1921]). Among other subjects, his theoretical writing addressed marginal artistic genres, film, and photography, and it strongly influenced the avant-garde's stance toward modern media forms (see the collection *Nejskromnější umění* [The humblest art, 1920]).

Čapek, Karel (1890–1938) – prose writer, dramatist, poet, journalist, and brother of Josef Čapek. Beginning in 1921, Čapek worked as an editor at *Lidové noviny* [People's news], where he published his distinctive columns and editorials. He maintained close political ties with Czechoslovak president T. G. Masaryk and his circle. His literary works include dramas (e.g., the 1920 *R.U.R.* and *Věc Makropulos* [The Makropulos secret, 1922], collections of short stories (e.g., *Boží muka* [Wayside crosses, 1917]; *Trapné povídky* [Painful tales, 1921], detective stories (including the 1929 *Povídky z jedné kapsy* and *Povídky z druhé kapsy*, published together in English as *Tales from Two Pockets*), the novel trilogy *Hordubal* (1933), *Povětroň* [*Meteor*, 1934] and *Obyčejný život* [An ordinary life, 1934], science fiction novels (such as *Továrna na absolutno* [The absolute at large, 1921] and *Krakatit*, 1924), translations of modern French literature, and children's books. His works contain unique elaborations on neoclassicism, pragmatic philosophy, cubism, and relativism, and espouse ideas of pragmatic humanism, proclaiming human solidarity over ideological and class prejudices. At the end of the 1910s and during the 1920s, he wrote several fundamental studies of film both independently and with his brother. He also wrote the script for the film *Zlatý klíček* [The little golden key, 1921] and a number of his works were adapted to film (e.g., *Loupežník* [The brigand, 1931]; *Bílá nemoc* [*Skeleton on Horseback*, 1937]; *Hordubalové* [The Hordubals, 1937]). Other essays deal with subjects such as technological civilization, modern art, and marginal or popular genres of literature (e.g., *Marsyas čili na okraj literatury* [Marsyas or margins of literature, 1931]).

Černík, Artuš (1900–1953) – journalist and film critic, organizer for the avant-garde movement, and poet. Černík was also a co-founder of Devětsil, chairman of the Club for the New Film (Klub za nový film) and an editor of *Lidové noviny*, avant-garde journals *Disk* and *Pásmo* [Zone] as well as the film journal *Český filmový svět* [Czech film world, 1926–1928]. After the film industry was nationalized in 1945, he was named secretary of Dramaturgy for State Film Production (Státní výroba filmů) and chairman of the import commission for Czechoslovak State Film (Československý státní film, or ČSF, 1946–1950). He was the author of State Film's statistical study "Annual Report on Czechoslovak film" (Výroční zpráva o čs. filmovnictví, 1947–1951).

Hackenschmied, Alexander (1907–2004) – central figure of the Czech cinematic avant-garde, documentary filmmaker, cinematographer, editor, photographer, critic, and organizer of avant-garde activities. In his theoretical articles, he formulated the concept of "independent film" in reaction to the crisis of the film avant-garde in the early 1930s. In the same decade, he directed experimental films such as *Bezúčelná procházka* [The aimless walk, 1930] and *Na Pražském hradě* [Prague Castle, 1932], which rank among the most important examples of Czech avant-garde filmmaking from the period. He also worked, together with directors such as Otakar Vávra, Gustav Machatý, and Karel Plicka, as a cinematographer, art director, and film editor. In the latter half of the 1930s, he worked as a director and cinematographer for the newly established film studios of the Baťa shoe company in Zlín, where he made a number of successful advertisements and documentary films. The Baťa studios participated in the production of Herbert Kline's 1939 documentary *Crisis*, addressing the political and social tensions in the Czechoslovak border regions immediately prior to World War II, a film that Hackenschmied co-directed, shot, and edited. That same year, Hackenschmied emigrated to the United States, where he worked under the name Alexander Hammid and made a number of successful experimental and documentary films, including *Meshes of the Afternoon* (co-directed with his then-wife Maya Deren, 1943), which became a key work of American experimental cinema, and the short film *To Be Alive!* (1964), for which he won an Oscar.

Honzl, Jindřich (1894–1953) – theater director, drama theorist, and pedagogue, member of Devětsil, and defining figure of the leftist branch of the Czechoslovak interwar avant-garde. Together with Jiří Frejka, in 1926 he founded the experimental Liberated Theater, where he directed performances by the famous writer-actor duo Jiří Voskovec and Jan Werich. In the 1920s, inspired by the Soviet avant-garde, he advocated the principles of constructivism, which included introducing filmic elements into theatrical productions (see, for example, his 1925 book of programmatic articles *Roztočené jeviště* [The spinning stage]). In his theoretical writing on film and theater from the 1930s, he came to terms with surrealism and structuralism. He directed films with Jiří Voskovec and Jan Werich (*Pudr a benzin* [*Powder and Petrol*, 1931] and *Peníze nebo život* [Your money or your life, 1932]), and worked with Otakar Vávra on detailed plans for a film school (see their 1939 publication *Navrhujeme školu pro výchovu filmového dorostu* [We propose a school for the education of future filmmakers]). After World War II, he published the journal *Otázky divadla a filmu* [Film and theater issues]. During this period, his inclinations toward Marxist ideology and the principles of Soviet theater culture became more pronounced. Also at that time, he became a member of the National Theater and a pedagogue at both the Philosophical Faculty of Charles University and the Faculty of Theater of the Academy of Performing Arts (DAMU) in Prague.

Hošek, Arne (born Ernest Hoschek, 1895–1941) – architect, urbanist, acoustician, researcher of synesthesia, and creator of abstract "Musicalist" paintings. A member of the Union of Architects (Svaz architektů), he also belonged to the group associated with the avant-garde review *Stavba* [Construction] and was active in musical circles. He published his thoughts on music in the independent review of contemporary music *Klíč* [Key] and in the journal *Česká hudba* [Czech music]. In his theoretical studies on synesthesia and acoustics, he speculated on the correspondences between colors and musical tones, and contemplated the possibilities for creating melodic structures according to the geometric laws of various types of architectural spaces. He conceived of synesthesia as a metaphysical science and a pathway to an absolute art that would establish harmony between the external and the spiritual world. Like music, he saw film as a medium in which it is possible to achieve the goals of synesthetic theory and thereby the ideal of an absolute art.

Jakobson, Roman (1896–1982) – world-renowned linguist and Slavist. Born in Moscow, he lived and worked in Czechoslovakia from 1920 (first in Prague, and after 1933 as a professor in Brno) before escaping to Denmark in 1939 and later (via Norway and Sweden) to the United States. Together with Nikolai Trubetzkoy and Sergei Kartsevskii, he initiated structural linguistics and co-founded the Prague Linguistic Circle. His article "Is the Film in Decline?" (Úpadek filmu?, 1933) made him a pioneer of structuralist film theory. It originally appeared in a magazine as a chapter from the book "Předpoklady českého filmu" [The preconditions of Czech cinema], which was never published. Jakobson's interest in film is also evidenced by his membership in the Club for the New Film and by his collaboration with Vladislav Vančura on the screenplay for the film *Na sluneční straně* [On the sunny side, 1933].

Kučera, Jan (1908–1977) – film theorist, critic, historian, editor, and documentary filmmaker; one of the leading representatives of leftist film criticism and the Czech film avant-garde of the 1930s. Kučera edited the film section for the daily newspaper *České slovo* [Czech word] from 1934 to 1938. He was a key figure in Czech newsreel production: from the end of the 1920s, he worked for the weekly newsreel *Elektajournal*, and after 1931 for *Československý filmový týdeník* [Czechoslovak weekly newsreel], eventually becoming editor-in-chief of its follow-up project *Aktualita* from 1937 to 1943. Following the war, he became editor-in-chief of Czechoslovak Newsreel (Československý zpravodajský film), a state-controlled enterprise that produced several newsreels, but was stripped of his function after the communist takeover in 1948. From then until the early 1950s, he was an advisor in the Czechoslovak Film Institute (Československý filmový ústav). In the 1950s and 1960s, he taught at the Film Academy in Prague (FAMU) and from the 1960s he worked for Czechoslovak Television (Československá televize) and became a theorist of television. His theoretical books on film and television—*Kniha o filmu* [A book on film, 1941] and *Střihová skladba ve filmu a televizi* [Editing composition in film and television, 1969]—are based on concepts developed within the frameworks of avant-garde aesthetics, structuralism, and social critique, and in the latter, he elaborates his own theory of editing composition, describing how the temporal and spatial organization of a film functions in creating the dynamic whole of the work. His systematizing and synthesizing work on film poetics is analogous to the film grammar developed by well-known author of the same period Raymond J. Spottiswood. Some of his most significant film projects (although none of these was ever completed) are the experimental works *Burleska* [Burlesque, 1933] and *Pražský barok* [Prague baroque, 1934].

Langer, František (1888–1965) – dramatist and prose writer. During World War I, Langer fought in the Austro-Hungarian Army and was captured by the enemy at the front in Galicia. He joined the Czechoslovak Legions in Russia and lived through the ordeal of the Siberian anabasis with them. After the war, he worked as a military doctor, and then, from 1935 to 1938, as dramaturge for the Vinohrady Municipal Theater. He lived in exile from 1939 to 1945, serving in the Czechoslovak Foreign Army in France and Great Britain as a general in the health services division. He was a member of the Group of Fine Artists (Skupina výtvarných umělců) and co-editor of their magazine *Umělecký měsíčník* [Artist's monthly], which propagated ideas of cubism. His dramatic works explore themes such as crime and punishment (*Periférie*, [Periphery, 1925]) and deal with his experiences in the Czechoslovak Legions (*Jízdní hlídka* [Mounted patrol, 1935, adapted for film in 1936]). He also wrote a number of successful comedies such as *Velbloud uchem jehly* [Camel through the eye of a needle, 1923; film adaptation in 1936], *Grandhotel Nevada* (1927; film adaptation in 1934), and *Obrácení Ferdyše Pištory* [Ferdyš Pištora turns over a new leaf, 1929; film adaptation in 1931]. His prose works often depict life on the periphery of the city (*Předměstské povídky* [Suburban stories, 1926]). In his theoretical works from the 1910s, he advocated the new artistic directions of neoclassicism and cubism and praised film as a new form of realism for recording the mundane elements of people's everyday lives. His early interest in film is also evidenced by the film *Noční děs* [Night terror, 1914], for which he wrote the scenario.

Linhart, Lubomír (1906–1980) – leftist theorist and historian of film and photography, journalist, diplomat, and translator of Russian film-theoretical texts. In 1928, Linhart became the coordinator of the film section for the newspaper *Rudý večerník* [Red evening paper]. In 1930, he took part in the Second International Conference of Proletarian and Revolutionary Writers in Kharkov, and from 1931 to 1934 he led the the Film-Photo Group of the Left Front (Filmfoto skupina Levé fronty) in Prague. He organized exhibitions of social photography, was an advocate of Soviet film, and actively participated in a number of cultural organizations. During the war, he collaborated on a project for nationalizing Czechoslovak cinema, and, after Slovakia was liberated, he became involved in the nationalization of cinema theaters there. From 1946 to 1948 he was the central director of the Czechoslovak Film Association (Československá filmová společnost, the predecessor of Czechoslovak State Film), and from 1948 to 1956 he worked for the Ministry of Foreign Affairs as an ambassador to the GDR and Romania. He lectured on film aesthetics at FAMU from 1956 to 1969, and beginning in 1969 he also lectured at Charles University, where he founded and directed the Department of Film Studies. His main theoretical-critical works include

Malá abeceda filmu [A brief guide to film, 1930], *Sociální fotografie* [Social photography, 1934], *Sovětský film* [Soviet film, 1936], and a number of monographs on photographers.

Mukařovský, Jan (1891–1975) – world-renowned literary theorist and aesthetician, pioneer of the structural method in the areas of aesthetic theory and film semiotics. Mukařovský studied linguistics and aesthetics with Otakar Zich at Charles University in Prague, and became a member of the Prague Linguistic Circle in 1926. In the 1930s, he worked at Comenius University in Bratislava and Charles University. Initially, he worked specifically on linguistic problems, but gradually his interests expanded to include investigations of the signifying structures of literary and artistic works. His functional and dynamic conception of a work's structure enabled Czech art history to overcome its psychologizing approaches. After World War II, he attempted to revise his theoretical views by combining structuralism with Marxism. His main theoretical studies include *Máchův Máj: Estetická studie* [Mácha's May: an aesthetic study, 1923] and *Estetická funkce, norma a hodnota jako sociální fakty* [Aesthetic function, norm, and value as social facts, 1936]. His studies on Czech literature are collected in the three-volume book *Kapitoly z české poetiky* [Chapters from Czech poetics, 1941–1948]. Film occupied an important position within Mukařovský's studies of art as a sign system, and in addition to three essays dedicated specifically to film theory, Mukařovský also touches on aspects of film in a number of other aesthetic and literary studies. He was also interested in issues of film production and became a member of the Czechoslovak Film Association (Československé filmové společnosti) in 1936.

Neumann, Stanislav Kostka (1875–1947) – poet, journalist, and prose writer. Prior to World War I, Neumann was involved with the anarchist movement. After the war, he published the leftist journal *Červen* [June] and joined the communist movement, becoming active in the movement's cultural organizations Proletkult and Left Front (Levá fronta). Initially, his poetic works were influenced by decadence, symbolism, and anarchism, while the works from his mature period were informed by vitalism (e.g., *Kniha lesů, vod a strání* [Book of forests, watercourses, and hillsides, 1914]) and by an admiration for technological civilization (*Nové zpěvy* [New songs, 1918]). In his later period, he oscillated between politically agitational, amorous, and reflective poems (such as, respectively, *Rudé zpěvy* [Red songs, 1923]; *Láska* [Love, 1933]; and *Sonáta horizontálního života* [Sonata of a horizontal life, 1937]). He also wrote historical works (e.g., *Dějiny ženy I-IV* [The history of woman I-IV, 1931–1932]) and journalist articles in which he advocated new artistic directions, collected in *Ať žije život!* [Long live life!, 1920]).

At the time he wrote his poem "Film" (1919) Neumann was also engaged in public political discussions about the organization of the film industry within independent Czechoslovakia. With other representatives of the National Assembly (Národní shromáždění), he submitted a proposal to transfer cinema out of the jurisdiction of the Ministry of Interior to that of the Ministry of Education, whereby he hoped to increase to cinema's educational function. The Ministry of the Interior, however, had no desire to relinquish its authority over cinema, and the proposal went nowhere. In his articles from the 1920s, Neumann proposed the collectivization of all film activity, harshly criticized Czech film production, and discussed the purpose of film in the context of proletarian culture.

Nezval, Vítězslav (1900–1958) – one of the most significant Czech poets of the twentieth century, dramatist, and translator. Nezval joined Devětsil in 1922. In 1934, he was among the founders of the Czech surrealist group, but left the group in 1938. His poetic work progressed from proletarian poetry to playful poetism (of which his "Podivuhodný kouzelník" [The marvelous magician], is a key work), and finally to surrealism. His most important collections of poems from the 1920s include *Pantomima* [Pantomime, 1924] and *Básně noci* [Poems of the night, 1930], in which he explored new possibilities for poetic expression by employing rich metaphors and associative freedom with the logical structure of the poem. In the 1930s, his works acquired socially critical and existential dimensions (e.g., the collections *Skleněný havelok* [Glass inverness, 1932], *Sbohem a šáteček* [Farewell and a head scarf, 1934], and *52 hořkých balad věčného studenta Roberta Davida* [52 bitter ballads of Robert David, eternal student, 1936]) and, in the mid-1930s, they began to express surrealist tendencies (*Praha s prsty deště* [Prague with fingers of rain, 1936], *Žena v množném čísle* [Woman in the plural, 1936], *Absolutní hrobař* [Absolute gravedigger, 1937]). After the war, he fully accepted Stalinist literary norms (see, for example, his 1949 poem *Stalin*). During the 1920s, Nezval published thirty articles on film: from 1922 to 1923, he wrote mainly about American actors (Chaplin, Fairbanks, Hayakawa, etc.); from 1925 to 1926, he reflected on the notion of *photogénie* and also criticized the poor quality of Czech film production. In the 1930s, his writing on film became sporadic, but a number of his official speeches about the nationalization of the cinema in the post-war period are preserved in his literary estate. During the poetist period of the mid-1920s, he also wrote poetic film librettos, unrealized film screenplays that became key examples of the Czech avant-garde's attitude towards film in that decade. Some of his later screenplays, however, were written with practical intentions and were indeed filmed (e.g., *Varhaník u sv. Víta* [The organist at St. Vitus' cathedral, 1929]; *Erotikon*, 1929; *Ze soboty na neděli* [*From Saturday to Sunday*, 1931], of which the latter two were directed by Gustav

Machatý). His interest in film was also stimulated by his romantic involvement with film director Zet Molas (whose real name was Zdena Smolová). From 1945 to 1949, he served as the chief of the film section of the Ministry of Information, where, as the head of the Film Censorship Board, his duties included approving films for distribution. Although the film section was dissolved in February 1949, he continued to work for two more years as a ministerial advisor on film.

Obrtel, Vít (1901–1988) – architect, graphic designer, stage designer, architectural theorist, and poet. In 1922, together with Eugen Linhart, Jaroslav Fragner, and Karel Honzík, Obrtel co-founded the architectural group the Four Purists (Puristická čtyřka) and joined Devětsil in 1923. He designed a number of significant buildings, as well as sets for the Liberated Theater, prepared the graphic design for publications by Devětsil members, and began writing lyrical prose poems at the end of the 1930s. He was the director of *Kvart* [Quart, 1930–1937 and 1945–1949), a journal that espoused modernist trends and the establishment of closer contacts between the sciences and art. In contrast to orthodox functionalism (and in opposition to Karel Teige), his architectural theory and works called for a synthesis of functionality and emotion, a "harmony between man, nature, and buildings," which approaches the style known as organic architecture.

Pešánek, Zdeněk (1896–1965) – sculptor, architect, member of Devětsil, and pioneer of kinetic art, which he deals with in his theoretical work. Influenced by constructivism, Pešánek was interested in the phenomenon of artificial light in motion, and created experiments with color pianos, kinetic-light techniques, the illumination of architecture, light advertising, and abstract film. One of his kinetic sculptures became the subject of Otakar Vávra's and František Pilát's short film *Světlo proniká tmou* [Light penetrates the darkness, 1930]. He provides a summary of his theories in his 1941 book *Kinetismus* [Kinetic art].

Purkinje (Purkyně), Jan Evangelista (1787–1868) – the most important Czech natural scientist (physiologist, anatomist, biologist) of the nineteenth century, as well as a philosopher and organizer of science and culture. Purkinje was one of the founders of experimental physiology and psychology, and a researcher in the field of perception. Purkinje's 1819 dissertation, *Beiträge zur Kenntniss des Sehens in subjectiver Hinsicht* [Contributions to the knowledge of vision in its subjective aspect], named and established subjective sensory phenomena as a field of scientific study and had a great impact on a number of contemporary thinkers, including Johann Wolfgang von Goethe. (Purkinje, in fact, translated poetic works by Goethe, Schiller, and others, in addition to writing his own poetry, and was interested in German classical philosophy and the philosophy of nature, or

Naturphilosophie.) In 1823, Purkinje was made a professor of physiology in Wrocław, where he founded the first physiological institute focusing on experimental work, which became the model for many similar institutes established after it. He made several key discoveries that are named after him, including, among others, the Purkinje cells (or Purkinje neurons) in the cerebellar cortex, the Purkinje tree (a diagram of the blood vessels in the eye), the Purkinje effect (sometimes called the Purkinje shift), designating the changing brightness of colors at dusk, and Purkinje images (reflections of objects produced by the structure of the eye). After 1850, he became a university professor in Prague, where he tried to establish a Czech academy of sciences. In his work, especially in his observations and experiments regarding the perception of movement, Purkinje envisioned some of the principal developments in modern visual culture such as abstraction and the rise of media of moving pictures. Purkinje also contributed to the development of precinematic optical machines by introducing innovations that predated later inventions and applications such as intermittent motion and the use of photography.

Teige, Karel (1900–1951) – art critic and theorist, book and graphic designer. Teige was the most important spokesperson and organizer of the interwar Czech avant-garde, an intermediary for many current artistic movements from abroad, and a founding member of Devětsil in 1920. He initially advocated the concept of proletarian art, authored a number of manifestos on the uniquely Czech artistic program of poetism in the mid-1920s, and became a member of the Czech surrealist group in 1934. Teige participated in activities relating to all areas of avant-garde art, from film and photography to architecture, painting, and literature. In his programmatic writings on aesthetics, he rejected the educational function of art, and in the late 1930s he was one of the few leftist intellectuals to condemn the Moscow trials. After 1948, Teige was persecuted by the communist government of Czechoslovakia, yet managed to have a marked influence on the new generation of Czech surrealists led by Vratislav Effenberger. His most important theoretical publications include *Film* (1925), *Stavba a báseň* [Construction and poetry, 1927], *Svět, který se směje* [The laughing world, 1928], *Jarmark umění* [Art fair, 1936], and *Moderní fotografie v Československu* [Modern photography in Czechoslovakia, 1948]. In terms of artistic practice, he focused primarily on typography and photomontage. Teige's film-theoretical writing can be divided into two phases: in the early 1920s, he was inspired by Louis Delluc's theory of *photogénie* and developed the poetist conception of film based on the duality of construction and poetry; then, from 1929 to 1934, he focused on a critique of the commercial film industry and propagation of Soviet cinema as a political instrument.

Tille, Václav (1867–1937) – theorist and critic of literature, theater, and film; folklorist, prose writer, and professor of comparative literary history at Charles University in Prague. In addition to his critical and historical writings on literature, theater, and film, he also investigated folk literature and the relationships between high literature and fairy tales. His pioneering 1908 study "Kinéma" numbers among the world's first complex theoretical treatments of film. Between 1908 and 1936, he published nearly thirty articles on film, addressing issues such as the critical assessment of contemporary production, the relationship between film and theater, the educational effects of nonfiction film, and the introduction of sound.

Václavek, Bedřich (1897–1943) – Marxist literary theorist, historian, critic, and folklorist. Václavek was also an organizer of cultural events in Brno and a member of the section of Devětsil in that city. He joined the Communist Party of Czechoslovakia (KSČ) in 1927. From 1922 to 1923, he studied theater and literary theory in Berlin, and in the 1920s and 1930s he worked at the university libraries in Olomouc and Brno, where he took his higher-level doctorate (*habilitace*) at Masaryk University in 1939. He also worked as editor of the cultural section of the communist daily newspaper *Rovnost* [Equality, 1926–1928], and of the avant-garde journals *Pásmo* [Zone], *Revue Devětsilu* [Review of Devětsil or ReD] and *Index*. In addition, he was director of the section "Sociologie umění" [The sociology of art] in the magazine *Sociologická revue* [Sociology review]. Václavek's studies on poetry are collected in the 1930 book *Poesie v rozpacích* [Poetry in a quandary]. His most significant work of literary theory, *Česká literatura 20. století* [Czech literature in the twentieth century, 1935], is an attempt to formulate a synthetic sociological interpretation of modern Czech literature. His aesthetic orientation shifted from a focus on experimental art in the 1920s toward the propagation of socialist realism in the 1930s, and his theoretical works deal primarily with the sociology of literature, wherein, being a Marxist, his emphasis lies on the relationship between the structure of society and the structure of the artistic work. The analysis of art's social determination led him to an interest in folk literature and the modern mass culture associated with it, including film. In 1942, Václavek was arrested by the Nazis in 1942 and deported to Auschwitz, where he later perished.

Vančura, Vladislav (1891–1942) – prose writer, dramatist, film director, and member of Devětsil. During World War II, Vančura worked with the resistance until his arrest by the Gestapo in 1942 and subsequent execution. His prose work is characterized by a search for new forms, unique sentence structure, and lexical archaisms. His early works include social critiques (*Pekař Jan Marhoul* [Baker

Jan Marhoul, 1924]), tales of grotesque apocalypse (*Pole orná i válečná* [Fields of plough, fields of war, 1925]), humorous stories (*Rozmarné léto* [Summer of Caprice, 1926]), and experiments with language (*Hrdelní pře aneb přísloví* [Criminal dispute, or the proverbs, 1930]). In the 1930s, he turned toward epic (*Marketa Lazarová*, 1931) and continued writing his novels on social issues (*Konec starých časů* [The end of the old times, 1934]). He also wrote screenplays and directed films that experimented with acting and speech (*Před maturitou* [Before graduation, 1932]; *Na sluneční straně* [On the sunny side, 1933]; *Marijka nevěrnice* [Marijka the unfaithful, 1934]). In his texts on cinema, he advocated applying principles of experimental prose to film and defended the expressive possibilities of sound. He maintained close ties to the Prague Linguistic Circle and collaborated with Roman Jakobson, who contributed to the screenplay for *Na sluneční straně*. In addition, he co-founded the Club for the New Film (Klub za nový film) in 1927 and was chairman of the Czechoslovak Film Association. In 1937, he served as the latter organization's delegate on the Film Advisory Board (Filmový poradní sbor) of the Ministry of Commerce, the umbrella institution that regulated all aspects of cinema in the 1930s, and whose establishment initiated a process of centralization that increased the state's control over cinema.

Voskovec, Jiří (born Jiří Wachsmann) (1905–1981) – actor, dramatist, and director. Voskovec was a member of Devětsil until 1927, when he was expelled after he accepted a role in the film *Pohádka máje* [May tale]. With Jan Werich, he formed a writing and acting duo, and, after the successful premiere of their play *Vest Pocket Revue* in 1927, they worked together at the avant-garde Liberated Theater, which became the V+W Theater (Divadlo V+W) in 1929. The theater was shut down in 1938 on political grounds; Voskovec and Werich emigrated to the United States in 1939 to return in 1946 and attempt to revive the V+W Theater. Voskovec emigrated once again in 1948, living in Paris before returning to the United States in 1950, where he became an established actor in television, film, and theater. In the 1930s, he and Werich co-authored a number of well-known stage plays whose style ranged from dadaistic playfulness to social-political satire (examples include *Osel a stín* [The donkey and the shadow, 1933]; *Balada z hadrů* [Rag ballad, 1935], and *Rub a líc* [Pros and cons, 1937]). He and Werich also wrote and performed many songs set to music by Jaroslav Ježek, who was a member of their theater troupe. Voskovec and Werich performed together on the radio and appeared in the lead roles of four film comedies in the 1930s (*Pudr a benzin* [Powder and Petrol, 1931], *Peníze nebo život* [Your money or your life, 1932]), *Hej-Rup!* [Heave Ho!, 1934]; *Svět patří nám* [The World Belongs to Us, 1937]). In the 1920s, like many of his colleagues from Devětsil, he also created "picture poems" (i.e., collages), experimented with the genre of the film libretto (e.g.,

"Nikotin," 1925), and published a variety of essays and commentaries on American, French, and Czech cinema, which he often supplemented with hand-drawn caricatures of actors and film-themed jokes.

SOURCES AND COPYRIGHTS

Stanislav Kostka Neumann, "Film." Originally as "Film," *Červen* 2, no. 19 (July 10, 1919), 170–171. Present translation based on Stanislav Kostka Neumann, *Básně, III – Spisy Stanislava K. Neumanna, vol. 8* (Praha: Odeon, 1974), 300–302. © Stanislav Kostka Neumann – heirs.

Jan Evangelista Purkinje, excerpts from *Contributions to the Knowledge of Vision in its Subjective Aspect*. Originally as *Beiträge zur Kenntniss des Sehens in subjectiver Hinsicht* (Praha: Fr. Vetterl, 1819), 1–10, 166–176.

Václav Tille, "Kinéma." Originally as "Kinéma," *Novina* 1, no. 21 (October 6, 1908), 647–651; no. 22 (November 13, 1908), 689–693; no. 23 (November 20, 1908), 716–720.

František Langer, "Cinema All the Time." Originally as "Stále kinema," *Lidové noviny* 21, no. 234 (August 27, 1913), 1–2. © František Langer – heirs, c/o Aura-Pont, Prague.

Stanislav Kostka Neumann, "Pictures—Little Pictures—Tiny, Tiny Pictures." Originally as "Obrazy, obrázky, obrázečky," *Lidové noviny* 21, no. 306 (November 8, 1913), 1–2. © Stanislav Kostka Neumann – heirs.

Josef Čapek and Karel Čapek, "The Cinema." Originally as "Biograf," *Stopa* 1, no. 19 (November 4, 1910), 594–596. © Karel Čapek – heirs c/o DILIA, © Josef Čapek – heirs c/o DILIA.

Karel Čapek, "The Style of the Cinematograph." Originally as "Styl kinematografu," *Styl* 5, no. 5 (June 1913), 146–148. © Karel Čapek – heirs c/o DILIA.

Karel Čapek, "A. W. F. Co." Originally as "A. W. F. Co.," *Národ* 1, no. 4 (May 24, 1917), 73–75. © Karel Čapek – heirs c/o DILIA.

Josef Čapek, "Film." Originally as "Film," *Cesta* 1, no. 18 (October 4, 1918), 477–478. © Josef Čapek – heirs c/o DILIA.

Karel Teige, "Photo Cinema Film." Originally as "Foto kino film," in *Život: Sborník nové krásy* (Praha: Výtvarný odbor Umělecké besedy, 1922), 153–168. © Karel Teige – heirs c/o DILIA.

Karel Teige, "The Aesthetics of Film and *Cinégraphie*." Originally as "Estetika filmu a kinografie," *Host* 3, no. 6–7 (April 1924), 143–152. © Karel Teige – heirs c/o DILIA.

Bedřich Václavek, "On the Sociology of Film." Originally as "K sociologii filmu," *Pásmo* 1, no. 5–6 (1924), 4. © Bedřich Václavek – heirs.

Jiří Voskovec, "*Photogénie* and Suprareality." Originally as "Fotogenie a suprarealita," *Disk* 2 (spring 1925), 14–15. © Jiří Voskovec – heirs c/o DILIA.

Vítězslav Nezval, "*Photogénie*." Originally as "Fotogenie," *Český filmový svět* 3, no. 9 (June 1925), 5–6. © Vítězslav Nezval – heirs c/o DILIA.

Vítězslav Nezval, "Film." Originally as "Film," *Český filmový svět* 3, no. 10–11 (September 1925), 6–7. © Vítězslav Nezval – heirs c/o DILIA.

Artuš Černík, "The Tasks of the Modern Film Librettist." Originally as "Úkoly moderního filmového libretisty," *Pásmo* 1, no. 13–14 (1925), 6. © Artuš Černík – heirs.

Vít Obrtel, "Architecture and Film." Originally as "Architektura a film," *Český filmový svět* 4, no. 2 (March 1926), 10. © Vít Obrtel – heirs c/o DILIA.

Jan Kučera, "Advertising and Cinematic Art." Originally as "Reklama a umění kinematografické," *Filmový kurýr* 2, no. 29 (August 25, 1928), 1–2. © Jan Kučera – heirs.

Jan Kučera, "Film and Building." Originally as "Film a stavba," *Volné směry* 30, no. 2 (1933), 40–42. © Jan Kučera – heirs.

Lubomír Linhart, "The Proletarian Film Struggle in Czechoslovakia." Originally as "Proletarischer Filmkampf in der Tschechoslowakei," *Arbeiterbühne und Film* 2, no. 2 (1931), 28. © Lubomír Linhart – heirs.

Lubomír Linhart, "Newsreels Show Us the World...." Originally as "Filmové žurnály nám ukazují svět...," *Žijeme* 2, no. 7 (1932), 197–200. © Lubomír Linhart – heirs.

Emil František Burian, "Music in Sound Film." Originally as "Hudba ve zvukovém filmu," *Jak žijeme* 1, no. 2 (1933), 47–48. © Emil František Burian – heirs c/o DILIA.

Alexander Hackenschmied, "Film and Music." *Cinema Quarterly* 1, no. 1 (spring 1933), 152–155. © Tino and Julia Hammid.

Jindřich Honzl, "Contribution to the Discussion of Speech in Film." Originally as "K diskusi o řeči ve filmu," *Slovo a slovesnost* 1, no. 1 (1935), 38–40. © Jindřich Honzl – heirs c/o DILIA.

Vladislav Vančura, "Contribution to the Discussion of Speech in Film." Originally as "K diskusi o řeči ve filmu," *Slovo a slovesnost* 1, no. 1 (1935), 40–42. © Vladislav Vančura – heirs.

Alexander Hackenschmied, "Independent Film—A World Movement." Originally as "Nezávislý film – světové hnutí," *Studio* 2, no. 3 (April 1930), 70–75. © Tino and Julia Hammid.

Zdeněk Pešánek, "Postscript to *Light and the Visual Arts.*" Originally as "Doslov" in *Světlo a výtvarné umění v díle Zdeňka a Jöny Pešánkových* (Praha: Nákladem Elektrických podniků hlavního města Prahy, 1930), 134–135. © Zdeněk Pešánek – heirs.

Zdeněk Pešánek, "Kinetic Art: Film." Originally as "Film" in his *Kinetismus* (Praha: Česká grafická unie, 1941), 20–29. © Zdeněk Pešánek – heirs.

Arne Hošek, "Notes on the Aesthetics of Film." Originally as "Poznámky k estetice filmu," *Program D 40* 5, no. 1 (1939), 15–18. © Arne Hošek – heirs.

Jan Mukařovský, "An Attempt at a Structural Analysis of an Actor's Figure (Chaplin in *City Lights*)." Originally as "Chaplin ve *Světlech velkoměsta* (Pokus o strukturní rozbor hereckého zjevu)," *Literární noviny* 5, no. 10 (1931), 2–3. We follow the title format Mukařovský uses in his *Studie z estetiky* (Praha: Odeon, 1966). The present English translation by John Burbank and Peter Steiner first appeared in *Structure, Sign, and Function: Selected Essays by Jan Mukařovský*, ed. John Burbank and Peter Steiner (New Haven: Yale University Press, 1978), 171–177. © Jan Mukařovský – heirs, English translation © Yale University Press.

Jan Mukařovský, "A Note on the Aesthetics of Film." Originally as "K estetice filmu," *Listy pro umění a kritiku* 1, no. 4 (1933), 100–108. The present English translation by John Burbank and Peter Steiner first appeared in *Structure, Sign, and Function: Selected Essays by Jan Mukařovský*, ed. John Burbank and Peter Steiner (New Haven: Yale University Press, 1978), 178–190. © Jan Mukařovský – heirs, English translation © Yale University Press.

Jan Mukařovský, "Time in Film." Originally as "Čas ve filmu" (written in 1933 for the unpublished collection "Preconditions of Czech Cinema"). First published in Jan Mukařovský, *Studie z estetiky* (Praha: Odeon, 1966), 179–183. The present English translation by John Burbank and Peter Steiner first appeared in *Structure, Sign, and Function: Selected Essays by Jan Mukařovský*, ed. John Burbank and Peter Steiner (New Haven: Yale University Press, 1978), 191–200. © Jan Mukařovský – heirs, English translation © Yale University Press.

Roman Jakobson, "Is the Film in Decline?" Originally as "Úpadek filmu?," *Listy pro umění a kritiku* 1, no. 2 (1933), 45–49. The present English translation by Elena Sokol first appeared in Roman Jakobson, *Selected Writings*, vol. 3 (The Hague: Mouton, 1981), 732–739. © The Roman Jakobson Trust.

Petr Bogatyrev, "Disney's *Snow White*." Originally as "Disneyova Sněhurka," *Program D 39* 4, no. 2 (1938), 59–66. © Petr Bogatyrev – heirs.

INDEX

Index of names (individuals, organizations), titles (films, magazines, newspapers), and selected critical terms. Film title dates, according to year of production, are placed in parentheses. Film titles and publication titles are in italics.

313

Index

315

Index